The Hidden History
of Women's Ordination

The Hidden History of Women's Ordination

Female Clergy in the Medieval West

GARY MACY

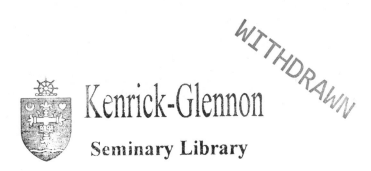

OXFORD
UNIVERSITY PRESS

2008

OXFORD
UNIVERSITY PRESS

Oxford University Press, Inc., publishes works that further
Oxford University's objective of excellence
in research, scholarship, and education.

Oxford   New York
Auckland   Cape Town   Dar es Salaam   Hong Kong   Karachi
Kuala Lumpur   Madrid   Melbourne   Mexico City   Nairobi
New Delhi   Shanghai   Taipei   Toronto

With offices in
Argentina   Austria   Brazil   Chile   Czech Republic   France   Greece
Guatemala   Hungary   Italy   Japan   Poland   Portugal   Singapore
South Korea   Switzerland   Thailand   Turkey   Ukraine   Vietnam

Copyright © 2008 by Oxford University Press, Inc.

Published by Oxford University Press, Inc.
198 Madison Avenue, New York, New York 10016

www.oup.com

Oxford is a registered trademark of Oxford University Press

Library of Congress Cataloging-in-Publication Data
Macy, Gary.
The hidden history of women's ordination : female clergy in the
medieval West / Gary Macy.
    p. cm.
Includes bibliographical references and index.
ISBN 978-0-19-518970-4
1. Ordination of women—Europe—History—To 1500.   2. Ordination—
History of doctrines—Middle Ages, 600–1500.   I. Title.
BV676.M33 2007
262'.1408209—dc22   2007004478

9 8 7 6 5 4 3 2 1

Printed in the United States of America
on acid-free paper

Ad omnes clericas praeteritas praesentes futurasque

Preface

The fact that women were ordained for the first twelve hundred years of Christianity will surprise many people. It surprised me when I first discovered it. Some of the people interested in learning about this deliberately hidden history will be scholars, specialists such as myself. Given the heated debates over the ordination of women in several Christian communities, however, the topic is likely to be of interest to many nonspecialists as well.

These two audiences, however, have different needs. Scholars will quite rightly demand to know on what grounds I am making the claims and interpretations that the book offers. Such argumentation requires accurate bibliographic references to and quotations from both the original sources as well as the secondary sources cited in the book. I have provided these necessary proofs in the original language. They are relegated, however, to the notes.

For most readers, this specialized information is inaccessible. Many don't read the Latin of the primary sources, and the secondary studies are often obscure texts difficult to obtain and decipher. For those readers I have tried to provide either a translation or paraphrase in the text of most of the Latin quotations cited. All the translations are mine unless indicated otherwise. Whenever possible, I have also directed readers to English translations of the Latin documents used in the study. When English translations are available for the secondary sources that I cite, I provide an initial reference to the source in its original language and then cite the English translation.

This double referencing can be cumbersome, I admit. It seemed the best way, though, to make the book as accessible as possible to everyone interested in the topic whatever their training in history and languages. Nevertheless, I readily admit an ulterior motive and that is a desire to share my own sheer joy of discovery. Not only do I want to introduce such fascinating sources to the wider audience they deserve, but I would also like to infect the uninfected reader with the delightful addiction of scholarship. Come on in, I would like to suggest, the water is fine. And if you aren't yet trained to face the heavy surf of deeper waters, well, there are marvelous discoveries to be made in tide pools as well. The ocean of learning is vast, beautiful, mysterious, and once you put your foot in the water, you may find it hard to resist its charms.

One further convention used in this book needs explanation. In ordinary American English usage, the terms "continence" "chastity," and "celibacy" are practically interchangeable. All generally refer to abstention from sexual activity, particularly abstention from sexual intercourse. For the purposes of this study only, however, the words will have distinct meanings, as indeed they do in most Christian theology. "Celibacy" will refer to the technical state of being unmarried. "Continence" will mean abstention from sexual activity, while "chastity" will mean moral sexual practice within one's state of life. So, for instance, a married person is chaste if she or he performs intercourse only with her or his own spouse, however she or he is not continent, and certainly not celibate.

The distinction is important for this study since some clergy during the Middle Ages were chaste, but not celibate or continent. These were the clergy who were married and continued to have conjugal relations. Some married clergy, as we will see, took vows of continence but remained married. These couples would not be celibate but would be both chaste and continent. If they broke their vows, and resumed conjugal relations, they would still be chaste but not continent. After the twelfth century, neither deacons nor priests nor bishops could contract a valid marriage. They were celibate by definition but were not necessary either continent or chaste, although they were certainly supposed to be so. Since celibacy was always recognized as a merely disciplinary law of the church, but not a divine command, clergy could be exempted from this law. Since they had taken no vows of chastity, as had clergy in religious orders, they were as free as any other Christian to live a chaste, and sexually active, married life once the law was lifted. Celibacy, chastity, and continence, therefore, are carefully distinguished for the purposes of the book. The difference is a bit tricky, but it seemed the best way to make the distinctions the medievals themselves were making.

With these few caveats out of the way, I would like to express the gratitude I owe so many people who have made this project possible. First, I would like to thank the National Humanities Center and the Luce Foundation. The bulk of this book was written while Senior Luce Fellow at the Center. I could not have had a more pleasant environment in which to work. The staff at the Center was professional, extremely helpful, and graciously welcoming. My thanks to everyone there.

Particular thanks are due to Jo Ann McNamara and Elizabeth Clark, who read what I thought was the finished text of the book. Their many thoughtful and challenging suggestions strengthened the book. Without their help, the study would have been much the poorer. If the text manages to rise above the usual boring scholarly recitation, it is in part due to Paul St. Amour, who read an early draft of the book. His comments helped me see a lively narrative in my drudging research.

At different stages of the project, numerous scholars offered critiques, references to sources, challenges, and encouragement. I owe them all more than I can say. Marcia Colish, Giles Constable, Mark Zier, Constant Mews, David Luscombe, Alastair Minnis, Anne Clark, Michael Clanchy, Marie Anne Mayeski, J. Frank Henderson, William W. Bassett, Donald Logan, and Teresa Berger deserve special mention here.

All studies rely on the work of others, and this does more than most. The early scholarship of Franz Gillmann, Joan Morris, and Ida Raming laid the foundations for this book. Without their work this book would not exist. In truth, this study only expands and strengthens the arguments they made quite some time ago. The notes and discussions will make it apparent how much I have also relied on more recent studies, especially those of the historians Jo Ann McNamara, Marie Anne Mayeski, Maureen Miller, Robert Swanson, Prudence Allen, Anne Barstow, Ute Eisen, John Hilary Martin, Alastair Minnis, Giorgio Otranto, and Suzanne Wemple, as well as the theologians, Yves Congar, Pierre-Marie Gy, Ludwig Ott, and Peter Hünermann. The story I tell is more a report of their findings than any original work of my own.

I also need to thank Jane Via, a true *clerica*, a minister, scholar, and friend of many years, who not only encouraged me to finish this work, but also told me in no uncertain terms that I better finish it. Then there are all my friends in San Diego who listened patiently and endlessly to presentations of different stages of my research.

Mostly, however, I want to thank my wife, Saralynn, for her wise patience in putting up with the alternatively whining, exuberant, moaning, manic, and petulant irrationality that always accompanies my research and writing.

A special thanks is also due to Cynthia Read and the wonderful people at Oxford University Press without whom the book would never have appeared.

Contents

Abbreviations, xiii

1. The State of the Question, 3

2. What Did Ordination Mean? 23

3. The Ministry of Ordained Women, 49

4. Defining Women Out of Ordination, 89

5. Conclusion, 111

Historical and Theological Postscript, 129

Appendix 1: Prayers and Rites for the Ordination
of a Deaconess, 133

Appendix 2: Ordination Rites for Abbesses from
the Early Middle Ages, 143

Notes, 157

Bibliography, 233

Index, 253

Abbreviations

Acta sanctorum	Johannes Bolland, et al. *Acta sanctorum quotquot toto orbe coluntur.* 1643–1940. Reproduced Cambridge: Chadwyck-Healey, 1999–2002.
CCSL	Corpus christianorum, series latina
CCCM	Corpus christianorum, continuatio medievalis
Denzinger	Peter Hünermann, ed. Heinrich Denzinger, *Enchiridion symbolorum definitionum et declarationem de rebus fidei et morum.* 39th ed. Freiburg im Breisgau: Herder, 2001.
Jaffé	Philipp Jaffé, et al., eds. *Regestra ponitificum romanorum ab condita ecclesia ad annum post Christum natum MCXCVIII.* 2nd ed. 2 vols. Leipzig: Veit, 1885.
LThK	Joseph Höfer, et al., eds, *Lexikon für Theologie und Kirche.* 2nd ed. 10 vols. Freiburg: Herder, 1957–1965.
Mansi	Giovanni Domenico Mansi, et al., eds. *Sacrorum conciliorum nova, et amplissima collectio.* 53 vols. Paris: H. Welter, 1901–1927.
MGH	Monumenta Germaniae Historica
NCE	*New Catholic Encyclopedia.* 2nd ed. 15 vols. New York: Thomson Gale, 2003.

ODCC   F. L. Cross and Elizabeth A. Livingstone, eds. *The Oxford Dictionary of the Christian Church*. 3rd ed. New York: Oxford University Press, 1997.

PL   Jacques Paul Migne, ed. *Patrologiae cursus completus . . . Series Latina*. 217 vols. 1844–1865. Reproduced Cambridge: Chadwyck-Healey, 1996–2006.

The Hidden History
of Women's Ordination

I

The State of the Question

This is not a book I ever intended to write. I was quite content to produce rather obscure articles on what people in the Middle Ages thought about the Christian ritual meal, called, variously, communion or the Lord's Supper or the Mass. In fact, until 1997, I never questioned the received wisdom that women had never been ordained in the Christian West. I got dragged into this question quite accidentally through a controversy not of my making.

In 1997, I gave an address at the Catholic Theological Society of America that suggested that women in the Middle Ages had presided over ceremonies during which they distributed the bread and wine consecrated during the communion ritual. It wasn't a very radical suggestion but seemed to touch a nerve with some people. My talk, along with the addresses of my colleagues John Baldovin and Mary Collins, earned the disapproval of Cardinal Avery Dulles in an issue of the Catholic journal, *Commonweal*. There was a bit of a kerfuffle that seemed to be fading when a colleague of mine, Evelyn Kirkely, stopped me in the hallway and remarked, "I heard you proved that women had been ordained in the Middle Ages." I was perplexed and a little annoyed. No, I protested, I had proved no such thing, and further, women never had been ordained in the Middle Ages.

Kirkley, not being Catholic, had not followed closely the minor uproar over the papers given at the CTSA. She was suggesting, nevertheless, a possible conclusion that could be drawn from the examples I had given. She was herself an ordained minister and an accomplished scholar. She doesn't voice opinions lightly. On the short trip back to my office, I reconsidered my hasty response. I had never checked the evidence. Maybe women were ordained. Maybe, as Kirkley intimated, women distributed communion because they were ordained to do so.

There is no point in rehearsing the fascinating hunt that followed. As so often happens in scholarship, one small clue led to another and yet another. Slowly, a pattern emerged. There was no shortage of evidence about ordained women and of secondary studies analyzing this evidence. But the sources were dismissed as anomolies, and the studies that argued that women had been ordained were attacked or marginalized. Mostly, though, both were ignored. Few historians questioned, as I had not, the assumption that women had not, and could not have been, ordained in the Middle Ages. The memory of ordained women has been nearly erased, and where it survived, it was dismissed as illusion or, worse, delusion. This was no accident of history. This is a history that has been deliberately forgotten, intentionally marginalized, and, not infrequently, creatively explained away. The pages that follow hope to expose this buried treasure, not only to excavate and expose the sources that survive concerning ordained women, but also to shed light on the brave scholars, mostly women, who have been insisting, against the odds, for decades that this is a legacy that should not, and cannot, be lost.

The story starts with theologians. They, rather than historians, have spent a great deal of time and ink over the question of whether women have ever been ordained. Most, but not all, have concluded that women have not. But we are getting ahead of our story. Since it is the theologians who have set the limits and the tone of the issue of women's ordination, it is with theologians that we must begin, and theologians have a very different set of questions than historians.

The Difference between Historians and Theologians

The history of Christianity is replete with references to the ordination of women. There are rites for the ordination of women; there are canonical requirements for the ordination of women; there are particular women depicted as ordained, and a number of roles limited to women are included among lists of ordained ministries. There is no question that women were considered to have been ordained by a large number of Christians over several centuries. Yet there remains a good deal of controversy over what exactly the sources that so describe women might have meant when they spoke of that ordination. That this controversy over the meaning of these sources exists at all tells us more about the later history of Christianity than it does of the period in which the sources appeared. In short, there is only a controversy because in later centuries Christians did not ordain women and some Christian groups still do not ordain women. During these later centuries and for these groups, women were often considered incapable of being ordained. According to this way of thinking, if women were (and are) incapable of being ordained, then they cannot have been ordained in the past. Therefore the texts that so describe them must be somehow mistaken. References to the ordination of women must either be not truly Christian (i.e., heretical) or they must really mean something other than what they seem to mean.

The most common explanation for the numerous references to the ordination of women in the first millennium of Christianity, at least for those who deny that women can be ordained, clarifies those references by describing them as referring to something other than a "real" ordination. They may denote a blessing, or consecration, but not what the words would appear to mean. This reading, of course, depends on the definition of a "real" ordination. The description of an ordination as "real" implies that there is a fixed definition of ordination in Christian history or, at least, that the definition of ordination from one particular period in Christian history is definitive for all of that history.

But to determine one particular definition of ordination as definitive is fundamentally a theological, not an historical, endeavor. Determining what counts as a valid ordination requires that theologians in each Christian denomination decide by what criteria an ordination is considered valid, and further, whether those criteria are eternally valid or mutable over time. Historians do not make such decisions. Historians ask, rather, what ordination meant at a particular moment in the past. Any ceremony called an ordination that fits the criteria established at that time and place *was* an ordination.

The distinction between the very different roles of theologians and of historians is crucial for this study.[1] Historians should not, in this case, assume that women were not ordained in the past simply because the ordinations women underwent then do not meet the criteria for ordination in the present. So, for instance, to ask the interesting historical question whether women ever led the eucharistic liturgy in the past should not be confused with the historical question whether women were ever ordained in the past. The first question is only relevant to the second if leading the eucharistic liturgy were constitutive of valid ordinations in the past.

This study is concerned first and foremost with the historical question whether women were ordained in the past, that is to say, whether they were considered ordained by their contemporaries according to the definition of ordination used at that time. Theologians may judge that definitions of ordination used in the past were inadequate or invalid or both. Those decisions are but a necessary part of each Christian denomination's self-understanding. Such decisions are not of immediate concern to historians, however, and the two separate tasks of theology and of history should not be confused. When they are so confused, some rather odd conclusions have been reached.

The strangeness of this approach can be more clearly seen when compared to the situation of men in Christian history. Throughout the history of Christianity, one finds references to the ordination of men. There are rites for the ordination of men; there are canonical requirements for the ordination of men; there are particular men depicted as ordained, and a number of roles limited to men are included among lists of ordained ministries. Yet no historians, of whom I am aware, question whether these references are, in fact, mistaken. Men are assumed to have been ordained in all such references because the references say they were and there has never been a period in history or a Christian group that ever denied (or denies) on theological grounds that men were (or are) capable of being ordained. One can then assume that if there had never been a period in the history of Christianity when women had been judged to be incapable of ordination, references to their being ordained would be as unproblematic as references to men being ordained.

The purpose of this book is to help uncover how it happened that women came to be considered as incapable of ordination. Implied in this question is the broader question of whether the definition of ordination changed in such a way that it excluded women and, if so, how it changed. In this sense, the purpose of this book is quite limited. It will not attempt to answer, or even to address, the theological question of whether women should now be ordained. Nor will it discuss whether the ordinations of women that took place in the past meet the criteria for ordination assumed in the present. This book will address only the meaning that ordination had for women in Western Christianity from roughly the sixth through the thirteenth centuries. The reasons for this limited focus are twofold. First a study of the Eastern and Oriental Christian Churches would require a much more extensive analysis than is possible in a single volume.[2] Second, the ordination of women during the early centuries of Christianity and particularly in the early centuries of Eastern Christianity has been more thoroughly covered in recent research then has the ordination of women during the medieval centuries in the West.[3]

What the Theologians Have Been Saying

The last forty years have produced an extraordinary amount of research on the question of whether women have ever been ordained within Christianity.

Several scholarly books and articles have discussed the historical background of, and the theological arguments for and against, the ordination of women. As a result, a great deal more is known now about the history of the roles women played in the official church during the early centuries of Christianity than during perhaps any other period in modern Christian history. Slightly less is known about the roles that women played in medieval Christianity, yet there, too, our knowledge has increased significantly. All of this research, however, has been conducted with two particular theological questions in mind. First, have women ever been validly ordained at any time in the two-thousand-year history of Christianity? Second, should women be ordained now? In fact, the first question has been asked mainly to answer the second question.

The fact that these two questions have shaped most of the research on the roles women have played in official Christian ministry has had a profound effect on the results of that research. Since the first question has so often depended on the second question, the criteria for determining whether women have ever been ordained in the Church are those required in answering the first question. To put it simply, what most scholars are asking in the first question is really, "Is there any evidence in the past that supports the ordina-tion of women in the present?" A review of the literature so far produced should help make this clear.

The Early Studies

Even the early modern studies that addressed this question did so from an explicitly theological stance. Jean Morin, the great liturgist, produced a mon-umental collection of ordination rites in Greek, Latin, and Syriac in 1655.[4] He included a separate section discussing the question of whether women had been ordained to the diaconate or not in the early church.[5] He concluded that since the same rites were used for deacons and deaconesses in the most ancient Greek rites, then deaconesses were indeed ordained.

> Three of the most ancient Greek rituals, uniformly one in agreement, hand down to us the ordination of deaconesses, admin-istered by almost the same rites and words by which deacons [were ordained]. Both are called ordination, χειρτονία, χειροφεσία. Both are celebrated at the altar by the bishop, and in the same liturgical space. Hands are placed on both while the bishop offers prayers. The stole is placed on the neck of both, both the ordained man and the ordained woman communicate, the chalice full of the blood of Christ placed in the hands of both so they may taste of it.[6]

Morin certainly knew that this would shock most theologians and re-counted the opinion of Epiphanius that women could not be priests. This opinion, according to Morin, should not mean, however, that other offices were not open to women. In fact, Morin was certain that his fellow theologians, however rigid they might be, would be won over by the force of the evidence Morin presented.[7]

Morin was the first, to my knowledge, to argue that the requirements for a true ordination require (1) that the ritual be called an ordination, (2) that the ritual be celebrated at the altar by the bishop, (3) that hands are laid upon the one to be ordained, (4) that the stole is placed on the one to be ordained, (5) that the ordained receive communion under the forms of both bread and wine, and most important (6) that the ordination be to one of the "major orders," that is, priest, deacon, or subdeacon. In short, the ancient ceremonies had to meet the requirements for ordination as they would have been understood in the seventeenth century.

Morin was in fact asking the theological question whether these women ordained in the past would be validly ordained in (his) present. This is precisely the confusion of theological and historical questions discussed above. What Morin did not ask is whether women in the past were validly ordained according to the definition of ordination used at the time they were ordained. Most scholars after Morin who addressed this issue would adopt a similar theological approach and apply the same criteria as Morin for determining whether women had ever been ordained.

The Jesuit, Jean Pien,[8] also wrote an early tract on deaconesses as an appendix to the 1746 volume of the *Acta Sanctorum*. In the second section of the tract, "Concerning the Ordination of Deaconesses," he began, "Before I undertake a word about the ordination of deaconesses, I wish to warn the reader that I am not treating here of ordination in the strict or sacramental sense of the word, but of that sense which might be ceremonial or improper as I will explain more fully later."[9] Pien then went on to list references to deaconesses found in literary and legal texts as well as in inscriptions. Several of these texts would indicate, as Morin had pointed out, that women were indeed described as ordained deaconesses and were so ordained by a laying on of hands. Pien, however, unlike Morin, described this ritual as "not strictly speaking sacramental, but merely ceremonial"[10] and went on to provide his own texts to support his claims. In conclusion, he quoted the twelfth-century Greek theologian Theodore Balsamon: "A deaconess is not ordained, even if some ascetic women improperly were called deaconesses."[11] Thus, the pattern for much of the discussion of the ordination of women was set. Scholars would undertake ever more elaborate dissections of the ancient texts that speak of the ordination of women in order to determine whether or not ordination rites for women and ministries of women in the past met the criteria for ordination and ministry required of men in the present.

A brief study of deaconesses was undertaken in the nineteenth century by Arcadius Pankowski.[12] A section of his study was dedicated to the question of the ordination of deaconesses. Pankowski reviewed the material, particularly that used by Morin, yet concluded with Pien that deaconesses had never been truly ordained. "A merely ceremonial ordination, in which we hold deaconesses to have been participants, was not the same [as that of deacons] as it does not give the power of public preaching in the church, ministering at the altar, sacrificing, or conferring the other sacraments. These offices of sacramental ordination alone were already forbidden to the female sex from the time of the apostles."[13] The criteria cited by Pankowski are, again, the criteria that would have been assumed to be eternally valid. The same criteria that applied in the nineteenth century would have applied from the very beginnings of Christianity.

In the early years of the twentieth century, a debate began among liturgists as to the status of the ancient deaconesses. One of the most complete collections of sources on this issue was compiled by Josephine Mayer in her *Monumenta de viduis diaconissis virginibusque tractantia* (*Records Treating of Widows, Diaconesses and Virgins*).[14] Containing both the original Greek and Latin sources, it remains one of the most complete collections of original material on these offices. Mayer herself concluded from her studies that deaconesses were set apart by their office in a special position between laity and clergy.[15]

The most complete of the early study of deaconesses from this period was Adolf Kalsbach's 1926 investigation of the rise and decline of that order. He made the important point that women could only be judged as truly ordained when rites of consecration had been fully developed in Christianity. According to Kalsbach, this occurred in the second half of the fourth century, and from that point on, women were not considered to be ordained.[16] Karlsbach insisted that ordination in the past needed to be judged as valid on its own terms. At the very least, it was inappropriate to make retrospective judgments on the validity of any ordination until the criteria for a valid ordination had been established.

Karlsbach's suggestion that any analysis of the ordination of women must also entail an understanding of the concept of ordination itself was taken up in 1954 by the Spanish scholar, Santiago Giner Sempere.[17] In a lengthy analysis of the most important sources, Sempere warned the reader that:

> It certainly produces anxiety to read the words "ordination,"
> "imposition of hands," etc. [in regard to the ordination of women].
> But one ought not to forget the inconsistency of those words,

particularly in the first centuries of the church, and the ease with which one encounters the phrase, "ordination of deaconesses," as synonymous with the expressions, "consecration," "benediction," "veiling," etc. which never appear when treating of the ordination of deacons or priests.[18]

Sempere realized, as had Morin, that the language of many ancient documents, taken at their face value, attested to the ordination of women. For Sempere, then, those documents must have meant something else in their own time and certainly did not mean the same as true sacramental ordination as it would become defined in later centuries. Sempere realized that a different definition of ordination must have been used in earlier centuries but assumed that this definition must have been incomplete, if not defective, since it included women.

The Recent Flurry of Scholarship

By the middle decades of the twentieth century, the rising social and political claims of women for equality began also to affect most Christian denominations. The discussion of the ordination of women began in earnest, spurred by the possibility that women would be allowed to be ordained. Several Christian denominations, including the Evangelical Church in Germany, the Anglican Communion, the Old Catholic Church, the Orthodox Churches, and the Roman Catholic Church, began to study the possibility of the ordination of women.[19] There were nearly eight hundred articles and books written on this subject between 1960 and 2001, and interest in the subject does not seem to have waned since then.[20] Not all of these discussions are immediately pertinent to the topic of this book since they do not address the ordination of women in earlier Christian history. Still, a comprehensive discussion of even all of the historical studies would constitute another book of equal length, so a brief overview of some of the major contributions to the question must suffice.

In 1960, in an article in the journal *Maison-Dieu*, the Jesuit scholar Jean Daniélou argued that the evidence showed that women had been ordained in the past. His approach was astonishingly similar to that of Morin over three hundred years earlier. "Above all in the East, we are face to face with Ordination rites which include a laying-on-of-hands, clothing with the deacon's vestments and the delivery of the chalice, offering remarkable parallels to the ordination of men."[21] Daniélou was quick to point out, however, that women had never been ordained to the priesthood.[22]

Another Jesuit scholar, Haye van der Meer, offered a different argument in favor of the ordination of women, in this case, to the priesthood rather than to the diaconate. Writing in 1969, van der Meer, after extensive historical analysis, argued that women had in the past been excluded from ordination to the priesthood, but that the grounds for this exclusion were historically conditioned and did need not necessarily apply in the present.[23] A year later, the German scholar Ida Raming completed her doctoral thesis investigating the medieval canonical background to the exclusion of women from the priesthood.[24] Raming, like van der Meer, did not argue that women had been ordained to the priesthood, but rather that the grounds for the exclusion of women from ordination were based on misogyny and, in some cases, on forged documents. In any case, reasons based on these authorities should no longer be used to validate the exclusion of women from ordination to the priesthood in the present.[25]

The argument had taken a decidedly different turn. First, van der Meer and Raming argued that women could, or should, be ordained as priests as well as deaconesses. Second, they did not seek to prove that women had been ordained in the past, but rather that the reasons for the exclusion of women from ordination in the past were no longer valid. These authors were not the first to argue that women should be ordained as priests, but they were perhaps the first to do so after an exhaustive study of the historical sources against such an ordination.[26]

Two of the most influential studies on the ordination of women as deaconesses were those of the French scholars Roger Gryson and Aimé Georges Martimort. Both analyzed at length the historical documents related to this office in the first centuries of Christianity in both Eastern and Western Christianity. Gryson's study covered evidence through the sixth century, while Martimort's study continued into the thirteenth century in the West. So thorough was the treatment of the subject by these two scholars that all later studies are either based on, or refer back to, these important contributions.

Yet the two scholars reached very different conclusions. Gryson's study, published in 1972,[27] discussed the ministry of women in general in the early history of Christianity, although as he stated, "Actually, women did not exercise any other ministry properly so called in the early Church except that of deaconesses and occasionally of widows."[28] Gryson found no evidence that widows were ever ordained since they played no role in liturgical services.[29] Deaconesses, however, "from the end of the 4th century, were definitely counted among the clergy like clerics, with the laying on of hands (*cheirotonia*), they received ordination under precise juridical conditions."[30]

Gryson made explicit the reasons for his study in his conclusions: "From a doctrinal point of view, since for several centuries a large portion of the Church followed this practice [of ordaining deaconesses] without raising a theoretical problem, it is perfectly conceivable to confer on women a diaconal type of ministry. Women deacons then receive a true ordination, with nothing distinguishing it formally from the ordination of their male colleagues."[31] Again, the criteria Gryson used to assess the ordination of deaconesses were the same as those first suggested by Morin, and he made quite it clear that the purpose of his study was to investigate the history of the early church to help determine present practice. Like van der Meer and Raming, Gryson suggested that the fact that women did not function as priests in the early years of Christianity could be merely cultural.[32]

Gryson's study received a strong response from Martimort in the *Bulletin de littérature ecclésiastique*. Martimort argued that the *Apostolic Constitutions*, a fourth-century document upon which Gryson had partly relied for his evaluation of women deaconesses, was of questionable orthodoxy.[33] Further, the *Constitutions* also described the laying on of hands as part of the ordination ceremonies of subdeacons and readers, orders that modern theology would not consider capable of being truly ordained. Martimort went on to suggest details in the rite of ordaining deaconesses that diverged from that of deacons. In short, the *Constitutions* did not provide proof that women were ordained.[34]

Gryson answered Martimort's challenge in his own article in *Mélanges des science religieuse*.[35] Gryson disputed the heretical status of the *Apostolic Constitutions* as described by Martimort but also insisted that his analysis depended on more than this one source. He further found that the differences between the rites of ordination for deacons and deaconesses were too slight to designate one a true ordination and the other not. Most important for our study, Gryson took issue with Martimort's concern with modern theological concepts: "I believe that 'the concepts of our modern theology' have nothing to do with determining how the *Apostolic Constitutions* regarded the ordination of deaconesses. One cannot say that because our theology is reluctant to accept this ordination as sacramental, the same as that of the male deacons, the *Apostolic Constitutions* could not consider it such."[36] Gryson, however, did not leave the matter there. Even if one used modern criteria for ordination, the ancient documents of the Eastern Church described a true sacramental ordination.

> Concerning the theological appreciation, I would certainly never have hazarded a conclusion on the sole basis of the testimony of the *Constitutions*. But actually, this evidence is not isolated; it appears in a series of concordant testimonies tending to prove that, in the

milieu termed "Syrian-Byzantine," from the end of the fourth century in any case, women deacons received an ordination analogous to men deacons, and, as a consequence, if one refers to the "concepts of our modern theology," it was a sacramental ordination. Since this was not a marginal fact or a fantasy rejected by legitimate authority, but, on the contrary, an institution peacefully accepted by a large part of Christianity for several centuries, one can deduce from it, it seems to me, that when the Church judges it relevant, women can receive the sacrament of orders for a ministry of the diaconal type, whose limits the Church can establish.[37]

Despite the fact that Gryson was well aware that the author of the *Apostolic Constitutions* did not use the same concept of ordination that modern theologians would use, in the end, he insisted that it was the modern criteria that must be met for women to be considered as ordained in the past. On this one issue, both sides of the dispute over the ordination of women in the past agreed. In order for women to be considered as ordained in the past, the ordinations of those women must pass muster as ordinations as they exist in the present. Martimort and Gryson did not disagree over the criteria for evaluating ordinations in the past; they disagreed whether those criteria had been met or not. And so the debate continued.

Writing shortly after Gryson, and dependent to some extent upon both Gryson and van der Meer, Jean Galot produced a comprehensive study of women and ministry in the church.[38] After a careful study of the documents and of the theological requirements for ordination in the Roman Catholic Church of the twentieth century, Galot took the position that the ancient deaconesses of the Eastern church were in fact sacramentally ordained.[39] This ordination, however, stood at the very edge of the clerical state, almost between the clergy and the laity.[40] This was because no women, not even the ancient deaconesses, ever did or ever could have access to the priesthood. Despite the obvious prejudice against women in the scriptural and historical sources, the divine plan clearly forbade women access to the sacerdotal order.[41] Galot was much clearer than any previous writer that he was deliberately applying the twentieth-century laws governing ordination to evaluate the ordination of women (and men by implication) in the past. His purpose, as the final chapter of his book makes clear, was purely theological. He wished to outline the possible roles for women in the present Roman Catholic Church.[42]

Joan Morris, a British theologian and journalist, published a study of the quasi-episcopal role of women particularly in the medieval church in 1973.[43] Although her study was concerned mostly with the jurisdictional power that women exercised in Christian history, she included an appendix entitled "The Ordination of Abbesses," in which she presented extensive references to documents that referred to abbesses as ordained. Among the references were rites for the ordination of abbesses. "We can conclude," Morris noted, "that women from earliest times were ordained to an administrative position within the Church. They at times received the titles of *Episcopa, Sacerdos Maxima, Praeposita,* and *Custos* of churches. They had all the powers of a bishop with regard to the jurisdiction of churches and people within their territories."[44]

Morris reasoned that abbesses were validly ordained as bishops because they did what bishops did, and so were given the titles usually reserved to men who were ordained. She did not address the validity of women's ordinations in the past but did raise in a very pointed way the problem of how to explain references to abbesses in the past that clearly spoke of them as ordained.

In 1982, Martimort produced his own extensive study of the history of deaconesses. It remains the most comprehensive study of the sources on the role of deaconesses in Christianity from its beginning through the attempted renewal of the status of deaconess among the Carthusians of the seventeenth century. In general, Martimort presented his sources without bias, but his conclusions make clear his position on the ordination of women. Martimort found that the differences between the rituals for the ordination of deacons and of deaconesses were based on the inability of deaconesses to serve at the altar and to continue on to ordination as priests.[45] He concluded that the ordination of deaconesses was "merely ceremonial," not sacramental, using Pien's phrase. In his conclusion, Martimort admitted, "It is difficult to avoid anachronism when one wishes to resolve present problems with the solutions of a past long gone: the ancient institution of deaconesses was, in its time, burdened with several ambiguities, as we have seen."[46] Unfortunately, despite this warning, he concluded his study with a continued use of modern theological categories to assess the validity of the ordination of deaconesses. Deaconesses could neither serve at the altar and nor aspire to the priesthood. The equivalence between ordination and service at the altar was assumed to have been equally important in the past as it is in the present.

In the same year, the Italian scholar Giorgio Otranto suggested that women had actually functioned as priests in Italy and in Brittany in the fifth and early sixth centuries.[47] He based this conclusion on a letter of Gelasius I, dated 494, in which the pope condemned the practice of bishops allowing women to officiate at the altar. A similar condemnation was sent by the bishops in Gaul to two Breton priests who allowed women to serve at the altar with them. Otrantro found confirmation that women had served as priests during this period in epigraphs dedicated to *presbyterae* in Calabria, Dalmatia, and Poitiers. Otranto concluded, "Although specific attestations of women priests are few, the frequent and always polemical treatment of the question of the admission of women to the priesthood, both in Christian authors and in the *Acta* of councils, leads us to conclude that the cases of women participating in liturgical service must have been more numerous than those attested in the literary and epigraphical testimonies."[48] Otranto was the first scholar to argue that women had been ordained and served as priests (*presbyterae*) within orthodox Christianity. As had Martimort, however, Otranto assumed that service at the altar implied ordination, and vice versa. The link between the Eucharist and ordination was not questioned.

Questioning the Definition of Ordination

Marie-Joséphe Aubert's lengthy study of deaconesses in 1987 relied heavily in its historical analysis on the work of Gryson and Martimort.[49] Aubert agreed with Gryson that the ordination of female deacons in the Greek church was a true sacramental ordination.[50] Aubert admitted, however, that asking whether deaconesses were so ordained was simply the wrong question. In a long quotation from Yves Congar, the Dominican theologian and historian, Aubert made his position clear:

> This is a bad question. I think that there is a certain *quiproquo* about the notion. Order in the ancient church, *"ordo," "ordinare"* meant to establish a certain "order" in the Church. The question does present itself as knowing whether this is the sacrament of Orders. Without doubt one might ask that today if one thinks of things in this way. But the ancients did not work like that. The question solely to be established about an *"ordo"* was whether it is *authentic,* the "order" of the female diaconate.[51]

Aubert repeated this position in the conclusion to his study: "Theologians pose themselves the question if eastern deaconesses received the sacrament. In fact, this would be for them to read an ancient institution using a much later frame of analysis for this institution that is relatively inadequate for it."[52]

In short, Aubert insisted that, historically speaking, one cannot answer the question of whether women had received a true sacramental ordination in the fourth century because the concept of a true sacramental ordination simply did not exist then. The "ordination" to which the ancient document alluded was not at all the same concept that the modern question implies. The continued use of the word "ordination" (in Latin, *ordinatio*) for rites of initiation into Christian ministry gives the illusion of perfect continuity. Yet for men and women, ordination had a far different meaning for the first half of Christian history than it would come to have in the twelfth and thirteenth centuries.

Aubert only briefly alludes to what an early concept of ordination might have been. According to Aubert, ordination in the ancient church did not involve the conferral of priestly power but was rather the installation (*ordinatio*) into a new job or position (*ordo*) in the church. Ordination was not limited to the priesthood and so was less sacramental than functional, and this, according to Aubert, marked a profound difference.[53] Aubert's insight, based on that of Congar, was extremely important. Yet few scholars picked up on it, and the investigation into the ordination of women in the past continued to be driven by the question whether women should be ordained in the present.

A collection of essays on the subject of women and the liturgy edited by Teresa Berger and Albert Gerhards in 1990 contained a review by Dirk Ansorge of the role of the ordination of women in Christian history as it had so far developed.[54] Using the work of Gryson, Galot, Martimort, and Aubert, Ansorge concluded that at least in some places and at some times in the history of the church, women had received a true sacramental ordination based on the modern definition of that term.[55] Ansorge, again, specifically asked the historical question in order to address the modern issues associated with the ordination of women.[56]

A year later, Joseph Ysebaert wrote an article addressing the origin of deaconesses in the Western church of late antiquity.[57] He concluded that the rite of ordaining deaconesses was adopted from the Eastern Christian practice. Further, despite the objections of some councils in Gaul, a proper ordination ceremony, including the laying on of hands and the invocation of the Holy Spirit, was practiced in the West.[58] Just as earlier studies, Ysebaert's article was consciously inspired by the modern debate over the restoration of the practice of ordaining deacons in the Roman Catholic Church. Ysebaert was looking for signs that women in the past had been ordained in the same way as they would need to be ordained in the present.[59]

In 1997, Peter Hünermann, Albert Biesinger, Marianne Heimbach-Steins, and Anne Jenson edited a thorough discussion of the ordination of deaconesses from both theological and historical perspectives.[60] Although the edited volume was fundamentally concerned with the modern issue of the ordination of deaconesses, four of the essays summarize the scholarship on the history of women's ordination. A brief overview of the history of the ordination of deaconesses was included as part of a longer theological essay on the revival of the female diaconate by Albert Biesinger. Like Ansorge, Biesinger argued that the history demonstrated that women had once been ordained as deaconesses.[61] Hans Jorissen and Peter Hünermann summarized the arguments for and against the ordination of deaconesses in contrasting articles.[62] Both scholars agreed that the basic historical argument against the ordination of deaconesses was based on the definition of ordination as service at the altar. Since deaconesses had never served at the altar, then any ceremony that they may have undergone could not be a true ordination.[63] Finally, Heike Grieser in a brief summary article contended that the evidence would suggest that women had been ordained in the past.[64]

Contributions from Eastern Christianity

Although the subject of this book is limited to ordination in the Western church, some mention should be made of the discussion concerning the ordination of women in the past among scholars in the Greek Orthodox Church. An excellent summary of the Orthodox positions on this question was compiled by Kyriaki Karidoyanes FitzGerald in her book *Women Deacons in the Orthodox Church*.[65] The opposition to the ordination of deaconesses in the Eastern church, according to FitzGerald, was based on a very similar argument to that detailed by Jorissen and Hünermann. The diaconate, in this understanding, is part of the fullness of priesthood shared by the three orders of bishop, priest, and deacon. Since women cannot be ordained as priests, then they cannot be ordained as deacons, as the diaconate is merely the first step in the process of becoming a priest.[66] Conspicuously for our study, FitzGerald noted that "this understanding of ordained ministry finds its roots in the medieval West."[67]

The Holy Synod of the Orthodox Church of Greece decided to restore the female diaconate on October 8, 2004, thus ending at the least the modern debate over the possibility of the ordination of women to the diaconate in the Greek Church. Yet, historical investigation of the role of women in the Byzantine church continues. Particularly notable are the recent studies by Valerie Karras. Holding that women were ordained deaconesses in the past, Karras reiterated the view of FitzGerald that opposition to this recognition was due to an understanding of the diaconate that tied it firmly to the priesthood. If women could not be ordained as priests, then it must follow that they cannot be ordained as deacons either.[68]

The findings of FitzGerald and Karras strengthen the position of earlier scholars that the meaning of ordination, both in the past and in the present, centers for many scholars on the question of service at the altar. The three "major orders" of deacon, priest, and bishop perform that service, and it is that service that defines what it means to be ordained. Those who argue that women have never been truly ordained base this judgment on the evidence that women have never served at the altar, and therefore, by definition, they have never been ordained. The proponents of the ordination of deaconesses assert that deaconesses can be ordained into the major order of the diaconate despite the fact that they have never served at the altar. They are ordained into a separate ministry of service that does not include such ministry at the altar.[69] It is significant that the Greek Orthodox scholars understand the tie between service at the altar and true ordination as a medieval Western innovation. Unfortunately, they do not elaborate on this assertion.

The Most Recent Studies

In 1996, Ute Eisen produced an exhaustive compilation of the epigraphical evidence of women ministers in the early centuries of Christianity.[70] Although her concerns were mainly with the historical evidence, Eisen did address briefly the issue of the validity of the ordination of women in the past. While carefully insisting that historical remains be understood in their contemporary setting, Eisen concluded, "It is clear that women were active in the expansion and shaping of the Church in the first centuries: they were apostles, prophets, teachers, presbyters, enrolled widows, deacons, bishops, and stewards.... In short, to the question of whether there were women officeholders in the Church's first centuries our study returns a resounding answer: yes!"[71] Eisen provided important historical information on the role women played in the first five hundred years of Christianity but did not investigate the link between those roles and ordination.

The most complete study of the modern debate concerning the ordination of women is certainly Dorothea Reininger's *Diakonat der Frau in der Einen Kirche,* which appeared in 1999. Reininger's major concern rested with the theological arguments advanced in the Roman Catholic Church for and against the ordination of women; although in the process of presenting this material, she offered a thorough discussion of the debate in the Evangelical Church in Germany, the Anglican Communion, the Old Catholic Church, and the Orthodox churches.[72] As background to this larger discussion, Reininger summarized the arguments over the validity of the ordination of deaconesses in the early church. She concluded that evidence from history neither mandates nor fundamentally rules out the restoration of the female diaconate.[73] On the difficult question of the validity of the ordination of deaconesses in the past, Reininger noted that some scholars simply found the question unanswerable. The criteria necessary even to ask the question were not developed until the twelfth century. Echoing the sentiments of Yves Congar, as quoted by Aubert, she considered the question anachronistic.[74] Reininger noted that other authors, notably Peter Hünermann, while accepting these caveats, would yet find enough equivalence between the past and later criteria to attempt a theological judgment on the ordination of women in the past.[75]

Reininger's study detailed the growing awareness among scholars that since the understanding of ordination changed significantly in the twelfth and thirteenth centuries in the West, any judgment about ordinations in earlier centuries was, at best, problematic. Certainly one could, and indeed had to, make a theological judgment concerning the relevance of earlier ordinations to the present issue of the ordination of women. Yet the question of the meaning of such ordinations in the past was not, and could not be, the focus of these studies since their purpose remained precisely the issue of ordaining women now. For those Christian groups for whom tradition played an important theological role—particularly Roman Catholics, the Anglican Communion, and the Orthodox churches—if women in the past were ordained according to criteria as presently accepted by those groups, this would constitute a strong traditional argument in favor of ordination in the present.

In 2000, three studies appeared that discussed the ordination of women in the early history of Christianity. The most emphatically theological of these was Gerhard Müller's *Priesthood and Diaconate*. The subtitle, "The Recipient of the Sacrament of Holy Orders from the Perspective of Creation Theology and Christology," makes this abundantly clear.[76] At least partly in response to Dorothea Reininger's work, Müller specifically addressed the question of the validity of historical ordinations of women. According to Müller, the criteria for reading all historical documents must be the official teaching of the present magisterium of the Roman Catholic Church.[77] The church has determined that the three offices of deacon, priest, and bishop constitute a sacramental unity and hence are significantly different from any other function in the church. This sacramental unity is of the essence of ordination.[78] "If the deaconess and the subdeacon are not allowed to carry out the duties of the presbyter or the deacon, then they have not received such a commission in their blessing or consecration either, and thus *are* not deacons."[79]

As Jorissen and Hünermann had pointed out some years earlier, the decisive argument against the validity of ordination of women in the past relied on criteria for ordination developed in the twelfth and thirteenth centuries. Müller was well aware of this and, in fact, specifically alluded to this development, arguing that the touchstone for ordination was the later understanding since this was the position approved by official church teaching.[80]

A second study from the year 2000 was also based on theological grounds but reached the opposite conclusion from that of Müller. Phyllis Zagano, in *Holy Saturday: An Argument for the Restoration of the Female Diaconate in the Catholic Church*, urged that the ministry of women in that church be formalized through the ordination to the diaconate. As part of that argument, Zagano summarized the discussion concerning the validity of women's ordinations in the past and concluded that "there are stronger arguments from scripture, history, tradition, and theology that women may be ordained deacons than that women may not be ordained deacons."[81]

A third study from 2000 was my article, "The Ordination of Women in the Early Middle Ages."[82] The article reviewed references to ordination in the literature of the early Middle Ages in Western Christianity and then argued that the understanding of ordination used in these sources was quite different from that of later centuries. Based on studies by earlier scholars, the article asserted that ordination in this period referred to any ceremony by which a person moved to a new role or ministry (ordo) in the church. Given that understanding of ordination, then, nuns, abbesses, and queens in their own historical setting were described as, and indeed considered as, ordained.[83] To use other criteria to determine if these women were "really" ordained was a theological decision that had to be justified on theological, not historical, grounds.[84]

This article offered two new perspectives to the ongoing debate. First, although many scholars had noted that a different notion of ordination had been used before the twelfth century, I attempted to describe what precisely that understanding was. Second, I attempted to separate more clearly the theological questions raised in this debate from the purely historical issues.

John Wijngaards has been a contributor to the discussion about the ordination of women for many years through his web site, perhaps the most extensive source for bibliography on the subject.[85] In 2001 and 2002, Wijngaards published two books that detail the arguments he had been making for many years over the Internet. The first book, *The Ordination of Women in the Catholic Church*,[86] was fundamentally a theological argument refuting the papal statements justifying the refusal to admit women into ordination. Wijngaards, however, addressed his refutations not directly to the papal documents themselves, but to the late medieval sources upon which they were based.[87] His approach strengthened the contention of earlier writers, particularly Ida Raming, that it was Western medieval theology, particularly canon law, that provided the justification for the modern exclusion of women from the priesthood. Wijngaards included a discussion of the ordination of deaconesses and concluded that women did receive the sacrament of ordination. As proof, the author detailed the Byzantine rite for the ordination of a deaconess, highlighting the laying on of hands and the presentation of a chalice by the bishop that were part of this rite.[88]

The second book, *No Women in Holy Orders?* specifically discussed the validity of the ordination of deaconesses in the Byzantine church. *No Women in*

Holy Orders? contains an even more elaborate discussion of ritual for this ordination, including translations of the ritual along with other important early church witnesses to deaconesses.[89] Specifically addressing in detail the arguments against the validity of this ordination, Wijngaards concluded that "the ordination rite of a women deacon, set within the framework of a full Byzantine celebration of the eucharist, shows clearly that women deacons did receive the full sacramental holy orders of the diaconate."[90] Again, Wijngaards's arguments for the ordination of women in the present were based partly on his judgment that the ordination of women in the past met the criteria now used to judge the validity of orders.

Conclusion

This survey does not do justice to many insights offered by so many scholars, especially over the last forty-five years. I hope, however, it does delineate how concern over the ordination of women in the present has driven the historical question of whether women had ever been ordained in the past. This connection of past and present is inevitable, since scholars raised the issue of women's ordination in the past only in order to assist in determining whether women ought to be or even are capable of being ordained in the present. Theologians gradually became aware that the "ordination" of women, for instance, in the fourth century was understood quite differently than one would understand "ordination" in the present. Yet, theologically, the central question can, and indeed must, still be asked whether such ordinations, however different, offer any insight into how the tradition might view the ordination of women in the present.[91] The concern of theologians is necessarily how the past, understood as tradition, can justify or elucidate actions in the present.[92] On the issue of women's ordination, therefore, the essential question for theologians must be: Are ordination rites for women in the past similar enough to those in the present to serve as evidence of a tradition that would, in part, justify the ordination of women in the present? The question assumes, of course, that similar ceremonies in the past would indicate a similar intent to ordain women into the deaconate or presbyterate and that such ceremonies would effect such an ordination. The essential issue remains what constitutes a valid ordination and whether past ordinations of women fit those criteria.

It would be difficult, or at least unhelpful, merely to detail the understanding of the ordination in the past for theologians thus concerned with the question of the ordination of women in the present. Yet the study of the ordination of women in the past has been undertaken exclusively by theologians.

Historians, as will be detailed in chapter 3, have provided excellent studies of the role of women in the early medieval church but do not, in general, refer to the theological debate over the ordination of women during this period. If the topic comes up at all, they assume that women were not ordained since they were repeatedly refused access to altar and pulpit. It should come as no surprise, then, that theologians concerned with the ordination of women have done no more than suggest that the understandings of ordination in the past are quite different than those in the present and, further, that a significant change in the understanding of ordination occurred in the twelfth and thirteenth centuries.

The purpose of this study will be to pick up the hints and suggestions tantalizingly distributed throughout these several studies to uncover what it might mean to say that a woman was ordained in the early Middle Ages and then to investigate why twelfth- and thirteenth-century theologians came to assume that not only could women not be ordained but also that they in fact had never been ordained.

2

What Did Ordination Mean?

A significant number of the scholars who have written on the history of the ordination of women would agree that an important change in the understanding of ordination took place some time in the eleventh and twelfth centuries in Western Christianity. Since those scholars, as we hope to have shown, were interested in whether women had ever been ordained according to our present understanding of ordination, they did not pursue the question of what the earlier understanding of ordination might have been. Yet it is essential to know what ordination meant in those earlier centuries, since this is precisely the period in which one finds references to ordained women. What did it mean to be ordained during the period in which women were so designated? It is to that question that we now must turn.

What Ordination Was Not

Let us start with the criteria for a valid sacramental ordination laid down so long ago by Jean Morin. Such an ordination required (1) that the ritual be called an ordination, (2) that the ritual be celebrated at the altar by the bishop, (3) that hands be laid upon the one to be ordained, (4) that the stole be placed on those to be ordained, (5) that the ordained receive communion under the forms of both bread and wine, and, most important (6) that the ordination be to one of the "major orders," that is, priest, deacon, or subdeacon.

As suggested in chapter 1, most of these requirements were adopted in the second millennium of Christianity. Since the whole point of this exercise is to determine what "ordination" meant in the early Middle Ages, the first criterion is best left aside for the moment. After all, there is little value in simply calling a ceremony an ordination without first determining what the person using that term might mean. The next three criteria are specific actions that are required, or at least expected, in a valid sacramental ritual. Here the work of Jean Morin himself played an important role in establishing the criteria for a valid ordination. In 1655, when Morin wrote his study, some theologians assumed that the solemn delivery of some object connected with the ministry being conferred was essential for a valid ordination.[1] So in the case of a priest, the handing over of the chalice filled with wine and water and/or the paten with the host would constitute the "matter" (necessary action or symbol) for a valid ritual. This was the opinion, for instance, of Thomas Aquinas in the thirteenth century[2] and of Pope Eugenius IV in 1439.[3] Medieval positions did differ, however, and some medieval theologians argued that the laying on of hands constituted all or part of the matter of the sacrament. The issue, however, was far from settled even at the end of the Middle Ages.[4]

Morin demonstrated that the practice of handing over some ritual objects, known technically as the *traditio instrumentorum* (handing on of the instruments), was in fact a practice added to the ordination ritual for priests in Western Christianity after the fifth century and not essential for ordination.[5] Only in 1947 did Pope Pius XII rule that the laying on of hands was the only "matter" necessary for the ordination of a priest for Roman Catholics, deliberately excluding the *traditio instrumentorum* from the matter of the sacrament.[6] One can hardly expect that early medieval theologians and canonists would agree on any particular ritual as essential to ordination when such an agreement was only recently reached. At the very least one should suspect that the exact form of the ritual of ordination was not a fixed matter and that early medieval criteria for ordination are much more likely to identify the *traditio instrumentorum* than the laying of hands as essential for a valid ordination. To apply, therefore, the criterion of the laying on of hands, as so many modern theologians do, to adjudicate whether an ordination in the past was valid would be at best anachronistic.

The final and, for many scholars, the essential requirement for a valid ordination remains the last. Ordination can only be to the major orders of the episcopacy, the presbyterate, and diaconate. All other orders are "minor orders" and not true ordinations. Even the diaconate ought to be understood as a step on the way to becoming a priest and so shares in the priestly ministry. It is the priesthood that is the essence of all three orders.[7] Yet for most early medieval writers, the unity of these three offices as different stages of priesthood was not accepted as either obvious or inevitable. Surely, lists of those ministries that served under a bishop existed from the early centuries of the church, and these orders were ranked by the importance of their functions. These grades, however, were not the only ministries considered to be "orders," nor were they always considered to be stepping stones toward those orders that served at the altar.

Only in the eleventh century would there be a clear understanding that the minor diocesan orders led to the major orders of deacon, priest, and bishop in what would only then be named the *cursus honorum* (progression of honor). In fact this term was first used by Pope Alexander II in a letter to Romuldus, the bishop of Constance, in 1063.[8] Up until the eleventh century there was no necessary progression from deacon to priest to bishop. Deacons, even in the most important sees, could move directly to the episcopate and priests could be ordained without ever having been deacons. According to the excellent study of sequential ordination by John St. H. Gibaut, ten popes between the years 715 through 974 were ordained bishop directly from the diaconate and were never ordained priests at all.[9] This would mean that the bishops of Rome celebrated all the papal ceremonies without having ever been ordained to the priesthood. The first deacon chosen as pope who bothered to be ordained a priest before ascending to the See of Rome was Gregory VII in 1073.[10] Even in the twelfth century, popes Gelasius II (1118–19), Innocent II (1130–43), Celestine III (1191–98), and Innocent III (1198–1216) were all deacons when they were chosen to be pope. All were ordained priests and then bishop of Rome within twenty-four hours.[11]

Nor was there particularly a relationship between the presbyterate and the diaconate. Gibaut summarized the situation in the eighth through the ninth century: "While liturgical rites suggest that normally presbyters would have been deacons, the biographical and historical evidence, especially from the *Liber pontificalis*, suggests that there were many presbyters who had never been deacons."[12] The triumvirate of deacon, priest, and bishop did not always exist as the embodiment of the sacerdotal office. Each office existed independently of the other as a separate and independent position or vocation. Being a priest did not necessitate first being ordained a deacon, nor did being a bishop necessitate first being ordained a priest. Similarly, one could move from being a deacon directly to being a bishop.

Nor were the so-called "minor" orders fixed until the twelfth century. Medieval canonists, theologians, and liturgists often included seven such offices but sometimes counted six or eight or even nine ecclesiastical ministries.[13] Only through the influence of the late eleventh- and twelfth-century writers did the number of ecclesiastical orders become relatively fixed.[14] Some of the ministries also shifted position. The subdeacon, for instance, was sometimes considered a major order, sometimes a minor order, and sometimes does not appear in lists at all.[15] The eighth-century *Ordines Romani* does not include ordination rites for the three grades of doorkeeper, lector, or exorcist, possibly indicating that those ministries were not functioning at the time and place this liturgy was used.[16]

Gibaut described the situation succinctly: "In sum, the sequence of both the minor and major orders became fixed in the eleventh century, though considerable flexibility remained with regards to the ages of clerics and the interstices. Nevertheless, this period marks the final shape of the *cursus honorum* in the Western church until the sixteenth-century Reformation, and in the Roman Catholic Church, the 1972 Pontifical of Paul VI."[17] The understanding, therefore, of those ministries that served under the bishop as a fixed sequence leading up to the summit of the three orders of the priesthood (deacon, priest, and bishop) appeared only in the second millennium of Christianity and therefore would not and indeed could not have been used as a criterion for ordination before that period. In short, to be ordained was not necessarily to be a deacon, a priest, or a bishop. Nor were these three offices inextricably linked. Each was a separate vocation in itself, as indeed were the other orders in the church. Central to the argument denying the historical ordination of women, as described by Hünermann, Jorissen, and Müller, was that there is no evidence that women were ever ordained priests. Since, as should now be clear, the one office of priesthood did not exhaust all the offices to which one could be ordained, that argument in itself does not rule out the possibility of the ordination of women to the other offices. What were these "other offices," and how did early medieval Christians understand them? The plot thickens.

What Ordination Was

As discussed above, there has slowly developed a consensus among historians of Christianity that the understanding of ordination changed dramatically in the twelfth and thirteenth centuries. Some of those scholars have gone further than just pointing out that fact, and, while not discussing the implications for the ordination of women, they have outlined understanding of ordination assumed by the Christianity of the first millennium. A review of their findings will demonstrate how radically the understanding of ordination has changed in the course of Christian history.

In 1957, a group of studies on the sacrament of orders was published in the series *Lex orandi*.[18] Two articles touched on the meaning of *ordo* (order) and *ordinatio* (ordination) in Christianity. The first article, by Pierre-Marie Gy, offered some observations on the use of words *ordo* and *sacerdos* (priest) in Christian antiquity.[19] Gy argued that the term *ordo* originated with the political structure of the Roman Empire in which powerful societal groups were known as *ordines* (orders). Almost in passing, Gy noted that "*ordinare* (to ordain) and *ordinatio*, which in antiquity had a broader sense than *ordo* and which were applied without difficulty during the High Middle Ages to kings, to abbots and abbesses, supplanted the synonyms *consecrare* (to consecrate) and *benedicere* (to bless), and became the technical terms correlative to sacramental '*ordo*' conversely, it was customary to speak of the consecration of bishops and the benediction of abbots."[20] Gy attributed the change from a broader to a narrow understanding of *ordinare, ordinatio,* to the twelfth-century theologian Hugh of St. Victor.[21]

In this same collection, Gerard Fransen contributed an article on the treatment of the ordination of priests by medieval canonists.[22] At the very beginning of the discussion he noted, "For them [the medieval canonists] *ordinare* and *ordinatio* did not bear a sacramental reference. The election of the Pope, the nomination of archdeacon, canonical institution given to a monk to enable him to take charge of a parish, all are described as *ordinatio*."[23] Although both papers were offered as exploratory approaches to the subject, the authors suggested that ordination in the first half of Christian history was a much broader and looser concept than it would come to be in later centuries. Their early suggestions would be born out by later, more detailed studies.

In 1963, Vinzenz Fuchs published an examination of the appointment of ordained clergy.[24] He concluded that up until the twelfth century, there was a very close tie between ordination and the appointment to a particular congregation. Clergy came from and were assigned to a particular function within a particular community. Ordination in fact entailed and demanded appointment to a particular role in a particular church. Only in the twelfth century would ordination become an appointment for spiritual service not tied to any particular community. Fuchs's research pointed out that this appointment to a particular function within the community was the most important aspect of ordination during the early centuries of the church. Only later would an "absolute ordination," granting spiritual power to be exercised anywhere, appear in western Christianity.[25]

A few years later, René Metz completed a comprehensive study of the different terms used for the ritual acceptance of virgins into religious life.[26] Metz discovered several different terms were used for this ritual, including *consecratio, benedictio,* and *velatio* (veiling). More surprisingly, he encountered a number of instances in which the ritual was described as an *ordinatio.* Metz placed little importance on the use of the term, however, describing it as an exception.[27] He did point out though that one finds that the Roman pontifical of the thirteenth century also spoke of the "ordination" of doorkeepers, lectors, exorcists, and acolytes.[28] "These uses," Metz ventured, "can be explained by the imprecision of the terms; it is only at the beginning of the thirteenth century that there is an attempt to bring the required distinctions to the terminology of the sacrament of orders."[29] The terms *consecratio, benedictio,* and *velatio* seemed to be used interchangeably and indiscriminately in the early Middle Ages.[30] In area of rituals for religious women as well as those for religious males, the evidence was mounting that a different definition of what ordination entailed and who could be ordained was developed in the twelfth and thirteenth centuries.

In 1969, Ludwig Ott produced an extensive and detailed study of the sacrament of ordination.[31] He assumed that ordination included only the diaconate and presbyterate and excluded deaconesses from true ordination since they did not perform any liturgical roles ascribed to priest or deacon.[32] This is, once again, the central argument used to deny that women were ever ordained. Ott pointed out, however, that it was Pope Urban II at the Council of Benevento in 1091 who first described ordination as limited to the priesthood and diaconate[33] and that the first definition of *ordo* appeared in the *Sentences* of Peter the Lombard.[34] Peter's definition directly linked order with power: "If, however, one asks: what is that which is here called order (*ordo*), it can indeed be said to be a certain sign, that is, something sacred, by which a spiritual power and office is given to the one ordained."[35] His twelfth-century definition was modified by Alexander of Hales in the early thirteenth century. Alexander's definition limited orders to those offices linked to the Eucharist: "Order is a sacrament of spiritual power for some office established in the Church for the sacrament of communion."[36] These two definitions became the standard for late scholastic discussions of orders and ordination. Ott's study thus exposed the late date for the earliest systematic definition of order and the link of that definition to the bestowal of power, particularly the power to enact the liturgy of the Eucharist. Ott's study pinpointed the change. A redefinition of ordination was begun in the eleventh century and was completed by the early thirteenth century. Further, that definition tended to condense ordination to the power given to priests to consecrate the bread and wine in the Eucharist.

The Dominican theologian and historian Yves Congar looked back over his long career in an article published in 1972.[37] As a summary of the work he and others had done, he made the fascinating claim that, for the early church,

> ordination encompassed at the same time election as its starting-point and consecration as its term. But instead of signifying, as happened from the beginning of the twelfth century, the ceremony in which an individual received a power henceforth possessed in such a way that it could never be lost, the words *ordinare, ordinari, ordinatio* signified the fact of being designated and consecrated to take up a certain place, or better a certain function, *ordo,* in the community and at its service.[38]

Congar claimed, without much further explanation, that the definitions of ordination proposed by Peter the Lombard and elaborated by Alexander of Hales were new and something quite different from the earlier understanding of ordination.

Support for Congar's position came from Pierre van Beneden in his study of the concept of *ordo* in the first three centuries of Christianity. Contrary to the opinion offered by Gy in 1957, Beneden demonstrated that Christians adopted the concept of *ordo* from everyday usage and not from Roman social structure. According to Beneden, *ordinatio* for the early Christian indicated the appointment and consecration of a person to a particular charge or function.[39] Ordination was linked not to an irrevocable power, but to a particular mission to a particular community. "One searches in vain for indications of an inherent and unchangeable (*character indelibilis*) attached to the power of orders (*potestas ordinis*)."[40] Beneden concluded, "If then in the spirit of the first Christians, ecclesiastical service is able to be characterized, in a certain sense, as 'sacramental,' the essential 'functional' character that has been attributed to it by this period constitutes nevertheless a clear and profound divergence with regard to the teaching of the Catholic church today."[41] Although Beneden's study only covered the first three centuries of Christianity, it clearly showed that earlier centuries had a very different understanding of ordination than would appear in the early scholastic period and supported the conclusions of Fuchs's earlier study.

Pierre-Marie Gy updated and expanded his 1957 article in a study that appeared in French and English in 1979.[42] Examining the ancient prayers of ordination, Gy noted that the both the prayers themselves and the theological understanding of ordination changed in the twelfth and thirteenth centuries. It is the theological change that most concerns this study. Gy summarized:

> When they [the theologians] circumscribed the seven sacra-
> ments, they generally thought that priesthood was an *ordo* (and they
> gave to this word a sacramental meaning), and that the episcopacy
> was a *dignitas* (dignity), in a non-sacramental sense. A further dis-
> tinction was made between *ordinare* (in a sacramental sense) and
> *consecrare* (which was not sacramental when it applied to persons).
> This new vocabulary, and also the related terms *ordinator* (one who
> ordains)/*consecrator* (one who consecrates), *ordinandus* (the one or-
> dained)/*consecrandus* (the one consecrated), comes into the Roman
> pontifical in the thirteenth century and replaces almost completely
> the former vocabulary by the time of the pontifical of Durandus
> (thirteenth century).[43]

This later approach contrasts markedly from the earlier understanding, a
change that Gy eloquently encapsulated:

> In the ancient vocabulary there was not much difference between
> *ordinare, consecrare,* and *benedicere.* Nevertheless, at least in the pa-
> tristic era, *ordinare* had a broader sense than *consecrare* or *benedicere,*
> and it meant not only the ordination prayer, but the whole process
> which this prayer terminates. At the same time *ordinatio* was also
> used, in the high middle ages, for kings, abbots and abbesses, and by
> Christian Roman law for civil servants.[44]

Based on earlier studies, Gy made clear the important and dramatic
change that occurred in the twelfth and thirteenth centuries. Before that period, ordination was fundamentally a dedication to a particular role or ministry, not the granting of a special power linked to the liturgy of the altar.
Further, the terms *ordination, benediction,* and *consecration* were used nearly
interchangeably, and only after the change did theologians and canonists
distinguish between nonsacramental consecration reserved, for instance, for
religious women and sacramental ordination reserved exclusively for priests
and deacons.

A short note by Yves Congar published in 1984 offered an important
contribution to the understanding of ordination.[45] In a densely referenced text,
Congar proved that ordination originally included the entire process whereby
a candidate was selected and appointed by the larger community to a particular
service to the community. Congar pointed out, for instance, that *ordination*
is the term used for the appointment to an ecclesiastical post by a secular
ruler. He also noted the many instances in which contemporaries referred to
secular rulers as ordained. Charlemagne, Otto II, and Otto III were all so

designated;[46] and, according to Congar, " 'To be ordained' was the official formula of the Capetians for their coronations."[47] For the eleventh-century reformers, Peter Damian and Humbert of Silva Candida, ordination referred above all to the appointment of a pope or bishop to a particular post. The actual ceremony was termed *consecration* by both.[48] Although Gregory VII was more likely to use *ordination* for the liturgical ceremony, he also retained the older usage, whereby ordination referred to the entire process of selection and appointment to an ecclesiastical post.[49]

Congar pointed out, once again, that the definition of ordination changed in the twelfth and thirteenth centuries. "When the treatment of the sacrament of orders was developed in the second half of the twelfth century, then formulated in the works of the great scholastics of the thirteenth century, it was dominated by reference to the Eucharist, by the power of consecrating it, *potestas conficiendi* (power of confecting [the Eucharist]). This power was given by a indelible and personally possessed character."[50] Thus the practice began of separating the liturgical rite from both the selection and appointment processes so central to the earlier understanding of ordination. Ordination became the name for the rite alone.

Edward Schillebeeckx contributed an influential book on ministry in Christianity in 1980.[51] Although his immediate concern was not the concept of *ordo* in Christian history, he did emphasize the change that took place in the twelfth and thirteenth centuries in the role of the priest. His findings augment the previous studies on *ordo* but take a slightly different approach. According to Schillebeeckx, as for Fuchs, the important change in ordination took place when priests were understood to receive a spiritual power in ordination rather than an appointment to a particular function within a particular congregation. Schillebeeckx pinpointed the change to the Third and Fourth Lateran Councils (1179 and 1215 respectively).[52] These councils allowed for the ordination of priests without any appointment to a particular congregation.[53]

Schillebeeckx understood this change to be rooted in the feudal system and above all in the concepts of law borrowed from the newly discovered texts of Roman law. "The priesthood was seen more as 'a personal state of life,' a '*status*,' than as a service to the community; it was personalized and privatized. In particular the new conceptions of law, *ius*, and thus of jurisdiction, brought about a division between the power of ordination and the power of jurisdiction, in my view one of the most fundamental factors which marks off the second millennium from the first."[54]

Something quite new in Christianity appeared, an ordination apart from any particular congregation and tied instead to the power to celebrate the

Eucharist, that is, to make present the risen Christ. Once again to quote Schillebeeckx,

> In comparison with the ancient church, circumstances here have taken a fundamentally different direction: a priest is ordained in order to be able to celebrate the eucharist; in the ancient church it is said that he is "appointed" as minister in order to be able to appear as leader to build up the community, and for this reason he was also the obvious person to preside at the Eucharist. This shift is of the utmost importance: at all events, it is a narrower legalistic version of what the early church believed.[55]

Schillebeeckx's work confirmed the conclusion of earlier scholars that there was a fundamental and significant change in the understanding of what constituted Christian ministry in the twelfth and thirteenth centuries. Schillebeeckx did offer something new, however. He suggested a cause for this change. It was the introduction of Roman law and hence a more legalistic approach to ministry that caused the change, a change that occurred at the conclusion of and partly as a result of the eleventh-century reform movement.[56]

Two historians have also addressed the ambiguous nature of the term *ordo* in the early Middle Ages. Giles Constable, in an extensive study of the different schemas used in the eleventh and twelfth centuries to organize medieval society into *ordines*,[57] noted the same characteristics of ordination recognized by the authors already cited:

> It is often hard to tell in exactly what sense *ordo* was being used, and especially to distinguish the social and sacramental senses of the term; but its root meaning remained row, rank, or grade, usually in a collective sense, which distinguished it from an individual honor or dignity as these terms are now used. One entered into rather than received an order, which was marked by a way of life and an internal discipline as well as exterior distinctions and obligations.[58]

Constance Berman undertook an extensive study of early Cistercian documents and concluded that before the middle of the twelfth century, the Cistercians used the term *ordo* to refer to a way of life rather than to an administrative unit.[59] Her conclusions again fit the general picture that an *ordo* was a way of life, a ministry, a vocation, rather than particular clerical states: "This reconsideration of terminology shows that in the earliest years, Cistercian *ordo* had more to do with how people lived within communities and with regulating social conditions within monasteries than with conformity to the administrative decrees of a larger group. Early Cistercian ideals about monastic *ordo* centered on notions of charity with little concern for administrative conformity or unanimity."[60] Although Constable and Berman were not concerned directly with ordination in the narrower sense of the process of moving into a new *ordo* in the service of the church, their studies of both the larger societal use of *ordo* and the narrow use of that term by the early Cistercians support the general conclusions of scholars surveyed above. Sometime during the twelfth century, the term *ordo* acquired a new and narrower definition.

Ordinations in the Early Middle Ages

A clear picture of ordination in the early Middle Ages emerges from these studies. To repeat the definition of Congar, "The words *ordinare, ordinari, ordinatio* signified the fact of being designated and consecrated to take up a certain place, or better a certain function, *ordo,* in the community and at its service."[61] Ordination within the church encompassed the entire process of selection and appointment of candidates to a particular position and was almost exclusively an appointment to a particular community; often selection was made by that particular community. There were many different functions that were deemed to require ordination, not only those connected with service at the altar. In fact, based on medieval examples given in the *Novum glossarium mediae latinitatis,* the words *ordinatio* and *ordinare* were used to describe the ceremony and installation not only of bishops, priests, deacons, and subdeacons but also of porters, lectors, exorcists, acolytes, canons, abbots, abbesses, kings, queens, and empresses. The terms could also apply to the consecration or establishment of a religious order or a monastery, or to admission to the religious life.[62]

The *Rule of Benedict* used *ordinatio* frequently to refer to the installation of an abbot.[63] The chapter in the *Rule* concerning the choosing of an abbot is simply entitled "*De ordinando abbate* (On the ordaining of an abbot)," and the chapter begins: "In the ordination of an abbot...."[64] Abbots, monks, and others entering the religious life were referred to as ordained throughout the early Middle Ages.[65] Kings and emperors were also considered to be ordained by themselves or by their contemporaries. As noted by Congar, the Capetians referred to their coronations as ordinations.[66] Pope Urban II in a letter dated 1089 to Rainold, archbishop of Rheims, affirmed the archbishop's power to ordain the kings and queens of France.[67] The Western rite for the coronation of the emperor is called in the tenth-century Romano-Germanic Pontifical "The blessing for the ordaining of the Emperor according to the West."[68] In an example of the use of *ordinatio* for a queen, the *Annales Altahenses maiores* for the year 1043 described how King Henry led his bride to Mainz and here arranged for her to be consecrated queen, and then "having completed the days of ordination (*diebus ordinationis*) in Ingelheim, the region made preparations for the marriage."[69] The coronation rite contained in a Florentine sacramentary from the second half of the tenth century introduces the blessing of the empress with the words, "the ordination of the Empress at the entrance to the church."[70]

Kings and queens, emperors, and empresses often considered themselves, and were considered by their contemporaries, to be validly ordained into an important *ordo* of the church. To quote Henry Chadwick, "So Western a writer as Pope Leo the Great can tell the orthodox Greek emperor that he is invested not only with *imperium* but with a priestly office (*sacerdotium*) and that by the Holy Spirit he is preserved from all doctrinal error."[71] No doubt such claims were more impressive when they were backed up with an army; nevertheless, kingship (and queenship) represents a historical example of ecclesiastically supported ordination that later theology would judge not to be ordination at all.[72]

Ordination, particularly understood as the selection of a candidate to a particular ministry, could be performed by laity. The editors of the *Annales Camaldulenses* recorded a charter from the year 867 granting lands to establish a convent of twenty nuns. The donors, Count Winigris and his wife Richild, insisted that the selection and ordination of the abbess remain firmly in their hands and the hands of their successors.[73] Even more dramatically, Orso, bishop of Olivolo near Venice, in 853, appointed his sister, Romana, as the administrator of his will. He further directed her to watch his successor closely, and if he should mismanage episcopal property, "she would have the most firm power to ordain the monastery [the basilica of St. Laurence] to any person she wished" after the death of the miscreant bishop.[74]

So, too, an *ordo* did not necessarily refer to a particular clerical state. Innocent III described canon lawyers as a separate *ordo* in the early twelfth century.[75] At least as late as the fourteenth century, *ordo* could also be used to designate the sacrament of extreme unction, and marriage would be referred to as an *ordo* as late as the fifteenth century.[76]

Each order had its own function, of course, and not all orders were equally important. The most prestigious of the clerical orders were bishop and priest. Many of the other orders, such as deacons, subdeacons, porters, lectors, exorcists, and acolytes, served under their care. These were the orders that served in diocese and parishes. Eventually these orders would become stages in training on the way to becoming a priest, but, as pointed out above, that process would not be complete until the high Middle Ages. Women served in three of these orders, bishop, priest, and deacon, although the attributions concerning the first two orders are highly controversial, as the next chapter will discuss. Most women, however, served in orders not under the direct care of a bishop. Women in religious life were also considered ordained into their own orders. These would include abbesses, canonesses, virgins, widows, and nuns.

Ordained Women

Clearly ordination served quite a different function in the early Middle Ages than it would come to serve from the later Middle Ages on. The criteria for ordination laid down by Morin, and followed by most modern scholars, simply would not have applied in the early Middle Ages. First, the term "ordination" was used interchangeably with "consecration" and "benediction," so "ordination" was not the only term used for a ceremony whereby one took up a new ministry in the church. Second, as pointed out earlier, the rituals that comprised an ordination did vary over the centuries, and, in any case, there was not yet the legal mindset to ask which ceremonies constituted a "valid" ordination.[77] Finally, ordination was not limited to only those ministries that served at the altar, that is, the priesthood and the diaconate.

Ordination comprised a much larger group of ministries in the early Middle Ages, including ministries reserved for women. Given the understanding that prevailed in the early centuries of the Middle Ages in western Christianity, a woman was just as ordained (as a deaconess or an abbess, for instance) as a man (as a priest or a deacon). One should not assume, therefore, that all references to "clerics" or "the ordained" from that period imply only men. Women were frequently also referred to as ordained and occasionally as clerics.

Popes and Bishops

Women's orders appear along with the orders of men in lists of orders included in many early medieval documents. When popes in the eleventh and twelfth centuries made lists of the different orders, they included those of women. In 1018, Benedict VIII conferred on the Cardinal Bishop of Porto the right to ordain bishops, priests, deacons, deaconesses, subdeacons, churches, and altars.[78] This privilege was repeated by John XIX in 1025[79] and by Leo IX in 1049.[80] In 1026, John XIX conceded to the bishop of Silva Candida "consecrations of the altar of the church of St. Peter and of other monasteries, also the consecration of churches, altars, priests, clerics, deacons, or deaconesses for the whole Leonine City."[81] Benedict IX continued this privilege in 1037 and also exempted from lay control "priests, deacons, monks, housekeepers, clerics of whatever order or dignity, all holy women or deaconesses."[82] Calixtus II, in a privilege of 1123 to the convent of the Holy Savior and St. Julia in Brescia, granted the abbess the right to seek the ordination of abbesses, nuns, and all other clerics advanced to sacred orders from any bishop she wished.[83]

Not only popes but also bishops included women among the ordained. Bishop Gilbert of Limerick included in his *De usu ecclesiae* (*On the Practice of the Church*) the injunction, "The bishop ordains abbots, abbesses, priests, and the six other grades."[84] The chronicle of Thietmar, Bishop of Merseburg (d. 1018), recorded that "the same woman who at that time was twelve years old was veiled on Sunday, the kalends of May and on the next day ordained abbess."[85] A tenth-century letter of Atto, Bishop of Vercelli, described the initiation of deaconesses in the early church as an ordination: "Therefore for the aid of men, devout women were ordained leaders of worship in the holy Church."[86]

Philip of Harvengt, the Praemonstratentian abbot, wrote a treatise on clerics in the second half of the twelfth century. In it he offered an example of how the popes and bishops quoted above would have included religious women when referring to clerics in general. Once, Philip noted: "A man came into a church, and I was there, and the man found a learned holy women reading from a book in front of the altar to other religious women. The woman explained that she was reading the life of a virgin. The man remarked, 'she was a good cleric.' "[87] He used the masculine (*clericus bonus*), however, and Philip went on to explain that although one does not often find the term *bona clerica,* the feminine for "good cleric," early Church writers knew of many learned and holy women who were certainly clerics, by which Philip meant that they were learned.[88] Later on in his book, Philip would include holy women and nuns among the clergy, even though they didn't earn their living from serving at the altar, but rather from donations.[89]

Rituals of Ordination

Several medieval books of rituals term the commissioning rites for women as ordinations. Of course, since *ordinatio* was used interchangeably with *consecratio* and *benedictio,* any rite that uses these or other phrases does not indicate a rite that is different from, or lesser than, an *ordinatio.* More important, these rites are contained among the ordination rites for men.

THE MOZARABIC LITURGY. A group of manuscripts dating from the eighth to the fourteenth centuries preserves the rites of the Mozarabic or Visigoth Church of Spain. These rites would have been practiced from the fifth century roughly through the eleventh century for many parts of Christian Spain and in the diocese of Toledo up to the present day. The critical edition of the oldest manuscript, however, would represent rites from roughly the seventh through the eleventh century.[90]

The section that contains the rites for ordination consists of the following rituals:

> Ritual for ordaining a cleric
> Ritual for ordaining a sacristan
> Ritual for ordaining the person who is committed to the care of books and writing
> Ritual over a person who wishes to cut his beard
> Ritual for ordaining a subdeacon
> Preface for ordaining a deacon
> Ritual for ordaining an archdeacon
> Blessing for the consecration of the head cleric
> Preface for ordaining a priest
> Ritual for ordaining an archpriest
> Ritual for ordaining an abbot
> Blessing for a garment dedicated to God
> Ritual for the blessing of a virgin
> Ritual or blessing for a veiled woman dedicated to God
> Ritual for the ordaining of an abbess[91]

Here the rites for ordaining an abbess and for the blessing of a virgin appear with the rites for ordaining abbots, archpriests, subdeacons, librarians, sacristans, clerics, priests, deacons, and archdeacons. Included are blessings for head clerics, vestments, and young clerics shaving for the first time. Ordination is certainly not limited to priests and deacons in these rites, and "blessing" seems to be used interchangeably with "ordination" to describe the rites of initiation into the various ministries listed.

THE PONTIFICAL OF EGBERT, BISHOP OF YORK. Another pontifical has survived from the eighth century, that of Egbert, bishop of York from 732 to 766.[92] Egbert included in his pontifical prayers for the ordination of psalmists, doorkeepers, lectors, exorcists, acolytes, and subdeacons. All of these rituals were called ordinations.[93] Under the section entitled "On the ordaining of deacons," Egbert's pontifical included a prayer, "Another blessing of a deacon or a deaconess."[94] Under the larger rubric "on the ordaining of priests," the pontifical included "prayers for the mass in behalf of himself on the day of his ordination or consecration."[95] In a separate section on the episcopal blessings, the pontifical included blessings for the ordination of deaconesses, for the ordination of deacons, and for the ordination of priests.[96] Also included among the prayers are those for the blessing and for the consecration of widows.[97]

The pontifical exhibits the same characteristics of the early medieval approach to ordination as does the Mozarabic pontifical. The terms "ordination," "consecration," and "blessing" are used interchangeably. The rites for the commissioning of deaconesses are called ordinations and included along with the rites for deacons and for priests.

THE GREGORIAN SACRAMENTARY. One of the most influential sacramentaries of the early Middle Ages was the so-called "Gregorian Sacramentary," attributed to Pope Gregory the Great. The sacramentary appeared in several different forms but is based on a Roman sacramentary that was adopted and adapted by the Carolingian court and from there spread throughout much of Europe.[98] The section on the rites of ordination starts with the phrase, "Here begins the ritual of sacred orders,"[99] and includes rites for doorkeepers, lectors, exorcists, and acolytes.[100] These are followed by rituals for the ordination of subdeacons and deacons.[101] The rites for priests are simply described as "ritual for priests" in just the same manner as the minor orders.[102] The rites for bishops are described as "a blessing for bishops"[103] and are followed by "a prayer for the making of a deaconess"[104] and "a prayer for the making of an abbot or abbess."[105] "A prayer for the ordaining of an abbot or abbess"[106] offers another ritual for monastics, and a set of prayers for virgins and widows completes the rites for the installation into ministry.[107]

Once again the rites for initiation into a new ministry include several ceremonies including those for women and are variously designated as blessings, makings, or ordinations. The understanding of ordination uncovered by Gy, Congar, and other scholars seems justified in the actual books of prayers used for ministry in the early church. Many more rituals were considered ordinations than just those rituals to the priesthood and diaconate. Different terms are used interchangeably with ordination for the commissioning to a new *ordo*. Women's *ordines* are included along with those of men, with no indication that they were considered different from those reserved to men.

THE ROMANO-GERMANIC PONTIFICAL. The famous Romano-Germanic Pontifical (RGP) from the tenth century (sometimes called the Mainz Pontifical or the Pontifical of Otto the Great) is a vast compilation of prayers and rites that had earlier appeared in separate books but were brought together in one large volume. The pontifical, originally compiled in Germany between 950 and 962, was rapidly diffused throughout Europe. It was used in Rome as early as the tenth century and continued to be used there at least until the time of Gregory VII (1073–85). Copies exist from as late as the twelfth century, and the Pontifical had a profound influence on later liturgical collections.[108]

The ordination rites in the RGP include several rites for the ordination of women, and these rites are again included among those for men. The ordinal discusses the different orders subject to the bishop (c. 14 and 15), then the rites and prayers for the ordination of priests, deacons, or subdeacons in the Roman Church (c. 16–19). These are followed by the rites for the consecration of a virgin (c. 20–21), the rite for the ordination of an abbess (c. 22), another rite for the consecration of a virgin (c. 23), the rite for the "making" of a deaconess (c. 24), and the rite for the consecration of a widow (c. 25). Immediately after these rites for women appear the rites for the ordination of an abbot (c. 26–27), followed by another rite for the "making" and ordination of a monk (c. 28–31). A further rite for the ordination of an abbess (c. 32) concludes the section on ordination and is followed by a series of prayers for the blessing of churches.

A list of the ordination rites reads as follows:

14. Concerning the offices, chapter on the seven grades of Isidore [of Seville]
15. Ritual for how the holy orders in the Roman Church were [i.e. psalmist, doorkeeper, lector, exorcist, acolyte]
16. Ritual for how priests, deacons or subdeacons are chosen in the Roman Church
17. Prayers for these at mass
18. Also a mass for the anniversary of the consecration of a deacon
19. Also how a priest ought to celebrate a mass on the anniversary of his consecration
20. The consecration of holy virgins that is celebrated on the Epiphany or Easter season or on the feast of the apostles.
21. Also a mass on the anniversary of a virgin
22. Ordination of an abbess professing a canonical rule
23. Consecration of virgins who converted from the world and having taken the habit of chastity wish to practice privately in their homes
24. On the making of a deaconess[109]
25. Consecration of widows who have professed chastity
26. Ordination of an abbot
27. Mass for an abbot
28. Ritual for the making of a monk
29. Ordination of monks
30. Other prayers for monks

31. Prayers and intercessions for monks at mass
32. Ordination of abbesses professing a monastic rule[110]

Besides these complete liturgical rites, one also finds an interesting reference to the blessing of *presbyterae* (women priests). A chapter entitled "On the grades of the Roman Church" describes an ordination mass lead by the pope. The following instructions are included as part of the ritual, "in the same way, likewise women, deaconesses and *presbyterae* who are blessed on the same day."[111] The reference tells little about these *presbyterae*, but it is significant that they are included in the liturgy.

First, the RGP offers an excellent example of the use of *ordinatio* during the early Middle Ages. The term is used interchangeably with *consecratio* and even *faciendam* (making) for both the orders of women and the orders of men. Second, these rites include those for priests, deacons, deaconesses, subdeacons, psalmists, doorkeepers, lectors, exorcists, acolytes, virgins, widows, abbots, abbesses, and monks. Just as in the earlier rites cited, the pattern holds. Ordination was not understood to be limited to the priesthood and the diaconate, but rather celebrated and effected the move into a new ministry or *ordo* in the church.

TWELFTH-CENTURY PONTIFICALS. In the twelfth century, a series of pontificals was produced for use in the Roman church. They were based on the RGP but simplified the liturgies and eliminated those no longer in use. In short, they attempted to adapt the RGP for use in the context of twelfth-century Rome.[112] The list of ordination rites found in these books once again includes those for virgins, widows, abbesses, and deaconesses. They follow in order:

I. In the name of the Lord, there the ritual begins of the seven ecclesiastical grades. First, the preface for the making of a cleric.
II. For the cutting of a beard
III. On the psalmist
IV. The ordination of a doorkeeper
V. The ordination of a lector
VI. The ordination of a exorcist
VII. The ordination of an acolyte
VIII. The ordination of a subdeacon
IX. The ritual for how deacons and priests are chosen in the Roman church
X. Here the ritual begins for the calling and examination or consecration of a person chosen for the episcopacy according to the custom of the Roman church

XI. The proclamation that the pope gives to a bishop whom he blessed, mention of which has been made above

XII. Here the ritual begins for the blessing of a virgin (alternatively: Ritual for the consecration of a holy virgin)

XIII. The blessing of a widow

XIV. Mass for the consecration of a deaconess

XV. The ritual for blessing an abbot or abbess

XVI. The ritual for making a monk[113]

As in the other liturgical books, the words "ordination," "blessing," "making," and "consecrating" are used indiscriminately to describe the rituals of initiation into a new *ordo* in the church. In fact, the word *ordinatio* is used in these titles only for the subdeacons and the other "minor" orders.

As late as the twelfth century, rituals for ordination considered far more ministries as ordained, included several for women, than would be the case from the thirteenth century on.[114] Ordination was not reserved for those ministries that served at the altar. Certainly each of the ordained ministries performed different functions. Some were clearly more prestigious than others. Yet there is no indication that any of the orders were somehow less ordained than others. All were, in the words of Congar, "designated and consecrated to take up a certain place, or better, function, *ordo,* in the community and at its service."

Development of the Power of the Priest

Several interesting implications follow from the definition of ordination current in the first millennium of Christianity. First and foremost, the power to perform the rituals of the church was not the essential purpose of ordination. The question of who had the power to perform rituals was less important than whom the community had chosen as their ministers. The central role of the priest as administrator of the sacraments became essential to ordination only with its redefinition. Not surprisingly, just at the time when this redefinition was taking place, and for the same reasons, the power of the priesthood was expanding to take over almost all ritual roles in the church. As we will see shortly abbots and abbesses in earlier centuries preached, heard confessions, and baptized, all powers that would be reserved to the priest in the twelfth and thirteenth centuries. The most important function reserved to the priest in this new understanding, however, was the power to celebrate the Mass. The new exclusionary definition of ordination was specifically defined by the function of the priest (and to a lesser extent that of the deacon and subdeacon) to preside at the Eucharist. The role of the priest as special mediator of God's grace rested most importantly on his ability to confect the presence of the risen Christ in the Eucharist. Just as important, therefore, as the redefinition of ordination in accomplishing a definitive change in the understanding of Christian ministry would be the theological teaching that only a properly ordained priest could make the risen Christ present in the Eucharist.

This was not at all a settled issue until the end of the twelfth century. From the viewpoint of the older definition of ordination, of course, this is not surprising. Such a question would not necessarily even be an interesting one in earlier centuries. A person led the liturgy (or baptized or preached or heard confessions) within a particular community because that person was chosen to lead that community. In the word of Schillebeeckx, "in the ancient church it is said that he (or she) is 'appointed' as minister in order to be able to appear as leader to build up the community, and for this reason he (or she) was also the obvious person to preside at the eucharist."[115] The question of exactly by whom and how the bread and wine is consecrated would only be of interest when that action became the central power bestowed by ordination. Indeed, it would become the central purpose of ordination itself. In the older definition of ordination, one officiated at ceremonies because one had been chosen by the community to lead the community; in the later understanding, one led the community because one was empowered to perform the ceremonies.

It is very important to keep this in mind when reviewing the evidence for female ministry in the early centuries. There was no understanding during those early centuries that only priests could lead a liturgy or that only priests were truly ordained. Other leaders could, and did, perform many of the functions later reserved to the ordained priesthood. The next chapter will review the roles attributed to women during this period. Before such a review can be properly assessed, though, it is important to have an appreciation of just how late the concept of a powerful mediatory priesthood appeared.

At the beginning of the twelfth century, for instance, scholars were not at all in agreement that a priest alone could effect the transformation of the bread and wine into the body and blood of Christ. At least three twelfth-century scholars are known to have put forward the theory that the words of consecration themselves confect, regardless of who says them.

Abelard, writing in his *Theologia christiana* (*Christian Theology*), described their position: "I know of two brothers who are numbered among the highest masters, the other of whom imputed such power to the divine words in the confecting of the sacrament that by whomever they are pronounced, they have the same efficacy, so that even a woman or someone of whatever order or condition through the words of the Lord is able to confect the sacrament of the altar."[116] The great medieval scholar Marie-Dominique Chenu has identified these two brothers as the famous brothers Bernard and Thierry of Chartres.[117]

The Chartranians, however, were not the only theologians to teach that the words of consecration alone confect the sacrament. Teaching in Paris in the early 1160s, the liturgist John Beleth described the secret of the Mass in the following terms:

> The secret is so-called because it is recited secretly, although in the past it was said aloud so that it was known by lay people. It happened, therefore, that one day shepherds placed bread on a rock which, at the recitation of those words, was changed into flesh, perhaps the bread was transubstantiated into the body of Christ since vengeance was most rapidly taken against them by divine agency. For they were struck down by a divine judgment sent from heaven. Hence it was decreed that in the future it be said silently.[118]

The story originally appeared as a cautionary tale in the sixth-century *Pratum spirituale* (Spiritual Meadow) of John Moschius.[119] The story was repeated by the anonymous *Speculum de mysteriis ecclesiae* (Mirror of the Mysteries of the Church), written c. 1160–75. In this version, there is no mention of transubstantiation; however, the shepherds were punished by divine vengeance for their lack of reverence for such a great mystery.[120] This version of the story was copied into the *De missarum mysteriis* (On the Mysteries of the Mass) of Cardinal Lothar of Segni (c. 1195). Lothar was careful to point out that it is only a priest who says the words of institution and that the shepherds' use of them was against the practice of the church.[121] He was soon to be elevated to the papacy as Pope Innocent III. Although neither author speaks of the words of institution consecrating of themselves, as did the brothers from Chartres and John Beleth, they ascribe to the words great power apart from their enunciation by an ordained priest.

The position of the brothers from Chartres and that of Beleth may have formed the basis of the teaching of some of the heretical Waldensians who argued in the late twelfth century that if no worthy priest could be found, a layperson, even a woman, could lead the liturgy and consecrate the bread and wine.[122] Their position is reflected in the creed written for those Waldensians returning to the church in 1208 by Innocent III. "Therefore we firmly believe and confess that however honest, pious, holy or prudent someone may be, he [the adjectives are masculine as only a male is intended here] is not able to nor ought to consecrate the Eucharist nor perform the ritual of the altar, unless he is a priest regularly ordained by a bishop in a visible and tangible way."[123] The words are quite similar to those used to describe the position of Bernard and Thierry and so suggest that this was not just an isolated academic opinion, but one that found resonance among at least one Christian community.

Along with the discussion of the power of the words of consecration, a further discussion occurred in the twelfth century over which words could be used for consecration. Gregory the Great, writing in the sixth century, explained in a letter to John, the bishop of Syracuse, the liturgical customs of the Roman church. "We say the Lord's Prayer immediately after the intercession (the Kyrie) for this reason because the custom of the apostles was that they consecrated the sacrifice of offering by this prayer alone. It seemed exceedingly unsuitable to me that we would say an intercession over the offering which a scholar had composed and that we would not say the very tradition that our Redeemer had composed over his body and blood."[124]

In the late eleventh century, Bernold of Constance produced a lengthy commentary on the papal liturgy. While explaining the history of the canon, he referred to the letter of Gregory, adding that Gregory inserted the Lord's Prayer into the liturgy since this was the prayer that "the apostles themselves were believed to have used in the confection of these sacraments by the institution of the Lord."[125] By the twelfth century, Gregory's teaching had been slightly changed. While scholars continued to teach that the Lord's Prayer was the original prayer over the gifts, they added that the blessings of Jesus over the bread and wine were also part of the original prayer of consecration. One of the most fascinating of these accounts comes from an anonymous work found in a thirteenth-century manuscript in the British Library. The author gives a history of the prayers used in the Mass that begins, "Saint Peter the first celebrated Mass in Antioch in which only the words of the Lord and the Lord's Prayer were said."[126] Less colorful explanations of Gregory's teaching appeared in the Gemma animae (Jewel of the Soul) of Honorius Augustodunensis written ca. c. 1102–33: "The Lord Jesus, priest according to the order of Melchisedech, at first instituted the mass when he made his body and blood from bread and wine, and ordered this to be celebrated in his memory. The apostles added to this when they said the words which the Lord said and the Lord's Prayer over the bread and wine."[127]

Rupert of Deutz, writing in 1111, explained that the elaborated liturgy was not holier than earlier times, "when it was consecrated by the words of the Lord alone and by the Lord's Prayer alone."[128] Robert Paululus, writing ca. 1175–80, copied this teaching of Honorius.[129] John Beleth taught that the apostles originally simply recited the words of institution but then added the Lord's Prayer.[130] Sicard of Cremona, writing ca. 1185–95, taught that the words of institution transubstantiated the bread and wine but added that the apostles added the Lord's Prayer to the words said over the bread and wine.[131] Once again, the Waldensians appeared to have used this teaching in their liturgies. According to Alexander of Alexandria, the Dominican friar who recorded early practices of the Waldensians, the heart of their liturgy was a sevenfold repetition of the Lord's Prayer.[132]

The Lord's Prayer was not the only element in the liturgy, however, that twelfth-century theologians considered as candidates for the power to consecrate. The *Speculum de mysteriis ecclesiae* was quite explicit concerning the role of the sign of the cross in the consecration:

> And by this everything is given in those words of the Lord given in the supper which the priest adds. But this about to be said, thus first he begins, "Who on the day before he suffered." With these words, he raises the still common bread from the altar and having raised it, he blesses and imprints the sign of the cross, and before he sets it down he reproduces the words of the Lord when he says, "He blessed and broke," and that which follows. Then he takes up the chalice and signs it and reproduces the words of the Lord saying, "And he gave it to his disciples saying, 'Take and drink from this, all of you.'" Here that extraordinary miracle is done. With these words food for the flesh becomes food for the soul. Through these words and through the sign of the cross nature is renewed, and bread becomes flesh and wine blood.[133]

Richard the Premonstratensian, writing ca. 1150–75, makes the power of the cross the central theme of his entire spiritual commentary on the liturgy. According to Richard, "The power of the mass is the cross of Christ which consecrates and sanctifies the sacrament of the altar and all the sacraments of the church."[134] Once again, it is the Waldensians who seem to have put this teaching into practice in their liturgies, as they are reported by Alexander of Alexandria to have consecrated the bread and wine by means of the sign of the cross.[135]

During the twelfth century at least, it appears that there was as yet no agreement as to what would be referred to as the "form" of the Eucharist. Many, if not most, theologians and notably Peter the Lombard would have agreed that the words of institution consecrate the bread and wine, transforming them into the body and blood of the risen Christ.[136] As demonstrated above, however, there was not unanimous agreement on that question. Some theologians, based on a tradition stemming from Gregory the Great, would argue that the Lord's Prayer was at least at one time part of the words of consecration. Other theologians would put forth the theory that the sign of the cross was still part of the formula of consecration.

At the great Fourth Lateran Council of 1215, the first article adopted by Pope Innocent III and the others gathered together was a creed directed against several heretical groups, including the Waldensians. In part, it reads:

> There is one Universal Church of the faithful, outside of which there is absolutely no salvation. In which there is the same priest and sacrifice, Jesus Christ, whose body and blood are truly contained in the sacrament of the altar under the forms of bread and wine; the bread being changed (*transubstantiatis*) by divine power into the body, and the wine into the blood, so that to realize the mystery of unity we may receive of Him what He has received of us. And this sacrament no one can effect except the priest who has been duly ordained in accordance with the keys of the Church, which Jesus Christ Himself gave to the Apostles and their successors.[137]

This section of the creed and first canon arguably contains the most discussed and debated words from that council. Scholars have particularly focused on the use of the term *transubstantiatis*, the first such use in an official church document.

Less noticed, but perhaps equally important, are the words that follow: "And this sacrament no one can effect except the priest who has been duly ordained in accordance with the keys of the Church, which Jesus Christ Himself gave to the Apostles and their successors." Most scholars assume that this statement merely repeats the standard orthodox position of the time. In fact, this statement may have been intended to quell twelfth-century debates on two issues: who could properly confect the sacrament and how that sacrament was confected. The creed of the Fourth Lateran Council could be seen not as a simple repetition of long-held Christian beliefs, but as a magisterial intervention to settle theological and pastoral discussions of real importance. The decrees of Lateran IV spread with remarkable speed throughout Western Christianity, and the implementation of those decrees created a very different church from that which preceded the council.

Seen in this light, Lateran IV provides a convenient demarcation between the older understanding of *ordinatio*, which described most of the functions and roles within the church as ordained, and the new understanding of *ordinatio*, which excluded from orders all except those who led the liturgy. Along with this change, and closely connected with it, was an understanding of the priesthood that greatly enhanced its power by insisting that only a properly ordained priest could consecrate the bread and wine at the altar.

Not that Innocent III would have understood himself as introducing anything new. He would have seen himself as restoring an older order, basing himself on the texts contained in the eleventh- and twelfth-century collections of canon law. We will discuss the considerable influence of these texts in more detail later. The teachings of Bernard and Thierry of Chartres, of John Beleth, and of the commentators on the liturgy mentioned above would be soon forgotten or explained away by later writers. Interestingly enough, though, none of these writers were ever accused of heresy, nor were their positions ever condemned either during their lifetimes or even after. If the Waldensians were in fact carrying on what they may have felt were older traditions based on the above teachings, they were condemned for holding them. The creed of Lateran IV was in part directed against them. What was a respectable or at least an acceptable academic position before the end of the twelfth century would become heretical in the thirteenth century. The church that emerged from Lateran IV was, despite the intentions of its creators, something new—a more clerical, more hierarchical, more centralized church than that which preceded it.[138]

A more detailed picture of how and when this new conception of the church emerged will be discussed in chapter 4. For now, it is important to emphasize that the concentration of sacramental power into the hands of the priest did not occur until the end of the twelfth century. Early writers could and did conceive of a different form of authority, an authority shared by several different *ordines*. We should not be surprised, given this earlier under-standing of both ordination and authority, to find both the men and women who constituted the leadership within their communities performing sacra-mental and even sacerdotal functions. They belonged to a different church and a different time, and however powerful the temptation, we should not attribute to them the clericalism that emerged in later centuries.

Conclusion

Ordination in the early Middle Ages did not have the same meaning that it would come to have after the twelfth century. Rather than the bestowal of a particular power and authority connected to the eucharistic liturgy and limited to those offices that performed that liturgy, ordination referred to the process by which one was chosen for a particular ministry or service in the church. Further, the term "ordination" was more or less interchangeable with the term "consecration" or "blessing" or even "making" or, in the case of nuns, "veiling." Many different ministries were considered to be ordained, including several ministries reserved for women. This did not mean that all those ordained were ordained to the same ministries, of course. In the next chapter, the various ministries that women did perform will be investigated in more detail. As will become clearer in the next chapter, women did indeed serve at the altar as priests and deacons, but that service was not a determining factor in judging whether they were considered ordained or not by their contemporaries. To argue that women were not ordained because they either did not or should not have served at the altar would be to impose definitions developed in the twelfth and thirteenth centuries on this earlier period. To do so requires a theological judgment that only the later definition encompasses "true ordination." As described in chapter 1, this may be theologically justified in order to determine what authority this past brings to present debates on the ordination of women. As history, however, it is simply anachronistic.

The evidence that a broader understanding of ordination existed in the early Middle Ages is widespread. Popes, bishops, theologians, and the book of rituals used in ordinations bare witness to this more inclusive understanding of ordination. According to this definition of ordination, women were certainly considered to be ordained. However, the sources discussed here are deliberately limited. They were chosen to show that the ordained ministries of women were included among those for men and that the ministries for women were included among lists of clergy. There exist many other references to the ministry of women during this period, references that offer a much more detailed picture of the actual ministries that women performed during this period. It is time now to turn to those sources to better understand to what services women were ordained.

3

The Ministry of
Ordained Women

The Roles of Ordained Women

Women were commissioned for several different *ordines* in the early
Middle Ages. The vocations of widow, virgin, and deaconess were a
continuation of earlier Christian practices.[1] References to the ministries of *episcopae, presbyterae,* deaconesses, abbesses, canonesses,
nuns and holy women also appear.[2] While the term "ordination" was
used to designate the commissioning rite for many holy women,
this book will focus on the particular ministries of *episcopae, presbyterae,* deaconesses, and abbesses. Since the purpose of the study is
to demonstrate why and how women were removed from the ordained ministry, the most useful examples for this purpose will be
those female ministries that performed functions later reserved to
male clergy.

The limitations of this study should not be understood to imply,
however, that the ministries of the other orders of holy women were
less important, nor that liturgy exists only in those practices later
reserved to the male presbyterate and diaconate. If ordination in the
early Middle Ages meant appointment to a particular ministry in the
church, then women were ordained to several functions, some of
which they continued to perform even after the ceremony initiating
them into that role had ceased to be considered a true ordination.
Religious women continued to pray the liturgy of the hours, to offer
extensive charitable services, and to wield considerable administrative

jurisdiction long after those services no longer qualified them to be included among the ordained clergy. Surely one would not want to minimize the importance of these ministries or deny that such ministries were considered as ordained in these early centuries.

Rather our purpose here will be to clarify as precisely as possible which ministries were forbidden to women as well as acknowledge that the ministries left to women were no longer considered as "ordained" ministries. There was a twofold process, therefore, that needs to be addressed. First, women were denied any status as ordained ministers; in short, they were laicized. Second, some functions once performed by women were reserved to male priests and deacons. This chapter will focus on the second of these movements in order to highlight more clearly the change that laicization effected in the status of religious women.

Reading the Sources

It should not be too surprising that few sources exist concerning the ordained ministry of women during this period. Once women were no longer ordained and, moreover, were considered never to have been ordained, there would be no reason to continue to reproduce liturgies for their ordinations. Exemplars of liturgies for the ordination of women, therefore, pretty much ceased to exist by the end of the twelfth century. The same would be true for liturgical texts used by women. There would be no need to go through all the expense of producing a liturgy to be used by women once they ceased to perform it. Nor were ancient texts of rites that never were supposed to have happened be would worth preserving. Of the texts that may possibly have been used by women for a eucharistic liturgy, for example, only a few fragments remain.

Once women were considered never to have been ordained, all references to their once being ordained would be either expunged or quietly dropped. The ecclesiastical laws that were copied into the great canonical collections of the eleventh and twelfth centuries were those that supported the reform movement of that period. Our picture of earlier periods is shaped by what survives, and what survives has been carefully selected and preserved to reflect and support the views of those doing the selecting and preservation.[3] It was not in the interests of those males who produced the vast canonical and theological collections of the twelfth and thirteenth centuries to "remember" either that women were ever ordained or that they ever performed liturgical functions reserved for males. Laws denying women access to the altar or to ordination would be preserved and would eventually be understood to be the true and only tradition. Sources that suggested otherwise were quietly dropped, or in the rare cases in which they were preserved, they were assiduously explained away. We are left with fragments to demonstrate that women played a more formal and public role in ministry than the tradition would suggest. The scarcity of the evidence, however, provides only hints of what those roles might have been.

The Role of History

These caveats suggest that a particular model of histor[y is being] used for this study. History, as understood here, is a contemporar[y construct]ion of more or less plausible scenarios, none of which accurately r[eflects] what actually occurred in the past. As such, all history is driven by [present c]oncerns and exists only in the present and for the present. This study is [no e]xception. The purpose of the study is more carefully to delineate the roles women played in Western Christianity in the past so as to better understand how women came to inherit the roles they presently play in Christianity and in the wider Western society. Hopefully understanding this history will empower those in the present by freeing them from the seeming inevitability of the constructed pasts that dominate our understanding of who women were and thus who they might become.

More precisely this study hopes to create an alternative scenario to the dominant picture that suggests that (1) ordination as presently defined has always been so defined and that (2) women's ministries were never considered to be ordained ministries given that definition. Scholars have clearly demonstrated that the first claim is mistaken, although a more detailed analysis of how the change in the definition of ordination occurred will be offered in chapter 4. The second issue is more difficult. An alternative scenario must be glimpsed through the cracks in the dominant story; places where the surviving evidence threatens to undermine the narrative. If women were never ordained, why are they so designated? If women never served at the altar, why were women called deacons and priests in the past? Why does past legislation forbid women from performing liturgical functions that they were never supposed to have performed at all? In short, what kind of Christianity allowed and even embraced women as deacons and priests? What kind of Christianity allowed abbesses to hear their nuns' confessions, preach, and distribute communion? Evidence survives that describes all of the above, and yet such evidence should not have survived. It should never have existed at all, if the dominant narrative were consistent.

This chapter will be an attempt to piece together such evidence as exists to suggest one possible scenario to explain the anomalies that continually threaten to crack open the common perception that religious women in the early Middle Ages were not ordained. The suggestion is, at the very least, that this assumption about religious women in the early Middle Ages is no longer credible. The fragments of women's ministry that have survived are presented here with a possible scenario that those fragments seem to suggest. It is a little like imagining a finished picture puzzle based on a few scattered pieces. A little sky here, a bit of green grass there, perhaps a patch of colored clothing—the picture can only be guessed at. Therefore it must be stressed that this is only one exploratory attempt to create such a plausible alternative scenario. It will have its own problems, some of which will be pointed out at the end of the chapter. Other possible scenarios are both welcomed and encouraged.

There are problems as well with the evidence that remains. The sources will, of necessity, have been compiled by an elite, almost exclusively male, intelligentsia. They wrote the documents and preserved them. The illiterate did not write, and the poor could not afford to preserve their writings even if they could write. Universities, monasteries, convents, dioceses, and the Roman curia had the means and motive to preserve particular records, and modern scholars, of necessity, rely heavily upon them. Because of this clear bias, the picture presented here cannot be, and will not be, complete. This study will be an attempt to uncover a hidden history—one deliberately and systematically denied an existence.

Other limitations add to the exploratory nature of the study. First, not all possible sources have been tapped. Many other sources—for instance, the lives of saints, wills, and charters—have still to be mined for references to women's ministries and theology. The formal university theology often used for this study was not the only theology formulated in the Middle Ages, and church laws referred to in the book were often more desires than implemented decrees. Often sources used will therefore more accurately represent what some male church officials wished the church to be like rather than describe any church that actually existed. One must tread warily here.

Many of the legal sources used are also local. They address local concerns and should not, and cannot be, generalized as even the desires, much less the "official teaching" of "the church." As I have argued elsewhere, there was no "the church" even in the high Middle Ages, much less in the earlier periods.[4] Disagreement among canonists, theologians, and church officials were common and bitter. "The church" rarely spoke with one voice on any issue. The later power and authority ascribed to the councils and synods quoted here were the result of being included in the great canonical and theological collections of the eleventh and twelfth centuries, particularly the *Decretum* of Gratian and the *Sentences* of Peter the Lombard. These statutes should not be seen as more or as less than they were—efforts by local bishops to handle local problems. As such, they tell us little about the larger church in Western Europe. They were certainly not decisions of some centralized authority immediately operative throughout Europe, as they too often have been read.[5]

Episcopae and the Wives of Bishops

Episcopae

As in earlier studies, I am going to use the Latin terms episcopae and presbyterae for the feminine forms of what might be better termed simply bishops and priests.[6] I use this terminology so that it is immediately clear that I mean women bishops and women priests. However, to refer to these offices as "women bishops" and "women priests" might imply that these are different offices from simply bishops and priests. Since part of what I want to argue is that this differentiation is not all that clear for the period under discussion, such terminology may not be useful. "Priestess" is also a possibility, but this title is still associated most commonly in English with non-Christian religions and can therefore be misleading. The usual titles for the ministries of deaconesses and abbesses do not present these problems and will be used throughout.[7] Although scholars disagree about both the relative importance and about relations among these different groups, they do agree that women who assumed these roles played an active part in the church.[8]

There are only five known references to women bishops in Western Christianity. By far the most famous is the ninth-century mosaic of "Theodora episcopa" in the Chapel of St. Zeno in the Church of Santa Prassede in Rome. An inscription on a reliquary in the same church identifies Theodora as the mother of Pope Paschal I (817–824). This inscription dates the translation of the relics contained therein to July 20, 817. The Liber pontificalis named the father of Pascal I as Bonosus without further title. More than likely, if Bonosus had clerical status, this would have been noted, so it is unlikely that Theodora was the wife of a bishop.[9]

The other epigraphic inscription offers less information. A tomb dating sometime between the fourth and the sixth century is inscribed to the "venerable woman, episcopa Q." Eisen identifies the inscription as originally from Umbria and points out that there are also inscriptions to presbyterae from the same period and location that may indicate a pattern of female leadership in fifth-century Umbria.[10] Madigan and Osiek locate the inscription in Rome and suggest a date of 390. They also offer a tentative identification of "Q" as that of the mother or wife of Pope Siricius (384–99).[11]

Brigid of Ireland was described not only as a bishop but also as having successfully undergone ordination to the ranks of the episcopacy. The ninth-century Celtic life of Brigid, the *Bethu Brigte*, described how it happened: "The bishop being intoxicated with the grace of God there did not recognise what he was reciting from his book, for he consecrated Brigid with the orders of a bishop. 'This virgin alone in Ireland,' said Mel, 'will hold the episcopal ordination.' While she was being consecrated a fiery column ascended from her head."[12] The reference is extraordinary for several reasons. First, Brigid was described as actually ordained to the episcopacy. She was referred to as a bishop not out of courtesy or metaphorically. She was really ordained, even if by accident and even if uniquely. Second, there is no question that the ordination took. As Bishop Mel realized, Brigid, once consecrated, was a bishop. At least for this ninth-century Irish writer, a woman could be ordained and even be ordained as bishop.

Hildeburga, the wife of Segenfrid, bishop of Le Mans from 963–996, was described as an *episcopissa* in the account of Segenfrid's death. The bishop was remembered disparagingly in the mid-eleventh-century continuation of the *Acts of the Bishops of Le Mans* because he married and because he bequeathed a large portion of the church's property to his son. Churches were treated as hereditary during this period, and so it is difficult to know if Segenfrid really abused church property or whether the author simply disapproved in general of married clergy. The story was clearly meant to encourage clergy to adopt continence. "When the blood-letting had been done, he slept with his *episcopissa* (little female bishop) the next night. The wound from the [blood-letting] began to grow and the pain advanced to the interior of his heart. The bishop, seeing truly that now he was to perish, asked to be made a monk of St. Peters. When he had been made a monk, he immediately died."[13] Although the use of the diminutive here was probably meant to be derogatory, it may harken back to a time when the term *episcopa* was one of respect.

Wives of Bishops

The only reference that does not designate a particular woman as a bishop is canon 14 of the Council of Tours held in 567. The law reads, "No crowd of women should follow a bishop who does not have an *episcopia*. Of course, a man is saved through the fidelity of a woman as a woman is saved through the fidelity of a man, as the apostle said (1 Cor. 6:16)."[14] Eisen has argued that since the wife of a bishop was called *coniux* (wife), but not *episcopa* in the literature of the early Middle Ages, this reference should not be understood as referring to the wife of a bishop.[15] Yet the context of the law would almost certainly indicate that it is the wife of the bishop that the law intended. The canon preceding this one states that a bishop who has a wife or sister should govern his house and church so that there might be no reason for suspicion of impropriety. This second law follows for those bishops who do not have *episcopiae,* that is, bishops who don't have wives. Finally the council urged those bishops without wives or sisters who need household help to use clergy rather than outside women.[16] The council was then covering all the bases. First, it dealt with the propriety of bishops with wives, then with the propriety of bishops without wives. Finally, it suggested ways that bishops might handle household chores without having unrelated women as part of episcopal households.

If indeed the reference was to the wives of bishops, then the statute would seem to uphold the sanctity and importance of married bishops. The bishops of the Council of Tours were not alone in their respect for married clergy. Brian Brennan in an article in *Church History* described the high regard in which the wives of bishops were often held in sixth-century Gaul.[17] Well they might be held in such regard, since the lives of married clergy could be rather awkward. According to the Council of Agde in 506, ordination to the higher married clergy (bishops, priests, and deacons) could only take place if the spouses mutually agreed to live together chastely.[18] The ideal, as expressed by Pope Leo, was for the couple to change their relationship from a carnal to a spiritual marriage.[19] The requirement that married clergy no longer practice intercourse was repeated and reinforced in the Merovingian councils of the sixth century.

Gregory of Tours, who in general had nothing good to say about the wives of clergy, did offer an engaging picture of the wife of Namatius, a fifth-century bishop of Clermont-Ferrand. Not only was she distinguished for her piety and humility, but she was also the donor of the church of St. Stephen. As donor, she took charge of the decorations:

> The wife of Namatius built the church of Saint Stephen in the suburb outside the walls of Clermont-Ferrand. She wanted it to be decorated with coloured frescoes. She used to hold in her lap a book from which she would read stories of events which happened long ago, and tell the workmen what she wanted painted on the walls. One day as she was sitting in the church and reading these stories, there came a poor man to pray. He saw her in her black dress, a woman already far advanced in age. He thought that she was one of the needy, so he produced a piece of bread, put it in her lap and went on his way. She did not scorn the gift of this poor man, who had not understood who she was. She took it, and thanked him, and put it on

one side. She ate it instead of her other food and each day received a blessing from it until it was all eaten up.[20]

Humble, learned, and personally concerned with both building and furnishing the church, the wife of Bishop Namatius was a model of an episcopal partner.

Sidonius Apollinaris, bishop of Clermont (471/2–487/9), was asked his advice on the choice of a new bishop for Bourge. Married himself to Papianilla, the daughter of Emperor Avitus,[21] he strongly recommended Simplicius, another married man, objecting that a monastic candidate would not be able to deal with worldly affairs. Part of his recommendation includes praise of Simplicius's wife. With a character beyond reproach, she came from a prominent family and was herself the descendant of bishops. The fact that she and her husband had raised their children successfully boded well for his future as a bishop.[22]

The sixth-century poet Venantius Fortunatus (c. 530–c. 610) wrote in praise of several of the bishops whose hospitality he shared.[23] At least two of their wives received particular notice. Venantius praised Eufrasia, widow of Namatius, bishop of Vienne (c. 599/60). Of noble birth, she entered the religious life upon the death of her husband and devoted herself to the care of the poor.[24] Placidina, wife of Leontius II of Bordeaux (c. 546–c. 573), received a great deal of attention by the poet. She was also a descendent of Emperor Avitus, as well as of Sidonius Apollinaris, and lived in continence (and contentment) with her husband as a model of virtue.[25] Placidina, like the wife of Bishop Namatius, helped furnish churches, in this case with wall hangings, a chalice, and a gold and silver reliquary cover.[26] Leontius's epitaph movingly recorded Placidina's love for him: "Sweet still to your ashes, Placidina gives to you a funeral observance, thus a consolation for her great love."[27]

The wives of bishops generally faired much more poorly at the hands of Gregory, bishop of Tours, who ripped into several clerical wives. They are particularly described as seductresses who tempted their husbands to renounce their vows of continence. The wife of Urbicus, the fourth-century bishop of Clermont, practically broke down the door of his bedroom to get at him. "The Bishop's wife burned so hot with passion, and was so overwhelmed by dark thoughts of such a sinful nature, that she made her way through the pitch-black night to the church-house. When she found that everything was shut up for the night, she started to beat on the doors of the church-house and shout."[28] Urbicus let his wife in, and they had intercourse, for which he repented. He was buried, however, with his wife and daughter in honor.[29] Susanna, the wife of Bishop Priscus, also entered the bedroom of her husband, and, according to Gregory, both she and her husband were severely punished by God for this indiscretion.[30] Bishop Felix of Nantes, another celibate, told Gregory of another bishop whose wife attempted to seduce him after he had become bishop. The story is worth relating in full as it offers an example both of the tension that mandatory continence would introduce into a marriage as well as the propaganda used by celibate bishops to enforce the canons:

> [Felix] said that there had been a cleric in his city who had had a wife; but when this man advanced to the honor of the episcopacy, in accordance with the requirement of catholic custom, he had set his bed apart. His wife received this separation with great difficulty. Although everyday she argued with him that they might sleep in one bed, the bishop did not assent to such wicked behavior that the decrees of the canons did not permit. One day she burned with rage and said to herself: "I do not think that the fact that I have been so rebuffed from my husband's embrace happened without his own complicity. But I will go and see that he is not perhaps sleeping with any other woman for whose love he has rejected me." Immediately she went to the bishop's chamber and found him taking an afternoon nap. She approached his bed and saw a lamb of overpowering brightness lying on his breast. She was terrified with fear and quickly removed herself from the saint's bed. Nor longer did she continue to ask what the man who was filled with God was doing in secret.[31]

As Suzanne Wemple has so clearly pointed out, Merovingian Gaul witnessed a struggle to impose celibacy upon the higher clergy, and these stories demonstrate the tensions this enterprise induced.[32] Many clergy continued an older tradition of dioceses constituted as noble households. Indeed, Brennan describes this period in precisely those terms:

> The virtual inheritance of some Gallic sees by members of the same senatorial families is a phenomenon that long has been commented upon by historians. Indeed, some of the episcopal epitaphs written by Venantius illustrate the concept of the episcopacy as a type of family inheritance. The Ruricii, grandfather and grandson, both bishop of Limoges, are accorded a joint epitaph that lays great stress on family ties. Likewise the epitaph written for Bishop Eumerius of Nantes highlights the succession of his son to the see. The most fulsome expression of this concept of the episcopacy as a family inheritance comes in the epitaph written for Bishop Cronopius of

Périgueux, who is descended from bishops on his father's side and on his mother's side as well—a matter for obvious pride.[33]

For these bishops, wives were in effect partners. Equal in status and virtue, they formed an aristocratic team, ruling the family inheritance for the good of the church.[34] However, for those bishops intent on establishing a continent, if not celibate clergy, wives were a terrible impediment. They were a constant source of temptation to their husbands and their co-adjudication of ecclesiastical property in favor of their families threatened the hierarchical model of the church envisioned by the reformers.

Conclusion

What then can be gleaned from these few references to *episcopae?* First, some few women received the title, an unusual occurrence in itself. Second, two references are to women clearly not married to bishops; one reference certainly is to wives of bishops, and one reference is uncertain. What these five references may have in common, however, is that they seem to be women who administered church property. Both Theodora and the wives of bishops mentioned in the literature of Merovingian Gaul built and furnished churches. Brigid was described as deeply involved in the administration of the church in Ireland.[35] The wives of bishops came from noble families and were held in high esteem by those bishops who supported a married clergy. We have only a few pieces of the puzzle, but one possible picture is that of a husband and wife team, or of individual women, who administered the goods of the church as bishops, thus meriting the title *episcopa*.[36] Like Brigid, the great abbesses of this period will continue to exercise extensive jurisdiction and in fact continue to do so even into the nineteenth century.[37] At least in this area, women shared in the ministry of the episcopate.

Presbyterae and the Wives of Priests

This setting will help to provide a framework for the references to *presbyterae* and deaconesses that also come from this period. Although only one reference to *episcopia* might refer to the wives of bishops, several references to these other offices come from the legislation of the early Middle Ages and clearly refer to *presbyterae* as the wives of priests and deaconesses as the wives of deacons. Unfortunately, little information about individual *presbyterae* or deaconesses has survived, so the references that do survive about the role of the wives of bishops from the fifth and sixth centuries provide one of the few glimpses into the lives of married clergy that has survived.

References to *presbyterae* are more numerous than those to *episcopae*. As noted above, the term often appears to refer to the wives of priests, but this does not always seem to be the case. A list of forbidden marriages was drawn up at a synod held under Pope Zachary (741–52) in 743: "No one should presume to join himself physically to an abominable consort, like a *presbytera*, deaconess, nun or female monk or a godmother (*spiritualem commatrem*)." The penance for an infraction of this rule was excommunication.[38] The law was repeated in a letter of Pope Leo VII (c. 937–39) to the French and German bishops in answer to a question about marriage to godmothers and godfathers.[39] A similar set of laws was later ascribed to Pope Gregory II and included in the ninth-century Pseudo-Isidorian decretals. Two of the laws read: "If anyone leads a *presbytera* into marriage, anathama sit" and "If anyone leads a deaconess into marriage, anathema sit."[40] The laws also anathematized a particular deaconess, Ephifania, and her husband, Hadrian, for just such an offense.[41] According to Michel Andrieu, as well as Madigan and Osiek, these injunctions forbade *remarriage* for the wives of priests and deacons.[42] This seems somewhat odd considering the juxtaposition with nuns and might be seen as enforcing a requirement for celibacy equivalent to that ascribed to single male priests and deacons. A set of laws spuriously ascribed to Pope Nicholas I (858–67), included in several eleventh-century collections of canon law, lists penances for intercourse with several *ordines* of holy women. *Presbyterae* and deaconesses are included among virgins, nuns, "brothers and sisters in Christ," godparents, and "women who have taken the habit."[43] Again, *presbyterae* are numbered among those who have taken vows of continence or are forbidden by canon law from intermarriage. There is no suggestion here that remarriage is an issue. If therefore, the laws do not refer to remarriage, they must refer to single women who held the position of *presbytera*.

Further, an interpolated translation of canon 10 of the Council of Laodicea (mid- to late fourth century), included in the ninth-century Pseudo-Isidorian decretals, forbade the installation of *presbyterae* in a church as if they were appointed to it (*ordinatas*).[44] Although the canon pertained originally to the fourth-century Greek Church, the interpolation may indicate that a contemporary situation required the repetition and explanation of the earlier canon.[45] The interpolation described *presbyterae*, however, not as the wives of priests, but as "women who are called *presbyterae* among the Greeks, but by us, however, they are called elder widows (*viduae seniores*), a once-married women (*univira*) and little mothers (*matriculariae*)."[46] The role that these laws seek to curtail appears to include more than just outliving a husband priest and does not, in fact, mention these women as specifically widows of priests.

Presbyterae

Five inscriptions found in the West introduce us to actual women who were *presbyterae*. Two of them are from Italy, one is from Poitiers, and two are from Croatia. All are dated from the fourth through the sixth century. An inscription in Greek from Sicily marks the tomb of the *presbytera* Kale. No indication is given of her marital state.[47] A second Italian tomb inscription comes from Tropea in Calabria and was erected for the *prebytera* Leta by her husband. No mention is made of his being a priest.[48] A graffito found near Poitiers commemorates that "Martia the presbytera made the offering together with Olybrius and Nepos."[49] Scholars who have studied it agree that this inscription refers to Martia as a minister who celebrated the Eucharist along with two men, Olybrius and Nepos.[50] The two remaining inscriptions both come from Solin (ancient Solana) in Croatia. One fragment simply mentions a *sacerdotae*, in this instance using the feminine form of the Latin for "priest" rather than the Greek word for "presbyter.[51] The final inscription is dated to 425 and refers to the *presbytera* Flavia Vitalia from whom the tomb was purchased.[52]

Who were these women and what did they do? Both questions are difficult to answer given the paucity of sources, but scholars have made some educated guesses. There is good evidence that at least some of these women were the wives of priests. The Second Council of Tours held in 567 first specifically referred to *presbytera* as the wife of a priest. The Council decreed that "if a priest has been found with his *presbytera* or a deacon with his deaconess or a subdeacon with his subdeaconess," they were to be excommunicated for a year and deprived of any clerical office.[53] The Council of Auxerre in 578 held that after ordination, no priest was allowed to sleep in the same bed with his *presbytera* or "unite in carnal sin." The same held true for deacons and subdeacons.[54] Gregory the Great in the fourth book of his *Dialogues* described how a priest and his *presbytera* lived chaste and separate lives.[55] On his deathbed, his *presbytera* leaned over him to see if the priest was still alive. The old man shouted at her, "Get away, woman: a little fire is still left, take away the straw."[56] Once again, like the wives of bishops described by Gregory of Tours, the *presbytera* was offered as a temptress who threatened the chastity of her pure husband.

The Ministry of Presbyterae

Some of these references clearly refer to *presbyterae* as the wives of priests. But does this mean that they were "merely" the wives of priests, or did they have their own ministries? In other words, would they have been understood to be ordained by the standards of the time, that is, commissioned for a particular ministry? Several sources would seem to indicate that this was indeed the case. The Council of Nîmes, held in 394, noting that "women seemed to have been assumed into levitical service," ordered that "such ordination should be undone when it is effected contrary to reason. It should be seen that no one so presume in the future."[57] It is quite likely that the ordination and ministry of women into the priesthood was being discussed here, although some scholars have argued that it was the diaconate rather than the presbyterate that the Council intended to forbid.[58] A hundred years later, in 494, Pope Gelasius, in a letter to the bishops of southern Italy and Sicily, also spoke out against bishops who were allowing women to serve at the altar. Gelasius had heard that "women are confirmed to minister at the sacred altars and to perform all matters imputed only to the service of the male sex and for which women are not competent."[59] Otranto makes clear in his analysis of this letter that Gelasius was directing his ire at the bishops who were ordaining women to function as priests, not at the women themselves.[60]

Fifteen years later, bishops Licinius, Melanius, and Eustochius of northern Gaul wrote to two priests from Brittany. They were furious to learn that the priests traveled with women who assisted them at the altar, "so that, while you are distributing the Eucharist, they hold the chalices and presume to administer the blood of Christ to the people of God."[61] The women were referred to by their companions as *conhospitae* ("housemates"), indicating that the women were living with the priests if indeed they were not their wives. The bishops upbraided the priests for "this novelty and unheard-of superstition" that "brings infamy upon the clergy and ... incurs shame and horror for the holy religion." The bishops demanded that "silly little women (*mulierculae*) of this sort not pollute the holy sacraments by illicit assistance" and forbade the priests to continue to live in the same house with them.[62] However, the letter implied that at least these priests and their congregations accepted the women as coministers of the Eucharist.

In 599, Pope Gregory the Great wrote to Januarius, the bishop of Caligliari, to explain his concerns about the former abbess of the monastery of saints Gavinus and Luxurius. In her will, the abbess, Sirica, had left property of the monastery to other people. Gregory forbade this but also noted "that the above-mentioned abbess, up to the day of her death, had been unwilling to wear the monastic habit, but had kept on wearing the kind of dresses used by *presbyterae* in that place."[63] This is the only extent reference indicating that *presbyterae* wore a distinctive habit, clearly different from that worn by abbesses or nuns. The fact that Sirica "kept on wearing" the habit of a *presbyterae* indicates that she was a *presbyterae* before she was an abbess. It is clear from the letter that she came to the monastery with her own property and that this is the property that she left as a legacy in her will.[64] She could, then, have been a married *presbytera* before entering the convent, although the text does not specifically say so.

In 747, Pope Zachary wrote to the Frankish authorities who wished to know if nuns could read the Gospel or sing at Mass. Zachary replied in the negative and added, "Nevertheless, as we have heard to our dismay, divine worship has fallen into such disdain that women have presumed to serve at the sacred altars, and that the female sex, to whom it does not belong, perform all the things that are assigned exclusively to men."[65] Women, it would seem, were still ministering at the altar in the late eighth century. In the early ninth century, Bishop Haito of Basle included in his collection of laws the injunction, "women should have no access to the altar and are not to join in any ministry of the altar, even if dedicated to God." Women were not even allowed to approach the altar with washed linens or the offering brought to the altar.[66] Forbidding women to touch the altar or the instruments used on the altar may have been inferred from earlier legislation,[67] but Haito seems to imply more here. There still seem to have been women ministering at the altar, and Haito was careful to forbid this.

Support for this interpretation of Haito's concern comes from the statutes from the Council of Paris held in 829. The bishops were appalled to learn that "in some provinces, in contradiction to the divine law and to canonical instruction, women betake themselves into the altar area and impudently take hold of the sacred vessels, hold out the priestly garments to the priest, and—what is still worse, more indecent and unfitting than all this—they give the people the body and blood of the Lord and do other things which in themselves are indecent."[68] As in the sixth century, it appears that at least some priests and bishops were allowing women to minister at the altar. Perhaps they were participating as deaconesses or perhaps as *presbyterae*. This depends on whether the "things which it would be shameful to mention" referred to saying the Mass itself. A report to the bishops of the acts of the council from the same year makes it clear that some bishops had been allowing the practice: "doubtless it occurred through the carelessness and negligence of some bishops . . . [they] have given themselves to carnal passions and illicit actions, so that women, without anyone preventing them, betake themselves into consecrated houses and therein have been able to introduce unpermitted things."[69] The reference to the bishops' "carnal passions" might indicate as well that these bishops were married, and so the slur against the bishops that it was only lust that forced the clergy to allow the women to serve at the altar has to be taken with a grain of salt. In this case, the sources might be speaking of married *presbyterae* or deaconesses who shared in the liturgy with their spouses.

Surviving Rites

Women certainly did distribute communion in the tenth, eleventh, and perhaps the twelfth centuries. Texts for these services, with prayers written with feminine word endings, exist in two manuscripts of this period.[70] One was copied in the eleventh or twelfth century at the Abbey of Saint Sophia in Benevento for use by the nuns in that community.[71] The second dates from the tenth or eleventh century and, although the provenance of the manuscript is unknown, the use of the feminine word endings leads scholars to believe that it too was used by nuns.[72] Jean Leclercq notes: "It is never said or supposed that the one who recites [these prayers] is a priest. Nevertheless, in their ensemble they really constitute a long eucharistic prayer."[73] The rite consists of a series of prayers, followed by a communion service and prayers after communion. Again, according to Leclercq: "Note that this ensemble [which makes up the opening prayers] corresponds more or less to the series of texts which serve as an introduction to the Mass: entrance psalm, litany, penitential rite, collect and profession of faith."[74]

Although these rites for women do not seem to be masses, they are very close to them and indicate that women were still involved in service at the altar despite the many injunctions against them doing so. Further, since the books that preserve these rites are liturgical books, we can presume, again to quote Leclercq, that "one did not incur the expense of copying manuscripts which would not be used; thus we have every reason to suppose that they were used, and in more than one place."[75] While these *ordines* were used by nuns who are not specifically named as *presbyterae,* they do demonstrate that the practice of women serving at the altar persisted long after legislation had forbidden it.

No ordination rites exist for *presbyterae,* but as mentioned in chapter 2, there is a reference to the blessing of them in the Romano-Germanic Pontifical of the tenth century. *Ordo* 36 describes the ordination of priests and deacons.[76] As part of the ceremony, "the bishop [of Rome], rising from prayer, sits in his seat, individually placing his hand on the head of each of them and blesses them."[77] Those ordained as deacons are given the proper ritual objects representing their *ordo,* as are those ordained as priests. The ceremony having concluded, the procession from the church commences. The pope leads the way on his white horse with the people following. The text then adds, "in the same way, likewise women, deaconesses, and *presbyterae* who were blessed on the same day."[78]

Two interpretations are possible. The one most often given, or assumed, is that the wives of priests and deacons were given a episcopal blessing separate from the ordinations some time during or after the ceremony.[79] Another possibility, however, is that the women ordained as *presbyterae* and deaconesses had been included in the ordination ceremony; that is, those "who were blessed on the same day" were those blessed by the bishop during the laying on of hands.

That a separate ritual for the ordaining of *presbyterae* does not exist does not necessarily mean that they were never ordained. The same rite used for men might also have been used for women. Sometimes, in fact, rites were so designated in the medieval pontificals. As mentioned in chapter 2, the eighth-century pontifical of Egbert of York contained a blessing suitable for deacons or deaconesses. The text uses the masculine case throughout for those to be blessed even though the rite can be used for men or women.[80] The Gregorian sacramentary contains a "prayer for the making of an abbot or an abbess" that can be adapted for either male or female use.[81] The eighth-century *Liber sacramentorum Gellonensis* also includes a "prayer when an abbot or abbess is ordained in the monastery." The prayer refers only to an abbess, although the prayer could be used for an abbot as well and uses the masculine case throughout.[82] The ninth-century *Liber sacramentorum Augustodunensis* contains as well a "prayer when an abbot or abbess is ordained in a monastery." This pontifical, however, provides both the masculine and feminine forms of the prayer.[83] Finally the twelfth-century Roman sacramentary includes a ritual for the blessing of an abbot or abbess, in which the prayers occur in the masculine case only.[84] It is possible, then, that ordination rites for deacons and priests were also used for deaconesses and *presbyterae* even though they only refer to deacons or priests in their *tituli* and use the masculine voice throughout. One is reminded of the description of the virgin recounted by Philip of Harvengt as a *bonus clericus* (good cleric) in the masculine and of the use of the rite for the ordination of a (male) bishop to ordain Brigid.[85]

Some further evidence for *presbyterae* and deaconesses is contained in three manuscripts from the ninth and tenth centuries that include commentaries on church law. All three offered the following gloss:

> A deaconess is an abbess; she is ordained through the imposition of hands by a bishop but not before the age of forty years, the law by Paul of twenty years being abrogated, in order to instruct all Christian women in the faith and law of God, as they did in the old law. Of this the apostle [said] "Widows ought not be chosen less than forty years old." And there were *presbyterisse* (*presbyterae*) in the gospel, [for

instance] Anna the octogenarian; now truly the law of Calcedon allows forty years.[86]

This commentary would indicate that the Carolingian Church recognized both *presbyterae* and deaconesses as scriptural institutions and that they still functioned in the church.

Conclusion

What possible pictures emerge from such fragments? Slightly more is known about *presbyterae* than about *episcopae*. Some women did minister at the altar as priests and they did so with the support of at least some bishops at least until the ninth century. The women who so served were not specifically called *presbyterae*, however. Another group of women were so titled and at least some of these were the wives of priests. It is certainly plausible that the women who are recorded as serving at the altar were in fact the same as the women who were called *presbyterae*, some of whom were the wives of priests. As in the case of *episcopae*, the most likely reason for women to be given the title of *presbyterae* is because they performed the function of priests.[87] Therefore, it seems reasonable to assume that references to *presbyterae* and to women who serve at the altar are references to the women in the same *ordo* and with the same ministry. The clearest example of this is the reference to Martia the *presbytera* who ministered with Olybrius and Nepos in Poitiers some time in the fourth through sixth centuries.

Like their male counterparts, they were expected to be chaste even in marriage. In fact, Merovingian legislation was quite clear on this point. Married clergy, bishops, priests, deacons, and subdeacons were expected to live chastely in separate quarters from their wives. The legislation forbidding marriage to *presbyterae* and deaconesses can be understood to enforce the same requirement as for men. If married, they must remain chaste; if unmarried, they must remain celibate and chaste.[88]

By the tenth century, *presbyterae* appear to have all but disappeared from the ecclesiastical scene. References to them still existed, however, and required explanation. One such explanation survives in a fascinating letter by the tenth-century bishop Atto of Vercelli. Asked why ancient laws speak about *presbyterae* and deaconesses, Atto responded that in the early church, because of a shortage of workers, devout women were ordained (*ordinantur*) to help men in leading the worship. Not only men, but also women, presided over the church because of the great need. Women had been long familiar with pagan cults and been educated in philosophy and so, when converted, were well suited to teach religious practice. Atto explained, basing his opinion on the law of the Council of Laodicea discussed above, that *presbyterae* were no longer allowed by the church. Atto described deaconesses as those who prepared other women for baptism through catechesis and then assisted at their baptism. Since most people are baptized as infants, Atto explained, this very rarely happens any more, and women in any case have been forbidden to baptize. Atto's description of the former role of *presbyterae* and deaconesses is interesting, however: "As indeed those called *presbyterae* assumed their office by preaching, commanding or teaching, so deaconesses sensibly assumed their office by ministering and baptizing."[89]

Atto did not completely rule out the existence of *presbyterae* and deaconesses in his own time. "I suppose that these *presbyterae* and deaconesses also exist, that is those who are joined in marriage to priests and deacons before ordination." Atto immediately pointed out that, according to law, these women should remain chaste once their husbands were ordained.[90] However, this is about the last one hears of *presbyterae* as a separate *ordo*. Deaconesses, though, were a different matter. Atto also alluded to some who claimed that the office once called "deaconess" is now called "abbess."[91] Atto disagreed, but only because the words "deaconess" and "abbess" come from very different roots. Atto's argument would be taken up again in detail by the twelfth-century canonists.[92] Deaconesses would continue to appear in different forms well into the twelfth century, and it is to these deaconesses that we now turn.

Deaconesses and the Wives of Deacons

Early Western References

Deaconesses present an even more detailed and interesting problem than *episcopae* and *presbyterae*. At least from the time of Morin, scholars discussing the ancient order of deaconesses have distinguished different kinds of deaconesses in the early medieval West. Morin spoke of widows called deaconesses, the wives of deacons and true deaconesses. Martimort also described three kinds of deaconesses: widow-deaconesses, wives of deacons, and deaconess-abbesses.[93] Unlike Morin, he held that none of the women called deaconesses functioned as such during this period.[94] Further, there are two words used for deaconess in Latin, *diaconia* and *diaconissa*. The terms were used indiscriminately in several different contexts in the several different kinds of texts in which they appear during this period. The terms, therefore, appear to refer to the same ministry.[95] In this study, rather than strictly distinguishing types of deaconesses, an attempt will be made to ascertain why different groups of women were given this title. In other words, what did these different women do that would cause their contemporaries to honor them with this title? What did they each have in common with the *ordo* of deaconess?

References to deaconesses in Western Christianity first appear with certainty in the fifth century. The anonymous commentator on scripture known as Ambrosiaster[96] and the Irish monk Pelagius[97] both knew of deaconesses when they wrote at the end of the fourth century, but they refer to this institution as an Eastern practice. As already discussed, the Council of Nîmes of 394 forbade women from being ordained to the levitical ministry, althouth this is just as likely to refer to the presbyterate as to the deaconate.[98] The First Council of Orange, held in 441, certainly did know of deaconesses and was not thrilled about them. "Deaconesses are by no means to be ordained. If there are any who have already been ordained, let them submit their heads to the benediction that is granted to the people."[99] It is very hard to know precisely which ministry the bishops were trying to proscribe here since there is no other evidence for deaconesses in the West during this early period. It is possible that these deaconesses were in fact from the East. Indeed, the Council of Nîmes in 394 had been concerned about "so-called priests and deacons coming from the far eastern parts" and decreed that they were not to be admitted to the ministry of the altar.[100] The First Council of Orange did approve of widows, however, and described how they were to be professed by bishops.[101]

Widows and Deaconesses

It was the widows in fact who seemed to have been doing some of the work ascribed to deaconesses. Sometime between 476 and 485, a set of laws was compiled, most likely by the priest Gennadius of Marseilles,[102] that describes the ministry of widows in a way reminiscent of the deaconesses of the early centuries of the church. In a list of the *ordines* of the church, Gennadius included "widows or holy women who are chosen for the ministry of baptizing women, [who] should be so instructed in that office that they are able clearly and wisely to teach ignorant and rustic women how they are to respond at the time of their baptism to the questions asked by the one baptizing and how they should live having been baptized."[103] The *Statuta* made clear, however, that women were not to do the baptizing, nor were they to teach men publicly.[104]

The Council of Epaon, held in 517, conflated the ministries of widow and deaconess when the bishop there annulled throughout the region the consecration of widows "who are called deaconesses."[105] There seems to have been, therefore, widows who were also deaconesses. Indeed it may be to such women that the Second Council of Orange addressed itself in 533: "Women

who, up to this point, against its interdiction by the canons, received the benediction of the diaconate, if they be proven to have again entered into marriage,
are to be banished from communion."[106] The council fathers then went on
once again to attempt to abolish the office of deaconess, justifying this decision on the basis of the fragility of women.[107] The Merovingian bishops for
nearly one hundred years had then continuously attempted to ban the ordination of deaconesses. Their ambition in this was notably frustrated as the
sixth century witnessed a number of women who were deaconesses.

Deaconesses

Remigius, the long-lived bishop of Reims (c. 433–c. 533),[108] left a testament in
which he bequeathed the servant named Noca and part of a vineyard to "my
blessed daughter, Helaria the deaconess."[109] This last will and testament of
a Merovingian bishop not only names one early deaconess in the Western
medieval church but also provides a fascinating insight into Remigius's understanding of the church. Here the model for the church would be that of a
diocese as an extended family. Remigius left several bequests to his nephews
and their families.[110] His "brother" bishop, his priests, deacons, subdeacons,
and other orders all receive bequests from the diocesan lands and goods.[111] One
is reminded of the will of Orso, bishop of Olivolo, who appointed his sister
Romana, in 853, to guard the family property from future bishops who might
not be worthy.[112] This model of church can be discerned as well in the descriptions of the wives of the Merovingian bishops discussed above. In such a
model, the wives of bishops, priests, and deacons could play an important role
in safeguarding and administering diocesan property, and it would seem from
the evidence that they joined with their husbands in liturgical functions as well.

Venantius Fortunatus, the poet and bishop, has already been introduced
as an extoller of the virtues of the wives of the Merovingian bishops. He also
wrote a life of his contemporary, Queen Radegund, the wife of King Clothar I
(511–58).[113] Radegund left the king c. 550 and was consecrated a deaconesses
by Médard, bishop of Noyen. Fortunatus dramatically described the event:

> She left the king and went straight to the holy Médard at Noyon.
> She earnestly begged that she might change her garments and be
> consecrated to God. But mindful of the words of the Apostle: "Art
> thou bound unto a wife? Seek not to be loosed," he hesitated to garb
> the Queen in the robe of a *monacha* (nun). For even then, nobles
> were harassing the holy man and attempting to drag him brutally
> though the basilica from the altar to keep him from veiling the king's

spouse lest the priest imagine he could take away the king's official queen as though she were only a prostitute. The holiest of women
knew this and, sizing up the situation, entered the sacristy, put on
a monastic garb and proceeded straight to the altar, saying to the
blessed Médard: "If you shrink from consecrating me, and fear
man more than God, Pastor, He will require His sheep's soul
from your hand." He was thunderstruck by that argument and, laying his hand on her, he consecrated her as deaconess.[114]

Helaria and Radegund are not the only deaconesses whose names are
known from this period. Inscriptions have left us memorials to three other
deaconesses. Anna, a deaconess from Rome in the sixth century;[115] Theodora,
a deaconess from Gaul buried in 539;[116] and Ausonia, a deaconess from Dalmatia in the sixth century. Ausonia mentioned her children, thus making her
the only one of the three deaconesses who left evidence that she was married.[117]

Nor did all the councils from this period explicitly condemn the *ordo* of
deaconess. The Second Council of Tours held in 567 is one of the few contemporary references that clearly referred to the wives of deacons as deaconesses when it decreed that priests, deacons, or subdeacons who were found with
their wives would be excommunicated for a year and removed from office.[118]
The council accepted the fact of deaconesses but wished that they would forgo
sexual intercourse with their husbands once they were ordained. There was
extensive and repeated legislation concerning the wives of deacons, as there
was for the wives of bishops and priests. The title of deaconess for those wives
appears, however, only this once.

References to deaconesses continue to appear in the seventh through ninth
centuries. In the second half of the seventh century, the anonymous author of
the life of St. Sigolena described how she was consecrated deaconess after the
death of her husband.[119] The story may simply be copying that of Radegund,[120]
but it does indicate that the author could conceive of such an ordination. In a
charter from 636, Deacon Grimo of Trier referred to his sister Emengaud as a
deaconess.[121] In the registry of Pope Gregory II, there is a collection of grants
written by Gregory between 715 and 730. In it are three letters addressed to
deaconesses. Two are addressed to the deaconesses of St. Eustachius and one to
Matrona, a religious deaconess, and her sons and nephews.[122] Sergius, after
becoming archbishop of Ravenna in 753, "consecrated his wife, Euphemia, a
deaconess."[123] When Leo III returned to Rome in 799, he was greeted by the
entire population of Rome including "holy women, deaconesses and the most
noble matrons."[124] The Council of Rome held in 826 forbade certain illegal
marriages, including those with any veiled woman or deaconess.[125]

Already noted in the discussion of *presbyterae* was the prohibition by Pope Zachary (741–52) in 743: "No one should presume to join himself physically to an abominable consort, like a *presbytera*, deaconess, nun or female monk or a godmother (*spiritualem commatrem*)." Pope Leo VII (c. 937–39) repeated this prohibition, and the ninth-century Pseudo-Isidorian decretals similarly forbade the marriage of deaconesses. The decrees of the Council of Paris in 829 thundered out against women who were distributing communion and performing "other things which it would be shameful to mention."[126] These may have been women functioning as *presbyterae*, as suggested above, or as deaconesses. Much depends on what the bishops considered to be unmentionable acts. Again, the communion services for nuns contained in the tenth- and eleventh-century manuscripts may have been performed by deaconesses ordained for this purpose. Deaconess existed in the diocese of Lucca at least up until the time of Ottone, bishop from 1139 to–1146.[127] Abbesses were considered deaconesses by many twelfth-century writers as well, particularly because they could read the Gospel during liturgies, a task that belonged to the diaconate.[128]

Ordination Rites for Deaconesses

Along with the continuous references to deaconesses from the fifth through the twelfth century exist the rituals for the ordination of deaconesses.[129] The earliest of these rituals in the West comes from the eighth-century pontifical of Bishop Egbert of York. The pontifical contains a prayer for the ordaining of either a deacon or a deaconess that appears in the middle of the ordination rite for a deacon. The impression given is that the ordination rite for a deacon is the same as that used for a deaconess since the prayer for the ordination of a deaconess occurs within the ordination rite for a deacon, and the prayer can be used for ordaining either a deacon or a deaconess. The prayer is masculine in form, again reinforcing the assumption that it was meant as part of the entire rite of ordination for either male or female. This prayer will appear often in rituals for the both deacons and deaconesses and constitutes the most frequent prayer of consecration for both offices. The prayer reads: "Give heed, Lord, to our prayers and upon this your servant send forth that spirit of your blessing in order that, enriched by heavenly gifts, he [or they] might be able to obtain grace through your majesty and by living well offer an example to others. Through [our Lord Jesus Christ]."

Egbert's pontifical also contains a prayer for the blessing of a deaconess and a prayer for the blessing of a deacon. They differ substantially. The prayer over a deaconess stresses her virginity, referring to the wise virgins who waited for the bridegroom with the oil of virtue. The prayer over deacons begs God for peace and prosperity, promising the blessing of God on the image that God formed in the deacon.

There are then both similarities and differences in the *ordines* of deacon and deaconess as expressed in the pontifical of Egbert. Both deacons and deaconesses appear to receive the same consecration during their ordinations, but their state of life as described in the episcopal blessings given to each differs. Deaconesses are clearly to live as virgins and to be honored as such. The role of deacons is not altogether clear in the blessing they receive. In fact, the prayer is more one for communal support than individual office.

The ninth-century Gregorian sacramentary gives precisely the same prayer for the making of a deaconess as did the pontifical of Egbert, "Give heed, O Lord." The prayer appears again as an alternate prayer in the ceremony for the ordaining of a deacon. In this case, the prayer for the making of a deaconess appears separately from the ordination rite for deacon. However, as no complete ceremony is given for the ordination of a deaconess, it seems that the same ritual was used for the ordaining of a deacon and of a deaconess. There would be no reason to repeat the entire ritual for both offices unless they were different. Only the ordination prayer would need to be included as a separate item, as indeed it is.

The tenth-century Romano-Germanic Pontifical (RGP) contains the complete liturgy for both the ordination of a deaconess and the ordination of a deacon.[130] The ordination rite for a deaconess takes place within the Mass and begins with the instructions, "When the bishop blesses the deaconess, he places the orarium on her neck. However when she proceeds to the church, she wears it around her neck so that the ends on both sides of the orarium are under her tunic." The *orarium* is a form of stole that, according to the Council of Toledo in 633, was worn by bishops, priests, and deacons. Again, according to the Council, the deacon was to wear his *orarium* on his left side when he "prayed, that is preached."[131] The *orarium* would be one of the instruments of the deaconess, indicating her function, which in this case would be preaching. This would make sense in light of the ninth-century canonical commentaries that describe deaconesses as "ordained through the imposition of hands by a bishop . . . in order to instruct all Christian women in the faith and law of God, as they did in the old law."[132] Following the gradual (a prayer between the first reading of the liturgy and the Gospel reading), the deaconess prostrates herself before the bishop during the litany, after which he recites the prayer "Give heed, O Lord." The directions for the ritual continue with a prayer of consecration that strongly emphasizes the chastity of the deaconess, comparing her to Anna, the widow, mentioned in Luke 2:36–38, and indeed this prayer had been used in early sacramentaries as a consecration prayer for widows.[133]

According to the prayer, the office of deaconess was instituted by the apostles for the instruction of young women. The deaconess is to be anointed with chrism by the hand of the bishop.

The bishop then places the *orarium* around the neck of the deaconess, calling it a *stola*, the same word used for the stole of deacon. Since in the rite for a priest in the same sacramentary, the stole is called an *orarium*, the two terms seem to be interchangeable. The deaconess herself takes the veil from the altar and places it on her own head. Finally, the deaconess accepts a ring and a crown from the bishop. The reception of the veil, the ring, and the crown are also part of the ritual used in the consecration of virgins. The prayers for the collect (n. 3 in the service), the secret (n. 18 in the service), and the post-communion (n. 23 in the service) appear as well in an eighth-century sacramentary as part of the ritual for vesting a virgin. The Mass continues with a reading from the Gospel of Mark, after which the deaconess is presented to the *ordo velatarum* (the *ordo* of those who are veiled). The rest of the Mass follows, during which the deaconess receives communion. After Mass, the bishop confirms her new position by pastoral proclamation in order that she might live in peace and security.

A picture of how a deaconess who participated in this rite would appear is preserved in a twelfth-century manuscript illumination of the annunciation contained in the Gengenbach Gospel (Cod. bibl. fol. 28, at Wuerttembergische Landesbibliothek, Stuttgart). In the miniature, reproduced on the cover of this book, Mary, at the moment of the annunciation, wears a dalmatic, the distinguishing vestment of a deacon. She has the *orarium* tucked under her tunic, as would a deaconess before ordination. Mary already wears the veil, however, as would a deaconess after ordination.

An almost identical liturgy appeared as well in the twelfth-century Roman pontifical. This version, however, appeared without rubrics, so it is difficult to know exactly how the ritual proceeded. Further, the prayer "Give heed, O Lord" does not appear. The fact that the liturgy was included in the pontifical is important, however. According to Vogel, "the Roman liturgists aimed as eliminating a good deal of archaic and unnecessary material from the Mainz Pontifical [the RGP]...the rites that were retained were either simplified by the elimination of a good deal of exuberant or interchangeable *formulae* (series of *aliae*) or adapted to the peculiar conditions of the Church of Rome."[134] This would indicate that the rite was indeed used, contrary to the opinion of Martimort who believed the rite was simply "preserved as a result of rote recopying by scribes."[135] As late as the end of the thirteenth century, the pontifical of William Durandus included the rite "On the ordination of a deaconess," although Durandus made it clear that this rite was performed in the past. The rite as he described it included the prayer "Give heed, O Lord" and the handing over of the *orarium* by the bishop.[136]

These liturgies differ significantly from that for a deacon. There are, however, some similarities. Both rites usually contain the prayer "Give heed, O Lord," as indeed does the rite for a priest, and both include that prayer before the prayer of consecration. Both receive a form of stole from the hands of the bishop as signs of their respective offices.

The differences are more marked. The deaconess receives a ring and crown, the mark of a virgin. The deacon receives the Gospel book and dalmatic, the signs of his liturgical office. Many of the prayers used for the ordination of a deaconess come from the rite for the veiling of a virgin.[137] The clear message is that a deaconess is a consecrated widow or virgin pledged to continence for the rest of her life.

The ritual would suggest then that the *ordo* of deaconess stands in a position between that of deacon and virgin. Of course, this does not mean that she is any less ordained than either of them, given the definition of ordination at the time the rites being discussed were used. There is an indication in the rite that a deaconess taught other younger women, and the bestowal of the *orarium* may indicate some liturgical role as well.

Ysebaert would describe these ordination rites as true ordinations.

> The practice in the West of ordaining deaconesses has been adopted from the churches in the East, where there is full evidence of old for the rite of laying on of hands and an invocation of the Holy Spirit. The bishops ordained deaconesses in spite of the prohibition by some councils in Gaul, and they did so in the proper way, as is clear in the case of Radegund, who was ordained during a ceremony in a chapel by an imposition of hands and from the Gregorian sacramentary.[138]

Ysebaert would also caution against making the assumption that the wives of deacons were not also ordained. "These texts show a great similarity of the wives of ministers to the deaconesses in the strict sense of the word, and the benediction of either group had the same purpose."[139]

Conclusions

What possible picture emerges from these disparate sources concerning deaconesses? Again, women certainly existed who performed functions that earned for them the title of deaconess. Further, the rites for the ordination of these deaconesses exist in at least three pontificals from the early Middle Ages. In the very few references we have to the ministry of deaconesses, it seems they may have assisted at the altar with the approval of at least some bishops. There is more evidence that they taught younger women and prepared rural women for baptism. They may have preached and read the Gospel, as the bestowal of the *orarium* would indicate. Can these extant remains supply enough information to form a plausible picture of a medieval deaconess? If they are joined with similar information about *episcopae* and *presbyterae*, certain outlines do emerge. It is to this larger portrait that we now turn.

Episcopae, Presbyterae, and Deaconesses: An Alternative Portrait

Before discussing the ordination of abbesses and their ministry, it might be worthwhile to look back over the references to *episcopae, presbyterae,* and deaconesses presented above. What kind of church would accept these ministries? Can a larger picture be imagined from the many separate pieces of the puzzle that history has left? No doubt any such picture can only be one possible way of sensing a pattern in the random bits of data that remain. Yet, as stated above, there is value in presenting alternative views of history, even when the evidence is insufficient to reach any final conclusion. Such alternatives challenge the received tradition and offer the possibility that our past may be more diverse, perhaps even more liberating, than expected. This is such an exploration.

The wives of bishops, priests, and deacons were obliged by church law to separate from their husbands and live lives of continence similar to that of widows, virgins, or nuns. Both spouses mutually agreed to enter into such an arrangement.[140] The Councils of Orange in 441, of Agde in 506, of Arles in 524, and of Toledo in 633 all called that mutual decision a "conversion" or "profession," common terms for entering a religious order. As late as the mid-eleventh century, Pope Leo IX would require the consent of both spouses before a minor cleric could become a subdeacon.

Both parties in effect were expected to enter the religious, vowed life. Once women entered this *ordo*, they were, in practice if not in reality, widows. At the Council of Lyon in 583, spouses were enjoined not to share daily activities; and at the Council of Gérone in 517, the spouses were encouraged to live in separate houses. Several councils punished priests who fathered children or punished those who returned to their wives for conjugal relations.[141] Some couples were at least described as living in separate establishments. The wife of Bishop Urbicus, according to Gregory of Tours, had to race from her house through the night to bang on the door of his house, begging to share his bed once again. It would make perfect sense, therefore, for the ritual of ordination for a deaconess in the RGP to borrow prayers from the ordination rites for widows. It would also make sense that *episcopae, presbyterae,* and deaconesses would enter convents after their husbands' deaths, as did Abbess Sirica who continued nevertheless to wear the garb of a *presbyterae.* These women would join their husbands in the "third gender" of the continent.[142]

However, not all bishops, priests, and deacons separated from their wives or undertook a life of continence. The bishops and wives of bishops who prided themselves on descending from episcopal families alone undermine this notion. According to Jo Ann McNamara: "These clerical proponents of the chaste marriage were, however, an elite. They provided an example that could hardly have been expected to suit the vast majority of the clergy."[143] Clergy continued to marry and live normal, active married lives well into the twelfth century. If there were ceremonies whereby the wives of bishops, priests, or deacons took on a life of continence and vows, perhaps only those women who separated from their husbands and underwent such a ceremony were called *episcopae, presbyterae,* and deaconesses. Since the ceremony celebrated the change to this new *ordo,* it would be a true ordination in the contemporary understanding of this term.[144] In this reading of the evidence, not all wives of bishops, priests, or deacons were *episcopae, presbyterae,* or deaconesses, but only those who mutually agreed with their husbands to undertake the continent religious life.

The legislation of the period can be read in this way. After all, since all married bishops, priests, and deacons were supposed to live separately from their *episcopae, presbyterae,* and deaconesses (all theoretically ordained to these positions), then regulations concerning the married life of clergy would use these terms when referring to wives of bishops, priests, and deacons after their ordinations. The only legislation on *episcopae,* that of the Council of Tours in 567, forbade marital relations after ordination, as did the legislation on *presbyterae* and deaconesses from Tours in 567 and Auxerre in 578. Laws forbidding the marriage of *presbyterae* and deaconesses from the eighth and ninth centuries listed these *ordines* along with other vowed women. This would indicate that the vows of these women now forbade them both from returning to conjugal relations with their own husbands and marrying again after the death of their husbands. This is not to say that these are the only terms used for spouses of ordained bishops, priests, and deacons in medieval legislation. Canon law frequently referred to the wives of priests and deacons as either *conjux/conjunx* (spouse) or *uxor* (wife), for instance, in the canons of the Council of Orange in 441,[145] the Council of Clermont in 535,[146] and the Council of Orléans in 538.[147] Interestingly, however, the titles *episcopa, presbytera,* and deaconess are not used for the spouses of clergy before their ordination, for instance, in those laws requiring mutual consent of the spouses before ordination.

Jo Ann McNamara has described just such a role for clerical spouses:

> Spiritual marriage not only assured the purity of priests but
> provided purified partners qualified for some share in their sacred
> activities. Thus, it undermined the alterity that precluded the sacra-
> mental activities of women. In the sixth and seventh centuries,
> clerical wives joined celibate virgins in housekeeping chores that
> extended to the sacred precincts of the altar. They took up church
> design and at least one bishop's wife took over the supervision of the
> building works of the cathedral. They ranged from baking the eu-
> charistic bread, handling altar vessels and lighting candles to litur-
> gical services like ringing bells and distributing communion. . . .
> Consecrated women encroached closely on sacramental preserves by
> anointing the sick with blessed oil.[148]

Clerical spouses played these roles, we have argued, because they were
ordained to do so.

The orders of *episcopa, presbytera,* and deaconess then were clerical orders
to which the wives of bishops, priests, and deacons could aspire, but they did
not always do so. Given the understanding of ordination at that time, however,
these women were not just *episcopae, presbyterae,* and deaconesses because they
were the wives of bishops; they were so because they took on a certain function
or role or ministry in the church. It is quite possible that single women were
also ordained into these ministries, especially that of deaconess. In the tenth,
eleventh, and twelfth centuries in particular, abbesses would be considered
deaconesses because they performed the ministry of deaconesses. This is an
extremely important point. For these centuries, ordination was to a particular
function rather than to a particular metaphysical or personal state. It was what
they did, not who they were, that made women *episcopae, presbyterae,* and deaconesses. Any woman who performed that ministry and was ordained to it,
married or single, could be an *episcopa, presbytera,* or deaconess. This would
explain why both single and married women were described as *episcopae* and
deaconesses, although no unequivocal references to unmarried *presbyterae*
survive. This would also explain why widows and later abbesses were called
deaconesses. They did what deaconesses did and were ordained to joint ministries, as it were.

These were in fact all separate *ordines. Presbyterae* had their own distinctive
garb that, according to Gregory the Great, was different from that of abbesses.
Presbyterae and deaconesses may have shared the same ordination rite as priests
and deacons up until the tenth century, and this would distinguish them from
other holy women. Deaconesses, at least by the tenth century, had a quite

distinctive ordination rite, different from both deacons and abbesses or other holy women.

As discussed above, there is good evidence that, despite legislation to the contrary, some bishops allowed women to participate at the altar either as priests or as deacons. Martia the *presbytera* was so described in the graffito from Poitiers. She was, however, the only woman who led a liturgy who was identified as a *presbytera*. The other references to women doing so were deliberately insulting, for instance "the silly little women" mentioned by the bishops of northern Gaul. These prohibitions were not likely to give such women any title, certainly not one attached to a legitimate ministry. Still, it does not take much of a stretch of the imagination to equate these women with the *ordines* who performed the functions that these women are described as performing. One wonders what the bishops who did allow this ministry would have called these women. There is also evidence that deaconesses taught other women, prepared them for baptism, and read the Gospel at Mass. All of these functions were functions or ministries assigned to priests and deacons, so it should not be surprising that *presbyterae* and deaconesses performed similar functions when their local bishops approved of that ministry.

Very clearly, not all bishops did so approve, and their disapproval has survived in documents that later came to form the received tradition of the church. Yet their very record of disapproval demonstrates that there was more than one opinion on the matter. To what kind of church would these "other" bishops belong? What alternative portrait of the church might be derived from the hints and suggestions uncovered so far in this investigation? The experiment continues.

An Alternative View of Church

In a challenging and provocative essay on late ancient Christian devotion,[149] Kim Bowes describes, among other phenomena, the rise of the importance of estate churches in the fifth and sixth centuries in Italy, Spain, and Gaul.

> While private church concerns sounded a periodic refrain
> throughout the period's regulatory documentation, crescendos of
> concern punctuated certain times and places. Once such time and
> place was the later fifth and sixth century in the western provinces,
> where particular concerns about estate churches seem to have trou-
> bled the churches of Gaul, Hispania, and Italy. Rural landowners
> had seemingly carved out a highly self-sufficient Christian experience

for themselves and their dependents through their estate churches, which provided all manner of services throughout the liturgical year. A worried episcopate insisted that the landowners and their immediate family make periodic appearances in the urban episcopal church, particularly on important feast days such as Easter and Epiphany. It similarly sought to wrest the sacraments of baptism, ordination, and consecration out of the hands of estate clergy, who had seemingly appropriated them, and to place them back under exclusive episcopal control.[150]

The "families" that these estate churches served were actually "the larger estate community of blood relations and dependents."[151] According to Bowes,

> Given the expansive community and wide variety of liturgical services provided by some estate churches, a clerical staff was clearly requisite. Certainly by the later fifth century and probably earlier, a landlord claimed the right to nominate his own clergy, for ordination if need be, while the final choice of such clerics remained with the local bishop. Nominees were frequently estate tenants or other working dependents. A variety of sources, from a disgruntled holy man-cum-villa-presbyter who lost his job, to disciplinary cases against dissolute estate clerics, make it likely that the clergy staffing these churches were permanent staff, rather than occasional visitors.[152]

The church described here reminds one strongly of the community captured in the will of St. Remigius. His extended household included not only his immediate family, but also his priests, deacons, deaconesses, and other *ordines*. It is a model of church as the kind of extended household to which the estate churches of this very same time and location ministered. Perhaps, and the evidence permits no more certainty than this, two separate understandings of church were in conflict here.

Some bishops and estate owners understood the church as an extended household or family. These bishops would be more open to married clergy and to the possibility that both spouses had a role in ministry. Bishops such as Sidonius Apollinaris or those described by Venantius Fortunatus valued the partnership of spouses and saw that partnership as an advantage in managing the larger extended family that was the church. Some of these bishops continued to live normal married lives and expected that their sons and daughters would continue serve as bishops and wives of bishops inheriting the family business, as it were. Other bishops placed a higher value on the ascetic and monastic model of the church. They would be either monks themselves or married bishops who lived separated lives of continence from their wives that still remained marriages, but without hope of offspring to continue the episcopal line. In this portrait, the wives would be vowed religious, not just wives, but *episcopae*. These two competing models of the church would remain in tension until the Gregorian reforms of the eleventh and twelfth centuries eventually made clerical marriage impossible.

We have little evidence of the lives of married priests and deacons, but such competing models might easily extend down from the bishops to the lesser clergy. Some priests and deacons married and passed along their vocation to their sons and daughters.[153] One can imagine them serving on estate churches, or for those bishops sympathetic to the model of church as extended family. Priests and *presbyterae*, deacons and deaconesses, lived the separated lives of continence their ordinations required. Both would be ministers with similar if not quite identical vocations. Again, here are two models of the church. One envisioned the church as an extended family that values marriage and is a ministry in the world, so to speak. The other model valued continence and understood the church as a monastery that stands over against, even if in service to, the larger world.[154]

Married clergy existed in both models, and both continued to function until clerical marriage was declared invalid in the twelfth century.[155] From that point on, at least technically, no clergy were married in Western Christianity, and if clergy did wish their offspring to inherit their jobs, they had to apply for an exception for their sons from their state of bastardy. An era had passed. But the office of deaconess continued, since this ministry does not seem to be limited to the wives of deacons. In fact, sometime before the tenth century, the separate *ordines* of deaconess and abbess seem to have merged, at least in the minds of some authors. Before addressing that merger, however, the ministry of the ordained abbess needs to be addressed.

Before closing this section, it is important to reiterate that this portrait offers only an exploration of one possible framework for the limited sources available. It is an admittedly rough fit. As indicated earlier, it is valuable to point out areas where this model, too, may not quite fit the evidence. The distinction between those wives of bishops, priests, and deacons who took vows and those who did not seems too harshly drawn. In reality, the two forms of clerical marriage were probably not so clearly distinguished. There is no indication that the women accused of leading liturgies, for instance, ever took vows or were even married. They could just as easily have been single women, perhaps belonging to another *ordo*, such at that of abbess.[156] The terms *episcopa, presbytera,* and "deaconess" could well have been used much more loosely than suggested here to refer to any wife of a bishop, priest, or deacon as well as refer to a women who performed the ministry suggested by the title.

Still, two suggestions made here seem to frame the sources better than other possible portrayals. First, the titles of *episcopa, presbytera,* and deaconess are better understood as referring to ministries performed by women, whether married or single, that correspond with the ministries of bishop, priest, and deacon. Second, the admittedly modern construct that envisions competing models of the church operative in the early Middle Ages can be very helpful in understanding some of the tensions of the period, as well as in breaking open the sometimes monolithic model of the church presented in the traditional histories of ordination discussed in chapter 1. The models suggested here—that of the church as an extended family within the world and the church as a monastery over against the world—do not capture all the complexity and subtlety that the sources present, but they do help frame the sources in a way that aids in understanding the role women played in that world and how the role that women played in the church would change drastically in the twelfth and thirteenth centuries.

Abbesses

Abbesses were described as ordained in several books of ritual in the early medieval period. This is not surprising given the definition of ordination as the ceremony celebrating and effecting entry to a new ministry in the church. Abbesses were an important and influential ministry throughout the Middle Ages. As in the case of *episcopae, presbyterae,* and deaconesses, they performed functions that were later reserved to the male offices of bishop, priest, and deacon. These functions, in themselves, did not constitute them as ordained. They were ordained because of their new role as the head of a monastic community, just as an abbot was ordained when he took up such a role.

The role of abbesses in this period is much clearer and less controversial than that of their sister ministers.[157] As will be discussed in the next chapter, *episcopae, presbyterae,* and deaconesses were not supposed to have existed, at least not as the functional equivalent of bishops, priests, and deacons. Once the definition of ordination became limited only to those who served at the altar and only to males, women could not be ordained and therefore had never been ordained. Abbesses, however, could be made to fit the new definition of ordination, as long as they were not considered really ordained and as long as they did not perform any of the liturgical functions now reserved to the male clergy. Once these parameters were established, their past existence would not be a threat.

Ordination Rites

The early medieval church, however, did think of abbesses as ordained as any other clergy in this period. Several rites for their ordination exist from this period, and they are quite impressive.[158] The Mozarabic rite has separate ordination rites for abbots and abbesses. Both rites begin with a vesting in the sacristy: "When an abbess is ordained, she is vested in the sacristy by one dedicated to God and the religious miter is placed on her head." In the ordination rite for an abblot, the abbot also is vested in the sacristy, where the bishop hands him regular monastic clothing, but no miter. The prayers for ordination are quite distinct, but at the conclusion of the rite, both received from the bishop a staff and a copy of the rule of the order as well as the kiss of peace from the bishop. The eighth-century *Liber sacramentorum Gellonensis* and the ninth-century *Liber sacramentorum Augustodunensis* combine the ordination rites for abbots and abbesses. Three alternative prayers are offered, but no rubrics are given. Two of the prayers are suitable for either an abbot or an abbess, but the third is clearly only to be used for abbesses as it refers to Mariam, the sister of Moses, and is worded completely with feminine word endings.

The RGP has two separate ordination rites for abbesses as well as a rite for abbots that can be adopted for abbesses. The two rites for abbesses differ in that one is for the ordination of an abbess of a congregation of canonesses and the other is for the ordination of an abbess to a congregation using a monastic rule. Although all the rites are similar, there are differences. All three rites should take place within a Mass. After the antiphon, the elect prostrates herself or himself at the altar in front of the bishop. The bishop then blesses him or her. In the case of either kind of abbess, one possible blessing is "Give heed, O, Lord," the same prayer used for the blessing of a deacon or deaconess. This is not an option for an abbot. Except in the case of a canoness, the bishop then places his hands on the head of the one to be ordained and intones a prayer in the form of a preface. One alternate prayer for an abbess reads: "It is truly just, right, and salutary that we always and everywhere give thanks to you, O Lord, holy Father, almighty and eternal God. Look favorably, we beseech you, upon this your servant, whom, acting in your name, we ordain guardian of your nuns." The bishop then presents the new abbess or abbot with the rule of their order. In the case of the abbess, the bishop then offers the prayer reserved for the ordination of abbesses in the Mozarabic rite. The abbot, but not the abbess, then receives a staff from the bishop as a sign of his office. If the abbess had been ordained outside her convent, she then processed back to it with cross, holy water, incense, and Gospel. Following the rite for the ordination of an abbot, there is an ordination rite for either abbots or abbesses in a monastery. It is simply a repetition of the blessing that the bishop gives when he places his hands on the heads of the elect. Once again, an alternative prayer for this ordination for abbesses alone is the prayer used in the Mozarabic liturgy.

The twelfth-century Roman liturgy contains a rite for the ordination of either an abbot or an abbess. As the ritual explains, "The blessing for both is the same, except that the abbess does not wear other than her customary vestments nor does she receive the staff." The ritual follows the pattern described above, and once again, the Mozarabic prayer for abbesses is appended as a special blessing.

The rites for the ordination of abbots and abbesses for this period were similar in some ways to the ordination to the other *ordines* of the church. Both were blessed with a laying on of hands by the bishop, and both received the signs of their offices from his hands. In the Mozarabic rite, the abbess received a miter, a staff, and a copy of the rule of the order. In the RGP and in the twelfth-century Roman ordinal, the abbess did not receive either a crown or a staff, but she did receive the rule and was processed back to her convent with the Gospel book. In the case of abbesses, the same prayer used for deacons and deaconesses is included in some forms of the rite.

Liturgical Functions

If the rites for ordination of abbots and abbesses were similar to those of other orders of women, so too were the roles that abbesses played within their communities. The main duty of an abbess was very similar to that of an abbot. Abbots and abbesses were quite powerful, sometimes as powerful as bishops. Given their high standing in the Christian community it is not too surprising that throughout this period, abbesses exercised functions later reserved to the male diaconate and presbyterate.

The best example would be the responsibility, indeed duty, of the abbess to hear her nuns' confessions.[159] This is mentioned by at least two of the rules for nuns from the early medieval period. The writers go on at great length about the necessity of the abbess (or her designate) to hear daily confessions.[160] One of the main virtues required of an abbess was a merciful yet firm use of penance to train the nuns under her care. Abbesses heard their nuns' confessions, gave them penances, and reconciled them back into the community. There is no provision in either monastic rules or canonical legislation for nuns to confess to anyone other than their abbess or her delegate. For all intents and purposes, abbesses played the same role for their communities in hearing confession and in absolving from sin as did bishops or priests for their communities. The abbesses' power to remove nuns from either table or the divine office or both is regularly termed "excommunication" and parallels within the community of nuns the power of bishops to excommunicate within the larger community of the church.[161]

Abbesses sometimes even heard the confessions of and gave penances for people other than the nuns of their immediate communities. According to her hagiographer, St. Bertila heard confessions for the entire surrounding area. "[Bertila] drew the family of the monastery or the surrounding neighbors through holy communion, so that, hearing their confessions, they would do penance for their sins."[162] The "family of the monastery" would include, in this case, all those who worked in and for the monastery including the peasant farmers in villages owned by the monastery. St. Ite heard the confession and gave penance to a murderer who sought her out to hear his confession. When he refused to complete his penance, she had to give him another penance that he finally fulfilled.[163]

Abbesses then for several centuries were recognized as the ordinary ministers of penance for their own monastic community and sometimes even exercised that power outside that circle. This was one of the most important liturgical functions attached to the *ordo* of abbess.

According to Gisela Muschiol, abbesses and nuns in general had far more access to the altar than laywomen. Despite laws of church councils and warnings of penitentials, abbesses and holy nuns were regularly described ministering in and around the altar area.[164] They brought up the gifts at the offertory and received communion with their bare hands, unlike laywomen who, at least according to church law, were supposed to cover their hands with a cloth when accepting the consecrated bread.[165] The abbess-elect also came up to the front of the altar along with two or three other nuns during her ordination ceremony.[166] According to the *Life of Matilda,* the wife of the emperor Henry I: "In fact, the custom of the holy lady was to present daily to the priest the offering of the bread and wine at Mass for the health and benefit of the entire holy church."[167] Matilda even miraculously produced the altar wine when it was lost. Clearly, the eleventh-century authors of Matilda's life had no problem imagining a women regularly serving at Mass. The purity concerns evoked by medieval legislation against women seem to find no echo in the lives of saintly women as described in their *vitae.*[168]

The most dramatic appearance of an abbess at an altar was that of St. Aldegundis. The saintly abbess appeared after her death to one of the young nuns.

After the nocturnes and matins one sister from that monastery, when she had fallen asleep, God showed her a mystical vision as if the holy Aldegunda of blessed memory had stood before the altar in the place of the priest, and broke the mass offerings with her hands into the chalice. And turning to the aforementioned sister, she said, "Go and tell the priest that over this chalice he should say the solemnities of the Mass because yesterday a serious illness in my body prevented me from communicating, today with the help of the Lord, I desire to participate in the body and blood of the Lord.[169]

The nun did as she was told, and when the priest said Mass for her, they both saw a vision of the chalice hanging in the air above them. Aldegunda did not say the Mass; for that, the priest had to be called, but she did appear at the altar, touching the consecrated bread and the chalice.

The *Canons of Theodore*, dating from the mid-eighth century, proscribed that "women, that is the servants of Christ, are allowed to read the readings and execute the ministry of the reliquary (*confessionem*) of the most holy altar except only those [ministries] that specially belong to the priest or deacon."[170] The convent of Monheim witnessed several such services offered to pilgrims at the altar by nuns. They would give pilgrims a drink of wine from the chalice at the altar, or allow pilgrims to place their hands on the votive light on the altar or touch their eyes with the wand of the patron saint and former abbess, Walpurgis. Most strikingly the blessing of the pilgrims would at times be accompanied by a gift of bread blessed by the abbess.[171]

The liturgies for the distribution of communion by women religious, discussed above, demonstrate that at least in some convents, communion services were held without a priest, and the most likely person to lead such a liturgy would be the abbess.[172] One example of such a communion service was mentioned by the ninth-century hagiographer of St. Odilia. The holy woman died while her sisters were in prayer. Alarmed that Odilia had died without receiving the body and blood of Christ, they prayed that her soul would return to her body. The miracle was granted (although Odilia was annoyed about it): "And when the chalice in which the Lord's body and blood were contained was ordered to be brought to her, accepting it with her own hands, and participating in the holy communion, she handed over her soul while all watched."[173] The hagiographer seems to have had no problem with nuns handling the consecrated species, with St. Odilia touching the chalice, and with nuns performing their own communion rites.

One of the *Regula ad virgines* included readings from the Gospel as part of the Divine Office to be said by the nuns.[174] Several of the rules designated carefully to whom the keys to the Gospel book were to be entrusted.[175] The gospels and letters of Paul were read by the nuns during vigils for deceased members, and the daily reading of the nuns most certainly included all of scripture.[176] In fact, several twelfth-century canonists argued that the reading of the gospel by abbesses was proof that they were the successors to the earlier *ordo* of deaconess.[177]

Abbesses preached, as indeed did other religious women in the Middle Ages.[178] Two of the rules indicate that abbesses may have baptized children brought to the monasteries.[179] The General Admonition of Charlemagne (829) noted that abbesses gave blessings to lay people and consecrated those nuns who entered their monasteries. He ordered these abuses to be corrected, but the reports of such activities indicated that at least some abbesses were practicing this "sacerdotal blessing."[180]

Abbesses as Deaconesses

Abbesses were sometimes deaconesses. Sigolena, for example, was ordained as deaconesses but also became abbesses. A group of ninth- and tenth-century commentators on canon law presumed that abbesses were somehow all deaconesses, simply stating, "A deaconess is an abbess."[181] Similarly, Atto of Vercelli spoke of writers who claimed that the ministry called "deaconess" in the past is now named "abbess."[182] It seems that over time the two roles of deaconess and abbess were understood to have merged, at least in the minds of some contemporaries. Or to put it more accurately, abbesses were deaconesses, the living continuation of the ancient ministry founded by the apostles. At least from the ninth through the twelfth centuries, authors would make this claim, sometimes, we shall see, with great learning and passion. In this sense, then, in the eyes of the medievals, deaconesses did not die out, as had *presbyterae*. They continued to function in the church continuously from the time of Christ. It is easy to understand why they might have held this opinion. The prayers for the ordination of a deaconess and an abbess are not greatly different, and, more important, abbesses did many things deaconesses had done. They read the gospel. They sometimes distributed communion. They certainly taught young women and sometimes taught young men. They confessed their own nuns and sometimes others as well, gave penances for sin, and absolved from sin once the penances were complete. In this sense, the *ordo* of deaconess lived on long after the *ordo* of *presbyterae* seems to have faded from the ecclesiastical scene.

The lives of abbesses and their ministries would soon dramatically and drastically change. However, before that story can be told, it might be wise to offer a summary of the earlier history of the ministries performed by women before the great changes of the twelfth and thirteenth centuries.

Conclusion

First and most important, women were ordained in the early Middle Ages. According to the understanding of ordination held by themselves and their contemporaries, they were just as truly ordained as any bishop, priest, or deacon. The ordination rites for deaconesses and abbesses have been preserved, and they closely parallel those for deacons and abbots when they are not in fact interchangeable. The rites for *episcopae* and *presbyterae* have been lost, although it is possible that rites for bishops and priests were also used for women. At the very least, there are references to rituals of "conversion" during which the wives of bishops and priests took on lives of continence after the ordination of their husbands. In all these cases, women moved to another ministry, or *ordo*, in the church, and the ceremony for that move was an ordination.

To argue that these ordinations were not "true" ordinations since they were not ordinations to service at the altar, or because they did not always involve the laying on of hands or lead inexorably to the ministry of priesthood, would be at best a theological judgment based on the standing these women would now have in some Christian communities (if they were alive), and is anachronistic. A theological judgment that such ordinations do not meet modern criteria is itself fraught with problems peculiar to the discipline of theology and raises its own concerns.[183] Historically, however, there can be no question of the validity of such ordinations. There are rites for the ordination of women; there are canonical requirements for the ordination of women; there are particular women depicted as ordained; and a number of roles limited to women are included in lists of ordained ministries. The evidence is simply overwhelming.

Further, the ministries to which these women belonged encompassed ritual actions that came to be reserved only to the male diaconate and presbyterate. Some bishops allowed women to serve at the altar leading the Mass or at least celebrating with men at the Mass. Some bishops allowed women to distribute communion, and the liturgies for these services have survived. Abbesses at least certainly heard confessions, gave penances, and absolved from sin. Both abbesses and *episcopae* administered churches that were the equivalent of, and sometimes were, dioceses. Some abbesses wore the miter and wielded the staff as powerfully as bishops, and one, Brigid, was held to have been ordained a bishop in hagiological lore.

Of course a number of council members, bishops, and popes were appalled that women were serving at the altar and condemned such activity. These are contained particularly in the councils of the Merovingian bishops cited so frequently in this chapter. The decrees of these councils, as well at the *History of the Franks* by Gregory of Tours, are most important sources for the history of the church during this period. They dominate the scene in a way that gives them disproportionate weight in understanding the role of women in the early church. As important as they are, they need to be carefully put in their proper places. They are not "the church," but at best speak for one party within the church They represent the wishes of a group of reforming bishops from one area of Europe, and the decrees of these councils were not binding outside their own diocese. The same is true for the letters of the popes. They were the bishops of Rome who at times claimed a much wider authority. Some bishops agreed with those claims; some did not. The claims and counterclaims for papal power have a long and checkered history. What is clear from the evidence is that the reforms of the Merovingian councils mostly failed. Clergy did not become celibate or chaste. They continued to marry and continued to have active sex lives with their spouses. We have much less evidence from this party within the church, and so their views tend to fade in importance. Yet they may well have been the majority. In the same way, the evidence shows that the laws banning women from the altar, or from touching any of the objects associated with the altar, were ignored or unknown to the women discussed above. One simply cannot assume that the statement of a pope or a council from this period represented a decree of some unified "church" or that such statements were known or followed even within the area from which they originated. Statements by popes and councils are often wish lists, and not all wishes are fulfilled.

It is the history of the decrees of the popes and councils that misleads. They were gathered up by the reforming bishops first of the Carolingian period and then of the eleventh- and twelfth-century reformers into massive collections of church law that gave the impression of unity and uniformity, as indeed they were meant to do. Once so gathered, the wish lists of disparate councils and popes were understood as descriptions of how the past once was and now, once again, ought to be. The program of reform of the Merovingian bishops was taken up by the Carolingians (among other reform projects). The Carolingian reformers seemed to have been no more successful in imposing celibacy and/or continence on the clergy than were the Merovingian bishops, nor did they seem to have much success in deterring abbesses and deaconesses from ritual roles that had, by then, become traditional. The eleventh- and twelfth-century reformers, however, were more successful in their attempts, and we will turn to them in the next chapter.

This chapter has been an attempt, given the limited evidence available, to imagine that other church, the church that did not agree with the reformers. This was a church where bishops, priests, and deacons continued to marry, and thought it perfectly acceptable to do so. This was a church were *episcopae, presbyterae,* deaconesses, and abbesses performed particular ministries with the approval of their local bishops. Some of these women were clergy married to clergy; others were not. They did not perform exactly the same functions as bishops, priests, and deacons, for they were different *ordines* from that of bishop, priest, and deacon. Yet the ministries were similar enough to be called by the same name.

It is a difficult picture to recover as so few pieces survive. The picture that emerges, or rather one possible picture that emerges, should not be romanticized. The early church was not an idyllic environment in which women served alongside men in a church of equals.[184] Women served in a different way under different church structures in the centuries that followed. What is important for this study is not so much whether those structures were more or less open to women, but rather that they were very different. One of the main differences was that women were ordained in the earlier period; in the later period, they were not ordained, and, further, they were thought to be incapable of being ordained. The story of that change deserves a separate chapter.

4

Defining Women
Out of Ordination

A New Definition

A seismic shift in Christianity began with a slight rumble barely
noticeable amid more dramatic clashes. According to Bernold of
Constance, Pope Urban II called a synod in Benevento in 1091 in
order to anathematize once again the anti-Pope, Clement III.[1] The
Council receives little attention by scholars of the larger movement
of which it was a part.[2] Only four canons were passed, a minor
skirmish in the much larger battle that constituted the eleventh- and
twelfth-century reform movement traditionally identified with one of
its most ardent advocates and Urban's mentor, Pope Gregory VII.
The first canon of the synod states that "no one is to be elected bishop
unless he has been found to be living devoutly in holy orders (*ordines*)."
The law continues on to describe more precisely what that would
entail. "We call sacred orders the diaconate and the presbyterate. These
only the early church is read to have had; upon these alone do we
have the commands of the apostles."[3]

There is nothing radically new here. Bishops were usually,
although not always, chosen from precisely the two *ordines* mentioned, those of the diaconate and the presbyterate. This canon was
simply reinforcing the trend in the eleventh century to insist on
a proper progress within the diocesan orders.[4] The Council of
Clermont-Ferrand in 1095 was more succinct: "No layman, cleric
or even subdeacon is to be chosen as bishop."[5]

This law, like all laws, was part of a larger history. The canon expressed the opinion, popular among the eleventh-century reformers, that Jesus only established two *ordines,* the diaconate and the presbyterate. All other orders were established later by the church, including the *ordo* of bishop. This theory was held in opposition to those who argued that the episcopacy was itself an *ordo* separate from the *ordo* of the presbyterate. The statement of the Council of Benevento on this issue was widely copied in the numerous French collections of canon law that were compiled in the first half of the twelfth century.[6] Gratian of Bologna, in turn copying them, included the law in his massive collection of church law known as the *Decretum.*[7] Gratian completed the first recension of his work before the 1130s; and in its second recension, c. 1150, it soon became the standard textbook for canon law schools throughout Western Europe and formed half of all church law at least until the Reformation.

The canon would have another life, however, outside the world of canon law. In the early twelfth century, a *sententia* attached to the School at Laon would insist: "The presbyterate and diaconate only are called sacred orders, because the Spirit is given only in them and therefore under no necessity ought they be received by inferiors, but others are possible, as the apostle can be read."[8] Since the *sententia* is given without further context, it is difficult to be sure what is meant, but it would seem that something more is being said here than what was intended by the Council of Benevento. Here the meaning would seem to be that the only sacred orders that exist are the priesthood and the diaconate since only they receive the Holy Spirit, although the last enigmatic qualification might mean that exceptions can apply. If this is what is intended, then this is the first indication that the traditional definition of ordination was to be challenged by a new and narrower approach.

The canon of Benevento was copied into the influential canonical collections compiled by Ivo, the bishop of Chartres in the late eleventh century,[9] and both Ivo and the School of Laon became extremely important in the development of a theology of orders in the twelfth century.[10] Both influenced the important master, Hugh of St. Victor, who taught in Paris from c. 1120 until his death in 1141.[11] All of these authors supported the theology of the presbyterian approach to orders; that is, they believed that bishops were part of the *ordo* of priests and not a separate *ordo.* The teaching that Jesus only founded two orders—that of deacon and of priest—was fairly widespread among influential canonists and theologians by 1140. This teaching would have a long and successful career. An important step had been reached in what would prove to be a rather short march to a change in the understanding of ordination. All other orders could, and eventually would, be seen as not truly orders at all, and their ordinations as not ordinations at all.

This change did not affect all *ordines* of women, however. Deaconesses were part of the diaconate and were understood still to be ordained in the church, especially as abbesses were understood to be deaconesses by at least some contemporary writers. Abbesses would be validly ordained deaconesses even under this new understanding. The teaching, then, that Jesus only founded the orders of deacon and priest would not necessarily exclude women from the ordained ministry.

However, another change was also underway at the same time that would seriously challenge the right of women to any ordination. Early twelfth-century scholars began to copy a commentary on the letters of Paul produced by an anonymous fourth-century writer whom medievals identified as the great saint, Ambrose of Milan. The writer known by modern scholars as "Ambrosiaster" argued that Paul in fact never intended to speak of any ministry for women either in his Letter to the Romans, in which Paul mentioned the "deaconess Phoebe," or in the First Letter to Timothy, in which Paul outlined the requirements for office in the church, including that of deaconess.[12]

John Hilary Martin summarizes Ambrosiaster's position succinctly:

> Paul does not intend to say [in 1 Timothy] that "women likewise are *deacons*," Ambrosiaster insists, but rather that they likewise should be *respectable*. What Paul wants is that the people should be holy just as the clergy are (the bishops and the deacons) and that this level of holiness should even be found among women who might seem to be of little importance. Seizing on the words of Paul, he continues, the Cataphrygians tried to twist them out of context to imply that Paul talked about the deaconesses as well as the deacons at the church. For Ambrosiaster, it is clear that Paul should not be interpreted in this way since he had already commanded women "to keep silence in the church" in the previous passage. Besides, the Cataphrygians were tendentious in proposing their view since they knew very well that the Apostles had chosen seven male deacons even though there were holy women in their company.[13]

The first of the medieval commentaries so to use Ambrosiaster was that attributed to Bruno the Carthusian dating from the early twelfth century. The commentator insisted that Paul was not speaking of a separate order of deaconesses in 1 Timothy but rather was inserting a section on the wives of deacons in the middle of a discussion of deacons.[14] With a bow to an older tradition, however, he added that perhaps deaconesses are intended here, but the term "deaconesses" refers to nuns.[15]

A much more influential commentary on Paul was produced at the School of Laon in the early twelfth century, quite possibly by the two great masters of that school, Anselm and Ralph of Laon. This commentary was known as the *Glossa ordinaria* (usual commentary) on scripture since it was so frequently used throughout the Middle Ages. The *Glossa ordinaria* on the Letters of Paul even more clearly ruled out the possibility of a female ministry. The *Glossa* noted the usual reservation, "Now he [Paul] says that the office of teaching is suitable for only males alone."[16] One early exemplar of the *Glossa* continues, however, "because he does not say that women ought to be ordained into the offices of the church, but he says that the wives of those ordained, that is of deacons and priests, [ought] to be chaste."[17] Following Ambrosiaster, some versions of the *Glossa* denied that 1 Timothy gave any reference to deaconesses, asserting that only the Cataphyrigian heretics would so read the text.[18]

If we grant that the *Glossa* on Paul most likely came from the School at Laon, then the *sententiae* attached to the School at Laon becomes an additional possible witnesses to Anselm's teaching on ordination.[19] The teaching of the *sententia* would exclude all except priests and deacons from true ordination and further would insist that the diaconate precede the priesthood in the stages of ordination. The commentary on Paul in the *Glossa* would exclude women from the possibility of ordination to the diaconate. In effect these two teachings would remove any possibility of women being considered as ordained. The teachings from the School at Laon were widely copied, and, according to Marcia Colish, "The School of Laon plays a critical role in the development of the sacramental understanding of the priesthood in the twelfth century."[20]

In the early decades of the twelfth century a theology was developing that would completely remove women from any ordained ministry. The teaching of the Council of Benevento, as understood by the School of Laon, would reduce true ordination to only the presbyterate and the diaconate. The teaching of the Ambrosiaster, especially as related again by the School of Laon, further argued that scripture contains no references to women deaconesses, and in fact only heretics allowed them. The dual message was clear. The only ministry open to women at that time that could be considered truly ordained was the diaconate, and according to these theologians, orthodox women never were deacons.

This teaching took its most abrupt and dogmatic expression in Gratian's *Decretum*. In *causa* 15, *questio* 3, Gratian asked if a woman can give testimony in a case against a priest. He answered that she cannot give such testimony since "those who are not in the same *ordo* cannot accuse nor testify against a priest, nor are they able to do so. Women are not able to advance to the priesthood or even to the diaconate, therefore they are capable of neither accusing priests nor of testifying against them."[21] Here was a clear and unambiguous statement that women could not be ordained either as priests or deacons, the only *ordines* recognized as truly ordained in this new definition of ordination. Within a fifty-year period, the centuries-old tradition of the ordination of women had been reversed and denied.

The Last Defense

This theology would not go uncontested. One of the School of Laon's most famous and most controversial students was the contentious scholar Abelard. While a student at Laon, he had challenged the school's most celebrated scholar, Anselm, and did not hide his contempt for his former teacher.[22] As a student of the School of Laon, Abelard was in an excellent position to know the school's teaching on the ordination of women. As in his student days, Abelard sharply disagreed with the teaching contained in the *Glossa* as well as in the *sententia*.

In several of his works, Abelard passionately and learnedly defended the position that deaconesses were an ancient order of the church and that abbesses were now deaconesses.[23] He defended the status of women religious in his commentary on Paul's Letter to the Romans, in his sermon on the feast of St. Stephen, and in his *Theologia christiana*. A further presentation of the issue is contained in the *Commentarius Cantabrigiensis*, written by a student who had himself heard Abelard lecture. His most extended defence came, however, at the instigation of his wife, the abbess Heloise. She had written him asking him to provide her and her nuns with a history of the *ordo* of holy women (*sanctimonialia*). His reply paralleled his other discussions and strongly insisted that women belonged to the diaconate as much as men.[24] All of these works date roughly between 1122 and 1137.[25]

Abelard's commentary on the Letter of Paul to the Romans contains a collection of scriptural citations authorizing the *ordo* of deaconess. Abelard pointed out that Phoebe, to whom Paul wrote, was a deaconess who ministered to the church "an example of the holy women who had done so much for the Lord and apostles." Abelard then quoted Origen who asserted the women had been constituted in the church by apostolic authority. Two quotes from Jerome followed, one that detailed the role of deaconesses in the Eastern Church, the other that read 1 Timothy as referring to deaconesses. Abelard quickly followed this up by explaining, "We now call abbesses, that is mothers, those who in early times were called deaconesses, that is, ministers." The authority of Cassiodorus was called upon to affirm the role of deaconesses in the Eastern Church, and Claudius of Turin was quoted to prove that this passage teaches that women were established in the ministry of the church.[26] Later in his commentary, Abelard added a quote from Epiphanius that demonstrated that this honored churchman had himself ordained deaconesses.[27]

The *Commentarius* contains notes on Abelard's teaching on 1 Timothy, and that teaching disagreed completely with the teaching of the *Glossa ordinaria:* "Now after deaconesses, [Paul] returned to deacons, both are treated the same by him as they are the same office." A little later he added, "And therefore the apostle teaches about deacons and deaconesses in turn, because they have such related offices, after deaconesses again returning to deacons."[28] The *Commentarius* also repeated Abelard's teaching that the institution of deaconesses dated from the beginning of the church[29] and his conviction that abbesses were the deaconesses of his own time: "And this *ordo* of women began a long time ago because we read in the Old Testament and in the New that there were deaconesses, that is women who ministered to the saints."[30]

In his sermon on the feast of St. Stephen, Abelard praised the widows who ministered to the apostles, "whom the holy teachers are accustomed to call *diaconas* or *diaconissas.*"[31] Again, Abelard quoted the "holy teachers" including Cassiodorus and Claudius and the apostle Paul, who included women in the *ordo* of deacons in his Letter to the Romans.[32] Abelard also claimed that Paul, in his First Letter to Timothy, "after he regulated the lives of bishops and deacons, joined to those the institution of deaconesses." Abelard once again invoked Jerome to substantiate this reading of the letter.[33] Abelard seemed then to be very carefully choosing his authorities to refute the reading of Anselm and his authority, "Ambrose."

It was Heloise who requested that Abelard produce a history of her *ordo* of holy women (*sanctimonialium*). Might Heloise have known of the attack on the very existence of that *ordo*? Possibly she did. After all, on at least one occasion, she called herself a deaconess,[34] and she included herself among the ordained clerics of the church.[35] Her request may have been a cry for defense, or at least clarification, of the status of her *ordo* by her husband and the patron of her convent. Abelard responded with possibly the most thorough and passionate defence of women's orders of the high Middle Ages. Abelard's response to Heloise's request for a history of and justification for women's orders has been described by both Jean Leclercq and Mary Martin McLaughlin as "unique in medieval literature."[36]

All in all, this work comprises a detailed, learned, and even passionate plea for the *ordo* of holy women. Abelard argued that this *ordo* was established by Jesus himself and not by the apostles, specifically rejecting the teaching that only the male priesthood and diaconate were part of the original church.[37] Further, this *ordo* predates even the Lord in the great Jewish women of Hebrew scripture, and in Anna and in Elizabeth, whom Abelard dramatically described as prophets to the prophets.[38] The holy women who followed Jesus and who supported him from their material goods were the equivalent of the apostles (*pariter cum apostolis*).[39] Mary Magdalene, indeed, was the apostle to the apostles, since it was she who first announced the resurrection of Jesus to the apostles. Not only the Magdalene, however, but "from this we infer that these holy women were constituted as if they were female apostles superior to the male ones, since they were sent to the male apostles."[40] The Samaritan woman in the Gospel of John is described as the first preacher to the Gentiles, one of several references demonstrating that Abelard had no problem ascribing the role of preaching to women in the early church.[41] As in his scripture commentaries and his sermon, Abelard quoted Origen, Claudius, and Cassiodorus in describing Phoebe as a deaconess of the Church in Corinth whose praise by Paul proves that women held important ministries in the early church.[42] Once again, Abelard described the third chapter of the First Letter to Timothy as including the requirements for the *ordo* of deaconesses in parallel with those for the other clerical orders of bishop and deacon.[43]

Finally, in a passage in his *Theologia Christiana*, Abelard described the veiling of virgins, the leaders of whom are deaconesses by the hands of the highest priest, that is, Christ.[44] The language Abelard used here resonates with a prayer used in the ordination of abbesses in the liturgies discussed in chapter 3.[45]

Abelard repeatedly and pointedly asserted that the title "abbess" was the new name for the ancient order of deaconesses. The identification of abbesses as the successors of the deaconesses of the early church so thoroughly dominated Abelard's and Heloise's thought that both used the title "deaconess" interchangeably with the title "abbess."[46] Heloise and Abelard quoted sources who referred to deaconesses/abbesses as an *ordo* and as ordained. Both Abelard and Heloise considered abbesses to be the successors to the ancient order of deaconesses, an ordained clerical office established by Christ himself. Abelard's repeated defense of this position could not be clearer, and even the way in which Heloise phrased her request to her husband suggests that this is precisely the position that she wished him to defend. In the words of Mary McLaughlin, "[Abelard] could hardly, it seems, have gone to greater lengths in his quest for arguments, testimonies and examples that would exalt and dignify both the sex and the vocation of religious women."[47] Heloise and Abelard would be the last to mount such an extended defence of the ordination of women in medieval Western Christianity.

They were not the last or only theologians to adhere to the older definition of ordination, however, and they did have an extensive tradition on which to draw. As already mentioned, Origen, Claudius, and Cassiodorus all advanced the position that women held ministries in the church and that Paul's Letter to the Romans offered the proof of this.[48] Following their illustrious lead, Rabanus Maurus,[49] Sedulius Scotus,[50] and the anonymous eleventh-century *Expositiones Pauli epistolarum ad Romanos, Galathas et Ephesios*[51] all understood Paul's letters as establishing the ministry of women in the church. Abelard's contemporary, Herveus de Bourg-Dieu, also argued in his commentary on Romans that according to Paul's teaching the apostles established women such as Phoebe in church ministries.[52] Herveus further understood the women Prisca and Junia mentioned by Paul in the same letter to be among the seventy-two disciples named by Jesus and established to preach by the apostles.[53] Herveus likewise construed 1 Timothy as establishing the order of deaconess alongside that of deacon.[54] Another twelfth-century theologian, Gilbert of La Porrée, also adopted this position in his gloss on 1 Timothy, holding that Paul is speaking here of deaconesses.[55] As already mentioned, the Premonstratensian abbot Philip of Harvengt included nuns among the clerics in his *De institutione clericorum.*[56]

Despite their quotation of the Council of Benevento, Ivo of Chartres (c. 1040–1115) continued to refer to the minor orders as ordained, as well as did Hugh of St. Victor (d. 1142). Their works were frequently copied by later twelfth-century writers.[57] Writing between 1160 and 1170, Master Gandulf of Bologna continued to describe all seven ecclesiastical grades as clerics and as ordained. He would also categorize the installation ceremonies to all the grades as sacraments and as ordinations.[58] The *Speculum de mysteriis ecclesie,* an anonymous commentary on the Mass associated with the School of St. Victor and written c. 1160–75, also described the minor orders as ordained.[59] Even Peter the Lombard copied Ivo and Hugh in continuing to refer to exorcists and acolytes as ordained in his *Sentences.*[60]

The Canonical Debate

The situation in the second half of the twelfth century, then, was in flux. If theologians were divided in their understanding of ordination, the canonists were deeply engaged in a discussion over the question of the ordination of deaconesses. Gratian did include in the *Decretum* laws that referred to deaconesses, and the canonists were the first to discuss in depth to what those references could possibly mean if women could not in fact "advance to the priesthood or even to the diaconate" as Gratian had claimed. The majority of the twelfth-century canonists followed Gratian in arguing that women could not be ordained.[61] There was an inherent problem with this position, however. Five references to *presbyterae* and deaconesses managed to find their way into the *Decretum*. Interestingly, three of the four references come not from the Western Church, but from the East. *Causa* 27, *questio* 1, *caput* 23 of the *Decretum* quoted a law from the Council of Chalcedon of 451 that requires deaconesses to be forty years of age and celibate.[62] Two other references to deaconesses were included in the *Decretum* from the sixth-century *Novellae* of Justinian.[63] Finally, two references to *presbyterae* were included in *distinctio* 32, cc. 18 and 19. The first came from the *Dialogues* of Gregory the Great.[64] The second, used in later editions of the *Decretum* to explain the first passage, came from the Council of Laodicea.[65]

These references are interesting for two reasons. First, they kept alive the memory of both *presbyterae* and deaconesses and in doing so required that the canonists somehow explain their existence. Second, it is curious that these are the only references to *presbyterae* and deaconesses that survived in the *Decretum*. None of the Merovingian legislation on these two ministries or in any other of the several references discussed in chapter 3 managed to find their way into the *Decretum*. The memory of the earlier ministry of women, whether unintentionally or not, was being expunged from official ecclesial sources.[66]

The erasure did not happen immediately, however. The early commentors on the *Decretum* of Gratian could still acknowledge the existence of ordained women in the past. The influential canonist Rolandus, writing before 1148, agreed that "there is no doubt that it was the custom in the past to ordain deaconesses, that is readers of the gospel, who were not to be ordained before forty years of age, nor were they allowed to be married after ordination."[67] Stephen of Tournai (writing in the 1160s) copied Rolandus but added concerning deaconesses that "perhaps we call them abbesses and they ought not to be ordained before forty years of age."[68] Stephen suggested that the deaconesses were holy women who were called deaconesses because they were permitted to read the Gospel.[69]

A few canonists held that not only were the ordinations of deaconesses in the early church valid, sacramental ordinations, but so too were contemporary ordinations of holy women. According to the *Summa Monacensis* (written between 1175 and 1178), "the consecratory (imposition of hands) on religious [women] is appropriate only for the bishop and is a sacrament and ought to be done only at certain times."[70] Further, "as it is a sacrament, it cannot by law be repeated."[71] Cardinal Sicard of Cremona, writing between 1179 and 1181, copied this opinion of the *Summa,* and so it might seem that he too accepted that women religious were ordained.[72] When Sicard questioned whether a Jew or a pagan or a woman could be ordained a bishop, however, he gave the rather cryptic answer, "Again how could that which is outside be ordained? Further would not it be retracted if a servant would give a ruling?" He did admit, though, that some thought the ordination would be valid.[73]

Huguccio, writing c. 1188, recorded the opinion of certain scholars that women had indeed once been ordained as far as the diaconate but that the church later disallowed this earlier practice.[74] The *Apparatus* on the *Decretum* written by Joannes Teutonicus after the Fourth Lateran Council of 1215 also recorded the opinion of scholars who held that when nuns are ordained, they truly receive the character of orders.[75] This opinion of the *Summa Monacensis* and the few followers it inspired was certainly the minority opinion, but that this opinion existed at all indicates that at least some scholars taught that women could be ordained up until the early thirteenth century.

Most canonists, however, argued that women could not be ordained and, in fact, had never been ordained. Rufinus (writing between 1157 and 1159) was the first of many canonists who were to rely heavily on the interpretation of Paul offered by the *Glossa ordinaria.* His comments on deaconesses were brief but marked a turning point in the understanding of the ordination of women.

> We are led to sufficiently wonder how a council ordered that deaconesses ought to be ordained after forty years of age, when Ambrose said that to ordain deaconesses is against authority. Indeed, he said on that text in the First Letter to Timothy, "Women similarly respectable," etc.: "Using the pretext of these words, the Catafrigians said that deaconesses ought to be ordained, which is against authority." But it is one thing for a women to be ordained by sacrament as far as the office of the altar is concerned, as deacons are ordained; this is somewhat prohibited. It is another [to ordain] in another way to some other ministry in the church which is permitted here. Today however deaconesses are not found in the church in this way, but certainly abbesses are ordained in place of them.[76]

Rufinus was faced with a dilemma. The Council of Chalcedon had clearly referred to the ordination of deaconesses, yet Ambrose (actually Ambrosiaster) had forbidden such ordinations. In order to resolve this class of authorities, Rufinus defined real ordination as ordination to the altar and distinguished it from an "ordination" that is really just a commissioning for a particular ministry. The "ordination" of deaconesses, or of abbesses, was clearly of the non-sacramental variety. Such a distinction assumed a far different understanding of ordination than that used in earlier centuries. For the early understanding, as we have seen, all ordinations were commissions to a particular ministry, not just those to the altar.

Rufinus's solution was ingenious. It carefully "distinguished away" a thousand years' worth of references to women's ordination. His distinction was legitimated by the Council of Benevento's definition of ordination as limited to priesthood and the diaconate. If early Christian sources or authorities referred to women as ordained, then the references must be really referring to some sort of blessing or commissioning that was not a true ordination. If early Christian sources or authorities referred to women deacons or to *presbyterae*, the references could not be referring to a position equivalent to the sacramentally ordained male diaconate or presbyterate, but to some lesser ministry since Gratian forbade the ordination of women to the diaconate and priesthood. Abbesses, too, then were blessed but not ordained since they did not serve at the altar. Rufinus's careful distinction between "true" ordination and mere blessing was a huge success. Most canonists and theologians followed him in using this distinction to explain away any reference to women's ordination in early Christian history, and, as demonstrated in chapter 1, this remains to the present day a potent stratagem for denying the ordination of women in the past.

At the time he was writing, in the late 1150s, Rufinus's approach was just one of many. As demonstrated above, other canonists did accept that women had once been ordained, and some even suggested that they still were ordained as abbesses. But the future lay with Rufinus. The majority of canonists and theologians followed his lead in not only denying that women could be ordained, but also in believing that women had never been ordained. Not only were the practices of Western Christianity to be changed, but also history itself. In one of the most successful propaganda efforts ever launched, a majority of Christians came to accept that ordination had always been limited to the priesthood and the diaconate and that women had never served in either ministry. A thousand years of Christian history would have been dramatically altered to fit a new understanding of ordination and ministry.

The most influential canonist of his age, Huguccio of Bologna, would expand and solidify the suggestions of Rufinus in his commentary on the *Decretum* written after 1188. Following Rufinus, Huguccio preferred the opinion of "Ambrose" that women cannot be ordained over the Council of Chalcedon that assumed they could be. In any case, references to the "ordination" of deaconesses was not a true ordination, but merely a ceremony appointing women to some diaconal roles, such as reading the Gospel at matins. Huguccio conceded that these roles were still performed by nuns, and so nuns might be considered the successors of deaconesses.[77] As mentioned above, Huguccio was aware that there were scholars who disagreed with his opinion.[78]

Huguccio took the initiative, however, and went further than any of his predecessors in arguing that women could not be ordained: "But I say that a woman is not able to receive orders. What impedes this? The law of the church and sex, that is, the law of the church made on account of sex. If therefore a female is in fact ordained, she does not receive orders, and hence is forbidden to exercise the office of orders."[79] In other words, even if a woman were to be ordained, it would not "take." The mere fact of being a woman would negate any effect that an ordination might have.

Huguccio made this point even clearer in his discussion of whether a hermaphrodite could be ordained: "If therefore the person is drawn to the feminine more than to the male, the person does not receive the order. If the reverse, the person is able to receive, but ought not to be ordained on account of deformity and monstrosity."[80] Whenever the female prevails, ordination is completely ineffectual. This was not just a matter of the church deciding that women should not be ordained. Women could not be ordained, even if the church should decide to do so. The mere fact of being a woman would negate and nullify any effect such an attempt at ordination might intend. For Huguccio, then, women not only were never ordained, but also could never have been ordained. Of course, it would go without saying that women could never be ordained in the future.

In a mere one hundred years, from the Council of Benevento in 1091 until the publication of Huguccio's commentary, some time after 1188, teaching on the ordination of women had been dramatically transformed. Despite opposition from Abelard and a few other writers, canonists moved from conceding that women were once ordained, to teaching that women never were ordained, to teaching, finally, that women never could and never would be ordained. This final position is what canon law students would be taught for the rest of the Middle Ages.

The majority of canon lawyers merely repeated the teachings of Rufinus and Huguccio. Robert of Flamesbury in his *Poenitentiale,* written after 1208, declared, "Sex is of the substance of orders since women are blessed, not ordained. Granted that it is found that at one time there were deaconesses, but they were called deaconesses in another sense than a deacon today. A female certainly never had that office in the way a deacon has."[81] The most influential commentary on Gratian, however, was produced by Johannes Teutonicus

(John the German) sometime after the Fourth Lateran Council in 1215.[82] His *Apparatus* became the *Glossa ordinaria* (usual commentary) on the *Decretum* and as such was used by generations of teachers of canon law. Johannes was emphatic about the ordination of women: "I answer that women do not receive the character [of orders] by impediment of sex and the law of the church."[83] Further, women may exercise no functions reserved to those who are ordained, although "some blessing surely can be bestowed upon her from which some special office follows that is not allowed to others, perhaps the reading of homilies or the Gospel at matins."[84] Johannes did record, perhaps copying Huguccio, the opposing opinion that held that nuns could and did receive the character of orders when they were ordained,[85] but this was very much the minority opinion by the early thirteenth century and was soon to disappear altogether from canonical and theological teaching.

Guido de Baysio, writing between 1296 and 1300, produced a late commentary on the *Decretum* called the *Rosarium*. In it he followed the teaching of Huguccio but added what had become the mainstream theological and canonical teaching about women: "Add this: you say that [a women] is not able to be ordained as has been said above and this is the reason because orders are for the more perfect members of the church since it is given for the distribution of grace to an other. A women however is not a perfect member of the church, but a male is."[86]

By the beginnning of the thirteenth century, the majority of canon lawyers were convinced that women never had been ordained and never could be ordained. Gratian had created a slight problem for them, however, by including laws in his collection that mentioned deaconesses and even *presbyterae*. The canonists moved, as we have seen, from agreeing that there had once been ordained deaconesses in the church to arguing that these "deaconesses" were really just abbesses or nuns who were not ordained but were blessed so that they could perform certain special functions, such as read the Gospel at matins.

The problem of the *presbyterae* was similarly solved. The very first canonist to comment on the *Decretum*, Paucapalea, writing before 1148, set the tone for the future. A *presbytera* was the wife of a priest, "whom he had been taken while in minor orders. . . . Or we understand *presbyterae* to be those dedicated to the church, and who are called little mothers (*matricuriae*) because they perform the chores which mothers are accustomed to perform; for they wash vestments, make bread and prepare the cooking."[87] Stephen of Tournai copied Paucapalea on the meaning of the word *presbyterae*,[88] as did the *Summa Parisiensis*.[89] The *Summa Coloniensis*, written c. 1169, also followed the teaching of Paucapalea, asserting that "the wife of a priest is able to be understood not as one whom was taken while a priest, but one to whom a lay person was joined or while in minor orders." It is to such a person that *presbytera* referred when that title was used by Pope Gregory.[90] The glossator added that *presbyterae* might also refer to powerful women who converted to the religious life, an act forbidden by the Council of Laodicea.[91]

The *Rosarium* of Guido de Baysio summed up the teaching of the canonists nicely: "You say that this *presbytera* is not so called because she had been ordained; for if a women would be ordained, she would not receive the character by impediment of her sex and the law of the church. . . . But in this case she is so called because she is the wife of an ordained man."[92] The canonists were correct in describing *presbyterae* as the wives of priests, as indeed they were, at least sometimes. However, the canonists were suggesting more than this. They were suggesting that *presbyterae* were merely the wives of priests who neither received ordination of any sort nor performed any ecclesial ministry or function. In short, they did not even receive the special blessing of a deaconess. Since priests could no longer legitimately marry by the end of the twelfth century, the question would be moot in any case. *Presbyterae* no longer existed under any definition of that term.

Within roughly a century, women lost all standing as ordained clergy. They could not be ordained even if they underwent a ceremony of ordination. They had never been truly ordained either as *presbyterae,* deaconesses, or abbesses, despite any authorities to the contrary. All women were now simply laity and, as we shall see in chapter 5, lower in standing than any layman. Further, they had always been laity and would always be laity. It was metaphysically impossible for them to be ordained, to have been ordained, or ever to be ordained.

There was one more blow to come. Since abbesses were now simply laywomen, several of their earlier liturgical functions were now clearly inappropriate. In 1210, Innocent III thundered out against abbesses:

> News of certain things recently have reached our ears, about which we are not a little amazed, that abbesses, namely those constituted in the diocese of Burgos and Palencia, bless their own nuns, and hear the confessions of sins of these same, and reading the Gospel presume to preach publicly. Since then this is equally incongruous and absurd (nor supported by you to any degree), we order through the apostolic writing at your discernment so that, lest this be done by others, you take care by the apostolic authority firmly to prevent [these actions] because even though the most blessed virgin Mary was more worthy and more excellent than all of the apostles, yet

not to her, but to them the Lord handed over the keys to the kingdom of heaven.[93]

These were precisely the roles that traditionally belonged to an abbess, particularly the role of hearing her nun's confessions. No longer. As a laywoman, an abbess did not have the right to hear her nuns' confessions, to bless them, or to preach to the larger household that made up her abbey. The consequences of having been defined out of ordination were beginning to be felt. Innocent IV reiterated this legislation when he empowered a Cistercian abbot to enforce the prohibition against nuns confessing to anyone other than to the abbot.[94]

Innocent also limited the right of an abbess to excommunicate her own nuns. In 1202, the pope ruled that in cases in which physical violence had occurred, the abbess could not absolve her own nuns from excommunication, but absolution must be obtained from the local bishop.[95] The precise jurisdiction of abbesses over their own property would continue to be debated by canonists, but the basic principles were clear. Abbesses could have no power implied by ordination. They could not hear confessions, preach, proclaim the Gospel at Mass, offer blessings, or impose or lift excommunications.

The canon law professors commented upon the new laws as they appeared and as they circulated in informal collections. In 1234, an official collection of all the new laws promulgated by the papacy was published by Gregory IX. Known as the *Liber Extra* (added book), this collection in turn received its own commentaries by the law professors.[96] A sample of these commentaries demonstrates the position to which women were relegated in the thirteenth and fourteenth centuries.

Raymond of Peñafort, who compiled the *Liber Extra* for Gregory IX, set the tone for later writers in his *Summa de paenitentia*, first compiled in 1225–27 and then expanded in 1235–36[97]:

> It should be noted that a female is not able to receive the character of any clerical order. Ambrose on that saying of the apostle in the first letter to Timothy, "similarly, women ought to be respectable," said "using the pretext of these words, the Cathafrigians say that deaconesses ought to be ordained, which is against authority," since women do not receive the character by impediment of sex and the law of the church. Hence even an abbess, however learned, holy or religious, is not able to preach, nor to bless, nor to excommunicate, nor to absolve, nor to give penance, nor to judge, nor to exercise the office of any order.... Some now, as the Cathafrigians, still consider females to receive even the diaconal and presbyteral character introducing in support of this *causa* 27, c. 23 and c. 30, in which

it seems expressly to demonstrate the diaconal order, the presbyteral order is shown through *distinctio* 32, c. 18, but those chapters (*causa* 27, c. 23 and c. 30) call a deaconess those over whom some blessing was clearly bestowed by reason of which some special office followed, clearly the reading of the homily at matins or some other [service] not allowed to other nuns; in that chapter (*distinctio* 32, c. 18) a *presbytera* is so named since she was the wife of a priest, or perhaps a widow, or a "little mother" (*matricuria*), that is, having care of the things of the church as after the fashion of the mother of a family.[98]

Here we have all the elements of the standard teaching on the ordination of women from the thirteenth century through the Reformation of the sixteenth century and, in some denominations such as Roman Catholicism, up to the present. Women cannot receive the irrevocable character of ordination. Since they cannot be ordained, they can exercise no function reserved for those who are ordained. The few references to deaconesses and to *presbyterae* that did survive cannot be understood as implying any kind of ordination. Deaconesses were women who were blessed in order to exercise some special function, and *presbyterae* were "merely" the wives of priests (when priests were still allowed to marry).

Raymond still included a memory of current authors who argued that women could be ordained. He may have been referring to the *Summa Monacensis,* or possibly even to Abelard. None of the writings of his contemporaries (or at least those that have survived), however, betray this opinion. By 1234, it would be unthinkable to write, as did the author of the ninth-century Celtic life of Brigid, that a woman over whom the proper rites were read actually would then be ordained.

Scholarly discourse of the time simply wrote ordained women out of the history of the church. It was easy to forget that women had ever been ordained. The references to the ordination of women seem to have been limited to those few included in the *Decretum.* Discussion of the many sources quoted by Abelard, or of the other sources discussed in chapter 3, simply don't appear in the literature. Nor were ecclesiastics likely to remember that rites for the ordination of women once existed. The ordination rites for deaconesses were not included in the new thirteenth-century pontifical prepared for the Roman Church.[99] There was no longer any need for such a ritual. The pontificals of Rome became the models for other dioceses, and the memory of the older rites faded. Of course, if antiquarians such as William Durandus in the late thirteenth century did uncover such rites, they could be explained away as merely referring to a blessing of the type described by Raymond of Peñafort.

Other canonists followed more or less precisely the teaching of Raymond.[100] Bernard of Botone's *Apparatus on the Decretales of Gregory IX,* written
in 1245, became the *Glossa ordinaria* for the *Liber Extra.* As such, it became
extremely influential on the teaching of later canon lawyers. Bernard included
a string of caveats in regard to women's involvement in any aspect of ecclesial
life:

> A woman in fact is able neither to preach, nor to teach because
> this office is foreign to women, nor to touch the sacred vessels...nor
> are they able to veil nuns...nor to absolve them...nor to judge,
> unless clearly some noble [woman] has this from custom...nor
> to take authority upon themselves...nor is she able to be a procu-
> rator in court...nor is she able to plead in court...and generally
> the office of males is forbidden to women.[101]

This catalog of caveats would be repeated in successive commentaries and
become the standard teaching in schools of canon law.[102] The debate over the
ordination of women was swiftly settled by the canonists. Gratian had stated
that women could not be priests or deacons, and his opinion prevailed. A few
canonists had objected, arguing that references in the *Decretum* itself to
presbyterae and deaconesses was proof that women had at least at one time
been ordained. These references were explained away in a threefold process.
First, the ordinations to which the literature referred were not true ordinations. Second, the *presbyterae* and deaconesses to whom the literature referred
were not true priests or deaconesses. Finally, a definitive argument was offered to remove any possibility that women ever had been or ever would be
ordained. Women, in their very existence as women, could not receive the
character of holy orders. Even if the rite of ordination were performed over a
women, it would simply have no effect.[103]

The Theological Position

Theologians, as opposed to canonists, do not seem to have discussed the
ordination of women in the second half of the twelfth century. One of the last
to include such a discussion was the famous Peter the Lombard, who, in his
commentary on Paul, followed the *Glossa* in teaching that Paul had no in-
tention of speaking of deaconesses in 1 Timothy since it would be against the
authorities to argue that deaconesses were ordained.[104] Following the lead
of the pseudo-Bruno and perhaps of the early exemplar of the *Glossa* found
in Bibliothèque nationale MS lat. 654, Peter claimed that the women Paul

mentioned here referred only to the wives of deacons.[105] Peter's commentary, written in the late 1140s, would be the last theological work to raise the question of women's ordination for nearly ninety years. Perhaps, as Peter of Poitiers noted in his *Five Books of Sentences* (c. 1179), "concerning orders, nothing is said here about those things the arguments about which are more of service to the decretists [canonists] than to the theologians."[106]

Theologians did, however, continue to discuss what ordination in general might mean. In fact, Peter the Lombard, in his *Sentences,* offered what is usually considered to be the first definition of the sacrament of orders: "If, however, one asks: what is that which is here called order, it can indeed be said to be a certain sign, that is, something sacred, by which a spiritual power and office is given to the one ordained. Therefore a spiritual character is called an *ordo* or grade, where the promotion to power occurs."[107] The definition, although based on Augustine and earlier medieval writers,[108] breaks decisively with the earlier understanding of ordination discussed in chapter 2. Here ordination became tied securely to power rather than to vocation. Ordination bestowed a power that could be used in any community at any time. No longer was it a vocation to a particular ministry in a particular church. Lombard's definition would have a lasting impact on both theology and church practice.

The role of the "character" bestowed on the one promoted into the power of orders would be both enlarged and clarified by scholars who copied Peter the Lombard's definition. Sicard of Cremona offered a slight but significant change to the Lombard's definition of orders: "*Ordo* is the character, by which spiritual power and office are handed over to the one who is ordained."[109] Here it is the character itself that gives the ordained person both power and office. This understanding of the character of orders would be strengthened by Praepositinus, a theologian at Paris writing c. 1190–94. He linked the character received in baptism to that received in ordination, thus setting those ordained irrevocably apart from ordinary believers.[110] Guido of Orchelle, writing c. 1215–20, specifically linked the character of baptism and confirmation with the ordination of a bishop.[111]

Rufinus seems to have been the first of the canonists to argue that the power of the priesthood could not be lost, and therefore the character of orders, like that of baptism, was irreversible. Proof of this for Rufinus was that priests were not reordained, even if they were once heretics.[112] Sicard of Cremona followed the teaching of Rufinus in his commentary on the *Decretum,*[113] as did the canonist Simon of Bisignano.[114] Huguccio continued the teaching of Rufinus[115] but added an important new component to the teaching on sacramental character. The character received in baptism, confirmation, and orders was a mark on the soul itself and therefore persisted even after death.[116] The *Glossa* of Bernard of Botone repeated the teaching of Huguccio and particularly noted that the character given in baptism, confirmation, and orders lasts eternally.[117] By the end of the twelfth century, canonists were teaching that ordination bestowed an indelible and eternal character on the soul that marked out a priest or deacon as different from all other Christians for eternity. Ordination made one metaphysically distinct from all other Christians, indeed from all other humans.

The character of orders was not yet understood by all scholars as irreversible. The canonists held two opinions. Those of the Bologna School, on the one hand, held that ordination was irreversible. Canonists from Paris, on the other hand, held that priests who were degraded lost power of orders entirely.[118] Theologians were equally divided. A commentary on the *Sentences* of Peter the Lombard, attributed to Peter of Poitiers, noted that it was customary for the canonists to discuss whether the orders can be withdrawn. Some—and Peter of Poitiers sided with them—agreed that it could, and other denied this.[119] A *Summa* attributed to Stephen Langton and written c. 1202–06 also pointed out that some theologians thought that the sacerdotal character is irreversible and other argued it could be lost.[120] Theologians, like canonists, however, soon came to describe the character given in orders as permanent.

Magister Simon, writing c. 1145–60, argued strongly that the sacerdotal character, like that the sacrament of baptism or the consecration of the Eucharist, is irreversible. Priests, even if degraded for excommunication, should not be reordinated upon reception back into the church.[121] William of Auxerre, in his *Summa aurea* (*Golden Summa*), written between 1215 and 1229, also closely linked the character received in baptism and orders.[122] He further described the priesthood as the most worthy of the orders because of the priest's ability to consecrate the body and blood of the Lord. The bishop holds his worth because he can consecrate priests to perform this powerful act.[123] The sacrament of orders began to be identified exclusively with service at the altar because only this service, as embodied in the priesthood, could make the risen Christ present in the liturgy.

The identification of orders with the liturgy of the Eucharist reached its full articulation in Alexander of Hales's commentary on the *Sentences* of Peter the Lombard. A contemporary of William of Auxerre, Alexander was the first of many Parisian theologians to lecture on the *Sentences* of Peter the Lombard. Alexander's commentary was written between 1220 and 1227.[124] For Alexander, orders was different from any of the other sacraments, even baptism and confirmation, the sacraments that also imprinted indelible characters on the soul. Orders not only imprinted such a character but also conferred spiritual power and the execution of that power to a particular member of the church.[125] The power that Alexander understood to be conferred was clearly the power to consecrate the Eucharist. So intimately connected are orders and the Eucharist, that Alexander defined orders as "a sacrament of spiritual power for some office established in the church for the sacrament of communion."[126] All of the other *ordines* are somehow related to the priesthood, the highest of the *ordines,* since this is the *ordo* that can make Christ present in the liturgy.[127]

The link between orders and the Eucharist was dramatically portrayed in a story included by Robert Courson in his lectures given in Paris c. 1208–12/3:

> For it proved this man was always a virgin when St. Thomas of Canterbury had lifted up St. Cuthbert from the earth in his coffin, and when he had patted each of [Cuthbert's] limbs and his face and all of his members so that he sensed no putrefaction. The king of that kingdom who was present, asked St. Thomas by what presumption he thus patted all the parts of the saint. He responded, "King, you should not be surprised about the fact that I touch this with my consecrated hands." Because by far the most preeminent of the sacraments, of course, the body of the most holy Lord handled by all priests every day on the altar, was entrusted to the ministries of the three ministers, of course, priest, deacon and subdeacon, as Pope Clement held in *distinctio 2, de consecratione, capitulo* "Tribus gradibus" (c. 23).[128]

Robert at least implied here that the power of a priest, deacon, and subdeacon surpassed that even of a king, and it was ordination that gave that power to those ministries established for the purpose of making present the body and blood of the risen Christ. To make his point, Robert markedly referred to canon law.

The definition of ordination that dominated the late Middle Ages and that is still the definition of orders accepted by most Christians was now complete.[129] Ordination was no longer a ceremony that marked the entry of a member of the church into some new service or ministry. Ordination was a ceremony empowering a member of the church for only one purpose, the consecration of the bread and wine during the liturgy in order to make the risen Christ present at that liturgy. All other *ordines* (now the minor orders) either led to the priesthood or, as in the case of the episcopacy, made the priesthood possible. Any *ordo* that did not relate directly to the priesthood (as did the diaconate) was not an *ordo* at all. Henceforth, only the ceremony empowering a priest or deacon would be a true ordination, and anything called an ordination in the past that was not an ordination to the priesthood or diaconate was not an ordination. This is precisely the criterion applied in present debates to determine whether women have ever been ordained in the past, as chapter 1 had hoped to prove. The older definition of ordination had been replaced and had been forgotten.

One further step was necessary to complete the late medieval picture of women's ordination. The question of the ordination of women would return to theological debate, not in the scripture commentaries, but in commentaries on the *Sentences* of Peter the Lombard. Theologians picked up this discussion from the canonists, but after the canonists had already settled the issue. The first theologian to ask once again if women could be ordained was Richard Fishacre, the first Oxford theologian to comment on Peter the Lombard's *Sentences*. In his commentary, completed before 1245, Richard simply copied directly from the canonists.[130] The masculine sex is necessary for ordination, and women are incapable of receiving orders.[131] Deaconesses were merely religious women who never shared in the diaconate of men.[132] Finally, Richard stated: "Let it be noted that a woman, if she should be ordained, would not receive the character [of orders], nor would she be ordained, and this because of the impediment of sex and the constitution of the church. Therefore abbesses are not able to preach or to bless, or to excommunicate, or to absolve, or to give penances, or to judge, or to exercise the office of any order."[133] Richard's interpretation of the canonists was based on the *Glossa ordinaria* of Johannes Teutonicus.[134] The theologians would continue to discuss the ordination of women in ever more sophisticated presentations.[135] They would be united, however, in their belief that women could not be ordained, nor were they ever ordained. This judgment rested firmly, of course, on the belief that ordination could only be to the priesthood or to the diaconate as a preparation for the priesthood that shared in the ministry of the altar. Theologians and canonists were now one in rejecting the possibility that women could ever be or ever were ordained.

Conclusion

Rarely in history has ritual practice and understanding changed so rapidly and so completely. In the 1130s, Abelard could still staunchly defend the *ordo* of deaconess as divinely instituted, as truly ordained, and as still functioning in the guise of abbesses, one of whom was his own wife, Heloise. By 1230, such a defense would have been most unlikely, if not, in fact, unthinkable.

Two changes comprised this shift. First, ordination was redefined. Rather than a ceremony that celebrated the move to a new ministry in a particular community, ordination became a ceremony that granted power and a new spiritual status to a particular individual. Second, ordination was focused on only one ministry and one power, the ministry of the priesthood and the power to consecrate the bread and wine during the liturgy of the Mass. Other roles were quite quickly relegated to the ordained, and only the ordained, such as hearing confessions and preaching. However, the central power and the central ministry of a priest (and to a lesser extent to a deacon) was the ability to make the risen Christ present on the altar. This power set aside priests from all other believers, marking them with an indelible character that made their ordinations irreversible. They became a different kind of believer, if not a different kind of human being.

This change in the definition of ordination did not automatically exclude women. After all, women had been and, according to Abelard, Heloise, and many others, still were deaconesses. If deaconesses were the same as deacons, then they too were ordained even under a definition that limited ordination to the presbyterate and the diaconate. But at the same time that theologians and canonists were redefining ordination, they also began a process of expunging the memory of ordained women from Christianity. First, commentaries on scripture denied that the apostle Paul had ever referred to deaconesses in his letters. In fact, only heretics could so read the letters. Next, Gratian, based on this reading of scripture, denied that women could aspire to either the priesthood or the diaconate. Commentators on Gratian debated this point, but the majority of writers and the prevailing opinion argued that women, in their very essence, were incapable of receiving the character of ordination and therefore could not receive the power or ministry that accompanied that character. If women could never be ordained, then they never were ordained. All references to *presbyterae* and to deaconesses were then carefully explained away. *Presbyterae* must refer to the women who baked the bread or did the laundry for the church. Deaconesses were really nuns who were given a special blessing that allowed them to read the Gospel during prayer. At best, these women were the wives of ordained men, when ordained men had still been allowed to marry. No real ordination had ever occurred for any woman at any time in Christian history. And so the situation stood for centuries and stands, even today, for some Christian denominations, as the survey of modern scholarship on the question hoped to demonstrate in chapter I.

That this change took place seems clear. What is not so clear is why it happened and why it occurred in the eleventh, twelfth, and thirteen centuries. What conditions prevailed at that time to allow for so dramatic, rapid, and thorough a reconstruction of both liturgy and history? It is to those questions that we will now turn.

5

Conclusion

An Essay on Context

Chapter 4 outlined the theological and canonical discussions that led to an abrupt and thoroughgoing change in the concept of ordination. Both canonists and theologians came to define ordination as imparting particular sacramental powers, powers that males alone could receive. Canonists and theologians, on their own, however, do not effect cultural change. Their ideas are just ideas until they are received and implemented in the larger society. The story of the implementation of this change is much too complex and varied to describe in detail here.[1] Nevertheless, recent research in several areas indicates that a particular confluence of influences facilitated the change and reinforced its acceptability. This chapter will try to outline the matrix in which the change in the concept of ordination appeared in order to ascertain how such a dramatic change could be accomplished so thoroughly and so quickly.

Research suggests the picture of women, never particularly flattering in the Middle Ages, changed significantly for the worse during the Gregorian Reform.[2] If women were denied even the possibility of ordination, it was partly because the understanding of women that developed during the high Middle Ages could not conceive of women responsibly holding any position of authority. This is not to say that women did not hold such positions, but rather that they were not supposed to hold them, or even be able to hold them, according to the respected authorities of the day.

Gregorian Reform and Celibacy

The innovations of Gratian, the *Glossa ordinaria* on the Bible, and the Lombard did not appear in a vacuum. In many ways, they can be seen as the logical result and in some sense the culmination of reforms of the eleventh century. Central to this reform was the insistence of the supremacy of the priesthood and particularly of the papacy over the secular lords. Emphasizing the difference between laity and priesthood was essential to this claim.[3] Throughout much of the twelfth century, the claims were at best tenuous, as papal and imperial claimants for the papal throne fought for control. Not until 1177 would there be one pope accepted by all of Europe, a papacy dedicated to the implementation of the reform agenda. Only then could the councils of Lateran III (1179) and Lateran IV (1215) begin to consolidate and enforce the claims of the reform movement. The struggle for the control of the church between lay lords and the papal office must be seen as the backdrop to the redefinition of orders that took place as part of the struggle between priest and lord.

In order to effect this separation, the reform movement insisted on the continence of the clergy. According to the reformers, sexual intercourse polluted the priests who administered the rituals necessary for human salvation.[4] At first there was strong opposition to this demand from the married clergy who saw no need to change a centuries-old practice. They particularly objected to the disinheritance of their sons who could now no longer succeed them in what was in effect a family business.[5] At least in England, such hereditary clerical dynasties existed into the thirteenth century.[6]

Of course, the reformers would not have understood themselves as innovators. They assiduously pored over church law, creating vast collections of those laws, culminating in the *Decretum* of Gratian. Their goal was to restore the church to the state envisioned by the laws they collected. They did not simply collect ancient laws, however. They consciously or unconsciously selected and highlighted those laws that most strongly upheld the sanctity of the priesthood and the power of the papacy.[7] Among those laws was the frequent demand that subdeacons, deacons, and priests live chastely and separately from their wives.[8] At first, the reformers sought merely to enforce those laws. By the time of Pope Gregory VII (1073–85), however, the reformers began to despair of ever enforcing continence upon the married clergy. Instead, they began to insist that the higher clergy be celibate, that is, that they never be married at all.[9] Finally, at the Second Lateran Council in 1139, any marriages contracted by the bishops, priests, deacons, subdeacons, canons regular, monks, professed lay brothers, and women religious were judged to be invalid.[10] In the end, the law was enforced only for subdeacons, deacons, and priests. If they attempted to marry, their wives would legally be concubines and their offspring bastards. This would provide a huge disincentive to women to marry priests and effectively undermined hereditary parishes and dioceses, as bastard children could not inherit without a special exemption of bastardry.[11]

Here we have clear attack on the understanding of the church as an extended family. The dominant model henceforth (or at least until the Reformation of the sixteenth century) would be that of the church as monastery. Deacons, priests, and bishops might live in the world, but they would adopt, at least in the part, the life of the ascetic. They were celibate, that is to say, they could not legally marry. According to Christian theology, this would imply continence since any sexual relationship outside one's own marriage was a serious sin. Continence could no longer be practiced between clerical married couples since no such couples could exist. The church that allowed for *episcopae, presbyterae,* and married deaconesses vanished from history. This was not only a change that affected the relationship between kings and bishops, emperors and popes; it also was a change that redefined what it meant to be a church. In fact, the term "church" slowly came to refer only to the ordained, that is, to the celibate clergy.[12] Abbots, abbesses, deaconesses, kings, queens, and all the minor orders became laity and therefore not really the church.

One of the tactics used by the reformers to encourage at first continence and then celibacy was to denigrate women. Peter Damian in particular described women in the most loathsome terms:

> I speak to you, o charmers of the clergy, appetizing flesh of the devil, that castaway from paradise, you, poison of the minds, death of souls, venom of wine and of eating, companions of the very stuff of sin, the cause of our ruin. You, I say, I exhort you women of the ancient enemy, you bitches, sows, screech-owls, night owls, she-wolves, blood suckers, [who] cry "Give, give! without ceasing" (Proverbs 30:15–16). Come now, hear me, harlots, prostitutes, with your lascivious kisses, you wallowing places for fat pigs, couches for unclean spirits, demi-goddesses, sirens, witches, devotees of Diana, if any portents, if any omens are found thus far, they should be judged sufficient to your name. For you are the victims of demons, destined to be cut off by eternal death. From you the devil is fattened by the abundance of your lust, is fed by your alluring feasts.[13]

Although Peter Damian was perhaps the most lurid and vicious of the reformers in his attack on women, he was not alone.[14] In the canonical literature of the twelfth century, women were similarly described as unclean.

Following the third-century writer, Julius Solinus, Paucapalea, the first com-
mentor on the *Decretum,* explained, "For only a woman is a menstrual animal
by contact with whose blood fruits do not produce, wine turns sour, plants die,
trees lack fruit, rust corrupts iron, the air darkens. If dogs eat [the blood], they
are made wild with madness."[15] The much more influential twelfth-century
law professor Rufinus of Bologna repeated the claim to prove that women who
were menstruating should not be allowed to enter churches.[16]

The cardinal and canon lawyer, Sicard of Cremona, held that women
should not enter a church after childbirth for the same reason. However, the
time that a woman had to refrain from entering the church varied depending
on whether the child was a boy or a girl.

> If a woman should bear a male, she should abstain from entering
> the church for forty days as one unclean since an infant conceived in
> uncleanliness is said to be unformed for forty days; and if [a woman
> bears] a female, the period of time is doubled. The menstrual blood
> that accompanies the child is held to be unclean since up until that
> time, as Solinus said, by its touch fruit withers and plants die. But
> why is the time doubled for females? Answer: because two-fold is
> the curse of the birth of a female; she has of course the curse of
> Adam, and over and above that "in sorrow are you born," or be-
> cause, as the knowledge of the physicians states, women remain un-
> formed in conception twice as long as men.[17]

How could the sacrifice of the altar be performed worthily by men who had
intercourse with such filthy beasts? The papal legate, John of Cremona, was
reported to have to urged the papal reforms in England in the early twelfth
century by stating that it was the greatest sin to rise from the side of a whore and
then go create the body of Christ at Mass.[18] The language of misogyny used to
encourage and justify celibacy provides an important background for the exclusion of women from ordained ministry. It is easy to understand why the reformers would wish to deny women the ordained state. They were portrayed as
impure, sinful, and lustful, thus clearly unworthy of ordination. Moreover, the
impurity of women would also make it difficult, if not impossible, to believe
that they ever were ordained. When theologians and canonists, then, set out to
prove that *presbyterae* and deaconesses were never really ordained, they found a
receptive audience, at least among those who accepted the idea that women
were so unclean that they could never have served at the altar.

The idea that sexual activity rendered a person unclean did indeed seem
to find a receptive audience. People demanded that only pure, that is, celibate,

priests provide them with the rituals necessary for salvation. The reformers urged people to abstain from masses said by married priests, and the response was impressive. As support for the celibacy of clergy grew among the laity, married priests and their wives were sometimes attacked, beaten, or driven from the town.[19] The ideas of purity formulated by the reformers, including their attacks on the impurity of women, found enough resonance among the laity to make the enforcement of clerical celibacy possible.

The large influx of recruits to the new religious orders of the twelfth century, particularly the Cistercians, and later to the mendicant orders, would also indicate that many lay men and women believed that the celibate life was holier than the married state.[20] Thousands of men and women fled from the impurity of marriage to enter the monastery or to join the new forms of the *vita apostolica*.[21] The married state was now identified with the laity, and the laity were definitely second-class citizens in the kingdom of heaven. Perhaps the reformers' insistence on purity also contributed to the attraction of the Albigensians' severe disapproval of sexuality. In any case, the connection between sex and impurity was strengthened by the reform rhetoric. At the same time, sexuality and impurity were identified with women.

A New Understanding of Women

The demand for continence and then celibacy among the clergy, however, does not immediately rule out the possibility of female clergy. Women, too, can be continent and celibate, as indeed it seems the *presbyterae* and deaconesses of earlier centuries were required to be. Women as well as men should have been able to achieve the status of a "third sex," as Robert Swanson has described it. No longer male or female, these individuals overcame their sexual nature to achieve an angelic state.[22] Ascetics of both genders could become members of a third category—ungendered persons—closer to the angels in their detachment.

Jo Ann McNamara describes a similar possibility in the formation of the syneisactic society of celibates that marked earlier centuries of the church, culminating in the double monasteries of the twelfth century.[23] If men and women could both achieve self-mastery of their sexuality, they could transcend gender roles. Both could govern the church and perform sacramental roles, if not precisely as equals, at least as partners. If the argument of this book is correct, men and women were also both equally ordained, albeit to distinct orders. The possibility existed, then—up until the reforms of the eleventh and twelfth centuries—of partnership, if not equality, of men and women in Western

Christianity. This partnership, however, was based on the premise that both men and women could overcome their own embodiment to forge a third, asexual identity.

Prudence Allen finds a theory of sexual complementarity in the works of the twelfth-century abbess Hildegard of Bingen, among others. According to Allen, the theory that the sexes are intellectually and spiritually equal, but different and complementary, evolved from the Benedictine practice of men and women having equal access to learning. The spiritual equality of the sexes also allowed for some mutual study and interaction in the double monasteries of the twelfth century:

> In attempting to assess why this breakthrough in the history of the philosophy of sex identity occurred in the twelfth century, several factors arise. The first one is the situation of women and men within the Benedictine tradition of education. For the first time in history, significant numbers of women and men together studied and discussed philosophy within the context of double monasteries. The example of Hilda of Whitby, Roswitha, St. Anselm, Heloise and Herrad all point to the release of creative energies and to the quality of writing that emerged within this situation in which women and men had equal access to the highest and broadest sources of knowledge.[24]

Allen has probably overstated the case for shared study between men and women during this period, but her point that women could be seen as the intellectual and spiritual equal of men is well taken. This assumption was nurtured by "a supposed environment of mutual respect of women and men in the monastic setting." The monastic setting, of course, presupposes continence and celibacy. The pursuit of continence, then, and the celibate life do not necessarily imply inequality of the sexes and, in fact, can, as both McNamara and Allen demonstrate, provide the ground for a form of gender complementarity or partnership based on respect, if not on complete equality.

Marie Anne Mayeski makes a similar argument that the new collections of canon law allied with the introduction of Aristotle significantly and negatively changed a society that had previously allowed women wider opportunities for learning and ministry: "During the early Middle Ages (roughly the fifth through the eleventh centuries) the social, political, and economic situation was fluid enough to allow at least some women to make an impact on ecclesiastical and social life, but at the beginning of the twelfth century a new stability led to a decline in opportunities for even the most extraordinary women."[25] Since both men and women were equally capable of continence and of celibacy, the demand of celibacy, in itself, would not necessarily result in the exclusion of women from the ordained ministry. A further element was needed. An argument would need to be made that women were not the intellectual and spiritual equals of men. This argument was already implicit in the misogyny of the reformers but would become explicit in the adoption in the twelfth and thirteenth centuries of certain aspects of Roman law and of the philosophy of Aristotle regarding sexual differentiation.

Roman Law

Ida Raming identified Roman law as one of the culprits in the exclusion of women from the priesthood.[26] Certainly Roman law had become closely interwoven with church law shortly after the first recension of Gratian's *Decretum* appeared. The second recension greatly expanded the use of Roman law in the *Decretum*, and this is the version that canonists in the Middle Ages came to use.[27]

Roman law in itself need not have restricted the role of women in church service. At least during the later years of the empire, women were not constrained from most public activities, nor were they banned from owning and controlling their own property. According to Annit Arjava, "Women living in the last centuries of the [Roman] empire had a greater legal capacity than their sisters in any historical period before the twentieth century."[28] Canon law chose to follow an early form of Roman law that stressed the control of the *paterfamilias* (the father of the family) over his children and spouse.[29] The selective use of the law greatly restricted the role of women, reducing their legal status to that of children or servants. According to Raming, the *Decretum* severely limited the legal rights of women:

> Simply because of her sex a woman is forbidden by canon law to accuse someone in court—there are a few exceptions (cf. *causa* 15, *questio* 3)—to be a witness in cases involving punishment and in matters relating to wills (*causa* 4, *questio* 2/3 c. 1 and c. 3, § 22), to postulate for someone (*causa* 3, *questio* 7 c. 2, § 2 and *causa* 15, *questio* 3 *princ.*). Likewise, she is excluded from the office of judge and from all functions connected with judgeship (such as *procurare, advocare, postulare.*) (Cf. *causa* 3, *questio* 7, *dict.* p. c. 2, § 2.) The determining factor in the possession or nonpossession of these important rights and functions and in the admission or nonadmission of persons to them both in Roman law and in canon law, is *before anything else the sex* of the persons in consideration.[30]

Gratian's teaching that a woman could not be ordained either to the priesthood or to the diaconate actually occurred in the context of a law that forbade women to testify against priests.[31] In canon law in general, women were not allowed to be witnesses because of their supposed unreliability. Gratian argued that even the word for women in Latin, *mulier,* comes from *mollities mentis* (softness of mind or character), while the Latin for male, *vir,* derives from *virtus animi* (strength of soul).[32]

Later canonists built on this foundation to create a portrait of women as incapable of reasoned discourse. The *Liber Extra* quoted the seventh-century bishop Isidore of Seville to prove that women cannot be witnesses: "For a female always produces untrustworthy and fickle testimony."[33] Aegidius de Bellamera, writing in the thirteen century, explained further: "But why are women removed from civil and public offices? The reason is because they are fragile and usually less discerning.... Again especially in making judgments the reason is because a judge ought to be constant and unchanging ... but a woman is fickle and fragile ... again because she is not prudent nor learned as a judge ought to be."[34] Nicolas de Tudeschis, a canonist writing in the fifteenth century, summed it up nicely:

> Note that a female is not of such credibility as a male, thus he is better able to persuade ... since in cases in which a female is admitted, she does not produce as much faith as a male, and therefore if two males are on one side and two women on the opposite side, the witness of the males is preferred; for a woman (*mulier*) is so-called, not from her sex, but from the softness of her mind (*a mollitiale mentis*) while a male (*vir*) [is so-called], not from his sex, but from the constancy and virtue of his soul (*a constantia et virtute animi*)."[35]

But surely the most sarcastic comment occurred in the *Glossa ordinaria* on the *Decretales* written in the thirteenth century. The author, Bernard of Botone, rejected any testimony by women in court with the snide comment, "What is lighter than smoke? A breeze. What [is lighter] than a breeze? The wind. What [is lighter] than the wind? A woman. What [is lighter] than a woman? Nothing!"[36] Bernard goes on to note however that women do have some advantages under the law. They are too stupid to know the law, so they cannot be held accountable to it. Based on Bernard's comment, Hostiensis noted that "nuns truly not only through ignorance, but also through simplicity, [ought to be excused] for it is permitted for women to be ignorant of laws."[37]

Men were given power over women because of their inability to make proper judgments for themselves. This power of husbands was strikingly demonstrated in Gratian's discussion of how a husband should treat an adulterous wife. The *Decretum* included a law regarding the adulterous wife of a cleric but assumed the law applied to all husbands and to other sins.[38] Gratian forbade a husband from killing his wife, but "if their wives sin, it is furthermore allowed for clerics to hold them in custody without the severity of death and to force them to fast, not however to weaken them to death."[39]

The canonist Johannes Teutonicus understood this law to apply to all husbands, giving them extraordinary powers to control their wives: "A husband is able to judge a wife, correcting her. . . . But not beating her . . . but he is able to chastise with moderation since she is of his family . . . as lord his servant . . . and likewise his hired hand."[40] Later in his commentary, John continued, "Wives are subjects to their husbands and children to their parents and servants to their lords, hence they are to be restrained by them and according to the law ought to be rebuked lest they enter into an offense worthy of excommunication." John does add, "not that they should be beaten immoderately however."[41] His commentary on clerics' right to punish their wives simply repeated his general opinion: "It is stated here that if the wives of clerics should sin, they should not kill them, but guard them lest they have the opportunity of sinning in something else, weakening them by beatings and hunger, but not to death."[42]

Women were considered as children or servants in canon law, subject to the protection and the correction of males. No longer were women considered the intellectual equals of men. They were flighty, unreliable, and hopelessly ignorant. They were, in fact, children who needed to be protected, disciplined, and governed by men. Women, as a class, were incapable of understanding the law and so were incapable of enforcing or even understanding it.[43] This selective use of Roman law was not inevitable. This portrait of women came from a narrow reading of Roman law that fit with other elements to create an identity for women that excluded equality with men. A second part of the picture would come from the newly discovered texts of Aristotle.

Aristotle on Women

At the heart of the late medieval church's concept of women was the firm belief that women were naturally inferior to men, and this understanding was based partly on the philosophy of Aristotle. Allen has traced the introduction of the philosophy of Aristotle on women into the theology, law, and medicine of the twelfth and particularly the thirteenth centuries, so there is no need to repeat her analysis.[44] Allen tags this particular approach to women as "polarity," as women are held to be the opposite of men. Men are rational; women are emotional. Men are cold; women are hot. Men are active; women are passive. A brief review of some of the most striking theological and canonical positions that resulted from the adoption of this approach should suffice to demonstrate the inferior position in which this placed women.[45]

Notes on the lectures on the Letters of St. Paul by the thirteenth-century theologian Thomas Aquinas offer an insight into his use of Aristotle in understanding women.[46] According to the notes, "three things are appropriate to women, of course, silence, discipline and subjugation as these three proceed from one reason, of course, the defect of reason in them . . . since it is natural that the body be dominated by the soul and reason (dominate) inferior powers. And for that reason, as (Aristotle) teaches, whenever any two thus are mutually constituted as soul to body . . . the other is subject to the principal one."[47] Women, then, are to men as the body is to the soul. Women need to be guided by men just as the body needs to be controlled by reason. Aquinas is quite explicit about this: "The reason why (women) are subject and not in command is because they are deficient in reason which is of the greatest necessity in presiding. And for that reason (Aristotle) said in his *Politics* (book 4, chapter 11) 'that corruption of government exists when government falls to women.' "[48]

Thomas was equally blunt about women's nature: "In respect to her particular nature, woman is something defective and accidental."[49] This is a reference, of course, to Aristotle's belief that women were "misbegotten or deformed males," that is to say, a female results from an imperfect reception of the male seed in the womb. All women are a mistake that occurs when something in nature goes wrong during conception.[50] Richard of Middleton, who taught in Paris in the later thirteenth century, put it succinctly: "A woman has a subject status in respect to the status of a male which is, furthermore, in agreement with her nature because the sex of a woman is naturally imperfect in respect to the sex of a male."[51] His sentiments were echoed in the fifteenth century by the theologian Gui Brianson: "A women truly has the status of subjugation in respect to a male. This is indeed consonant with nature since the sex of women is naturally imperfect as she is according to (Aristotle), a 'defective male' (*vir occasionatus*), that is, imperfect."[52]

Hostiensis went further than his fellow theologians in denigration of the natural state of women: "The sex of women is naturally worse, hence commonly she lives less [long] since she also has less natural heat and therefore as she is more quickly ended, so she naturally ought to come to completion (that is, mature) more quickly. . . . Plato truly said that therefore this is so since weeds grow more quickly than good plants."[53] Hostiensis's observation was repeated by Aegidius de Bellamera, who compares women to flies, since they mature and die quickly.[54]

Women were naturally inferior to men simply because they were women. Nothing they could do could correct this defect. The minds of women were not capable of controlling their emotions and passions as were those of men. There was no possibility that women, as a class, were the intellectual equals of men, as a class. This made it much more difficult, although not impossible by the grace of God, for a woman to reach that "third gender" of asexuality. She did not have the required intellectual or moral strength. Nor were women capable of the reasoned discourse of the new universities. Universities were from the beginning an all-male preserve, and the philosophy of Aristotle gave ample justification for this exclusivity.[55]

The reception of Aristotle's concept of women by medieval scholars was a conscious work of selection, just as was the appropriation of Roman law. Aristotle's philosophy was suspect and at first forbidden at the University of Paris. Even those theologians who promoted the use of Aristotle denied certain of his teachings, in particular his belief that the world was eternal.[56] Theologians could also have rejected his teaching on the natural inferiority of women. That they did not was a choice. The separation of men and women into separate spheres, as well as the relegation of women to the laity, resulted in women being shunted to the margins of the intellectual life of Western Europe. Those who chose the passages from Aristotle and from Roman law that shaped this new of definition of women were all men, of course.

Use of Scripture

Women were in effect considered to be monsters. Unnatural in birth, incompetent in mind, and disgusting in their bodily functions, they were clearly inferior to men. What they lacked in nature was equally matched by their divine defects. Supposedly quoting Augustine, the *Decretum* interpreted 1 Corinthians 10:7 as teaching that women were not made in the image of God:

> This image of God exists in the male that he might be made the one from whom all others originate having the dominion of God; in some sense as His representative as he has the image of the one God. And therefore woman is not created in the image of God. For indeed it is said, "And God made man; in God's image he made him." (Gen. 5:1) Here also the Apostle: "A male," he said, "ought not to cover his head, because he is the image and glory of God," for that reason a woman covers her head because she is not the glory or the image of God (1 Cor. 10:7).[57]

The teaching became a mainstay in both theological and canonical writing.[58] Thomas Aquinas agreed that in some sense, the image of God is found in both male and female, however, "in a secondary sense the image of God is found in a male that is not found in a woman; for a male is the source of a woman and her end, as God is the source and end of all creatures."[59] Thomas's student, Peter of Tarantase, the future Pope Innocent V, repeated his master's teaching: "A male is situated closer to God as a male is the image and glory of God; a woman, on the other hand, [is the image and glory] of a male. Thus women ought to be led back to God through males and not the reverse."[60]

Not only were women not made in God's image, but also women were dependent on men for their relationship with God. According to Huguccio, there are three reasons why a male, and not a female, is understood not to be the image of God:

> A male and not a female is said to be the glory of God for three reasons. First because God appeared more powerful and more glo-rious in the creation of males than of females, for the glory of God was manifested principally through man since [God] made him *per se* and from the slime of the earth against nature, but the female was made from the man [*homo*]. Second because the man was made by God with nothing mediating which is not the case for the female. Third because [a man] principally glorifies God, that is with nothing mediating, but a female [glorifies God] through the mediation of a male since a male teaches and instructs the female for the glorifi-cation of God.[61]

The consequence of this arrangement was that women were made to serve men. According to the *Glossa ordinaria* on the *Decretales*, "A women ought not have such power since she was not made in the image of God, but a male who is the image and glory of God [was so made]; and a woman ought to be subject to a male and to be somewhat like a handmaid to a male, as a male is the head of a woman and not the contrary."[62]

The condition of women, already one of subjugation to men, became worse with the Fall, since the Fall was fundamentally caused by Eve and only sec-ondarily by Adam. Medieval scholars based their teaching on 1 Timothy 2:11–15: "Let a woman learn in silence with full submission. I permit no woman to teach or to have authority over a man; she is to keep silent. For Adam was formed first, then Eve; and Adam was not deceived, but the woman was deceived and became a transgressor. Yet she will be saved through childbearing, provided they continue in faith and love and holiness, with modesty" (New Revised Standard Version). The *Decretum* included a passage from Ambrose that makes it clear that the Fall was Eve's fault: "Adam was deceived by Eve, and not Eve by Adam. The woman summoned him to sin; it is just that he take on the guidance of her, lest he be ruined again by female recklessness."[63]

The extremely influential thirteenth-century scriptural scholar and later cardinal, the Dominican Hugh of St. Cher, made the point in his commentary on 1 Timothy by noting that "the nature of all women was made in transgression through that (sin)."[64] Duns Scotus, the Franciscan theologian teaching at end of the thirteenth century, put it this way, "In fact, natural reason agrees with this saying which the apostle intimates in 1 Corinthians 14 [34]. For nature does not permit a woman, at least after the Fall, to hold the eminent grade in the human species, since indeed it was said to her for the punishment of her sins, 'Under the power of men you will be.' "[65] Guido de Baysio, writing at the same time, agreed, "a woman was the effective cause of damnation since she was the origin of lying and Adam was deceived through her."[66]

Since it was a woman who first seduced a man to sin, medieval scholars were very wary of the seductive powers of women. Thomas Netter, the fifteenth-century Carmelite and theologian, put it movingly, "The alluring voice truly entices and the species of woman inveigles and in the end the intellect is spun around in a net of sweet words. . . . On that account, it is not permitted to her to teach because she is a weaker sex than a male. And one should be warned lest as seduced through the serpent she brought about the death of the world, so likewise easily falling into error herself, she would lead astray others to the same error."[67] Raymond of Peñafort put it more bluntly: "A woman taught one time and the whole world was overthrown."[68]

Henry of Ghent, a thirteenth-century theologian, listed several reasons why a woman should not be allowed to preach. Among them, he noted, "A woman truly does not have the constancy for preaching and teaching and is easily seduced from the truth; and therefore after the Apostle in 1 Tim. (2:12) said, 'I do not permit a woman to teach,' after a bit he added in some sense for this reason, 'Adam was not seduced, a woman was, into a lie (1 Tim. 2:14).' " For good measure, Henry added, "a woman does not have the vivacity of words leading to mortification, but more provoking to sin; and therefore on that passage, 'I do not permit a woman to teach,' the Gloss (on the bible) says, 'if, in fact, she speaks, she incites more to wantonness and is enflamed; and therefore it is said in Ecclesiasticus 9 (Sir 9:11) 'Conversation with them inflames like fire.' "[69]

Of course, the canonists were quite aware that Jewish scriptures spoke of female leaders like Deborah and that women had been leaders in the early days of Christianity. They dismissed these occurrences as anomalies. Gratian understood the role of the strong women of the Old Testament as imperfections that God allowed in the past but that grace has now perfected: "In the Old Covenant much was permitted which today [i.e., in the New Covenant] is abolished, through the perfection of grace. So if [in the Old Covenant] women were permitted to judge the people, today because of sin, which woman brought into the world, women are admonished by the Apostle to be careful to practice a modest restraint, to be subject to men and to veil themselves as a sign of subjugation."[70]

Hugh of St. Cher admitted that Deborah had prophesied, but he understood this as a special unrepeatable exception.[71] Duns Scotus agreed, but in his case, it was Mary Magdalene who was the exception: "And if you object that Magdalene was an apostle and as it were a preacher and protectress over all women sinners, I respond that she was a woman unique in this regard, uniquely accepted by Christ, and for that reason the privilege personally followed that person and ceased with that person."[72] Henry of Ghent argued that God allowed women to become leaders in the Old Testament to mock the men who ought to been leading the community: "Grace was granted to such women publicly to prophesy in the Old Testament as a reproach to males because they were made effeminate so as to cause public rule over men to be allowed to women." Henry also felt that women were allowed to preach in the early church only because of a lack of personnel: "Similarly in the early church it was allowed to the women, Mary and Martha, to publicly preach and to the daughter of Philip to publicly prophesy because of the multitude of crops and the shortage of laborers."[73]

Once again, medieval theologians could have read scripture differently. The example of Abelard in the twelfth century demonstrates that the same scriptural texts (Romans, 1 Timothy) could be used to defend the ordination of women. Abelard read these texts as proof that women were established by Jesus as capable ministers in the church. His reading would find few followers, as the standard teaching on women mined scripture for passages that supported the subordinate picture of women equally mined from Roman law and Aristotelian philosophy. Perhaps one factor would not have been sufficient to create the misogynistic approach that resulted. The cumulative effect of a selective use of church laws, Roman laws, philosophy, and scripture combined to create a potent array of authorities, all in agreement on the natural incompetence, subordination, and danger of women. Men wanted to believe the worst about women, and so they found justification to do so. Perhaps women wanted also to believe it; although there is evidence that they did not.[74] It may well be that was a confluence of factors that together helped create a society that could not conceive of women as capable of ordination as it had come to be understood.

One more factor also played a role. During the twelfth century, as we have seen, the concept of sacramental ordination became limited to those who served at the altar, the diaconate and presbyterate. These roles were further limited to males. Concomitant with this redefinition was the establishment of the priest at the center of liturgical life.

The new and greater power given to the priesthood meant that the powers left to female religious leaders were that much diminished. Innocent III, it should be remembered, broke new ground in forbidding abbesses to hear confessions, preach, and bless their own nuns. Once women were reduced to lay status, and most sacramental functions were concentrated in the hands of the presbyterate, there was no official room left for women in the church.

Conclusion

Maureen Miller has criticized the suggestion that the reformers of the eleventh century wished to create an asexual third gender by enforcing celibacy upon the diocesan clergy. Rather, Miller contends, the reformers aimed to create a new understanding of masculinity that would equal, if not surpass, the masculinity of the lay lords. She sees the real struggle of the reform movement as a struggle of clerical men against laymen, rather than a struggle against women. Clerics attacked women to prove their masculinity over against the lay lords, and in this sense, misogyny was a consequence of the larger debate over masculinity between clerics and lords.[75]

From the vantage point of this study, the attacks by the reformers on both women and lords could be seen as part of the larger struggle to define and defend an exclusive claim for sacred power. In earlier centuries, as chapter 2 has described, kings, queens, emperors, and empresses were considered ordained. They too were laicized by default when the new definition reduced ordination to those who serve at the altar. The debate then was not so clearly between clerics and laity, but rather who was going to decide what constituted clergy and laity. The issue was power. Both women and lords had ancient claims to the ordained state, and the leaders of the reform movement denied both sets of claims. The reformers wished to create a clear distinction between those men who controlled the sacred and all other Christians. In doing so, they redefined both clergy and laity. All sacramental power was consolidated into the hands of the presbyterate, and the presbyterate defined itself to be exclusively male and celibate. Laity were defined as married, female (at least in relation to the power of the priest), and dependent on the priesthood for their salvation.[76] As McNamara, Allen, and Swanson all very clearly indicate, the possibility of constructing gender to achieve a form of spiritual and intellectual equality between men and women foundered on the new assertion of masculine dominance as described above.[77]

Curiously, abbots and monks, who were also technically laicized by the redefinition of ordination, retained their sacral power through ordination to the priesthood. Although abbots and monks, like abbesses and nuns, were now no longer ordained, most abbots and many monks were being ordained priests, an option closed to the *ordines* of holy women[78]: deaconesses, abbesses, and nuns. While the diocesan clergy was being "monasticized" through enforced celibacy, the male religious orders were being "clericalized" through ordination to the priesthood.[79] The chasm between male and female religious widened as the possibility of ordination was closed to women. Ordination was redefined as sacral power, and women, even religious women, were no longer defined as capable of exercising such power.

This was not a simple, well-planned, and crude grab for power. The reformers believed that they were purifying the church. They believed that they were merely enforcing laws long in place, but long ignored. They believed they were using the best and brightest legal sources available in Roman law.[80] They believed that they were using the most astute philosophy and best science available to them in the texts of Aristotle. They believed that scripture supported their position and that this is what God wanted and what God intended. They also found willing participants in churches around Europe, in which parishioners were willing to shun married priests and participate wholeheartedly in the growing eucharistic devotions that greatly enhanced the power of the celibate priesthood. Enough of Christian Europe accepted the reforms for them to become institutionalized at least until the reformation of the sixteenth century, and in many ways, far beyond.

The effects of this revolution on women were devastating. To quote McNamara:

> The Gregorian revolution aimed at a church virtually free of women at every level but the lowest stratum of the married laity. Once the secular clergy had been subjected to celibacy, the monastic orders were largely clericalized. The co-option of monks into the ordained priesthood doubly hedged religious women. Once priesthood became prerequisite of higher education, nuns were institutionally disqualified from following monks into new areas of learning and administration, regardless of their natural endowments.[81]

Allen would concur: "Women were excluded from academic study of philosophy and theology, as well as from the study and practice of medicine and law. In addition, women were excluded from the hierarchical, jurisdictional, and sacramental structures of the church."[82] Moreover, women were reconceived as the quintessential danger to men: irrational, unclean, sinful, passive, morally and physically weak, victims who at the same time tempted men to violate them. The definition says more about men, particularly celibate men, and their own fears and temptations, than it does about women. After all, this was a definition by men of women, and even then, of a particular group of men who were banned from marriage, one of the few institutions that allowed for frequent interaction between men and women. This redefinition of women also redefined men as rational, pure, salvific, active, morally and physically strong, constantly having to fight off the temptations of women.[83] The attempts by men to live up to this definition, and of women to either escape or embrace the definition, have shaped Western culture up to the present.[84]

In closing, it must be emphasized that both women and men did escape the definition of women created by the clerical and intellectual elite. This was, after all, an intellectual construct and, in some ways, wish fulfillment on the part of a male elite. It never completely corresponded to reality. Women were hardly the passive victims some men envisioned them to be. They found ways of gaining and retaining power even within the church. They formed their own spheres of influence. They created their own self-definitions and their own definitions of men. Some men, too, rejected the roles thrust upon them and created different ways of being male and of understanding the feminine. That is a story of defiance, bravery, creativity, and success and failure that is still being recovered.

Historical and
Theological Postscript

So, then, how does this new information change anything? The answer is not straightforward, since both historians and theologians have a stake in the answer. Historians will want to know how this study might change the picture of women in the Middle Ages. Theologians' first concern will be whether this new information strengthens or weakens the arguments for and against the ordination of women in the present. These concerns may be related, but they are not the same and therefore are best addressed separately.

Historical Implications

First, then, what impact would this study have for historians? Certainly it would not change greatly what historians already know about how women functioned in the church of the early Middle Ages. As I hope I have made clear, several authors upon whom this work depends have already established that women played a far greater role in both the sacramental and jurisdictional life of Christianity in these earlier centuries than they would from the eleventh century onward. What this study hopes to change is how historians classify those roles. Women functioned in their several liturgical and administrative roles not as laity, but as ordained ministers. They were not ordained, however, as ordination would come to be understood from the twelfth century on, that is, as receiving a personal irrevocable power to serve at the altar. They were commissioned for particular roles in particular communities. The important point to be made, however, is that so were men. Men during this period did not receive a different, superior form of ordination from women. Both men and women understood themselves to be ordained in the same way, although to different *ordines*. Nor were some *ordines* "truly" ordained and others not.

Certain implications would seem to follow. Women were considered clergy insofar as they were ordained. Debates about which functions women could fulfill as ordained persisted throughout the period, but there seems to be no evidence that women were considered to be incapable of ordination before the twelfth century, and a great deal of evidence that they were considered to be ordained clergy. Care should be taken, then, in assuming that women could not or did not legitimately perform liturgical or administrative functions simply because historians assumed that they were not ordained. Further, a cooperative and respectful, if not equal, relationship between men and women would be legitimated by their shared status as ordained. The "syneisactic communities," described by Jo Ann McNamara, could be accepted and even valued in a society that assumed that both genders were ordained. Such communities would understandably come under attack once women were considered not only as laity, but also as dangerous to ordained males. If the argument in this book is correct, it supports the studies of those historians who have long argued that the status of women declined dramatically in the period following the eleventh-century reform movement.

In this sense, the book adds little new to the picture of women in the early Middle Ages painstakingly recovered by the historians acknowledged in this study as well as many others upon whose work I have not relied so heavily. Reestablishing the ordained status of women in the early Middle Ages simply reinforces the discoveries already presented in their work. Women played a far more important role in the first millennium of Christianity than historians have ascribed to them in the past. This buried "City of Women" needs still further excavation. There appears to be even more treasure to be unearthed.

Theological Implications

The fact that women were once ordained does not directly argue for or against the ordination of women in the present. Those who oppose the ordination of women now will argue that the ordination described here is not a true ordination. True ordination must meet the criteria set down in the later Middle Ages, and the ordination of women as deaconesses and abbesses does not meet those criteria. The most important of the criteria is the ability of the ordained to consecrate the bread and wine in the Mass. The evidence that women did so is so scant that the scarcity of that evidence could be read to suggest that these occasions were anomalies that were quickly condemned.

Those who support the ordination of women would argue that the instances in which women served at the altar were accepted by at least some bishops and therefore constitute a valid witness to women's ordination even as presently constructed. Further, the ordination rites for deaconesses and abbesses are similar enough to the ordination rites for deacons that they meet the criteria for a valid ordination in the present.

It is quite possible that history alone cannot solve this impasse, unless some new and irrefutable evidence appears to support one or the other position. What is important to point out here is that both of these arguments depend on the theological judgment that the present definition of ordination is correct and unalterable. This position, however, has been seriously questioned by a number of theologians, as chapter 1 indicates. For over half of Christian history, a different definition of ordination prevailed. It cannot be automatically assumed that this earlier definition was merely a tentative or failed attempt at the present definition. The theological argument must be made that the definition of the late Middle Ages is proscriptive for the present. The usual theological defense of the later definition depends either on papal authority (for Roman Catholics) or scriptural support (for Reformed Christians). These defenses are not unproblematic. Different popes supported the different understandings of ordination, and scripture can be (and has been) read to support or deny ordination to women.

However, some theologians have argued that the earlier definition of ordination would better serve Christians in the present. These theologians point out that the position has deep roots in ancient tradition and counters the dangers of clericalism inherent in an understanding of ordination focused on an individual and sacral priesthood. Men and women should once again be commissioned for particular tasks for the particular communities in which they live and worship. Again, the theological case would have to be made for this position, and, again, the position is not unproblematic. There is a long tradition of perceiving ministry to the pulpit and altar as sacred and irreversible. This tradition must be addressed seriously and on theological grounds.

As will be clear to the discerning reader, the author finds the second of these theological positions the more convincing. I have expressly written in favor of this position on more than one occasion. However, I am not making that argument at present. My point is rather that the real theological debate centers not so much on whether women can or should be ordained, but rather what definition of ordination should be used to make that decision. For instance, the historical fact that women legitimately led liturgies in the past is theologically significant only if one adopts the definition of ordination that limits ordination to service at the altar. This again depends on the centrality of the priesthood as the exclusive paradigm for ministry. In this sense, the theological question (what constitutes ordination?) precedes the historical question (did women meet those requirements?). Historians as well as theologians should be careful not to let theological positions inadvertently determine historical investigations.

The Beginning

The purpose of this study is to begin a discussion. Historically, is there sufficient evidence to warrant the claim that women were considered to be ordained ministers in the Western church of the early Middle Ages? I have argued that there is. Theologically, does this claim affect how Christianity presently understands ordination? I have argued that it should. I hope the presentation is provocative enough to stimulate others to correct, redirect, refashion, refute, or abandon those positions. If you are intrigued by the questions, I consider the project a success.

Appendix 1

Prayers and Rites for the Ordination of a Deaconess

W. Greenwell, ed., *The Pontifical of Egbert, Archbishop of York, A.D. 732–766*, Surtee Society 27 (London: T. & W. Boone, 1853).

A) Under the Heading "Ad ordinandum diaconum"
Alia benedictio diaconi sive diaconissae (p. 19)
Exaudi, Domine, preces nostras, et super hunc famulum tuum (*vel* hos famulos tuos) Ill. spiritum tuae benedictionis emitte, ut coelesti munere ditatus (*vel* ditati), et tuae gratiam possit (*vel* possint) majestatis adquirere, et bene vivendi aliis exemplum prebere. Per.

B) Benedictio episcopalis in ordinatione diaconissae (p. 94)
Omnipotens Deus intercedentibus sanctis viriginibus suis vos dignetur benedicere, qui de antiquo hoste etiam per feminas voluit triumphare. Amen. Et qui illis voluit centesimi fructum, decoremque virginitatis, et agonem martyrii conferrre, vos dignetur et vitiorum squaloribus expurgare, et virtutum lampadibus exornare. Amen.
Quatenus virtutum oleo ita peccatorum lampades possint repleri, ut cum eis coelestis sponsi thalamum valeatis ingredi.
Quod ipse. Amen. Benedictio.

C) Benedictio episcopalis in ordinatione diaconi (p. 94)
Benedicat vos Deus misericordia plenus, pietate immensus, majestate gloriosus, virtute precipuus. Amen.
Mulitplicetur pax in diebus tuis, saturitas in tempore, temperies in aere, fructus in germine. Amen.
Ut dum te pius miserator locupletat in suam hereditatem propitious introducat.

Benedicat in te Dominus imaginem quia plasmavit, et det misericordiam quam promisit. Amen.

Custodiate animam tuam quam redemit servando gratiam quam profudit.

Ut et impleas que precepit, et ille custodiat quod donavit. Amen.

Quod ipse. Amen. Benedictio.

Amen.

Jean Deshusses, ed., *Le sacramentaire Grégrorien: Ses principales formes d'apres les plus anciens manuscripts*, 2nd ed., 2 vols., Spicilegium Friburgenses, 24 (Fribourg: Éditions Universitaires Fribourg, 1988).

D) Orationem ad diaconam faciendam (1:341)

Exaudi domine preces nostras, et super hanc famulam tuam *illam*, spiritum tuae benedictionis emitte, ut caelesti munere ditata et tuae gratiam possit maiestatis adquirere, et bene uiuendi aliis exemplum prebere. <per.>

E) Under the heading "Orationes ad ordinandum diaconum" (1:97)

Alia. Exaudi domine preces nostras, et super hanc famulum tuum spiritum tuae benedictionis emitte, ut caelesti munere ditatus et tuae gratiam possit maiestatis adquirere, et bene uiuendi aliis exemplum prebere. Per.

Cyrille Vogel and Reinhard Elze, eds., *Le Pontifical Romano-Germanique du Dixième Siècle*, Studi e testi, 226, 3 vols. (Vatican City: Biblioteca Apostolica Vaticana, 1963).

(In the edition of Vogel and Elze, the rituals take different forms in different manuscripts. The differences are preserved here. Each capital letter stands for a different manuscript following the original edition. For the key to these designations, see Vogel and Elze, *Le Pontifical Romano-Germanique du Dixième Siècle*, 1:2.)

F) XXIV. Ad diaconam faciendam (1:54–59)

1. Episcopus cum diaconam benedicit, orarium in collo eius ponit. Quando autem ad ecclesiam procedit, portat illud super collum suum sic vero ut summitas orarii ex utraque parte sub tunica sit.

C D T V	B G K L
	Oratio. *Exaudi domine, preces nostras et super hanc famulam tuam . . . praebere Per.* (ut infra.n.7)

2. Item missa ad diaconam consecrandam.

Deus in nomine tuo salvum. Ps. Quoniam alieni.

3. Oratio. *Deus castitatis amator et continentiae conservator, supplicationem nostram benignus exaudi et hanc famulam tuam propitius intuere, ut que pro timore tuo continentiae pudicitiam vovit, tuo auxilio conservet et sexagesimum fructum continentiae et vitam aeternam te largiente percipiat. Per.*

4. Lectio. Require in dominica post pentecosten, feria IIIIA.

Fratres, nescitis quoniam corpora vestra.

5. Graduale. *De necessitatibus meis.* Versus. *Ad te, domine. Alleluia.* Versus. *Amavit eam dominus et ornavit.*

CDTV	BGKL
6. Deinde prostrata illa ante altare, imponatur letania.	Letania. *Kyrie [eleison].*

7. Qua finita, dicit episcopus super illam hanc orationem: *Exaudi, domini preces nostras et super hanc famulam tuam spiritum tuae benedictionis emitte, ut caelesti munere ditata, et tuae gratiam possit maiestatis acquirere et bene vivendi aliis exemplum praebere. Per.*

7a. *Preces famulae tuae, quaesumus domine, benignus exaudi, ut assumpta castitatis gratiam, te auxiliante, custodiat. Per.*

8. Sequitur consecratio in modum praephationis. *Deus qui Annam filiam Phanuelis vix per annos septem sortitam iugale coniugium ita annos octoginta quatuor in sancta et intemerata viduitate servasti, ut noctibus ac diebus orationes ieiuniaque miscentem, usque ad prophetiae gratiam sub circumcisione Christi tui, iustus remunerator adduceres, quique deinceps per apostolicam intentionem, sanctarum huius ordinationis manibus feminarum sexum ipsius adolescentulas ac iuniores instrui cum sancti chrismatis visitatione iussisti, suscipere dignare, omnipotens, piissime rerum omnium Deus, huius famulae tuae arduum et laboriosum, nec satis discrepans a perfecta virginitate propositum, quia tu, creaturarum omnium conditor, probe nosti mundiales illecebras non posse vitari, sed cum ad te venitur per te, numquam animas semel vivificatas vel terribiles passiones vel deliciarum blandimenta sollicitant; nam sensibus quibus ipse dignaris infundi nihil est desiderabilius quam regnum tuum, nihil terribilius quam iudicium tuum. Da ergo, domine, ad petitionem nostram huic famulae tuae inter coniugatas tricesimum, cum viduis sexagesimum fructum. Sit in ea cum misericordia districtio, cum libertate honestas, cum humanitate sobrietas. Opus tuum die ac nocte meditetur, ut in die vocationis suae talis esse mereatur quales per spiritum prophetiae esse voluisti presta. Per dominum.*

CDTV	BGKL
9. Tunc ponat episcopus orarium in collo eius., dicens: *Stola iocunditatis induat te dominus.*	

10. Ipsa autem imponat velamen capiti suo palam omnibus de altari acceptum cum antiphona: *Ipsi sum desponsata.*

CDTV   BGKL

11. Oratio. *Preces famulae tuae,*
quaesumus, domine, benignus exaudi,
ut assumtam castitatis gratiam te
auxiliante custodiat. Per.

12. Ad anulum dandum.
Accipe anulum fidei, signaculum spiritus sancti, ut sponsa Christi voceris, si fideliter ei
servieris.

13. Ad torquem.
Accipe signum Christi in capite, ut uxor eius efficiaris et si in eo permanseris, in perpetuum
coroneris, prosequentibus illis que circumstant antiphonam. *Anulo suo.*

CDTV   BGKL

14. *Famulam tuam, quaesumus, domine,*
pia devotione iuvante, perducat ad veniam,
quatenus mereatur a cunctis mundari
sordibus delictorum et reconciliatam tibi
per Christum sereno vultu respicias et
omnia eius peccata dimittas, severitatem
quoque iudicii tui ab ea clementer suspen-
das et miserationis tuae clementiam super
eam benignus infundas. Per.

15. Tunc imponat evangelium secundum Mattheum. *In illo tempore, respondit Iohannes*
et dixit: Non potest homo accipere.

16. Post evangelium in ordine velatarum
ad manus episcopi offerat, choro imponente
offertorium.

17. Offertorium. *Miserere mei, domine.*

18. Secreta: *Munera, quaesumus, domine, famulae et sacratae tuae, quae tibi ob consecra-*
tionem sui corporis offert, simul ad eius animae medelam proficiant Per.

19. <Praefatio. *Vere dignum, aeterne Deus. Per ipsum te deprecamur omnipotens Deus, ut*
haec oblatio quam tibi pro famula tua offero, sit in oculis tuis semper accepta et sicut sanctis
tuis eorum fide recta pervenit ad coronas, ita eam devotio te iuvante perducat ad veniam, ut
mereatur per hoc sacrificium a cunctis enumdari sordibus delictorum et reconciliatam tibi per
Christum sereno vultu respicias et omnia eius peccata dimittas, severitatem quoque iudicii tui
ab ea clementer suspendas et miserationis tuae clementiam super eam benignus infundas. Per
Christum dominum>.

20. <Infra agendam>. *Hanc igitur oblationem servitutis nostrae, sed et cunctae familiae tuae, quaesumus, domine, quam tibi offero pro incolomitate famulae tuae, ob devotionem mentis suae pius ac propitius clementi vultu suscipias,tibi vero supplicantes libens protege, dignanter exaudi, diesque.*

21. Benedictio. *Benedic, domine, hanc famulam tuam pretioso filii tui sanguine comparatam.* **R**. *Amen.*
Benedictionis tuae gratiam quam desiderat consequatur et, sine ulla offensione, maiestati tue dignum exhibeat famulatum. **R**. *Amen*
Cursum vitae suae impleat sine ullis maculis delictorum et superet in bonis actibus inimicum. **R**. *Amen. Quod ipse praestare.*

22. Communio. *Servite domino in timore.*

23. *Bonorum, Deus operum institutor, famulae tuae cor purifica, ut nihil in ea quod punire, sed quod coronare possis invenias. Per.*

CDTV	BGKL

24. Diacona vero illa inter misteria sacra communicet et post missam episcopus ei pastorali banno pacem confirmet, ut sua cum securitate et quiete possideat.

G) Ordinatio diaconorum (1:24–28)

9. Ordinatio diaconorum. Diaconi cum ordinantur, solus episcopus qui eos benedicit, manum suam super caput illorum ponat, quia non ad sacerdotium sed ad ministerium consecrantur; et alloquatur populum his verbis:

10. Allocutio ad populum. *Commune votum communis oratio prosequatur, ut hi totius aecclesiae prece, qui in diaconatus ministerio preparuntur, leviticae benedictionis ordine clarescent et spirituali conversatione prefulgentes gratiam sanctificationis eluceant, praestente domino nostro Iesu Christo.*

B C D G K L T	A

11. Benedictio ad stolas vel planetas quando levitae vel presbiteri ordinandi sunt. *Deus invictae virtutis triumphator et omnium rerum creator ac sanctificator, intende propitius preces nostras et has stolas sive planetas leviticae an sacerdotalis gloriae ministris tuis fruendas tuo proprio ore benedicere ac sanctificare consecrareque digneris, omnesque tuis ministeriis a nobis*

indignis consecrandos eis utentes et tibi
in eis devote ac laudabiliter servientes, ap-
tos tibi et gratos effici concedas et nunc
et per infinita secula   seculorum. Resp.:
Amen.

12. Prefatio diaconorum. *Oremus, dilectissimi, Deum patrem omnipotentem, ut super hos*
famulos suos N., quos ad officium diaconatus dignatur assumere, benedictionis suae gratiam
clementer effundat

B O D G K L T V	A
eisque donum consecrationis indulgeat, per	*et consecrationis indultae propitius*
quod eos ad premia aeterna perducat.	*dona conservet et preces nostras*
	clementer exaudiat, ut quae nostro
	gerenda sunt ministerio, suo
	benignus protegatur auxilio et quos
	sacris mysteriis exequendis pro
	nostra intelligentia credimus
	offerendos, sua electione iustificet.

13. *Oremus. Et diaconus:*
Flectumus genua. Levate.
Sequitur oratio:
Exaudi, domine, preces nostras et super
hos famulos tuos N. spiritum tuae
benedictionis emitte, ut celesti munere
ditati et tuae gratiam possint maiestatis
acquirere et bene vivendi aliis exemplum
praebere. Per dominum.

13. *Oremus. Et diaconus: Flectamus.*

14. Consecratio eorum in
modum prefationis. *Omnipotens*
Deus, honorum dator,

14. Oratio. *Adesto, quaesumus,*
omnipotens Deus, honorum dator,

ordinum distributor, officiorumque dispositor, qui in te manens innovas omnia et cuncta
disponis per verbum, virtutem sapientiamque, tuam Iesum Christum filium tuum dominum
nostrum, sempiterna providentia preparans et singulis quibusque temporibus aptanda dis-
pensans, cuius corpus aecclesiam videlicet tuam caelestium gratiarum varietate distinctam
suorum conexam distinctione membrorum, per legem mirabilem totius compaginis unitam, in
augmentum templi tui, crescere dilatarique largiris, sacri muneris servitutem in tribus gradibus
ministrorum, nomini tuo militari constituens, electis ab initio Levi filiis, qui in misticis op-
erationibus domus tue fidelibus excubiis permanentes, hereditatem benedictionis aeternae sorte
perpetua possiderent, super hos quoque famulos tuos quaesumus, domine, placatus intende,
quos tuis sacrariis servituros in officium diaconi suppliciter dedicamus. Et nos quidem, tam-

quam homines divini sensus et summae rationis ignari, horum vitam quantum possumus aestimamus; te autem, domine, ea que nobis sunt ignota non transeunt, te occulta non fallunt; tu cognitor secretorum, tu scrutator es cordium, tu eorum vitam celesti poteris examinare iudicio quo semper praevales et admissa purgare et ea que sunt agenda concedere. Emitte in eos, quaesumus, domine, spiritum sanctum quo in opus ministrii fideliter exequendi septiformis gratiae tuae munere roborentur. Habundet in eis totius forma virtutis, auctoritas modesta, pudor constans, innocentiae puritas et spiritualis observantia disciplinae. In moribus eorum praecepta tua fulgeant, ut suae castitatis exemplo imitationem sanctae plebis acquirant et bonum conscientiae testimonium praeferentes, in Christo firmi et stabiles perseverant dignisque successoribus de inferiori gradu per gratiam tuam capere potiora mereantur. Per eundem dominum nostrum Iesum Christum filium tuum, qui in unitate eiusdem spiritus sancti.

14a. <Benedictio ad stolas vel planetas.

Deus invictae virtutis triumphator et omnium rerum creator ac sanctificator, intende propitius preces nostras et has stolas sive planetas leviticae sacerdotalis qloriae ministris tuis fruendas tuo proprio ore benedicere ac sanctificare consecrareque digneris, omnesque tuis ministeriis a nobis indignis consecrandos eis utentes et tibi in eis devote ac laudabiliter servientes, aptos tibi et gratos effici concedas et nunc et per infinita saecula saeculorum>.

15. Ad consummandum diaconi officium cum stola:

Accipe stolam tuam, imple ministerium tuum, potens est enim Deus ut augeat tibi qratiam suam. Qui vivit et regnat.

16. Alia. *Accipe stolam, candidatam de manu domini, ab omnibus vitiorum sordibus purificatus in conspectu divine maiestatis ut omnibus vita tuae conversationis praebeatur exemplum plepsque dicata Christi nomine possit, imitando te, imitationem acquirere iustam.*

B C D K T L T V	A

17. Tunc stola levae eius circumdata, det eis evangelium dicens:
Accipite potestatem legendi evangelium in ecclesia dei tam pro vivis quam pro defunctis in nomine domini. Resp. Amen.

17a. Benedictio post acceptam stolam.
Exaudi, domine, preces nostras et super hos famulos tuos N. spiritum tuae benedictionis emitte, ut caelesti ditati et tuae maiestatis gratiam possint acquirere et bene vivendi aliis exemplum praebere. Per.

18. Sequitur benedictio

Domine sanctae, spei, fidei, gratiae et profectuum munerator, qui in caelestibus et terrenis angelorum ministeriis ubique dispositis per omnia elementa voluntatis tuae diffundis effectum, hos quoque famulos tuos N. speciali dignare illustrare, aspectu, ut tuis obsequiis expediti sanctis altaribus tuis ministri puri accrescant et indulgentia puriores eorum gradu, quos apostoli tui in septenario numero, beato Stephano duce ac praeuio, sancto spiritu auctore, elegerunt, digni existant et virtutibus universis quibus tibi servire oportet instructi complaceant. Per. In unitate.

B C D G K L T V   A

19. Cum vero consecrati fuerint,
induantur dalmatica, et dent osculum
episcopo et sacerdotibus et stent ad
dexteram episcopi.

B C D G K L T   A V

20. Canon s. Theodori. In ordinatione
presbiterivel diaconi oportet episcopum
missam cantare; similiter greci faciunt
quando abbatem eligunt vel abbatissam.

Michel Andrieu, ed., *Le Pontifical Romain au moyen-âge*, vol. 1, *Le Pontifical Roman au moyen âge, Le pontical romain du XIIe siècle*, Studi e testi, 88 (Vatican City: Biblioteca apostolica vaticana, 1940): 168–69

H) XIV. Missa ad diaconam consecrandam

1. Introitus. *Deus in nomine tuo salvum me fac et in virtute tua libera me.* Ps. *Deus exaudi orationem.*

2. Oratio. *Deus castitatis amator et continentiae conservator, supplicationem nostram benignus exaudi et hanc famulam tuam propitius intuere, et quae pro timore tuo continentiae pudicitiam vovet, tuo auxilio conservet et sexagesimum fructum continentiae et vitam aeternam te largiente percipiat. Per.*

3. Lectio epistolae beati Pauli apostoli ad Corinthios [1 Cor. 6:15-20]. *Fratres, nescitis quoniam corpora vestra membra Christi sunt...et portate Deum in corpore vestro.*

4. Grad. *De necessitatibus meis.* Vers. *Ad te levavi.* Deinde letaniam. *Kyrie eleison.*

5. Oratio: *Preces famulae tuae, quaesumus, domine, benignus exaudi, ut sumptam castitatis gratiam te auxiliante custodiat. Per.*

6. Item consecratio. *Deus qui Annam filiam Phanuelis, quae vixit per annos septem sortita iugale coniugium, ita in annos octoginta quatuor in sancta et intemerata viduitate servasti, ut noctibus ac diebus orationes ieiuniaque miscentem usque ad prophetiae gratiam, sub circumcisione Christi tui, iustus remunerator adduceres, quique deinceps per apostolicam institutionem, sanctarum huius ordinationis manibus feminarum, sexum ipsius adulescentulas ac iuniores instrui cum sancti chrismatis visitatione iussisti, suscipere dignare, omnipotens, piissime rerum omnium Deus, huius famulae tuae aduum et laboriosum nec satis discrepans a perfecta viduitate propositum, quia tu creaturarum omnium conditor probe nosti mundiales illecebras non posse vitari, sed cum ad te venitur, per te numquam animas semel vivificatas vel terribiles passiones vel deliciarum blandimenta solicitant, nam sensibus quibus ipse dignaris infundi nihil est desiderabilius quam regnum tuum, nihil terribilius quam iudicium tuum. Da ergo, domine, ad petitionem nostram huic famulae tuae inter coniugatas tricesimum fructum, cum viduis sexagesimum. Sit in ea cum misericordia districtio, cum humilitate largitas, cum liberate honestas, cum humanitate sobrietas. Opus tuum die ac nocte meditetur, ut in die vocationis suae talis esse mereatur, qualem illam per spiritum prophetiae esse voluisti. Presta per dominum.*

6 [sic]. Grad. *Amavit eam dominus et ornavit eam stola.* Vers. *Induit eam dominus cyclade.*

7. Sequitur evangelium secundum Iohannem [John 3: 27-30]. *In illo tempore, respondit Iohannes et dixit: Non potest homo accipere quicquam . . . me autem minui.*

8. Offertorium. *Miserere mei, domine, secundum magnam misericordiam tuam. Dele iniquitatem meam.*

9. Secreta. *Munera, quaesumus, domine, famulae tuae ill., quae tibi obsecrationem sui corporis offert, simul ad eius animae et corporis medelam proficiant Per.*

10. Praefatio. *Vere dignum . . . Per ipsum te deprecamur, omnipotens Deus, ut haec oblatio, quam tibi pro famula tua N. offero, sit in oculis tuis semper accepta et sicut sanctis tuis eorum fide recta pervenit ad coronas, ita eam devotio te iubente perducat ad veniam, ut mereatur per hoc sacrificium a cunctis emundari sordibus delictorum et reconciliatam tibi sereno vultu respicias et omnia eius peccata dimittas, severitatem quoque iudicii tui ab ea clementer suspendas et miserationis tuae clementiam super eam benignus infundas. Per Christum.*

11. Infra canonem. *Hanc igitur oblationem servitutis nostrae sed et cunctae familiae tuae, domine, quam tibi offero pro incolomitate famulae tuae ob devotionem mentis suae pius ac propitius clementi vultu suscipias, tibi vero supplicantes libens protegens dignanter exaudi, diesque nostros.*

12. Communio. *Servite domino in timore et exultate ei cum tremore, apprehendite disciplinam ne pereatis de via iusta.*

13. A complendum. *Bonorum Deus operum institutor, famulae tuae corda purifica, ut nihil in ea quod punire sed quod coronare possis invenias. Per.*

14. Antequam vero legatur evangelium, dat ei anulum dicens: *Accipe anulum fidei, signaculum spiritus sancti, ut sponsa Dei voceris, si ei fideliter servieris.*

15. Ad torquem dandam: *Accipe signum Christi in capite, ut uxor eius efficiaris et, si in eo permanseris, in perpetuo coroneris. Per.*

Michel Andrieu, ed., *Le Pontifical Romain au moyen-âge, 3, Le Pontifical de Guillaume Durand*, Studi e testi, 88 (Vatican City: Biblioteca apostolica vaticana, 1940): 411.

I) XXII. De ordinatione diaconisse

1. Diaconissa olim, non tamen ante annum quadragesimum, ordinabatur hoc modo. Lecta etenim epistola, ea ad terram ante altare prostrata, dicebat episcopus super eam: *Adiutorium nostrum, etc. Oremus.*

Oratio. *Exaudi, domine, preces nostras et super hanc famulam tuam,* et cet., ut supra. Require supra, sub benedictione abbatis.

2. Deinde dabat ei orarium dicens: *Oremus.*

Oratio. *Famulam tuam, domine,* ut supra.

Appendix 2

Ordination Rites for Abbesses from the Early Middle Ages

José Janini, ed., *Liber ordinum episcopal [Cod. Silos, Arch. Monástico, 4]*, Studia silensia 15 (Burgos: Abadia de Silos, 1991).

A) XXIII Ordo ad ordinandam abbatissam (pp. 101–2)

Quando ordinatur abbatissa uestitur a deo uotis in sacrario ueste religionis et inponitur ei in capite mitra religiosa; et precedentes ac subsequentes eam alie deo uote cum cereis, tacentes ueniunt ad corum. Adplicans tamen eam episcopus ad altare, cooperit eam pallio per caput, et dicit super eam hanc orationem:

113b Oratio. Omnipotens domine deus aput quem non est discretio sexuum, nec ulla sanctorum disparilitas animarum; qui ita uiros ad spiritalia certamina corroboras, ut feminas non relinquas: pietatem tuam humili supplicatione deposcimus, ut huic famule tuae, quam sacrosancto gregi uirginum nostrarum inpositio<ne> manuum, et hoc uelaminis tegumento in cenobio matrem, fieri preobtamus, clementia tua roboratrix adueniat et adiutrix perpetuo non recedat. <D>a ei domine fortitudinem spiritalia bella gerenda, ut condam debbore bellatrici, procinctum certaminis contra sisare hostilem cuneum tribuisti. Ut sicut ducatu illius sraelitici populi aduersarii preire ita uigilantia huius multitudo daemonum <que> aduersus animas sanctas cotidie dimicatur et militat, uirtute tua penitus disturbetur et pereat. Adsit ei tua dextera consolatrix, que iudit uidue in perniciem non defuit olofornis. Ita domine sermonibus piis et tui adiutorio nominis exterminet usquequaque satan, ut ester humilis infestum tuis plebibus exterminauit aman. Dona ei domine castimonie custodiam indefessam, et karitatis sincerissimam dulcedinem gratiosam. Sit sollers in creditarum sibi regimine animarum, et celer in suarum correctione culparum. Ita subditas sibi spiritali zelo coerceat, et materne pietatis affectu refobeat, <ut> nec blanditia dissolute, nec nimia coercione reddantur pusillanimes aut proterue. Da ei christe domine spiritum discretionis omnimodae ut nec onesta dilaceret, nec inonesta delectetur. Atque ita te inluminante sibi creditam multitudinem tuo sancto nomini iugiter admonendo faciat inseruire, ut quum nube fla<m>miuoma mundum ueneris iudicare postrema subditarum profectibus gloriosa, et de nullius perditione confusa, tuae genetricis adiungatur gloriosa cetibus letabunda cum suis omnibus feliciter coronanda. Amen. Te prestante.

Qua explicita osculatur eam episcopus, et tradit ei librum regule et baculum. Ac post salutat oepiscopus et dicit diaconus: Missa acta est.

A. Dumas, ed. *Liber sacramentorum Gellonensis*, CCSL 159 (Turnhout: Brepols, 1981).

B) CCCLXXVI. Oratio qvando abba vel abbatissa ordinatvr in monasterio (pp. 399–401)

Cunctorum instituae deus, qui pro moysen famulum tuum ad gubernandas ecclesias prepositus instituisti, tibi supplicis fundimus preces teque deuotis mentibus exoramus ut hunc famulum tuum *ill.* que<m> conibentia et electio famularum tuarum abbatissam hodie <o>uium tuorum esse instituit si<c> qui regat subditus conmendatus et cum illis omnibus regna celorum adeptus quatenus te opitulante domine apostolicis iugiter fultu[a]s doctrinis, centissimo cum fructu[s] letus introeat portas paradisi atque te domine conlaudante audire mereatur: Euge euge [famola] serue bone et fidelis, quia super pauca fuisti fidelis, supra multa te constituam, intra in gaudium domini tui. Quod ipse. Per dominum.

Item alia benedictio. Omnipotens sempiterne deus, affluentem illum spiritum tui benedictionis super famulum tuum *ill.* nobis orantibus propitiatus infunde, ut qui per manus nostre hodie inpositione<m> abbatissa instituetur sanctificatione tua, dignitate electas permaneat, ut nunquam pusmodum de tua gratia separetur indigna. Suscipiat te largiente hodie domine hi bono opere [et] perseuerantiam, in aduersis constantiam, in tribulationibus tollerantiam, in ieiuniis desiderium, in [im]pietatibus misericordiam, in humilitatibus principatum, in superbia odium, in fide[m] dilectionem, in doctrina[m] peruigilantiam, in castitate[m] continentiam, in luxuria[m] abstinentiam, in uari<e> tatebus moderatione<m>, in moribus doctrinam. Te munerante domine talis hunc ministerium perseuerit qualis leuita electus ab apostolis sanctus sthephanus meruit perdurare. Tota ab odia diabolica conuersatione dispitiat; te domine benedictionem largitatem contempnat presentia[m], premia celestia desiderit sempiterna. Sit exemplum et furma iustitiae ad gubernandum regendamque ecclesiam fideliter, ut speculator idoneus inter suos collogiis semper efficiat. Sit magni consilii, industrie censure, efficatiae discipline. Ita te domine tribuente ut in omnibus mandatis tuis sine reprehensione tibi mundo corde deseruiens, ad pravium superne uocationis multiplicati fenore cum centisimo fructu coronamque iustitiam et celestium thesaurorum donatiua perueniat. Per dominum.

Item alia. Domine deus omnipotens, qui sororem moysen mariam pereuntem ceteris mulieribus inter aequorias undas cum thymphanis et choris letam ad litus maris uenire fecisti, te supplicis deprecamur pro fidele famola *ill.* que hodiae materna in cathedra uniuersis subditis sibi abbatissa esse constituetur, ut ita a monastica nurma tueatur cunctas famulas tuas quatenus aeternam ad gloriam te auxiliante[m] cum omnibus introeat leta tibique exultantes cum angelis, canentes cantica noua, sequantur agnum quocumque ierit prestante[m] <domino nostro>.

O. Heiming, ed., *Liber sacramentorum Augustodunensis*, CCSL 159 (Turnhout: Brepols, 1984).

C) CCCLXVIII Item Oratio quando abba uel abbatissa ordinatur in monasterio (pp. 193–4)

Cunctorum institutor deus qui per Moysen famulum tuum. ad gubernandas ecclesias praepositus instituisti. tibi supplices fundemus praeces teque deuotis mentibus exoramus ut hunc famulum tuum *illum* <hanc famulam tuam illam> quem <quam> conubentia et electio famulorum tuorum (famularum tuarum) abbatem (abbatissam) odie ouium tuarum. esse instituit. sicque regat subditus commendatus (subditas commendatas) ut cum illis omnibus regna caelorum adeptus (adepta) quatenus te opitulante domine apostolicis iugiter fultus (fulta) doctrinis centissimo cum fructu[s] laetus <laeta> introeat portas paradisi. atque te domine conlaudante. audire mereatur: *Euge euge. serue bone* (famula bona) *et fidelis quia super pauca fuisti fidelis super multa te constituam intra in gaudium domini tui.* quod ipse praestare digneris qui in trinitate.

Item alia benedictio.

Omnipotens sempiterne deus afluentem illum spiritum tuae benedictionis super famulum tuum *illum* (famulam tuam *illam*) nobis orantibus propitiatus infunde ut qui per manus nostrae hodiae inpositione abba (abbatissa) instituetur. sanctificatione tua digne a te electus (electa) permaneat. ut numquam postmodum de tua gratia separetur indignus (indigna) suscipiat te largiente hodiae domine in bono opere perseuerantiam. in aduersis constantiam. in tribulationibus tolerantiam. in ieiuniis desiderium. in pietatibus misericordiam. in humilitatibus principatum. in superbia odium in fide dilectionem. in doctrina peruigilantiam in castitate. continentiam. in luxoria abstinentiam in uarietatibus moderationem. in moribus doctrinam te munerante domine talis hunc ministerium. perseueret qualis leuita electus ab apostolis sanctus Stephanus meruit perdurare. tota ab hodie diabolica conuersatione. dispiciat te domine benedictionem. largiente[m] contempnat praesentia praemia caelestia desiderit sempiterna sit exemplum et forma iusticiae a<d> gubernandam regendamque ecclesiam fideliter ut speculator idoneus (speculatrix idonea) inter suis colligiis semper efficiat. Sit magni. consilii industrie censure efficatie discipline. ita te domine tribuente. ut in omnibus mandatis tuis sine repraehensione tibi mundo. corde deseruiens abbrauium superne uocationis multiplicato. fenore cum centissimo fructu. coronamque iusticiae et caelestium thesaurorum donatiua perueniat: praestante domino nostro.

Item benedictio.

Domine deus omnipotens qui sororem Moysen Mariam praeeuntem ceteris mulieribus inter aequorias undas. cum tympanis et choris laetam ad litus maris uenire fecisti. te supplices depraecamur profidele. famula tua *illa* que odie materna in cathedra uniuersus subditis sibi. abbatissa esse constituetur. ut ita a monastica norma tueatur cunctas famulas tuas quatenus eternam ad gloriam te auxiliante cum omnibus introeat laeta ibique exultantes cum angelis canentes cantica noua sequantur agnum quocumque ierit [Christus]: praestante domino nostro.

Jean Deshusses, ed., *Le sacramentaire Grégorien: Ses principales formes d'apres les plus anciens manuscripts*, 2nd ed., 3 vols., Spicilegium Friburgenses 24 (Fribourg: Éditions universitaires Fribourg, 1971-82)

D) 216 Oratio ad abbatem faciendum uel abbatissam (1:342)
Concede quaesumus omnipotens deus et famulum tuum *ill. uel illam* quem ad regimen animarum eligimus, gratiae tuae dono prosequere, ut te largient, cum ipsa tibi nostra electione placeamus. Per.

Cyrille Vogel and Reinhard Elze, eds., *Le Pontifical Romano-Germanique du Dixième Siècle*, Studi e testi, 226, 3 vols. (Vatican City: Biblioteca Apostolica Vaticana, 1963). (In the edition of Vogel and Elze, the rituals take different forms in different manuscripts. The differences are preserved here. Each capital letter stands for a different manuscript following the original edition. For the key to these designations, see Vogel and Elze, *Le Pontifical Romano-Germanique du Dixième Siècle*, 1:2.)

E) XXII. Ordinatio abbatissae canonicam regulam profitentis (1:48–51)
1. In ordinatione abbatisse episcopus debet missam canere et eam benedicere hoc modo.

2. Post antiphonam ad introitum et datam orationem et reliquum officium missae usque ad evangelium, prosternat se electa ante altare cum duabus vel tribus de soribus suis, fiantque ibi letaniae.

3. Quibus finitis, benedicit eam episcopus inclinato capite, dicens: *Dominus vobiscum.* **R.** *Et cum spiritu tuo.* Sequitur oratio. *Oremus.*
Exaudi, domine, preces nostras et super hanc famulam tuam spiritum tuae benedictionis emitte, ut caelesti munere ditata et tuae gratiam maiestatis possit acquirere et bene vivendi aliis exemplum praebere. Per dominum nostrum Iesum Christum filium qui tecum.

4. <Alia>. *Omnipotentiam tuam, domine, humiliter imploramus, ut super hanc famulam tuam quam ad sacrum ordinem assumere dignatus es benedictionis tuae donum dignanter infundas eique gratiam consecrationis tribuas, ut quod te donante percepit, te protegente inlesum custodiat. Per.*

5. Tunc dicat in altum: *Per omnia saecula saeculorum.* **R.** *Amen.*
Dominus vobiscum. **R.** *Et cum spiritu tuo.*
Et prosequatur istam orationem in modum prefationis.
Domine, sancte pater, omnipotens, eterne Deus, adesto precibus adesto votis, adesto famulationibus, adesto consecrationibus, qui omnia per verbum virtutis tuae mirabiliter dispensas et dispensanda ministras, qui diversis floribus tuam semper exornas ecclesiam, dum eam et virorum exemplis et illustrium feminarum irradias institutis; qui etiam de infirmiori sexu hanc famulam tuam servitutis tuae applicare dignatus es famulatui, effunde, quaesumus, domine, super hanc famulam tuam, quam in officium divinum fideliter dedicamus, gratiam spiritus sancti, ut tibi omnium tempore eius servitus dignanter complaceat, eamque dextra potentiae tuae benedicere et sanctificare sive consecrare digneris in opus ministerii tui condignum, quatinus actum ministrationis sibi creditae fideliter exequatur et eiusdem sancti spiritus septiformis gratiae virtute corroboretur. Requiescat ergo super eam, precamur, domine, spiritus sapientiae et pietatis, ac repleas eam spiritu timoris tui. Concede ei quoque gravitatem actuum censuramque vivendi, ut in lege tua die ac nocte meditetur; mandata tua custodiat, dictis tuis obediat, sacris lectionibus insistat, terrena et transitoria despiciat, atque omni tempore bonis operibus inserviat. Omnem libidinem pravae voluptatis superet, amorem honestae castitatis teneat, ut tibi sponso venienti cum lampadibus inextinguibilibus possit occurrere et praecedentium virginum choro iungi, et ne cum stultis excludatur, sed regalem ianuam cum sapientibus virginibus licenter introeat. Abundet in ea totius forma virtutis, auctoritas modesta, pudor constans, innocentiae puritas et spiritalis observantia displinae, in moribus eius praecepta tua fulgeant, ut suae castitatis exemplo cunctis sibi subditis imitationem praebeat puram et, bonum conscientiae testimonium ostendens, in Christo Iesu firma et stabilis perseveret atque ita perceptum ministerium, te auxiliante, peragat, qualiter ad aeternam remunerationem, te donante, pervenire mereatur. Per eundem.

6. Tunc det ei regulam, dicens:
Accipe regula sanctae conversationis, simulque gratiam divinae benedictionis, et ut per hanc cum grege tibi credito indistricti iudicii die, domino incontaminata representari valeas, ipse te adiuvare dignetur, qui cum Deo patre et spiritu sancto.

7. Sequitur oratio. *Domine Deus omnipotens, qui sororem Moysi Mariam praeeuntem cum caeteris mulieribus inter equoreas undas cum tympanis et choris letam ad litus maris venire fecisti, te supplice deprecamur pro fideli famula tua, quae hodie materna in cathedra super universas subditas sibi abbatissa constituitur, ut ita canonica norma tueatur cunctas famulas tuas, quatinus ad eternam gloriam, te auxiliante, cum omnibus illis introeat laeta, ibique exultans cum angelis, canens cantica nova sequatur agnum quocumque ierit Christum dominum nostrum. Qui tecum.*

8. *Alia. Famulam tuam, quaesumus, domine, tua semper gratia benedicat et inculpabilem ad vitam perducat aeternam. Per.*

9. Quod si ordinatio in domo sua facta fuerit, imponatur *Te Deum laudamus*, populo acclamante *Kirieleyson*.

10. Postea dicatur haec oratio pro adepta dignitate:
Omnium domine fons bonorum iustorumque provectuum munerator tribue, quaesumus, famulae tuae adeptam bene regere dignitatem et a te sibi, praestitam bonis operibus comprobare. Per.

11. Item si alibi consecrata fuerit, regressae ad monasterium omnis chorus virginum honorifice procedat ei obviam cum crucibus, aqua benedicta, incenso et evangelio, et in ipso ecclesie introitu imponant *Te Deum laudamus*, turba acclamante *Kirieleyson* et presbitero prosequente orationem ut supra: *Omnium domine fons.*

F) XXVI. Ordinatio abbatis [contains the following prayer for the ordination of an abbess (1:67–69)]

<14a. Consecratio quando abbas vel abbatissa ordinatur in monasterio.
Cunctorum operum institutor, Deus qui per Moysen famulum tuum ad gubernandas ecclesias praepositos instituisti, tibi supplices fundimus preces teque devotis mentibus exoramus, ut hunc famulum tuum N. quem conibentia et electio famulorum tuorum abbatem hodie ovium tuarum instituit, protectionis tuae gratia munire digneris, sicque regere subditos concedas, ut cum illis omnibus regna caelorum adeptus et, te, domine, opitulante, apostolicis iugiter fultus doctrinis, centesimo cum fructu laetus introeat portas paradisi, atque, te, domine, conlaudante, audire mereatur: Euge serve bone et fidelis quia in pauca fuisti fidelis, super multa te constituam, intra in gaudium domini tui. Quod ipse prestare digneris qui in trinitate perfecta vivis et regnas.

Tunc imponat ei manum super caput dicens orationem hanc in modum prefationis:
Omnipotens sempiterne Deus, affluentem spiritum tuae benedictionis famulo tuo N. nobis orantibus propitiatus infunde, ut qui per manus nostrae hodie impositionem abbas constituitur, sanctificatione tua digne a te electus permaneat, ut nunquam postmodum de tua gratia separetur indignus. Suscipiat, te, domine, largiente, hodie in bono opere perseverantiam, in adversis constantiam, in tribulationibus tolerantiam, in ieiuniis desiderium, in impietatibus misericordiam, in humilitate principatum, in superbia odium, in fide dilectionem, in doctrina pervigilantiam, in castitate continentiam, in luxuria abstinentiam, in varietatibus moderationem, in moribus doctrinam. Te munerante, domine, talis in hoc ministerio perseveret, qualis levita electus ab apostolis sanctus Stephanus meruit perdurare. Totam ab hodie diabolicam conversationem despiciat, tua, domine, benedictione largiente, contempnat praesentia, diligat caelestia, praemia desideret sempiterna. Sit exemplum et forma iusticiae ad gubernandam regendamque ecclesiam fideliter, ut speculator idoneus inter suos collegas semper efficatur, sit

magni consilii, industriae, censurae, efficaciae, disciplinae; ita te, domine, tribuente, in om-
nibus mandatis tuis sine reprehensione tibi mundo corde deserviat, ut ad bravium supernae
vocationis mulitiplicato fenore cum centesimo fructu coronaque iusticiae et ad celestium
thesaurorum donativa perveniat, praestante domino nostro.

14b. Alia. *Deus omnium fidelium pastor et rector, famulum tuum quem ecclesiae tuae praeesse*
voluisti, propitius respice, da ei, quaesumus, verbo et exemplo quibus praeest proficere, ut ad
vitam una cum grege sibi commisso perveniat sempiternam Per>.

15. Oratio pro adepta dignitate.
Omnium Deus fons bonorum iustorumque provectuum munerator, tribue, quaesumus Ill.
famulo tuo adeptam bene gerere dignitatem et a te sibi praestitam bonis operibus compro-
bare Per.

<15a. Item alia. *Deus cui omnis potestas et dignitas famulatur, da famulo tuo N. prosperum*
suae dignitatis effectum in qua te semper timeat tibique iugiter placere contendat. Per>.

16. Sequitur *Te Deum laudamus*, populo acclamante *Kyrieleyson*.

17. <Postea dicatur oratio:> *Deus aeternae lucis inventor, omnipotentiam tuam supplici*
prece deposcimus, ut famulum tuum N., quam ad regimen animarum elegimus, gratiae tuae
dono prosequaris, ut, te largiente, cum ipsa tibi nostra electione placeamus. Per unigenitum
tuum dominum nostum [sic] Iesum Christum, cum quo et spiritu sancto unus et verus es Deus,
vivens et regnans per omnia secula seculorum.

18. Et peragatur missa ordine suo.

<18a. Item benedictio proprie ad abbatissam. *Domine, Deus omnipotens, qui sororem*
Moysi Mariam pereuntem cum caeteris mulieribus inter aequoreas undas cum timpanis et
choris laetam ad litus maris venire fecisti, te supplices deprecamur pro fideli famula tua N.
quae hodie materna in cathedra super universas subditas sibi abbatissa esse constituitur, ut ita
monastica norma tueatur cunctas famulas tuas, quatenus ad aeternam gloriam, te auxiliante,
cum omnibus illis introeat laeta, ibique exultans cum angelis canens cantica nova sequatur
agnum quocumque ierit Christum dominum nostrum qui tecum vivit>.

G) XXXII. Ordinatio abbatisse monasticam regulam profitentis (1:76–82)

1. Capitulum ex canone Theodori Anglorum archiepiscopi.
In ordinatione abbatissae episcopus debet missam canere et eam benedicere hoc modo.

2. Post antiphonam ad introitum et datam orationem et reliquum officium missae
usque ad evangelium, prosternat se electa ante altare retro episcopum cum duabus vel
tribus de sororibus suis, fiantque ibi letaniae.

3. Sequitur *Pater noster* cum precibus: *Salvam fac ancillam tuam domine.* **R.** *Deus meus.*
<Dominus conservet eam et vivificet eam. **R.** *Et beatam faciat.*
Dominus custodiat introitum tuum et exitum tuum. **R.** *Ex hoc nunc et usque in saeculum.*
Dominus custodiat te ab omni malo. **R.** *Custodiat animam tuam dominus.*
Mittat tibi dominus auxilium de sancto. **R.** *Et de Syon tueatur te.*
Nihil proficiat inimicus in ea. **R.** *Et filius iniquitatis non nocebit eam.*
Esto illi domine turris fortitudinis. **R.** *A facie inimici.*
Exurge, domine, adiuva eam. **R.** *Et libera eam propter nomen tuum.*
Domine exaudi orationem meam. **R.** *Et clamor meus ad te veniat>.*

4. Precibus finitis, benedicat eam episcopus inclinato capite, dicens:
Dominus vobiscum. **R.** *Et cum.*
Sequitur oratio. *Concede, quaesumus, omnipotens Deus, affectui nostro <tuae miserationis effectum et famulam tuam, quam ad regimen animarum eligimus, gratiae tuae dono prosequere, ut, te largiente, cum ipsa tibi nostra electione placeamus. Per>.*

5. Alia. *Cunctorum bonorum institutor Deus <qui per Moysen famulum tuum ad gubernandas aecelesias praepositos instituisti, tibi supplices fundimus preces teque devotis mentibus exoramus, ut hanc famulam tuam N. quam coniventia et electio famularum tuarum abbatissam hodie ovium tuarum instituit, protectionis tuae gratia munire digneris sicque regere subditas commendatasque oves concedas, ut cum illis omnibus regna caelorum adepta et te, domine, opitulante apostolicis iugiter fulta doctrinis cum fructu centesimo laeta introeat portas paradysi atque te domine collaudante audire mereatur. "Euge ancilla bona et fidelis, quia in pauca fuisti fidelis, super multa te constituam, intra in gaudium domini tui". Quod ipse praestare dignetur>.*

BGKL

CDTV

6. *Exaudi, quaesumus, domine, preces humilitatis nostrae et super hanc famulam tuam N. gratiam tuae benedictionis effunde, quatinus per nostrae manus impositionem inter fideles dispensatrices inveniatur et cum subditis sibi gregibus placere tibi mereatur. Per.*

7. Hic excelsa voce dicit:
Per omnia saecula, usque *Vere dignum.*
Tunc imponat ei manum super caput, dicens hanc praephationem
Vere dignum, aequum ei salutare, nos tibi semper et ubique gratias agere, domine, sancte pater, omnipotens eterne Deus. Respice, quaesumus, super hanc famulam tuam, quam in tui nominis vice custodem monacharum ordinamus. Immitte ei,

domine, spiritum sapientiae et intellectus,
spiritum consilii et fortitudinis, spiritum
scientiae et pietatis, et reple eam spiritu
timoris tui, quatinus tua gratia praeventa
nihil contra tuum praeceptum faciat, doceat,
constituat vel iubeat, sed magis mentes
discipularum tam exemplis bonorum operum
quam verbis instuat, et quae discipulabus
docuerit esse contraria, in operibus suis
iudicet non agenda. Sit in omnibus suis
provida et considerata; sit sobria et casta; sit
vita probabilis; sit sapiens et humilis; sit
benigna et caritativa; sit in pauperum
peregrinorum susceptione assidua; sit in
hospitalitate hilaris; sit pia et misericors et
semper misericor-diam exaltet iudicio, et
ipsa ante aequissimum iudicem veniam
consequatur. Fac eam, domine, te solum
totis viribus suis diligere, ieiunium amare,
corpus castigare, delicias non appetere,
tribulantibus subvenire, neminem odisse,
zelum iniustum et invidiam non habere,
suspitionem omnimodo devitare, in tuo
nomine pro inimicis exorare. Fac eam semper
agnoscere quia tibi redditura est rationem
villicationis suae et quantas sub cura sua
animas habuerit, ipsas sine dubio ante sedem
maiestatis tuae sit latura. Quapropter tibi
piissimo pastori supplicamus, ut ad
humilitatis nostrae orationes cor eius gratia
tua illustres, quo possit quaeque singula ita
discernere atque temperare, ut fortes
habeant quod cupiant et infirmae quod
non refugiant. Da illi, domine, spiritum
compunctionis, ut caelestia semper diligat
et inextinguibilem gehennae ignem ante
mentis oculos proponat, quatinus
supernorum dulcedine gaudiorum et
infernalium amaritudine tormentorum
semetipsam inreprehensibilem custodiat,
ut cum creditis sibi ovibus in tremendo
examine gaudeat et cum omnibus sanctis tuis
inmarcescibilem caelestis regni coronam
accipiat. Per Christum.

8. Tunc inponat ei manum super caput dicens hanc orationem in modum prae-phationis:

Omnipotens sempiterne Deus, affluentem spiritum <tuae benedictionis famulae tuae N. orantibus nobis propitiatus infunde, ut quae per manus nostrae hodie impositionem abba-tissa constituitur, sanctificatione tua digne a te electa permaneat, ut numquam postmodum de tua gratia separetur indigna. Suscipiat te, domine, largiente hodie in bono opere perser-verantiam, in adversis constantiam, in tribulatione tolerantiam, in ieiuniis desiderium, in impietatibus misericordiam, in humilitate principatum, in superbia odium, in fide dilectio-nem, in doctrina vigilantiam, in castitate continentiam, in luxuria abstinentiam, in varie-tatibus moderationem, in moribus doctrinam. Te munerante, domine, talis in hoc ministerio perseveret qualis levita electus ab apostolis sanctus Stephanus meriut perdurare. Totam ab hodie diabolicam conversationem despiciat, tua, domine, benedictione largiente contempnat praesentia, diligat caelestia, praemia desideret sempiterna. Sit exemplum et forma iustitiae ad gubernandam regendamque aecclesiam fideliter, ut speculatrix idonea inter suas collegas semper efficiatur. Sit magni consilii, industriae, censurae, efficaciae, disciplinae. Ita te, domine, tribuente in omnibus mandatis tuis sine reprehensione tibi mundo corde deserviat, ut ad bravium supernae vocationis multiplicato foenore cum centesimo fructu coronaque iustitiae et ad caelestium thesaurorum dona tua perveniat. Praestante domino>.

9. Tunc det ei regulam, dicens: *Accipe regulam a sanctis patribus nobis traditam, ad re-gendum custodiendumque gregem tibi a Deo creditum, quantum Deus ipse te confortaverit ac fragilitas humana permiserit.*

10. Sequitur. *Domine Deus omnipotens qui sororem Moysi Mariam <pereuntem cum ceteris mulieribus inter aequoreas undas, cum tympanis et choris laetam ad litus maris venire fecisti, te supplices deprecamur pro fideli famula tua N. quae hodie materna in cathedra super universas subditas sibi abbatissa constituitur, ut ita monastica norma tueatur cunctas famulas tuas, quatinus ad aeternam gloriam, te auxiliante, cum omnibus illis introeat laeta ibique exultans cum angelis canens cantica nova, sequatur agnum quocumque ierit Christum domi-num nostrum. Qui tecum>.*

11. Alia. *Concede, quaesumus, omnipotens Deus, famulae tuae abbatissae, ut ostendendo et exercendo que recta sunt, exemplo bonorum operum animos suarum instruat subditarum et aeternae remunerationis mercedem a te piissimo pastore percipiat. Per.*

12. Alia. *Omnium, domine, fons bonorum, <iustorumque provectuum munerator, tribue, quaesumus, famulae tuae adeptam bene gerere dignitatem et a te sibi praestitam bonis op-eribus comprobare. Per>.*

13. Quod si ordinatio abbatisse infra monasterium suum facta fuerit, imponatur *Te Deum laudamus*, populo acclamante *Kyrie*.

14. Postea dicatur hec oratio pro adepta dignitate:
Deus cui omnis potestas <et dignitas famulatur, da famulae tuae N. prosperum suae dig-nitatis effectum in qua te semper timeat tibique iugiter placere contendat. Per.>

15. Item si alibi consecrata fuerit abbatissa, regressae ad monasterium, omnis chorus monacharum honorifice obviam procedat cum crucibus, aqua benedicta, incenso et e-vangelio. Et in ipso introitu ecelesiae imponant *Te Deum laudamus*, turba acclamante *Kyrieleison* et presbitero prosequente orationem ut supra: *Deus cui omnis potestas et dignitas*.

Michel Andrieu, ed., *Le Pontifical Romain au Moyen-Âge*, vol. 1, *Le Pontifical Romain du XIIe Siècle*, Studi e testi, 86 (Vatican City: Biblioteca apostolica vaticana, 1938). (In the edition of Andrieu, the rituals take different forms in different manuscripts. The differences are preserved here. Each capital letter stands for a different manuscript following the original edition. For full information on these manuscripts, see Andrieu, *Le Pontifical Romain du XIIe Siècle*, 21–114.)

H) XV. Ordo ad abbatem benedicendum vel abbatissam. (pp. 170–74)

BCO

1. Primum eligitur ab omni congregatione in praesentia episcopi et percepta ab eo donatione et roborata ab omnibus electione, episcopus pariter et electus veniant ante altare. Legitur tunc electio in ambone, ut audiatur et roboretur. Tunc, stratis ante altare tapetibus, sternant se simul pontifex et qui ab eo benedicendus est abbas. Deinde fiunt letaniae.

L

1. Consimilis est enim utriusque benedictio, nisi quod abbatissa in benedictione sua non induitur nisi consuetis vestibus, nec datur ei baculus. Postquam igitur electio facta est a congregatione et confirmata ab episcopo, die statuto accedat abbas ad benedictionem. Et tunc, ubi ab episcopo processum fuerit in missa usque ad evangelium, ille qui ab eo benedicendus est abbas, indutus super propria vestimenta albam et cappam de pallio, prosternat se super tapetia strata ante altare et episcopus procumbat super faudestolium suum. Deinde cantentur letaniae. Cum autem dicitur: *Ut abbatem istum benedicere digneris*, bis dicatur versiculus ille ab eo qui letaniam cantat. Et episcopus in singula responsione, quae fit a choro, signet super illum.

2. Quibus finitis, post orationem dominicam, erigat se solus pontifex, strato eo qui benedicendus est, et dicat:
Et ne nos inducas in temptationem. **R.** *Sed libera nos a malo.*
Salvum fac servum tuum, domine. **R.** *Deus meus, sperantem in te.*
<*Dominus conservet eum et vivificet eum.* **R.** *Et beatum faciat eum.*
Dominus custodiat introitum tum [sic] *et exitum tuum.* **R.** *Ex hoc nunc et usque in saeculum.*
Dominus custodiat te ab omni malo. **R.** *Custodiat animam tuam dominus.*>

2. Finitis letaniis, erigat se solus episcopus et dicat:

Mittat tibi auxilium dominus de sancto. **R.** *Et de Syon tueatur te.*
Hic accipiet benedictionem a domino. **R.** *Et misericordiam a Deo salutari suo.*
<Esto illi, domine, turris fortitudinis. **R.** *A facie inimici.*
Nihil proficiat inimicus in eo. **R.** *Et filius iniquitatis non apponat nocere ei.>*
Dominus vobiscum. **R.** *Et cum spiritu tuo.*

3. Oratio. *Actiones nostras, quaesumus, domine, aspirando praeveni et adiuvando prosequere, ut cuncta nostra oratio et a te semper incipiat et per te coepta finiatur. Per.*

4. His ita peractis,

BCO	L
dicit episcopus hanc orationem:	surgit ille qui benedicendus est et, ipso caput inclinante, prosequitur episcopus subscriptas orationes. Verumtamen sciendum est quoniam, iuxta ordinem romanum, praedicta omnia non dicuntur. Sed ubi episcopus processerit in missa usque ad evangelium, tunc praesentatur ei qui benedicendus est abbas et, ipso caput inclinante, prosequitur episcopus subscriptas orationes.

5. *Concede, quaesumus, omnipotens Deus, ut famulum tuum N., quem ad regimen anima-rum eligimus, gratiae tuae dono prosequaris, ut te largiente cum ipsa tibi nostra electione placeamus. Per.*

6. Alia. *Cunctorum bonorum institutor Deus, qui per Moysen famulum tuum ad guber-nandas ecclesias praepositos instituisti, tibi supplices preces effundimus teque devotis mentibus exoramus, ut hunc famulum tuum N., quem conventus et electio famulorum tuorum abbatem ovium tuarum esse instituit, protectionis tuae gratia munire digneris sicque regere subditos concedas, ut cum illis omnibus regna coelorum adipiscatur, quatenus te opitulante, domine, apostolicis fultus iugiter doctrinis, centesimo cum fructu lactus introeat portas paradysi atque a te, domine, collaudante audire mereatur: "Euge serve bone et fidelis, quia in pauca fuisti fidelis, supra multa te constituam, intra in gaudium domini tui". Quod ipse praestare digneris, qui vivis et gloriaris Deus, per omnia saecula saeculorum. Amen.*

7. Tunc imponit ei manus super caput eius et dicit hanc orationem in modum prae-fationis:
Omnipotens sempiterne Deus, affluentem spiritum tuae benedictionis super hunc famulum tuum N. nobis orantibus propitiatus infunde, ut qui per manus nostrae hodie impositionem abbas instituitur, sanctificatione tua digne a te electus permaneat, ut numquam postmodum de tua gratia separetur indignus. Suscipiat, te largiente, domine, hodie bono opere perseverantiam,

in adversis constantiam, in tribulationibus tolerantiam, in ieiuniis desiderium, in impieta-
tibus misericordiam, in humilitatibus principatum, in superbia odium, in fide dilectionem, in
doctrina pervigilantiam, in castitate continentiam, in luxuria abstinentiam, in varietatibus
moderationem, in moribus doctrinam. Te tribuente, domine, talis in hoc ministerio perseveret,
qualis levita electus ab apostolis sanctus Stephanus meruit perdurare. Totam ab hodie diabo-
licam conversationem despiciat. Tua, domine, benedictione largiente contempnat praesentia,
diligat coelestia, desideret sempiterna. Sit exemplum et forma iustitiae ad gubernandam re-
gendamque ecclesiam tuam fideliter. Ut speculator idoneus inter suos collegas semper efficiatur.
Sit magni consilii, industriae, censurae, efficaciae et disciplinae, ita te, domine, tribuente, ut in
omnibus mandatis tuis sine reprehensione tibi mundo corde serviens, ad bravium supernae
vocationis multiplicato fenore eum centesimo fructu coronaque iustitiae ad coelestium thesau-
rorum donativa perveniat. Praestante domino nostro. Qui venturus est iudicare.

8. Tunc tradit ei regulam dicens: *Accipe regulam a sanctis patribus nobis traditam, ad*
regendum custodiendumque gregem tibi a Deo creditum, quantum Deus ipse te confortaverit et
fragilitas humana permiserit. Per.

<9. Sequitur oratio. *Te, omnipotens et piissime deprecamur, domine.*>

10. Tunc tradit ei baculum dicens:

B O	C L
Accipe baculum pastoralis officii, ut sis in corrigendis vitiis pie seviens et, cum iratus fueris, misericordiae memoreris.	*Accipe baculum pastoralitatis, quem praeferas catervae tibi commissae ad exeplum iustae severitatis et correptionis.*

<11. Subsequatur ab episcopo
antiphona. *Confirma hoc, Deus, quod*
operatus es in nobis a templo sancto tuo
quod est in Ierusalem.>

12. Sequitur oratio. *Deus cui omnis*
potestas et dignitas famulatur, da
famulo tuo N. prosperum suae
dignitatis effectum, in qua te semper
timeat, tibique iugiter placere contendat.
Per.

13. Specialis benedictio abbatissae.   13. Oratio specialiter pertinens ad
benedictionem abbatissae.

Domine Deus omnipotens, qui sororem Moysi Mariam praeeuntem cum caeteris mulieribus inter
equoreas aquas cum tympanis et choris laetam ad litus maris venire fecisti, te supplices deprecamur
pro fideli famula tua N., quae hodie materna in cathedra subditis sibi abbatissa esse constituitur,
ut ita monastica norma tueatur cunetas famulas tuas sibi commissas, quatenus ad aeternam

gloriam, te auxiliante, cum omnibus introeat laeta, ibique exultantes et eum angelis canentes cantica nova sequantur agnum quocumque ierit, Christum dominum nostrum. Qui tecum.

14. Oratio communis abbatis et abbatissae pro adepta dignitate.

Omnium, domine, fons bonorum iustorumque provectuum munerator, tribue, quaesumus, N. famulo tuo adeptam bene gerere dignitatem, et a te sibi praestitam bonis operibus comprobare. Per.

Benedictione completa, episcopus ordine suo missam prosequatur.

Notes

CHAPTER I

1. For a discussion of this distinction, see Gary Macy, "The Ordination of Women in the Early Middle Ages," *Theological Studies* 61 (2000): 502–7, reprinted in Bernard Cooke and Gary Macy, eds., *A History of Women and Ordination*, vol. 1 of *The Ordination of Women in a Medieval Context* (New York: Scarecrow Press, 2002), 1–30; and Terrence Tilley, *History, Theology, and Faith: Dissolving the Modern Problematic* (Maryknoll, NY: Orbis Books, 2004).

2. For references to studies of the ordination of deaconesses in the Byzantine Church, see nn65–68 below.

3. There are many studies of the roles women played in the early centuries. Essential for the New Testament period is Elisabeth Schüssler Fiorenza, *In Memory of Her: A Feminist Theological Reconstruction of Christian Origins* (New York: Crossroad, 1983). Recent studies on women in the first three centuries of Christianity include Ben Witherington, *Women in the Earliest Churches*, Society for New Testament Studies, Monograph Series 59 (Cambridge: Cambridge University Press, 1988); Karen Jo Torjesen, *When Women Were Priests* (San Francisco: HarperSanFrancisco, 1993); Bonnie Bowman Thurston, *The Widows: A Women's Ministry in the Early Church* (Minneapolis: Fortress, 1989); Ross Shepard Kraemer and Mary Rose D'Angelo, eds., *Essays in Women and Christian Origins* (New York: Oxford University Press, 1999); and Ute Eisen, *Women Officeholders in Early Christianity: Epigraphical and Literary Studies* (Collegeville, MN: Liturgical Press, 2000), who provides an exhaustive bibliography on this subject on pages 227–95.

4. A second corrected edition was produced in Amsterdam in 1695. This later edition was reprinted in 1969 and is the edition used here. On Jean Morin, see P. Auvray, "Morin, Jean," *NCE* 9: 896–97.

5. "Exercitatio X De diaconissis, earum ordinatione et ministriis secondum ecclesiae graecae et latinae praxim" (Jean Morin, *Commentarius de sacris ecclesiae ordinationibus secundum antiquos et recentiores latinos, graecos, syros et babylonios in tres partes distinctus* [1695; repr. Farnborough: Gregg 1969], pt. 3, pp. 143–51).

6. "Tres illi antiquissimi rituales graeci uno consensu, et eodem tenore nobis tradunt diaconissae ordinationem, et similibus prope ritibus et verbis quibus diaconi, administratam. Utraque enim ordinatio χειρτονὶα, et χειροφεσὶα dicitur. Utraque ad altare a pontifice celebratur, et eodem liturgiae loco. In utraque manus imponitur dum adprecatur pontifex. In utraque stola collo apponitur, in altari ordinatus et ordinata communicantur, calix sanguine Christi plenus ut ex eo degustent, in manus traditur" (ibid., 143). See also "Nihil enim nobis perhibent rituales illi antiqui de diaconissis et earum ordinatione, quam quod exploratissimus testimoniis constat olim in ecclesia tam latina quam graeca suisse usitatissimum" (p. 144); "Diaconissas, et earum ordinationem multa alia monumenta eccclesiastica demonstrant" (p. 146); and "Manifestum est igitur diaconissas a patribus graecis ordinatas, et clericorum more punitas" (p. 147).

7. "Verum non existimant graeci ista ceremoniarum communicatione ullam mulieribus proprie dictam χειρτονὶαν infundi, ut disertissime testatur Sanctus Ephiphanius. . . . Nec opinor theologos aliquos ita severos fore, ut mulieres abdicare velint omni in ecclesia erga alias mulieres ministerio, et sacra aliqua ad illud suscipiendum et conferendum ceremoniali inauguratione. Si aliqua tam austerus et tetricus fuerit, ut nihil quod ad ordinationem ecclesiasticam spectat, mulieribus concedi posse contendat, facile anitiquissima multorum seculorum traditione revincetur, ejusque tetricitas retundur" (ibid., 143–44).

8. Jean Pien (Pinius in Latin) joined the group of Jesuits commonly known as the Bollandists who were editing the huge collection of the lives of the saints (*Acta sanctorum*) in 1713. See Hippolyte Delehaye, *A Travers Trois Siècles: L'oeuvre des Bollandists, 1615–1915* (Brussels: Bureaux de la Société des Bollandistes, 1920), 40–41.

9. "Priusquam de Diaconissarum ordinatione sermonem instituo, monitum volo lectorem, non agi hic de ordinatione stricti nominis seu sacramentali; sed de ea, quæ sit cæremonialis et impropria, sicut latius postea dicam" (J. Bollandus, et al, eds., *Acta sanctorum*, September, vol. 1 [Antwerp: Bernard Albert Vander Plassch, 1746], 1: iv, col. A). For a discussion of other early modern studies of the role of women in ministry, see Adolf Kalsbach, *Die altkirchliche Einrichtung der Diakonissen bis zum ihrem Erlöschen* (Frieburg im Breisgau: Herder, 1926), 2–3; Roger Gryson, *The Ministry of Women in the Early Church*, trans. Jean Laporte and Mary Louise Hall (Collegeville, MN: Liturgical Press, 1976), xi–xv; and Aimé Georges Martimort, *Les Diaconesses: Essai historique* (Rome: Edizione Liturgiche, 1982), 251–53. This work was translated by K.D. Whitehead as *Deaconesses: An Historical Study* (San Francisco: Ignatius Press, 1986), and this passage occurs on pp. 248–49. I will reference the English translation for this study. I would disagree with Martimort's assertion that Morin did not accept the

sacramental ordination of women. Martimort quoted as proof the quotation, "Verum non existimant graeci ista ceremoniarum communicatione ullam mulieribus proprie dictam χειρτονὶαν infundi," but the quotation in context demonstrates that this was an opinion of Ephiphanius with which Morin disagreed. See nn3–4 above.

10. "Ex jam dictis sequitur, ut diaconissæ ordinem quemdam in ecclesia constituerint, non quidem stricti nominis seu sacramentalem, sed mere cæremonialem" (*Acta sanctorum,* 1: v, col. D).

11. "Theodorus Balsamon, patriarcha Antiochenus, qui antea in hoc commentario sæpius occurrit, loco apud Morinum et superius apud nos citato habet ista: 'Quæ in præsenti canone tractantur (de Diaconissarum videlicet ætate, accurato delectu etc.) omnino exolevere.' Item 'Diaconissa non ordinatur, etsi quædam ascetriæ abusive Diaconissæ dicantur' " (ibid., 1:xxv, col. C). On Balsamon and his opinion on the ordination of women, see Ida Raming, *The Priestly Office of Women: God's Gift to a Renewed Church,* vol. 2 of *A History of Women and Ordination,* ed. Bernard Cooke and Gary Macy (Lanham, MD: Scarecrow Press, 2004), 21, 54n149, and 57n167.

12. *De Diaconisses: Commentatio archaelogica* (Ratisbon: George Joseph Manz, 1866).

13. "Ordinatio mere caerimonialis, cujus diaconisses participes fuisse ostendimus, non erat autem ejusmodi, ut ipsis publice docendi in ecclesia, ministrandi ad altare, sacrificandi vel aliquod sacramentum conferendi potestatem daret. Haec enim solius sacramentalis ordinationis officia omni sexui foemineo jam inde ab Apostolorum aetate interdictuntur" (ibid., 42).

14. Josephine Mayer, *Monumenta de viduis diaconissis virginibusque tractantia,* Florilegium patristicum tam veteris quam medii aevi auctores complectens 42 (Bonn: Peter Hanstein, 1938).

15. On this debate and on the contribution of Josephine Mayer, see Teresa Berger, *Liturgie und Frauenseele: Die liturgische Bewegung aus der Sicht der Frauenforschung,* Praktische Theologie heute 10 (Stuttgart: Kohlhammer, 1993), 83–88.

16. "Nach demselben konnte die Frage, ob klerikal, oder nicht, erst mit der Ausbildung eines eigenen Weiheritus auftreten, d. h. in der zweiten Häfte des 4. Jahrhunderts. Die Antwort lautet überall gleich: Ausschluss vom volklerus, Einordnung in den niedern Klerus, die Witwediakonisse eine Stufe höher." (Kalsbach, *Die altkirchliche Einrichtung,* 109). See also p. 49: "Die Analyse des Kanons ergibt also zwei sehr wichtige Resultate. Erstens spricht er klar den laikalen Charakter des Diakonissenamtes auf grund der mangelnden Weihe aus."

17. Santiago Giner Sempere, "La mujer y la potestad de orden: Incapacidad de la mujer. Argumentación histórica," *Revista española de derecho canónica* 9 (1954): 841–69.

18. "Ciertamente que puede producir inquietud el leer las palabras 'ordenación,' 'imposición de manos,' etc. Pero no se debe olvidar la inconstancia de los vocablos, principalmente en los primeros siglos de la Iglesia, y la facilidad con que se encuentran, como sinónimas a la frase 'ordenación de diaconisas,' las expresions 'consagración,' 'benedición,' '*velatio,*' etc. que nunca existen cuando se trata de la ordenación de diáconos o presbíteros" (ibid., 856).

19. For a thorough discussion of the issue in each of these different denominations, see Dorothea Reininger, *Diakonat der Frau in der Einen Kirche: Diskussionen, Entscheidungen und pastoral-praktische Erfahrungen in der christlichen Ökumene und ihr Beitrag zur römisch-katholischen Diskussion* (Ostfildern: Schwabenverlag, 1999). Also important for the Roman Catholic discussions is Teresa Berger, *Liturgie und Frauenseele.* For the official statements from different Christian and Jewish denominations on the ordination of women, see J. Gordon Melton and Gary L. Ward, eds., *The Churches Speak on Women's Ordination: Official Statements from Religious Bodies and Ecumenical Organizations* (Detroit, MI: Gale Research, Inc., 1991).

20. John Morgan and Terri Wall, eds., *The Ordination of Women: A Comprehensive Bibliography (1960–1973)* (Wichita, KS: Institute of Ministry and the Elderly, 1977) contains 612 items, while "Updated Bibliography for Women and Priestly Office (For the Years 1974 to 2001 in Chronological Order)," appendix 4, in Ida Raming, *Priestly Office,* contains 169 items.

21. Daniélou's article was revised and translated by Glyn Simon as *The Ministry of Women in the Early Church,* 2nd ed. (Leighton Buzzard, Bedfordshire: Faith Press, 1974), 31.

22. "On the one hand, there has never been any mention of women filling strictly sacerdotal offices. We never see a woman offering the Eucharistic Sacrifice, or ordaining, or preaching in the Church" (ibid., 7).

23. "This, then, is our conclusion: 1. There are certain texts which justify our saying: the ordinary magisterium has until now been against the priesthood for women. 2. But, seen from a scholarly-theological viewpoint, it is not at all certain that this still has an obligatory character for our time. That may be the case, but it is not proved" (Haye van der Meer, *Priestertum der Frau? Eine theologiegeschichtliche Untersuchung, Quaestiones disputatae* 42 [Freiburg: Herder, 1969], 130). The text is quoted from the English translation by Arlene and Leonard Swidler, *Women Priests in the Catholic Church: A Theological-Historical Investigation* (Philadelphia: Temple University Press, 1973), 105.

24. Raming's thesis was published in German as *Der Ausschluss der Frau vom priesterlichen Amt; gottgewollte Tradition oder Diskriminierung? Eine rechtshistorisch-dogmatische Untersuchung der Grundlagen von Kanon 968 1 des Codex Iuris Canonici* (Cologne: Böhlau, 1973) and was translated into English by Norman R. Adams as *The Exclusion of Women from the Priesthood: Divine Law or Sex Discrimination? A Historical Investigation of the Juridical and Doctrinal Foundations of the Code of Canon Law, Canon 968, 1* (Metuchen, NJ: Scarecrow Press, 1976). Dr. Raming produced a second edition of her work, *Priesteramt der Frau: Geschenk Gottes für eine erneuerte Kirche: Erweiterte Neuauflage von "Der Ausschluss der Frau vom priesterlichen Amt" (1973) mit ausführlicher Bibliographie (1974–2001)* (Münster: LIT, 2002), that was edited and translated into English as *A History of Women and Ordination,* vol. 2 Ida Raming, The *Priestly Office of Women: God's Gift to a Renewed Church* (New York: Scarecrow Press, 2004).

25. "We may conclude as the result of our investigation that the legal sources which support canon 968 § 1 (and the canons that are connected with it in content) imply a distinct concept of the essential and ethical inferiority of women; that the

biblical passages—concerning the subordinate position of women—which in part lie at the basis of these sources have been shown by historical-critical exegesis to be conditioned by the times and thus not convincing; that, further, the argument resulting from the traditional understanding of office and representation—that women must be excluded from them—carries no weight" (Raming, *Priestly Office*, 221).

26. For discussions of the progression of the argument for the ordination of women during this period, see Reininger, *Diakonat der Frau*, and for Roman Catholic thought, see Ida Raming, "Women Reject Discrimination and Disenfranchisement in the Church: The Formation and Development of the Women's Ordination Movement in the Roman Catholic Church in Europe," in Raming, *Priestly Office*, 265–89.

27. Roger Gryson, *Le ministère des femmes dans l'Église ancienne* (Recherches et synthèses, section d'histoire 4) (Éditions J. Duculot: Gembloux, 1972). An authorized English translation with added response appeared in 1976 as *The Ministry of Women in the Early Church* (Collegeville, MN: Liturgical Press, 1976).

28. Gryson, *Ministry of Women*, xiii.

29. "Widows were not 'ordained,' but simply 'enrolled' or 'established'; several documents make an explicit difference between 'to ordain' and 'to establish,' a distinction which the *Apostolic Tradition* justifies by the fact that the widow had no liturgical service" (ibid., 110–11).

30. Ibid., 110.

31. Gryson added, "Their functions, however, were less expansive and less important, and the most regularly attested one, which was of their assistance at the baptism of women for reasons of decency, has no reason to exist today. Consequently, unless it were given an object different from the ancient female diaconate, it is not certain that the restoration of the female diaconate today would make much sense" (ibid., 113).

32. "Therefore, one may ask once more whether the Fathers, sharing in a civilization which accorded women little place in the exercise of public duties, could envision with sufficient freedom of spirit the possibility of admitting women to the priestly ministry. These are the reasons why, in the eyes of many, the scriptural argument, as well as the traditional one, in the present state of their elaboration, are not sufficient to invalidate the issue of women priests and require, instead, to be put to good scholarly use to solve the prejudiced issues implicit in them" (ibid.).

33. Aimé Georges Martimort, "A propos des ministères féminins dans l'Eglise," *Bulletin de littérature ecclésiastique* 74 (1973): 103–8.

34. "En conclusion, il faut donc avouer que si l'on voulait reconnaître dans l'ordination d'une diaconesse d'après les *Constitutions apostoliques* un acte sacramental au sens morderne [*sic*] du terme, il faudrait l'affirmer pareillement de l'ordination des sous-diacres et des lecteurs" (ibid., 107).

35. The article was reprinted in translation as an appendix in Gryson, *Ministry of Women*, 115–20.

36. Ibid., 118.

37. Ibid., 120.

38. Jean Galot, *La donna e i ministeri nella chiesa* (Assisi: Cittadella editrice, 1973).

39. "In realtà, se confrontiamo il rito dell'ordinazione delle diaconesse, che le *Costituzioni Apostoliche* riferiscono al IV secolo, con la determinazione presa nel 1947 dal *Sacramentum Ordinis* per il diaconato, constatiamo che esso verifica gli elementi essenziali, ≪materia≫ e ≪forma≫, di quest'ultima: imposizione delle mani, preghiera in cui si chiede il dono dello Spirito santo per il copimento del compito diaconale. Si è dunque portati ad ammettere un valore sacramentale per il diaconato femminale" (ibid., 41).

40. "Questo stato di cose proveniva da una ragione essenziale: la donna non poteva avere accesso al ministero sacerdotale. Ora, con l'ammissione al diaconato, ella reciveva una carica in rapporto al sacerdozio, ma puramente ausiliare e marginale, di modo che era al tempo stesso nella sfera sacerdotale e al di fuori, al limite della distinzione tra clero et laici" (ibid., 212). See also the longer discussion of the ancient role of deaconesses on pp. 36–44.

41. "É vero che l'interpretazione dei testi biblici è stata influenzata da pregiudizi. Nondimeno resta il fatto che l'esclusione del sacerdozio femminile è fondata non su argomenti filosofici, psicologici o sociologici, né su motivi pratici di opportunità, ma sulla teologia dell'opera della salvezza. Il ricorso alla volontà divina costituisce l'essenziale dell'argomentazione" (ibid., 116).

42. Ibid., 203–18.

43. Joan Morris, *The Lady Was a Bishop: The Hidden History of Women with Clerical Ordination and the Jurisdiction of Bishops* (New York: Macmillan, 1973).

44. Ibid., 138. Morris, however, held that women were not consecrated for the celebration of the Eucharist.

45. Martimort, *Deaconesses*, 243–47.

46. Ibid., 249–50.

47. Giorgio Otranto, "Note sul sacerdozio femminile nell'antichità in margine a una testimonianza di Gelasio I," *Vetera Christianorum* 19 (1982): 341–60. The article was translated into English by Mary Ann Rossi in her article, "Priesthood, Precedent, and Prejudice: On Recovering the Women Priests of Early Christianity," *Journal of Feminist Studies in Religion* 7 (1991): 73–93. Otranto repeated his argument in a slightly extended version as chapter 2, "Il sacerdozio della donna nell'Italia meridionale," of his *Italia meridionale e Puglia paleochristiane: Saggi storici,* Scavi e ricerche 5 (Bari: Edipuglia, 1991), 94–121.

48. Otranto, "Priesthood," 89.

49. Marie-Joséphe Aubert, *Des femmes diacres: Un nouveau chemin pour l'église* (Paris: Beauchesne, 1987).

50. "Tous ces rites conduisent à conclure que cette ordination est de même nature que celles des clercs majeurs et donc qu'elle serait sacramentelle" (ibid., 122).

51. "*C'est une mauvaise question. Je pense qu'il y a un certain quipro/quo sur la notion. Ordre dans l'eglise ancienne, ≪ordo≫, ≪ordinare≫, c'était ètablir dans un certain ≪ordre≫ dans l'Église. La question ne se pose pas de savoir, est-ce le sacrement de l'Ordre? On le dirait sans doute aujourd'hui si on concevait les choses ainsi. Mais les anciens ne tra-vaillaient pas comme cela. La question était seulement être établi dans un ≪ordo≫ qui est*

original, «*l'ordo*» *du diaconat féminin*" (ibid., 127–28; italics are in the original). The comments by Chenu were quoted from a conversation with the author.

52. "Les théologiens s'interrogent pour savoir si la diaconesse orientale recevait un sacrement. En fait, il s'agit pour eux de lire une institution ancienne au travers d'une grille d'analyse bien postérieure à cette institution et que lui est relativement inadéquate" (ibid., 155). See also "Denière remarque: la théologie du sacrement de l'ordre s'esquisse seulement à cette époque. Elle est différent de celle qui commence à être acquise au XIIe siècle jusqu'à nos jours. Aussi n'est-il pas possible à l'historien et au théologien de tirer des conclusions définitives de l'interprétation de certain rites. Le risque d'anachronisme est constamment présent" (ibid., 101).

53. "Mais il est important de souligner que, dans l'église ancienne, l'ordination est d'abord la transmission d'un mandat, l'installation dans une charge" (ibid., 100). Also, quoting a study of Pierre van Beneden, "Si donc, dans l'espirit des premiers chrétiens, la charge ecclésiastique peur, dans un certain sens, être qualifiée de «sacramentelle», le caractère essentiellement «functionnel» qui lui était attribué à cette époque, constitue néanmoins une divergence évidente et profonde par rapport à l'enseignement de l'Église catholique aujourd'hui" (ibid.). We will return to the work of van Beneden in chapter 2.

54. Dirk Ansorge, "Der Diakonat der Frau: Zum gegenwärtigen Forschungsstand," in *Liturgie und Frauenfrage: Ein Beitrag zur Frauenforschung aus liturgiewissenschaftlicher Sicht*, Pietas liturgica, 7, ed. Teresa Berger and Albert Gerhards (St. Ottilien: Verlag Erzabtei St. Ottilien, 1990), 31–65.

55. "Wie im historischen Teil dieser Bestandsaufnahme deutlich wurde, ist der historische Befund zum Diakonat der Frau in der Geschichte der Kirche mindestens offen: Wenigstens in Teilkirchen der Christenheit und mindestens zeitweise hat es einen Diakonat der Frau gegeben, der eine »sakramentale« Wiehe voraussetzte" (ibid., 61–62).

56. Ibid., 62.

57. Joseph Ysebaert, "The Deaconesses in the Western Church of Late Antiquity and Their Origin," in *Eulogia: Mélange offerts à Antoon A. R. Bastiaensen à l'occasion des son soixante-cinquième anniversaire*, Instrumenta patristica, 24, ed. G. M. Bartelink, A. Hilhorst, and C. H. Kneepkens (Steenbruge: Abbatia S. Petri, 1991), 423–36.

58. "The practice in the west of ordaining deaconesses has been adopted from the churches in the East, where there is full evidence of old for the rite by laying on of hands and invocation of the Holy Spirit. The bishops ordained deaconesses in spite of the prohibition by some councils in Gaul. And they did so in the proper way as is clear in the case of Radegonda, who was ordained during a ceremony in a chapel by an imposition of hands and from the Gregorian sacramentary" (ibid., 435). On the ordination of Radegund as deaconess, see chapter 3, pp. 97–98. The Gregorian sacramentary, although based on earlier sources, was developed after the time of Radegund. See chapter 2, pp. 54–55.

59. "The second Vatican Council has restored the deaconate for men, but not for women. In fact, many texts from Antiquity dealing with ministry show, in

accordance with time and culture, a deprecating attitude toward women and marriage" (ibid., 436).

60. Peter Hünermann, Albert Biesinger, Marianne Heimbach-Steins, and Anne Jenson, eds., *Diakonat: Ein Amt für Frauen in der Kirche—Ein frauengerechtes Amt?* (Ostfildern: Schwabenverlag, 1997). The collection included as an appendix (pp. 367–409) a translation into German with commentary of thirty-seven of the most important documents on the ordination of women, starting with scripture and continuing on to the recent statements of popes and the German bishops. Most of the ancient documents also include a commentary.

61. Albert Biesinger, "Diakonat—Ein eigenständiges Amt in der Kirche. Historischer Rückblick und heutiges Profil" (in ibid., 53–77). For example, "Faßt man die historische Analyse gebündelt zusammen, dann kann man mit Abraham Andreas Thiermeyer folgendes festhalten: 'Der Diakonat der Frau is ein legitimes Amt in der Tradition der Kirche'" (ibid., 61).

62. Hans Jorissen, "Theologische Bedenken gegen die Diakonatsweihe von Frauen" (in ibid., 86–97); and Peter Hünermann, "Theologische Argument für Diakonatsweihe von Frauen" (in ibid., 98–128).

63. "Die Sakramentalität (im heutigen dognatischen Verständnis) eines eigenständigen Diakonats ohne inneren, in der Diakonatsweihe begründeten Bezug zum bishöflich-priesterlichen Amt läßt sich mit guten Gründen nicht historisch stützen" (Jorissen, "Theologische Bedenken," 95). "Ihre Argumentation folgt dem Schema: Männliche Diakone dienen am Altar und lehren. Frauen dürfen nich am Altar fungieren und lehren. Also können si auch nicht im eigentlichen Sinne Diakone gewesen sein, wenngliech sie so hießen, geweiht wurden oder die Rangabzeichen des Diakons trugen" (Hünermann, "Theologische Argument," 109).

64. "Betrachten wir unter all diesen Einschränkungen den Quellenbefund: Frauen werden vor allem in Osten des Römischen Reiches unter verschiedenen Titeln ≫ Jungfrau, Witwe, Diakonin oder Diakonisse ≪ öffentlich beauftragt oder geweiht und damit in den Klerus eingereiht" (Heike Grieser, "Gab es Diakoninnen in der Geschichte der Kirche? Zusammenfassung der Diskussionsergebnisse," in *Diakonat: Ein Amt für Frauen,* 190).

65. Kyriaki Karidoyanes FitzGerald, *Women Deacons in the Orthodox Church: Called to Holiness and Ministry,* rev. ed. (Brookline, MA: Holy Cross Orthodox Press, 1999). The book is itself an extended and revised edition of FitzGerald's "The Nature and Characteristics of the Order of the Deaconess," in *Women and the Priesthood,* rev. ed., ed. Thomas Hopko (Crestwood, NY: St. Vladimir's Seminary Press, 1999), 93–137. This collection first appeared in 1983. FitzGerald's article was included in the 1983 edition and was revised for the 1999 edition.

66. "Professor Karimis' [the leading opponent to the ordination of women in the Orthodox Church] perspectives on the women deacon appear to reflect his understanding of the priesthood. He emphatically affirms the 'priestly' character of the diaconate and viewed the diaconate as the 'first level' of the ordained priesthood which also included the presbyter and the bishop. His position is based upon a theological perspective which sees the ordained priesthood as a unified order with three

expressions. To this ordained priesthood, only certain men are called" (FitzGerald, *Women Deacons*, 112).

67. Ibid., 123. See also p. 129: "Professor Karmiris, basing his approach on an understanding of the 'three degrees' of priesthood, believes the ministry of the deaconess was strictly an 'auxiliary institution.' Professor Karmiris writes that the deaconess was 'set apart' through an act of installation or appointment (χειροφεσὶα). Orthodox theologians today recognize the essence of this ecclesiastical approach as deriving from the medieval Christian West."

68. "As for the modern scholarly debate over whether the female deacon was considered 'ordained' and whether that ordination was considered a major order, the naysayers predicate their opposition on two erroneous postulates. The first is the unsubstantiated presupposition—in truth, a tautological argument—that women were always excluded from major orders in the history of the church, and that to admit that they had been ordained to one major order then would open the door for their admission to the other two. The second is the assumption that, if the female diaconate was not identical to the male diaconate in liturgical function, then it was not a true diaconal office" (Valerie Karras, "Female Deacons in the Byzantine Church," *Church History* 73 [2004]: 315). See also Karras's "The Liturgical Functions of Consecrated Women in the Byzantine Church," *Theological Studies* 66 (2005): 96–116.

69. By "service at the altar" is meant the leadership of the liturgy of the word (reading of scripture and proclaiming the sermon) and of the eucharistic meal that constitutes the central Christian service. Traditionally, bishops, priests, and deacons have played this role. In chapter 3, I will argue that this role was also filled the female equivalents to these positions, that is, *presbyterae* and deaconesses.

70. Ute Eisen, *Amsträgerinnen in frühen Christentum. Epigraphische und literarische Studien* (Göttingen: Vandenhoeck & Ruprecht, 1996). An English translation was made by Linda Mahoney with the title, *Women Officeholders in Early Christianity: Epigraphical and Literary Studies.*

71. Eisen, *Women Officeholders*, 224. Eisen carefully placed her study within the larger setting of the role of Jewish and Greco-Roman women of the same period. See ibid., 6–18.

72. See n14 above.

73. "Somit lautet das Ergebnis: Die Tradition spricht nich zwingend für eine Zulassung von Frauen zur sakramentalen Diakonatweihe, steht aber auch nicht gundsätzlich dagegen" (Reininger, *Diakonat der Frau*, 126).

74. "Einige Autorinnen und Autoren halten eine Entscheidung in dieser Frage für nicht möglich mit der Begründung, daß bereits der Versuch einer Beanwortung dieser Frage von anachronistischen Voraussetzungen ausgehe, da die Unterscheidung zwischen Sakrament und Sakramentale erst in der Hochscholastik vorgenommen worden sei. Man könne nicht ≫ die Maßstäbe der seit Hugo von St. Viktor und Petrus Lombardus ab dem 12. Jahrhundert fortschreitend entfalteten Sakramententheologie ≪ an Weihehandlungen aus dem 4. bzw. 6.–8. Jahrhundert anlegen" (ibid., 95–96).

75. "Andere Autor/inn/en warnen zwar auch vor der Andwendung ≫hochmittelalterlicher oder moderner theologischer Kriterien ≪ auf altkirchliche Texte, versuchen aber dennoch—diese Erschwernisse und Bedingungen im Blick—sich einer Deutung anzunähern. Es gebe Gundlagen für eine solche Diskussion—so beispeilweise Hünermann in seiner Stellungnahme—, da man ≫sowohl in der lateinsichen wie in der östlichen Patristik gewisse Äquivalent ≪ finden könne, die die Formulierung erlaubten, daß wir heute als sakramental verstehen wurde, was in frühkirchlicher bzw. byzantinischer Zeit als Weihe prakiziert wurde" (ibid., 96).

76. This is the title from the English translation (San Franciso: St. Ignatius Press, 2002). The book orginally appeared as *Priestertum und Diakonat: Der Empfänger des Weihesakramentes in schöpfungstheologischer und christologischer Perspektive* (Freiburg: Johannes Verlag, 2000). Müller's work continued the argument made by Manfred Hauke, *Die Problematik um das Frauenpriestertum vor dem Hintergrund der Schöpfungs-und Erlösungsordnung* (Paderborn: Bonifatius-Drukerei, 1986), published in English as *Women in the Priesthood? A Systematic Analysis in the Light of the Order of Creation and Redemption* (San Francisco: St. Ignatius Press, 1988). Müller had already published an extensive study and translation of all the historical sources on the ordination of women, *Der Empfänger de Weihesakraments: Quellen zur Lehre und Praxis der Kirche, nur Männern des Weihesakrament zu spenden* (Würzgrug: Echter, 1999).

77. Müller, *Priesthood and Diaconate*, 58–61, 83–86.

78. Ibid., 92–93, 205–11.

79. Ibid., 150.

80. Ibid., 87–90, 161–75, 188–204.

81. Phyllis Zagano, *Holy Saturday: An Argument for the Restoration of the Female Diaconate in the Catholic Church* (New York: Crossroad Publishing, 2000), 203.

82. Macy, "Ordination of Women," 481–507; repr. in Cooke and Macy, eds., *History of Women and Ordination*, 1–30.

83. "In conclusion, then, whatever role they did play, either the full liturgical role envisioned by Hochsteller or the lesser role envisioned by Andrieu, women clearly were considered to form their own *ordines* during this period and were perceived to hold as much of an 'ordained' position in the Church as bishops, priests or deacons" (Macy, "Ordination of Women," 495–96; repr. in Cooke and Macy, *History*, 1:10).

84. "What cannot be said historically is that Christianity has never officially recognized women's ministry or that that ministry had no cultic function. Nor can it be denied that the Church once did accept an understanding of ordination as a vocation or ministry to the community from which that ministry arose. To deny any of these claims would be the result of a *theological* conclusion that affirms that these practices cannot be considered normative. That choice, however, must be justified theologically in the same way and with the same rigor as the opposing claim that such practices can play a normative function in present theological and ecclesiastical judgments" (Macy, "Ordination or Women," 507; repr. in Cooke and Macy, *History*, 1:18).

85. "Women Priests: The Case for Ordaining Women in the Catholic Church" available at http://www.womenpriests.org.

86. John Wijngaards, *The Ordination of Women in the Catholic Church: Unmasking a Cuckoo's Egg Tradition* (New York: Continuum, 2001).

87. Wijngaards listed the medieval sources he addressed in chapter 8 (ibid., 59–67) and then went on to refute their arguments in the subsequent chapters.

88. Ibid., 139–55.

89. John Wijngaards, *No Women in Holy Orders? The Women Deacons of the Early Church* (Norwich: Canterbury Press, 2002). The translations that Wijngards included make up half his text. Another useful set of English translations of historical documents dealing with the ordination of women was recently published by Kevin Madigan and Carolyn Osiek, *Ordained Women in the Early Church: A Documentary History* (Baltimore: Johns Hopkins Press, 2005). While the two sets of translations overlap, together they provide a very useful resource for those without access to the original languages.

90. Wijngaards, *No Women in Holy Orders?* 44.

91. See, for instance, the careful presentation of this problem in Peter Hünermann, "Theologische Argument," 98–128, as well as his "Conclusions Regarding the Female Diaconate," *Theological Studies* 36 (1975): 325–33.

92. For two recent studies of the role that tradition plays in theology, see Terrence Tilley, *Inventing Catholic Tradition* (Maryknoll, NY: Orbis Books, 2000); and Orlando O. Espín, "Toward the Construction of an Intercultural Theology of Tradition," *Journal of Hispanic/Latino Theology* 9 (2002): 22–59.

CHAPTER 2

1. Morin described five different opinions that theologians of his time held on this matter. See *De presbyteratus materia et forma* in Jean Morin, *Commentarius de sacris ecclesiae ordinationibus secundum antiquos et recentiores latinos, graecos, syros et babylonios in tres partes distinctus* (1695; repr. Farnborough: Gregg 1969), pt. 3:102–3G. For an overview of this issue, see *ODCC*, "*Instruments, Tradition of the*," 839.

2. "Materia autem huius sacramenti est illud materiale per cuius traditionem confertur ordo, sicut presbyteratus traditur per collationem calicis, et quilibet ordo traditur per collationem illius rei quae precipue pertinet ad ministerium illius ordinis" *De articulis fidei et ecclesiae sacramentis*, pt. 2; Gilles Emery, ed., *Saint Thomas d'Aquin, Traités Les Rasions de la Foi, Les Articles de la Foi et les Sacrements de l'Église* (Paris: Cerf, 1999), 262. English translation: *The Catechetical Instructions of St. Thomas Aquinas*, trans. Joseph Collins (New York: Joseph Wagner, 1939), 129–30.

3. "Sextum est sacramentum ordinis, cuius materia est illud, per cuius traditionem confertur ordo: sicut presbyteratus traditur per calicis cum vino et patenae cum pane porrectionem; diaconatus vero per libri Evangeliorum dationem; subdeaconatus vero per calicis vacui cum patena vacua superposita traditionem; et similiter de aliis per rerum ad ministeria sua pertinentium assignationem" (no. 1326 in Denzinger, 1439).

4. For a thorough discussion of this issue, see Ludwig Ott, *Das Weihesakrament*, Handbuch der Dogmengeschichte, nos. 4, 5 (Freiburg: Herder, 1969), 52–54, 92–96;

and Kenneth Carleton, "The Traditio Instrumentorum in the Reform of Ordination Rites in the Sixteenth Century," in *Continuity and Change in Christian Worship*, ed. Robert Swanson, Studies in Church History 35 (Woodbridge, Suffolk: Boydell Press, 1999), 172–77.

5. "Omnes codices post annos quigentos scripti hos habent additamentum uniforme in textu" (Morin, *De presbyteratus materia et forma*, 106).

6. "Now the effects which must be produced and hence also signified by Sacred Ordination to the Diaconate, the Priesthood, and the Episcopacy, namely power and grace, in all the rites of various times and places in the universal Church, are found to be sufficiently signified by the imposition of hands and the words which determine it" (*Sacramentum ordinis*, par. 3; Denzinger, 1076–77 no. 3859). English translation: Papal Encyclicals online, http://www.papalencyclicals.net.

7. On the importance of this criterion for modern theologians, see chapter 1.

8. "The letter of Alexander to Rumoldus marks the first instance in this study where the terminology *cursus honorum* is actually used in a papal (or any other) text" (John St. H. Gibaut, *The "Cursus Honorum": A Study of the Origins and Evolution of Sequential Ordination*, Patristics Studies 3 [New York: Peter Lang, 2000], 255; see also Ott, *Weihesakrament*, 40–43).

9. Gibaut, "*Cursus Honorum*," 235–39. During the earlier period of church history, priests and bishops were chosen directly from the laity, bypassing any other ecclesial office. "Although the list of *per saltum* ordinations noted is not exhaustive, it sufficiently demonstrates that it was possible for lay people to be ordained directly to the presbyterate and episcopate, for deacons and subdeacons to be bishops, for subdeacons to become presbyters, and at least in one instance, for a subdeacon to become a bishop" (ibid., 156; see also Ott, *Weihesakrament*, 21).

10. Gibaut, "*Cursus Honorum*," 296, 301.

11. Ibid., 296–98.

12. Ibid., 312.

13. Roger Reynolds, "'At Sixes and Sevens'—and Eights and Nines: The Sacred Mathematics of Sacred Orders in the Early Middle Ages," *Speculum* 54 (1979): 669–84.

14. "In sum, of the symbolic numbers attached to the grades, seven was clearly the most popular, and it was this number that was given wide broadcast through its use by the late eleventh- and twelfth-century authors, Peter Damian, Ivo of Chartres, Hugh of St. Victor, and Peter Lombard" (ibid., 676).

15. Gibaut, "*Cursus Honorum*," 185, 212, 218–29.

16. Ibid., 204–5, 241.

17. Ibid., 315. See also the "Excursus on Minor Orders: An Historical Survey," in Kenan Osborne, *Priesthood: A History of the Ordained Ministry in the Roman Catholic Church* (Mahwah, NJ: Paulist Press, 1988), 195–99.

18. *Études sur le sacrement de l'ordre*, Lex orandi, 22 (Paris: Éditions du Cerf, 1957), translated as *The Sacrament of Holy Orders: Some Papers and Discussions Concerning Holy Orders at a Session of the Centre de Pastorale Liturgique, 1955* (London: Aquin Press, 1962).

19. Pierre-Marie Gy, "Notes on the Early Terminology of Christian Priesthood," in *Sacrament of Holy Orders*, 98–126.

20. Ibid., 103.

21. Ibid., 102–3.

22. Gerard Fransen, "The Tradition in Medieval Canon Law," in *Sacrament of Holy Orders*, 202–18.

23. Fransen did add however, "Yet the term *ordo* is used with special reference to the sacrament, at least in the context with which we are concerned" (ibid., 204).

24. Vinzenz Fuchs, *Der Ordinationstitel von seiner Entstehung bis auf Innozenz III* (Amsterdam: P. Shippers, 1963).

25. "Es gab ordnungs mäßig nur mehr einen zur Ortskirche gehörigen und deren geistliche Vorsteherschaft bildenden Klerus; jeder Geistliche mußte für eine bestimmte Einzelkirche geweiht sein und einen Platz in ihrem Klerus einnehmen.... dem geistlichen Moment, der Bindung an die Kirche durch den geistlichen Dienst, allein es schob sich im Laufe der Jahrhunderte immer mehr in den Vordergrund und wurde endlich beherrschend. Diese Verschiebung war die treibende Kraft für die Umbildung von Begriff und Recht des Ordinationstitels um die Wende des 12. Jahrhunderts" (ibid., 280).

26. René Metz, "Benedictio sive consecratio virginum," *Ephemerides liturgicae* 80 (1966): 265–93.

27. "Pour notre cérémonial, le terme *ordinatio* n'a donc pas été d'un emploi courant. Il n'a pas retenu l'attention des compilateurs de recueils liturgiques. Il n'a été utilisé que de façon tout à fait exceptionnelle, contrairement à ce que nous avons constaté pour les autres expressions: *consecratio* et *benedictio*" (ibid., 285).

28. Ibid., 284–85.

29. "Les dénominations s'expliquent par l'imprécison des termes; c'est seulement à partir du XIIe siècle que l'on s'efforce d'apporter les distinctions voulues à la terminologie du sacrement de l'ordre" (ibid., 285).

30. "Les expressions *consecratio* et *benedictio* sont employées au hasard.... A notre avis, il ne faut pas y chercher le résultat de la précision qu'aux XIIe et XIIIe siècles les théologiens et les canonistes apportèrent au vocabulaire du sacrement de l'ordre" (ibid., 281–82). The source Metz gave for this statement is the article by Gy from 1957 discussed above.

31. See n4 above.

32. Ott, *Weihesakrament*, 39.

33. Ibid., 45.

34. "Die erste Definition des Ordo begegnet in den Sentenzen des Petrus Lombardus" (ibid., 48). See also the discussion of Osborne, *Priesthood*, 204–5. In the section of his book that treats of medieval theology, Osborne depends heavily upon Ott.

35. Ott, *Weihesakrament*, 48. The translation is by Osborne, *Priesthood*, 205.

36. Ott, *Weihesakrament*, 76. The translation is by Osborne, *Priesthood*, 206. According to Osborne, "The connection of order with the eucharist is, however, common and almost unanimous [in the later Middle Ages]. It seems that Alexander of Hales (d. 1245) was the first to highlight this." ibid.

37. Yves Congar, "My Path-Findings in the Theology of Laity and Ministries," *The Jurist* 32 (1972): 169–88.

38. Ibid., 180.

39. Pierre van Beneden, *Aux orgines d'une terminologie sacramentelle: Ordo, ordinare, ordinatio dans la littérature chrétienne avant 313*, Spicilegium sacrum Lovaniense, Études et documents, no. 38 (Louvain: Spicilegium sacrum Lovaniense, 1974).

40. "On chercherait en vain des indications d'une qualification inherent et inammovible (*character indelebilis*) attachée au pouvoir d'ordre (*postestas ordinis*)" (ibid., 163).

41. "Si donc, dans l'espirit des premiers chrétiens, la charge ecclésiastique peut, dans un certain sens, être qualifiée de «sacramentelle», le caractère essentiellement «fonctionnel» qui lui était attribué à cette époque, consitute néanmoins une divergence évidente et profonde par rapport à l'enseignement de l'Église catholique aujourd'hui" (ibid., 164).

42. Pierre-Marie Gy, "Les anciennes prères d'ordination," *La Maison-Dieu* 138 (1979): 93–122; and "Ancient Ordination Prayers," *Studia liturgica* 13 (1979): 70–93. The English version of this article was also reprinted in *Studies in Early Christianity: A Collection of Scholarly Essays*, ed. Everett Ferguson (New York: Garland Publishing, 1993), 122–45.

43. Gy, "Ancient Ordination Prayers," 80.

44. Ibid.

45. Yves Congar, "Note sur une valeur des termes «ordinare, ordinatio»," *Revue des sciences religieuses* 58 (1984): 7–14.

46. Ibid., 7–8.

47. Ibid., 8.

48. Ibid., 10–11.

49. Ibid., 11–12.

50. "Quand le traité du sacrament de l'ordre s'est élaboré dans la seconde moitié du XIIe siècle, puis formulé dans les oeuvres des grands Scolastiques du XIIIe siècle, il a été dominé par la référence à l'Eucharistie, par le pouvoir de la consacrer, *potestas conficiendi*. Ce pouvoir était donné par le caractère inadmissible et personnellement possédé" (ibid., 13).

51. Edward Schillebeeckx, *Kerkelijk ambt: Voorgangers in de gemeente van Jezus Christus* (Blemendaal: H. Nelissen, 1980). An English edition appeared shortly afterward under the title *Ministry: Leadership in the Community of Jesus Christ* (New York: Crossroads, 1981).

52. "A quite fundamental change in attitude from this view of the ministry in the early Church was sanctioned in principle by two Ecumenical Councils—though after the Photian schism they were in fact predominantly Latin: the Third and Fourth Lateran Councils in 1179 and 1215 respectively" (Schillebeeckx, *Ministry*, 52).

53. Ibid., 52–54.

54. Ibid., 56.

55. Ibid., 56–58

56. Ibid., 54–58.

57. Giles Constable, "The Orders of Society in the Eleventh and Twelfth Centuries," in *Medieval Religion: New Approaches*, ed. Constance Berman (New York: Routledge, 2005), 68–94. The article is a revised selection from "The Orders of Society," in Giles Constable, *Three Studies in Medieval Religious and Secular Society* (Cambridge: Cambridge University Press, 1995).

58. Constable, "Orders of Society," 69.

59. Constance Hoffman Berman, *The Cistercian Evolution: The Invention of a Religious Order in Twelfth-Century Europe*, (Philadelphia: University of Pennsylvania Press, 2000) 68–79.

60. Ibid., 79.

61. See n38 above.

62. See, for example, Charles DuCange, ed., *Glossarium mediae et infimae latinitatis* (Graz: Akademische Druck-U. Verlagsanstalt, 1954; repr. of the Paris, 1883–87 edition), 6:58–59, s.v. "ordinatio"; 6:60–62, s.v. "ordo." See also Franz Blatt and Yves Lefévre, eds., *Novum glossarium mediae latinitatis ab anno DCCC usque ad annum MCC*, vol. O (Copenhagen: Ejnar Munksgaard, 1983), cols. 696–708, s.v. "ordinatio"; cols. 714–29, s.v. "ordino"; and cols. 731–72, s.v. "ordo."

63. For a list of such references, see Timothy Fry, ed., *The Rule of St. Benedict in Latin and English with Notes* (Collegeville, MN: Liturgical Press, 1981), 532. I want to thank J. Frank Henderson for providing this reference. A thorough discussion of the ordination of abbots in the Rule can be found in Robert Somerville, "Ordinatio abbatis in the Rule of St. Benedict," *Revue benedictine* 77 (1967): 246–63.

64. "LXIV. De ordinando abbate. In abbatis ordinatione . . ." (Fry, *Rule of St. Benedict*, 280).

65. For references, see n58 above, esp. *Novum Glossarium*, vol. O, cols. 722–28.

66. See Congar, "Note sur une valeur des termes," 8.

67. "Primam praeterea praecipuamque tibi tuisque successoribus potestatem contradimus Francorum reges consecrandi: ut sicut beatus Remigius ad fidem Chlodoveo converso primum illi regno regem Christianum instituisse cognoscitur; ita tu quoque, tuique successores, qui ejusdem sancti Remigii vice in Remensi Ecclesia, Domino disponente, fungimini, ungendi regis et ordinandi sive reginae, prima potestate fungamini" (Urban II, *Epistola* 27, *PL* 151:310B).

68. "Ordo XLVII. Item benedictio ad ordinandum imperatorem secundum occidentalis" (Cyrille Vogel, *Medieval Liturgy: An Introduction to the Sources*, rev. and trans. William Storey and Neils Rasmussen [Washington, DC: Pastoral Press, 1986], 182).

69. "Mox convocata non minori multitudine profectus est rex Vesontionum urbem Burgundiae, et illic accipiens, quam praediximus, sponsam, duxit eam Mogonciacum ibique consecrari eam reginam curavit, consummatisque diebus ordinationis in Ingilenheim fecit nuptias regio, ut decuit, apparatu" (W. de Giesebrecht and E. von Oefele, eds., *Annales Altahenses maiores*, MGH, Scriptores rerum Germanicarum 1 [Hannover: Bibliopolii Hahniani, 1891], 33–34).

70. Reinhard Elze, ed., *Die Ordines für die Weihe und Krönung des Kaisers und der Kaiserin*, MGH, Fontes juris Germanici antiqui 9 (1960; repr., Hannover: Hansche Buchhandlung, 1995), no. 4b.

71. Henry Chadwick, *The Early Church*, rev. ed. (London: Penguin Books, 1993), 166.

72. Space does not allow further discussion here, but a study of sacral kingship and the rituals of coronation that embody it would be an important contribution to the early medieval understanding of ordination. The classic discussion of the sacred nature of kingship remains Ernst Kantorowicz, *The King's Two Bodies: A Study in Medieval Political Theology* (Princton, NJ: Princeton University Press, 1997), 42–86. See especially 44–45n6 on the clerical status of kings and emperors.

73. The selection process is quite complex and is repeated several times. One summary reads, "Nam et ipsa electione et ordinatione de ipso monasterio sine licentia et consensum de eredibus et proeredibus nostris stabilis esse non debeat." See Giovanni Mittarelli and Anselmo Costadoni, eds., *Annales Camaldulensis ordinis Sancti Benedicti*.... (Venice: Apud Jo. Baptistam Pasquali, 1755), vol.1, col. 23. See also col. 24: "Et quod ne permittat Deus fieri, si casus evenerit, quod de meo cispite, aut de Richil [*sic*] conjuge mea inventa non fuerit, que in suprascripto monasterio abbatissa esse possit, vel si fuerit, et abbatissa esse noluerit, tunc ipsa monachas de predicto monasterio habeat potestatem et licentiam una cum notitia de heredibus ac proheredibus nostris inter se abbatissam eligere et ordinare in ipso prefato almo loco, ut omnia statuta capitula faciat et adimpleat, ut supra legitur."

74. "Quod si hoc malum quod supra legitur ipsa predicta soror mea Romana se observaverit et custodierit se de malo vicio. et Dei servicio adimpleverit tunc habeat firmissimam potestatem post hobitum suum monasterio [recte: monasterium] hordinare a quocumque homine voluerit per vera virtute sicut et ego ei omnia hordinavit." (Andrea Gloria, *Codice diplomatico padovano dal secolo sesto a tutto l'undecimo*, Monumenti storici publicati dalla deputazione Veneta de storia patria 2, Serie prima documenti 2 [Venice: A spese della Società, 1877], 23).

75. James Brundage, *Medieval Canon Law* (London: Longman, 1995), 68.

76. For references to extreme unction, see DuCange, *Glossarium mediae et infimae latinitatis*, 58. For marriage: "Perrotin de Solier ... estant plevy en fiance à jeune fille ... et suidant velle esouser et recevoir l'Ordre de marriage, etc." (ibid., 60). Marriage was also called an *ordo* comparable to a religious order in the thirteenth century. See Nicole Bériou and David d'Avray, "Henry of Provins, O.P.'s Comparison of the Dominican and Franciscan Orders with the ≪Order≫ of Matrimony," in *Modern Questions About Medieval Sermons: Essays on Marriage, Death, History and Sanctity*, ed., Nicole Bériou and David L. d'Avray, Collano della "Società internazionale per lo studio del Medioevo latino," 11 (Spoleto: Centro italiano di studi sull'Alto medioevo, 1994), 71–75.

77. There was, however, a lively debate about the validity of ordination by schematics and heretics. See, for example, Ott, *Weihesakrament*, 31–39, 60–73.

78. "Pari modo concedimus et confirmamus vobis vestrisque successoribus in perpetuum omnem ordinationem episcopalem, tam de presbyteris quam diaconibus

vel diaconissis, seu subdiaconibus, ecclesiis vel altaribus, quae in tota Transtiberi necessaria fuerit" (Benedict VIII, "Quotiens illa" [1018 August 1], Jaffé, 4024, *PL* 139:1621B).

79. John XIX, "Quoniam semper" (May 1025), Jaffé, 4067, *PL* 141:1121B.

80. Leo IX, "Supplicantium desideriis" (1049 April 22), Jaffé, 4163, *PL* 143:602C.

81. "Consecrationes vero altarium ecclesiae sancti Petri, et aliorum monasteriorum, necnon consecrationes ecclesiarum, altarium, sacerdotum, clericorum, diaconorum, seu diaconissarum totius civitatis Leonianae, vobis vestrisque successoribus in perpetuum, sicut praelibatum est, concedimus et confirmamus" (John XIX, "Convenit apostolico" [1026 December 17], *PL* 141:1130D and *PL* 78:1056B, Jaffé, 4076).

82. "Super his autem non novum facientes, scilicet quod antecessores nostros sacrosanctis Albanensi, Ostiensi et Portuensi, et aliis ecclesiis fecisse cognoscimus, a praesenti indictione, per hujus nostrae apostolicae praeceptionis paginam statuimus et statuendo per auctoritatem apostolorum principis confirmamus, ut presbyteri, diaconi, monachi, mansionarii, clerici cujuscunque ordinis sint, vel dignitatis, sanctimoniales, seu diaconissae omnes, immunes sint a laicali servitio, judicio et publica datione in Galeria intra castellum, vel de foris habitantes, ita ut si imperator, aut marchio, sive missi eorum, aut successores nostri illuc venerint, nullo modo in jam dictis personis per publicos ministeriales expensa colligatur, neque aliquo modo eis injuria irrogetur" (Benedict IX, "Convenit apostolico" (November 1037), *PL* 141:1352A-B, Jaffé, 4110). For the repetition of the grant of John XIX, see *PL* 141:1365C. For a discussion of these papal documents, see Sempere, "La mujer," 854; and Aimé Georges Martimort, *Les Deaconesses: Essai historique* (Rome: Edizione Liturgiche, 1982), 214–15.

83. "Chrisma, oleum sanctum, consecrationes altarium sive basilicarum, ordinationes abbatissae, vel monacharum sive caeterorum clericorum, qui ad sacros fuerint ordines promovendi, seu quidquid ad sacrum mysterium pertinet, a quibuscunque catholicis praesulibus fuerint postulata, gratis concedimus, at absque reprehensione tribuenda, sicut Anselperga prima abbatissa ejusdem monasterii, a Paulo beatae memoriae, apostolicae sedis pontifice, pro fragilitate feminei sexus obtinuit" (Calixtus II, "Quae a praedecessoribus" [1123 April 3], Jaffé, 7049; Ulysse Robert, ed., *Bullaire du Pape Calixtus II, 1119–1124: Essai de Restitution*, 2 vols. [Paris: Imprimerie nationale, 1891], 2:165; *PL* 163:1284A–B). This same formula is used to remind abbots of the bishop's duty and makes clear that the *praesul* mentioned here would be the local bishop. Cf. Robert, *Bullaire*, 2:104 (*PL* 163:1264B); 2:131 (*PL* 163:1273A); 2:161 (*PL* 163:1281C); 2:163 (*PL* 163:1282C).

84. "Ordinat episcopus abbatem, abbatissam, sacerdotum et caeteros sex gradus" (*PL* 159:1002D). Gilbert was a student of Anselm of Canterbury and bishop of Limerick from 1001. He died c. 1140. Cf. A. Schmitt, "Gilbert v. Limerick," in *LThK*, 4:890.

85. "Postea vero archipresul, a cesare, patrino suo, rogatus, eandem cum iam duodecim esset annorum, II Kal. Maii die dominica velavit et in proxima die ad abbatissam in patris presentia ordinavit; quod postea eum nimis penituit" (Robert

Holtmann, ed., *Die Chronik des Bischofs Thietmar von Merseburg und ihre Korveier Überarbeitung*, MGH, Scriptores rerum germanicarum 9 (Berlin: Werdmannsche Bundhandlung, 1935), 93. An earlier edition is printed in *PL* 139: 1224A.

86. "Ad adjumentum virorum etiam religiosae mulieres in sancta Ecclesiae cultrices ordinabantur" (Atto of Vercelli, *Epistola ad Ambrosium sacerdotem*, *PL* 134:114A). The word *cultrices* is difficult to translate. Originally it would refer to a "female laborer" but could also mean "female worshiper" or even "female priest." See Charleston Lewis and Charles Short, eds., *A Latin Dictionary* (Oxford: Clarendon Press, 1969), 488; and P. G. W. Glare., ed., *Oxford Latin Dictionary* (Oxford: Clarendon Press, 1982), 466. On the problem of translating references to religious women in the Middle Ages, see Jo Ann McNamara and John E. Halborg, eds., *Sainted Women of the Dark Ages* (Durham, NC: Duke University Press, 1992), ix. Atto was the second bishop of Vercelli, governing from 924 until his death in 961. For recent information on Atto, see Edward A. Synan, "Atto of Vercelli," in *Dictionary of the Middle Ages*, ed. Joseph R. Strayer (New York: Charles Scribner's Sons, 1982–89), 1:641; and *NCE* 1:842.

87. "Inter eas quoque sanctimoniales, vel monachos a quibus Deo in Ecclesia labore litterario deservitur, si qua perfectius imbuta litteris invenitur, non proprio sed improprio sermone bonus clericus appellatur, in quo nihil aliud quam ejus scientia praedicatur. Cum aliquando, me praesente, vir quidam moribus et habitu religiosus in quamdam ecclesiam deveniret, et sanctimonialem, tam aetate quam scientia praematuram, coram altario tenentem libellum in manibus inveniret, inter caetera quae ad invicem mature contulerunt, sciscitatus est ab ea quid teneret, quid videlicet libellus quem tenebat in manibus contineret. At illa: 'Vitam, inquit, cujusdam virginis quam dictavi, quam scripto cum essem juvencula commendavi.' Et adjunxit: 'Fui enim bonus clericus.' In quo dicto nihil aliud intelligendum adnotavi quam quod bene litterata fuisset, cum junior vitam virginis descripsisset." Philip of Harvengt, *De institutione clericorum tractatus sex*, 110, *PL* 203:816D–817B.

88. "Sic et de quibusdam aliis quas scio admodum litteratas, vel esse, vel fuisse, recolo frequentius me audisse, ut cum de cujuslibet earum scientia sermo in medium versaretur, ipsa bonus clericus diceretur. Et miror cum in muliere clericalis scientia praedicetur, cur non bona clerica, sed bonus clericus nominetur, cum satis convenientius videretur, ut sicut a monacho monacha, sic a clerico clerica diceretur. Eas quidem quas sub religionis habitu constat in monasterio conversari, vel sanctimoniales, vel nonnas, vel monachas in Patrum opusculis invenio nominari; clericas vero utrum uspiam scriptum invenerim, non possum recordari, et a nullo sermonem Latinum proferente, aliquas audio sic vocari" (ibid.).

89. "In multis quoque monasteriis videmus feminas religionis gratia congregari, quas loquendi consuetudine, sanctimoniales vel monachas novimus appellari, ad usus quarum cum certum sit oblationes et decimas delegari, satis liquido declaratur non omnes esse clericos qui vivunt de altari. Denique Apostolus (1 Tim. 5: 9) vult ut vidua sexaginta annorum eligatur, quae de templi aerario temporalem alimoniam consequatur; et fidelem quemque ut ministret suis viduis diligentius adhortatur, ne gravata Ecclesia his quae vere sunt viduae minus sufficiens habeatur. Ex quo

patet quia, etsi proprium est clericorum vivere de altari, jam tamen non omnes clerici sunt qui vivunt de altari. Sicut autem non omnes qui vivunt de altari clerici sunt, sic e regione non omnes vivunt de altari qui tamen clerici sunt" (ibid., *PL* 203:811B-C).

90. "Mozarabic rite," in *NCE* 10: 42–47.

91. "Ordo ad ordinandum clericum
Ordo in ordinatione sacristae
Ordo in ordinatione eius, cui cura librorum et scribarum committitur
Ordo super eum qui barbam tangere cupit
Benedictio ad ordinandum subdiaconem
Praefatio ad ordinandum diaconem
Benedictio ad ordinandum arcediaconum
Benedictio ad consecrandum primiclericum
Praefatio ad ordinandum presbiterem
Ordo de arcipresbitero ordinando
Ordo in ordinatione abbatis
Benedictio de veste deo vote
Ordo ad benedicendum virginem
Ordo uel benedictio ad velandas Deo votas
Ordo ad ordinandam abbatissam."

José Janini, ed., *Liber ordinum episcopal [Cod. Silos, Arch. Monástico, 4]*, Studia silensia 15 (Burgos: Abadia de Silos, 1991), 63–64. The older but more commonly used version of this text is Marius Férotin, ed., *Le Liber Ordinum en usage dans l'église Wisigothique et Mozarabe d'Espagne du cinquième au onzième siècle*, Monumenta ecclesiae liturgica 5 (Paris: Librairie de Firmin-Didot, 1904), xl–xli.

92. "Egbert (Ecgbert) of York," in *NCE* 5:103.

93. W. Greenwell, ed., *The Pontifical of Egbert, Archbishop of York, A.D. 732–766*, Surtee Society 27 (London: T. & W. Boone, 1853), 8–16.

94. "Ad ordinandum diaconum," in ibid., 18. "Alia benedictio diaconi sive diaconissae," in ibid., 19.

95. "Item orationes ad missam pro ipsis in die ordinationis vel consecrationis eorum," in ibid., 24.

96. "Benedictio episcopalis in ordinatione diaconissae," "Benedictio episcopalis in ordinatione diaconi," and "Benedictio episcopalis in ordinatione presbyteri," in ibid., 94.

97. "Benedictio viduarum" and "Consecratio viduae," in ibid., 114–15.

98. For an introduction to the Gregorian sacramentaries, see Vogel, *Medieval Liturgy*, 79–106; Jean Deshusses, ed., *Le sacramentaire Grégorien: Ses principales formes d'après les plus anciens manuscripts*, 3 vols., Spicilegium Friburgenses, ns. 16, 24, 28 (Fribourg: Éditions universitaires Fribourg, 1971–82), 1:19–36 and in *NCR* 6:473–5.

99. "Incipit ordo de sacris ordinibus," in *Le sacramentaire Grégorien*, 3:215.

100. Ibid., 3:215–16. The headings are simply "ordo ostiariorum," etc.

101. Ibid., 3:216–17. The headings read "Ordo qualiter in Romana sedis apostolicae ecclesia prebyteri, diaconi, uel subdiaconi ordinandi sunt," "Ad subdiaconum ordinandum," and "Oratio ad ordinandum diaconum."

102. "Ordo praesbiterorum," in ibid., 3:218.

103. "Benedictio episcoporum," in ibid., 3:220

104. "Oratio ad diaconam faciendam," in ibid., 3:220. Both Martimort, (*Deaconesss*, 207) and Marie JosépheAubert (*Des femmes diacres: Un nouveau chemin pour l'eglise* [Paris: Beauchesne, 1987], 136) note this rite for the ordination of deaconesses. Martimort argued that since the rite only appears in the early copies of the pontifical, this "merely denoted the fidelity of the copyists to the text being copied." The rite itself, Martimort believed, was never used. The rite as edited by Deshusses, which was not available to Martimort and Aubert, is based on four manuscripts, three from the ninth century and one from the eleventh century. This is a wide enough distribution to assume the rite was used, especially given its existence in other pontificals.

105. "Oratio ad abbatem faciendum vel abbatissam," in *Le sacramentaire Grégorien*, 3:220.

106. "Oratio quando abbas aut abbatissa ordinatur," in ibid., 1:221–22.

107. Ibid., 1:222–28.

108. Vogel, *Medieval Liturgy*, 230–39.

109. Martimort, *Deaconesses*, 210–14, has an extensive discussion of this rite in the various forms it took in the transmission of the RGP. Martimort found that the rite so closely followed that for the blessing of a widow that "the ceremony as a whole is nothing more than the consecration of a widow, only more solemn than the formulary of that name" (p. 214). Even if this were the case, it would not invalidate the point being made here.

110. "XIV. De officils septem graduum Ysidori capitula

XV. Ordo qualiter in romana aecclesia sacri ordines fiunt [i.e. psalmista, ostiarius, lector, exorcista, acolytus]

XVI. Ordo qualiter in romana ecclesia presbiteri, diaconi vel subdiaconi eligendi sunt

XVII. Orationes pro ipsis ad missam

XVIII. Item missa in natali consecrationis diaconi

XIX. Item in natali consecrationis presbiteri qualiter sibi missas caelebrare debet

XX. Consecratio sacrae virginis quae in Epiphania uel in alvis paschalibus aut in apostolorum natalitiis celebratur

XXI. Item missa in natali virginum

XXII. Ordinatio abbatissae canonicam regulam profitentis

XXIII. Consecratio virginum quae a seculo conversae in domibus suis susceptun castitatis habitum privatim observare voluerint

XXIV. Ad diaconam faciendam

XXV. Consecratio viduae quae fuerit castitatem professa

XXVI. Ordinatio abbatis

XXVII. Missa pro abbate

XXVIII. Ordo ad faciendum monachum.

XXVIX. Ordinatio monachi

XXX. Aliae orationes pro monachis

XXXI. Orationes et preces pro monachis ad missam.

XXXII. Ordinatio abbatissae monasticam regulam profitentis"

Cyrille Vogel and Reinhard Elze, eds., *Le Pontifical Romano-Germanique du dixième siècle,* Studi e testi 226, 3 vols. (Vatican City: Biblioteca Apostolica Vaticana, 1963), 1:360.

111. "Similter etiam feminae diaconissis et presbiterissis, quae eodem die benedicuntur" (ibid., 2:150).

112. On the twelfth century Roman pontificals, see Vogel, *Medieval Liturgy,* 249–51.

113. The titles of the different sections are given in the critical edition by Michel Andrieu, *Le Pontifical Romain au moyen-âge, 1, Le Pontifical Romain du XIIe siècle,* Studi e testi, 86 (Vatican City: Biblioteca apostolica vaticana, 1937), 306–7.

"I. In nomine domini incipit ordo de septem ecclesiasticis gradibus. In primis praefatio ad clericum faciendum

II. Ad barbam tondendum

III. [De psalmista]

IV. Ordinatio ostiarii

V. Ordinatio lectoris

VI. Ordinatio exorcistae

VII. Ordinatio acoliti

VIII. Ordinatio subdiaconi

IX. Ordo qualiter in romana ecclesia diaconi et presbyteri eligendi sunt

X. Incipit ordo ad vocandum et examinandum seu consecrandum electum in episcopum iuxta morem romanae ecclesiae

XI. Edictum quod dat pontifex episcopo cui benedicit, de quo superius mentio facta fuit

XII. Incipit ordo ad virginem benedicendam . . . [or] Ordo ad consecrandum sacram virginem . . .

XII bis. Consecratio sacrae virginis . . .

XIII. Benedictio viduae . . .

XIV. Missa ad diaconam consecrandam

XV. Ordo ad abbatem benedicendum vel abbatissam

XVI. Ordo ad monachum faciendum"

114. This material first appeared in Gary Macy, "The 'Invention' of Clergy and Laity in the Twelfth Century," in *A Sacramental Life: A Festschrift Honoring Bernard Cooke,* ed., Michael Horace Barnes and William P. Roberts (Milwaukee: Marquette University Press, 2003), 117–35.

115. See n55 above.

116. "Novimus et duos fratres qui se inter summos connumerant magistros, quorum alter tantum uim diuinis uerbis in conficiendis sacramentis tribuit, ut a quibuscumque ipsa proferantur aeque suam habeant efficaciam, ut etiam mulier et quislibet cuiuscumque sit ordinis uel conditionis per uerba dominica sacramentum altaris conficere queat" (*Theologia christiana*, I. 4, c. 80, in *Petri Abaelardi Opera Theologia*, ed., Eligius M. Buytaert, Corpus christianorum, continuatio mediaevalis, 12 [Turnhout: Brepols, 1969], 302).

117. Marie-Dominique Chenu, "Un cas de platonisme grammatical au XIIe siècle," *Revue des sciences philosophiques et théologiques* 51 (1957): 666–68.

118. "Secreta dicitur, quia secreto pronuntiatur, cum olim tamen alta uoce diceretur, unde et ab hominibus laicis sciebatur. Contingit ergo, ut quadam die pastores super lapidem quendam ponerent panem, qui ad horum uerborum pro-lationem in carnem conuersus est, forsan transsubstantiatus est panis in corpus Christi, in quos diuinitus factus est acerrima uindicta. Nam percussi sunt diuino iuditio celitus misso. Vnde statutum fuit, ut de cetero sub silentio diceretur" (c. 44 in *Summa de ecclesiasticis officiis*, ed. Heribert Douteil, CCCM, 41A [Turnhout: Brepols, 1976], 78.

119. C. 196, *PL* 74: 225C–226D.

120. "In primitiva autem Ecclesia alta voce proferebatur, donec pastores memoriter ex quotidiano usu verba retinentes, in camnis eadem cantabant. Sed ipsi divina vindicta ibidem percussi sunt. Unde Ecclesia consuevit propter reverentiam tantum mysterium secreto agere" (*Speculum de mysteriis ecclesiae, c. 7, PL* 177:368C–D). On the dating of this work, see Gary Macy, *Treasures from the Storehouse: Essays on the Medieval Eucharist* (Collegeville, MN: Liturgical Press of America, 1999), 171.

121. "Caeterum ne sacrosancta verba vilescerent, dum omnes pene per usum ipsa scientes, in plateis et vicis, aiiisque locis incongruis decantarent, decrevit Ecclesia, ut haec obsecratio quae secreta censetur, a sacerdote secrete dicatur, unde fertur, quod cum ante consuetudinem quae postmodum inolevit, quidam pastores ca decantarent in agro, divinitus sunt percussi" (bk. 1, c. 1 of Lothar of Segni, *De missarum mysteriis, PL* 217: 840C–D). On the dating of this work, see Macy, *Treasures*, 171.

122. Euan Cameron, *Waldenses: Rejection of Holy Church in Medieval Europe* (Oxford: Blackwell, 2000), 33, 45–46, 129–131; and Gary Macy, *Theologies of the Eucharist in the Early Scholastic Period* (Oxford: Clarendon Press, 1984), 57.

123. "Unde firmiter credimus et confitemur, quod quantumcumque quilibet honestus, religiosus, sanctus et prudens sit, non potest nec debet Eucharistiam consecrare nec altaris Sacrificium conficere, nisi sit presbyter, a visibili et tangibili episcopo regulariter ordinatus" (Denzinger, 354, no. 794). The creed goes on to declare all those who do not believe so to be heretics: "Ideoque firmiter credimus et fatemur, quod quicumque sine praecendi ordinatione episcopali, ut praediximus, credit et contendit, se posse sacrificium Eucharistiae facere, haereticus est."

124. "Orationem vero Dominicam idcirco mox post precem dicimus, quia mos apostolorum fuit ut ad ipsam solummodo orationem oblationis hostiam consecrarent. Et valde mihi inconveniens visum est ut precem quam scholasticus composuerat super oblationem diceremus, et ipsam traditionem quam Redemptor noster

composuit super ejus corpus et sanguinem non diceremus" (Gregory the Great, bk. 11, *Epistola* 12, "Veniens quidam," *PL* 77:956C–957A). For an excellent summary of the tradition of using the Lord's Prayer in the Canon, see Joseph A. Jungmann, *The Mass of the Roman Rite: Its Origin and Development [Missa Sollemnia]*, 2 vols. [New York: Benziger Brothers, 1955], 2:278–81).

125. "Item [idem] quoque Gregorius Dominicam orationem se Canoni adjecisse in Registro suo asserit, ubi quibusdam inde murmurantibus, humili responsione satisfecit, inconveniens esse asserens ut oratio quam scholasticus composuit supero blationem diceretur, et illa praetermitteretur quam ipsi apostoli ex institutioneDominica in confectione eorumdem sacramentorum usitasse crederentur [creduntur]" (*Micrologus de ecclesiasticis observationibus, PL* 151:984D-985A). On Bernold and the *Micrologus,* see Macy, *Treasures,* 169.

126. "Sanctus petrus primus in antiochem missam celebravit in qua tantum verba domini et oratio dominica dicebantur" (London, British Museum, Royal MS. 5 F.xv, fol. 120r).

127. "Missam in primis Dominus Jesus, sacerdos secundum ordinem Melchisedech, instituit, quando ex pane et vino corpus et sanguinem suum fecit, et in memoriam sui, suis celebrare haec praecepit; hanc apostoli auxerunt, dum super panem et vinum verba quae Dominus dixit, et Dominicam orationem dixerunt" (*Gemma animae, PL* 172:572B). On Honorius and the *Gemma animae,* see Macy, *Treasures,* 170.

128. "Non quidem sanctius hinc est quam erat prius, cum ad sola uerba Domini solamque dominicam orationem consecrabatur" (*De divinis officiis,* l. 2, c. 21, in *Ruperti Tjuitiensis Liber de divinis officiis,* ed. Rhaban Haacke, CCCM, no. 7 [Turnhout: Brepols, 1967], 52). On Rupert and the *De divinis officiis,* see Macy, *Treasures,* 169.

129. "Apostoli missam auxerunt, dum super panem et vinum verba quae Dominus dixerat, et Orationem Dominicam dixerunt" (*De officiis ecclesiasticis,* bk. 2, c. 11, *PL* 177:416C). On Paululus and the *De officiis ecclesiasticis,* see Macy, *Treasures,* 171.

130. "Prius enim apostoli dicebant hec uerba tantum, que Dominus dixit: *Hoc est corpus meum* et cetera, et *Hic est sanguis novi testamenti* et cetera. Sed apostoli postea addiderunt dominicam orationem, et hec consuetudo apostolorum hic representatur" (*Summa de ecclesiasticis officiis,* c. 98, in Herbert Douteil, ed., *Johannis Beleth Summa de ecclesiasticis officiis,* CCCM, 41A [Turnhout: Brepols, 1976], 181).

131. "Missam instituit Dominus Jesus, sacerdos secundum ordinem Melchisedech, quando panem et vinum in corpus et sanguinem transmutavit, dicens: ≪Hoc est corpus meum, hic est sanguis meus;≫ ecce quod Dominus missam instituit, id est haec verba constituit, eisque vitam substantivam dedit; quibus panis in corpus, et vinum mittitur, id est transsubstantiatur in sanguinem. Item missam instituit et causam institutionis adjunxit, dum hoc faciendum esse mandavit, scilicet ob memoriam sui, dicens: ≪Hoc facite in meam commemorationem.≫ Unde licet apostoli hanc adauxerint, dum super panem et vinum, non solum verba quae Dominus dixerat, sed etiam Dominicam orationem superaddendam statuerunt" (*Mitrale,* l. 3, c. 1, *PL* 213:91B–C). On Sicard and the *Mitrale,* see Macy, *Treasures,* 171.

132. See Macy, *Theologies of the Eucharist*, 160nIII; and Gabriel Audisio, *The Waldensian Dissent: Persecution and Survival, c. 1170–c.1570* (Cambridge: Cambridge University Press, 1999), 105, 122–23, 134.

133. "Et hoc totum confertur in illis verbis Domini in coena prolatis, quae sacerdos subjungit. Sed ea dicturus sic prius incipit: *Qui pridie quam pateretur.* In his verbis sumit ab altari panem adhuc communem, et elevatum benedicit et signum crucis imprimit, et priusquam deponat repraesentat verba Domini dum dicit: *Benedixit et fregit*, et quae sequuntur. Postea tollit calicem et signat, et repraesentat verba Domini dicens: *Et dedit discipulis suis dicens: Accipite et bibite ex hoc omnes.* Hic fit illud insigne miraculum. In his verbis cibus carnis fit cibus animae. Per haec verba et per crucis signaculum novatur natura, et panis fit caro, et vinum sanguis" (c. 7, *PL* 177:370B–C).

134. "Virtus missae, crux Christi est, quae sacramentum altaris et omnia Ecclesiae sacramenta consecrat et sanctificat" (*Sermo in canone misse, PL* 177:459A). On Richard and his work, see Macy, *Treasures*, 170.

135. See Macy, *Theologies of the Eucharist*, 57.

136. "Forma vero est, quam ipse ibidem edidit dicens, *Hoc est corpus meum;* et post: *Hic est sanguis meus.* Cum enim haec verba proferuntur, conversio fit panis et vini in substantiam corporis et sanguinis Christi; reliqua ad Dei laudem dicuntur" (bk. 4, *dist.* 8, c. 4, in *Sententiae in IV Libris Distinctae*, 3rd. ed., 2 vols., Spicilegium Bonaventurianum 5 (Rome: Collegii St. Bonaventurae ad Claras Aquas, 1981), 2:282.

137. Denzinger, 358, no. 802.

138. For a different, but complementary, analysis of this power structure, see Robert I. Moore, *The First European Revolution, c. 970–1215* (Oxford: Blackwell, 2000), esp. 173–80.

CHAPTER 3

1. For studies of women in the early church, see the references given in n2 of chapter 1. On women in the early medieval church, see Suzanne Fonay Wemple, *Women in Frankish Society: Marriage and the Cloister, 500 to 900* (Philadelphia: University of Pennsylvania Press, 1981); idem, "Women from the Fifth Century to the Tenth Century," in *A History of Women in the West*, vol. 2 of *Silences of the Middle Ages*, ed. Christine Klapisch-Zuber (Cambridge, MA.: Harvard University Press, 1992), 181–213; Jo Ann McNamara, *Sisters in Arms: Catholic Nuns through Two Millennia* (Cambridge, MA: Harvard University Press, 1996), 91–229; Jane Schulenburg, *Forgetful of Their Sex: Female Sanctity and Society, ca 500–1100* (Chicago: University of Chicago Press, 1998); Lisa M Bitel, *Women in Early Medieval Europe, 400–1100* (New York: Cambridge University Press, 2002) and Marie Anne Mayeski, *Women at the Table: Three Women Theologians* (Collegeville, MN: Liturgical Press, 2005).

2. *Sanctimonialia* refers to any religious woman who is a consecrated virgin. The term will be translated here as "holy women" to distinguish *sanctimonialia* from the technical *ordo* of virgins found in the early church.

3. Kathleen Cushing makes this point in her excellent study of the eleventh-century collection of canons by Anselm of Lucca: "Even a preliminary examination of

the canonical sources indicate that Anselm set out to articulate a strategy for reform. He knew precisely what had to be achieved, and he selected, shaped, and ordered his sources accordingly" (see Cushing's *Papacy and Law in the Gregorian Revolution: The Canonistic Word of Anselm of Lucca* [Oxford: Clarendon Press, 1998], 102). See also Dyan Elliott: "In the eleventh century, the Western Clergy, Europe's intellectual elite, reinvented itself—an imaginative act necessarily accompanied by efforts to eradicate evidence of past identity" ("The Priest's Wife: Female Erasure and the Gregorian Reform," in *Medieval Religion: New Approaches,* ed. Constance Berman [New York: Routledge, 2005], 123). This article is a revised selection from Dyan Elliott, *Fallen Bodies: Pollution, Sexuality, and Demonology in the Middle Ages* (Philadelphia: University of Pennsylvania Press, 1999).

4. Gary Macy, "Demythologizing 'the Church' in the Middle Ages," *Journal of Hispanic/Latino Theology* 3 (1995): 23–41; and idem, "Was There a 'the Church' in the Middle Ages?" in *Unity and Diversity in the Church,* ed. Robert Swanson, Studies in Church History 52 (Blackwell: Oxford, 1996), 107–16.

5. For a fuller explanation of the methodology used here, see Gary Macy, "The 'Invention' of Clergy and Laity in the Twelfth Century," in *A Sacramental Life: A Festschrift Honoring Bernard Cooke,* ed., Michael Horace Barnes and William P. Roberts (Milwaukee: Marquette University Press, 2003), 117–35; idem, "The Future of the Past: What Can the History Say about Symbol and Ritual," in *Practicing Catholic: Ritual, Body, and Contestation,* ed. Bruce Morrill, S.J., Susan Rodgers, and Joanna E. Ziegler (New York: Palgrave-Macmillan Press, 2006), 29–37; and idem, "The Iberian Heritage of U.S. Latino/a Theology," in *Futuring Our Past: Explorations in the Theology of Tradition,* ed. Orlando O. Espín and Gary Macy (Maryknoll, NY: Orbis, 2006), 43–83.

6. Gary Macy, "Ordination of Women in the Early Middle Ages," *Theological Studies* 61 (2000): 502–7; and "Heloise, Abelard and the Ordination of Abbesses," *Journal of Ecclesiastical History* 57 (2006): 16–32.

7. Although, as discussed below, it is not altogether clear that deaconesses or abbesses were always considered differently than deacons or abbots in terms of jurisdiction or liturgical function.

8. For three recent discussions of the roles women played in the early medieval church, see Wemple, *Women in Frankish Society,* 127–48; Wemple, "Women," 186–201; Donald Hochstetler, *A Conflict of Traditions: Women in Religion in the Early Middle Ages: 500–840* (Lanham, MD: University Press of America, 1992); and McNamara, *Sisters in Arms.*

9. Ute Eisen, *Women Officeholders in Early Christianity: Epigraphical and Literary Studies* (Collegeville, MN: Liturgical Press, 2000), 201–5, has a complete description of the evidence for Theodora as well as an English translation of the inscriptions.

10. Ibid., 199–200. She also includes an English translation of the inscription.

11. Kevin Madigan and Carolyn Osiek, *Ordained Women in the Early Church: A Documentary History* (Baltimore: Johns Hopkins Press, 1005), 193. The inscribed stone now exists in the Basilican Cemetery of St. Paul's in Rome, and Madigan and Osiek assume a Roman origin. They do not discuss Eisen's identification of the inscription as Umbrian. They also include an English translation of the inscription.

12. "Ibi episcopus Dei gratia inebreatus non cognovit quid in libro suo cantavit. In gradum enim episcopi ordinis Brigitam. 'Haec sola,' inquid Mel, 'ordinationem episcopalem in Hibernia tenebit virgo.' Quandiu igitur consecratur columna ignea de vertice eius ascendat" (c. 19 in *Bethu Brigte*, ed. Donncha Ò hAodha [Dublin: Dublin Institute for Advanced Studies, 1978], 6). The translation is that given by Ò hAodha, 24.

13. "Audivimus miserabilem ejus vitam: audiamus pariter et finem. Quadam enim die cum aegrotare coepisset, placuit ut sanguinem minueret. Qui dum esset flebotomatus, nocte insecuta dormivit cum Episcopissa; que de re coepit vulnus intumescere, et dolor usque ad interiora cordis devenire. Videns vero Episcopus se ad occasum jam pertrahi, postulavit ad S. Petrum Culturae se Monachum fieri. Qui dum esset factus Monachus, statim mortuus est" (*Acta Pontificum Cenomannensis* in *Recueil des Historiens des Gaul et de la France*, vol. 10, ed. Léopold DeLisle, new ed. [Paris: Victor Palm, 1874], 385). Margarete Weidemann, *Geschichte des Bistums Le Mans von der Spätantike bis zur Karolingerzeit*, 4 vols., Römisch-Germanische Zentralmuseum, Forschungsinstitut für vor-und frühgeschichte, Monographien 56 (Mainz: Verlag des Römisch-Germanische Zentralmuseum, 2002), 1:16, dates this work to 1055/65.

14. "Episcopum episcopiam non habentem nulla sequatur turba mulierum; *uidelicet saluatur uir per mulierem fidelem, sicut et mulier per uirum fidelem*, ut apostolus ait" (Charles DeClercq, ed., *Concilium Turonense a. 567, Concilia Galliae*, CCSL, 148A [Turnhout: Brepols, 1963], 181).

15. Eisen, *Women Officeholders*, 200.

16. "Episcopus coniugem ut sororem habeat et ita conuersatione sancta gubernet domum omnem tam ecclesiasticam quam propriam, ut nulla de eo suspitio quaqua ratione consurgat. Episcopum episcopiam non habentem nulla sequatur turba mulierum; uidelicet saluatur uir per mulierem fidelem, sicut et mulier per uirum fidelem, ut apostolus ait. Nam ubi talis custodia necessaria non est, quid necesse est, ut miseria prosequatur, unde fama consurgat? habeant ministri ecclesiae, utique clerici, qui episcopum seruiunt et eum custodire debent, licentiam extraneas mulieres de frequentia quohabitationis eiecere" (DeClercq, *Concilia Galliae*, 180–81). The Council defined "outside women" as consecrated women or widows or servants in an earlier canon. "Nullus ergo clericorum, non episcopus, non presbiter, non diaconus, non subdiaconus, quasi sanctimonialem aut uiduam uel ancillam propriam pro conseruatione rerum in domum suam stabilire praesumat, quae et ipsa extranea est, dum non est mater aut soror aut filia, quae etiam pronior propinquauit ad culpam, dum dinoscitur subiecta dominatu" (ibid., 179). It should also be noted that the word *episcopia* is possibly a diminutive of *episcopa*. Since there are so few uses of either word, however, it is very difficult to know if the added "i" is significant or merely an error.

17. Brian Brennan, "'*Episcopae*': Bishops' Wives Viewed in Sixth-Century Gaul," *Church History* 54 (1985): 311–23.

18. "Sane si coniugati iuuenes consenserint ordinari, etiam uxorum uoluntas ita requirenda est, ut sequestrato mansionis cubiculo, religione praemissa, posteaquam pariter conuersi fuerint, ordinentur" (Charles Munier, ed., *Concilium Agathense a. 506*,

Concilia Galliae, CCSL, 148 [Turnhout: Brepols, 1963], 201). The first council to require continence from married clergy was the Council of Elvira in 306. On this Council and its decrees, see Samuel Laeuchli, *Power and Sexuality: The Emergence of Canon Law at the Council of Elvira* (Philadelphia: Temple University Press, 1972).

19. Leo was asked by Bishop Rusticus whether those who are married and minister at the altar are able to licitly have sexual relations. He responded: "Lex continentiae eadem est ministris altaris quae episcopis atque presbyteris, qui cum essent laici sive lectores, licito et uxores ducere et filios procreare potuerunt. Sed cum ad praedictos pervenerunt gradus, coepit eis non licere quod licuit. Unde, ut de carnali fiat spirituale conjugium, oportet eos nec dimittere uxores, et quasi non habeant sic habere, quo et salva sit charitas connubiorum, et cesset opera nuptiarum" (Leo I, *Epistola 167, Ad Rusticum Narbonensem Episcopum*, Jaffé, n. 544 [320]; "Si instituta ecclesiastica," *PL* 54:1204A).

20. "Cuius coniux basilicam sancti Stephani suburbano murorum aedificavit. Quam cum fucis colorum adornare velit, tenebat librum in sinum suum, legens historias actionis antiquae, pictoribus indicans, quae in parietibus fingere deberent. Factum est autem quadam die, ut sedente ea in basilica ac legente, adveniret quidam pauper ad orationem, et aspiciens eam in veste nigra, senio iam provecta, putavit esse unam de egentibus protulitque quadram [*sic*] panis et posuit in sinu eius et abscessit. Illa vero non dedignans munus pauperis, qui personam eius non intellexit, accepit et gratias egit reposuitque, hanc suis epulis anteponens et benedictionem ex ea singulis diebus sumens, donec expensa est" (bk. 2, c. 17 of Gregory of Tours, *Libri historiarum*, ed. Bruno Krusch and Wilhelm Levison, MGH, Scriptores rerum Merovingicarum, 1, 2, 2nd ed. [Hannover: Hahn, 1951], 64–65). Gregory of Tours, *The History of the Franks*, trans. Lewis Thorpe (New York: Penguin Books, 1974), 131–32; Brennan, "Bishops' Wives," 317.

21. *Sidonius domino papae Perpetuo salutem* in *Gai Sollii Apollinaris Sidonii Epistulae et carmina*, bk. 7, no. 9, Christian Lvetjohann, ed., MGH, Auctores anitquissimi 8 (Berlin: Weidmann, 1887), 112–17. On Sidonius, see *NCE* 13:104.

22. "Uxor illi de Palladiorum stripe descendit, qui aut litteram aut altarium cathedras eum sui ordinis laude tenuerunt. Sane quia persona matronae verecundam succinctamque sui exigit mentionem, constanter adstuxerim respondere illam feminam sacerdotiis utriusque familiae, vel ubi educta crevit vel ubi electa migravit. Filios ambo bene et prudenter instituunt, quibus comparatus pater inde felicior incipit esse, quia vincitur" (ibid., 117; see also Brennan, "Bishops' Wives," 318).

23. On Venantius's life and poetry, see Judith George, *Venantius Fortunatus, A Latin Poet in Merovingian Gaul* (Oxford: Clarendon Press, 1992); and idem., *Venantius Fortunatus, Personal and Political Poems* (Liverpool: Liverpool University Press, 1995).

24. Venantius Fortunatus wrote Eufrasia's epitaph, bk. 4, no. 27 in *Venanti Honori Clementiani Fortunati, Opera poetica*, ed. Friedrich Leo, MGH, Auctorum Antiquissimorum 6 (Berlin: Weidmannos, 1881), 99. Brennan, "Bishops' Wives," 321. On Venantius's epitaph for Eufrasia, see George, *Venantius Fortunatus, A Latin Poet*, 86–87.

25. Venantius praised Placidina in his poem on her husband, bk. 1, no. 15, lines 93–110, in Fortunatus, *Opera poetica*, 18; and in his dedicatory poem to her, bk. 1, no. 17 in Fortunatus, *Opera poetica*, 21 as well as the passages mention in n24 above. Brennan, "Bishops' Wives," 319–20. On Venantius's praise for Placidina and Leontius as well the career of both Placidina and Leontius, see George, *Venantius Fortunatus, A Latin Poet*, 31–32, 70–74.

26. Placidina's donation of wall hangings for the church of St. Martin was mentioned by Venantius in his poem on that church, in bk. 1, no. 6, in Fortunatus, *Opera poetica*, 11. The inscription of the chalice she and her husband donated was written by Venantius and preserved among his poems, in bk. 1, no. 14, in Fortunatus, *Opera poetica*, 15. The cover for the tomb of St. Bibianus was mentioned by Venantius in his poem on the church of the saint, in bk. 1, no. 12, lines 13–18, in Fortunatus, *Opera poetica*, 14. Brennan, "Bishops' Wives," 320.

27. "Funeris officium, magni solamen amoris, dulcis adhuc cineri dat Placidina tibi" (bk. 4, no. 10, lines 25–26, in Fortunatus, *Opera poetica*, 87); translation provided by Brennan, "Bishops' Wives," 321.

28. "Nam succensa mulier a libidine, operta peccati tenebris, pergit ad domum ecclesiae per tenebras noctis. Cumque obserata omnia repperisset, pulsare fores ecclesiasticae domus coepit" (bk. 1, c. 44 in Gregory of Tours, *Libri historiarum*, 29). See also Gregory of Tours, *History of the Franks*, 93.

29. See Book 4, c. 44 in Gregroy of Tours, *Libri historiarum*, 29; and Gregory of Tours, *History of the Franks*, 93–94.

30. Susanna was possessed by a devil, and Priscus and their son lost their wits. See bk. 4, c. 36 in Gregory of Tours, *Libri historiarum*, 168–69; and Gregory of Tours, *History of the Franks*, 231. See also Brennan, "Bishops' Wives," 315–16.

31. *Liber in gloria confessorum*, c. 77, in *Greogrii Turoneneis Opera*, vol. 2 of *Miracula et opera minora*, ed. W. Arndt and B. Krusch, MGH, Scriptores rerum Merovingicarum (Hannover: Hahn, 1885), 794. Translation is from Raymond Van Dam, *Gregory of Tours, Glory of the Confessors*, trans. texts for Historians, Latin series, vol. 4 (Liverpool: Liverpool University Press. 1988), 81. See also Brennan, "Bishops' Wives," 316–17.

32. Wemple, *Women in Frankish Society*, 127–48.

33. Brennan, "Bishops' Wives," 319.

34. This is precisely how the Placidina, the wife of Bishop Leontius, is described by George: "Placidina was an active partner with her husband [Bishop Leontius], eulogized in panegyric, and contributing her wealth and energies to his endeavours. She and Leontius jointly presented gifts of church plate and covered the shrine of St Bibianus with silver. She was also a patron of the poet [Venantius] in her own right, receiving verses of greetings from Fortunatus and commissioning his epitaph on her husband" (George, *Venantius Fortunatus, A Latin Poet*, 109).

35. On the extent of ecclesiastical authority claimed for Brigid by her hagiographers, see *Dictionary of the Middle Ages*, ed. Joseph R. Strayer (New York: Charles Scribner's Sons, 1982–89)2:376–77. The life of Brigid written by Cogitosus described

her monastery as head of all of the churches of Ireland: "Suum monasterium caput pene omnium Hibernensium Ecclesiarum, et culmen præcellens omnia monasteria Scottorum, cuius parochia per totam Hibernensem terram diffusa, a mari vsque ad mare extensa est" (*Acta sanctorum,* 1 Februrary, 1:135). See also Lisa Bitel, *Isle of the Saints: Monastic Settlement and Christian Community in Early Ireland* (Ithaca, NY: Cornell University Press, 1990), 157.

36. The tombstone of Mathilda, daughter of Otto I, describes her as *metropolitana* and abbess of Quedlinburg. *Metropolitanus* is commonly used for a bishop and so may indicate that Mathilda played such a role. See Edmund Stengel, "Die Grabschrift der ersten Abtissin von Quedlinbug," *Deutches Archiv für Geschichte des Mittelalters* 3 (1939): 36–70.

37. Joan Morris, *The Lady Was a Bishop: The Hidden History of Women with Clerical Ordination and the Jurisdiction of Bishops* (New York: Macmillan, 1973), gives numerous examples of the episcopal roles played by abbesses. See also McNamara, *Sisters in Arms,* 121, 126–28.

38. "Ut presbyteram, diaconum, nonnam aut monachum vel etiam spiritualem commatrem nullus sibi praesumat nefario conjugio copulare. Nam qui hujusmodi opus perpetraverit, sciat se anathematis vinculo esse obligatum, et Dei judicio condemnatum, atque a sacro corpore et sanguine nostri Jesu Christi alienum" (c. 5 of the Council of Rome, *Concilia aevi Karolini [742–842],* ed. Albert Werminghoff, MGH, Concilia 2,1 [Hannover: Hahn, 1906] 13–14). This is the translation given by Madigan and Osiek in *Ordained Women,* 173. I would suggest, however, that "spiritualem commatrem" might be better translated as "godmother." On this canon, see also, Aimé Georges Martimort, Les *Deaconesses: Essai historique* (Rome: Edizione Liturgiche, 1982), 201; and Peter Hünermann, Albert Biesinger, Marianne Heimbach-Steins, and Anne Jenson, eds., *Diakonat: Ein Amt für Frauen in der Kirche—Ein frauengrechtes Amt?* (Ostfildern: Schwabenverlag, 1997), 383.

39. "Post haec interrogavit de eo qui matrem et filiam spirituales in conjugio ducit, quod ne fiat, sacri canones per omnia vetant. In canonibus Zachariae ita habetur: Ut presbytera, diacona, monacha, vel etiam spirituali commatre, aut spirituali filia nullus utatur" (Leo VII, *Epistola Ad Gallos Et Germanos,* "Si instituta ecclesiastica," Jaffé, n. 3614 (2767), 1:457, *PL* 132: 1086D).

40. "Si quis presbyteram duxerit in coniugio, anathema sit." "Si quis diaconam duxerit in coniugio, anathema sit" (cc. 1 and 2, Paul Hinschius, ed., *Decretales Pseudo-Isidoriana* [1863; repr. Aalen: Scientia Verlag, 1963], *Decreta pape Gregorii iunioris,* 754). Hinschius believes these decretales may actually date back to Gregory II (p. cvii). On the dating of the *Decretales,* see Horst Fuhrmann, *Einfluß und Verbreitung der pseudoisidorischen Fälschungen,* 2 vols., Schriften der Monumenta Germaniae historica 24 (Stuttgart: Hiersemann, 1972), 1:182–83.

41. "Hadirano filio Exhilarati, qui praestito sacramento in apostolica confessione Ephiphaniam diaconam inlicito ausu in uxorem habet, anathema sit." "Epiphania diacona, quae post praestito sacramento cum Hadriano Exhilarati filio fuga lapsa est in uxorem, anathema sit" (cc. 14 and 15, Hinschius, *Decretales,* 754).

42. Michel Andrieu, ed., *Les Ordines Romani du Haut Moyen Age*, 4 vols., Spicilegium sacrum Lovaniense, Études et documents 28 (Louvain: Spicilegium sacrum Lovaniense, 1956), 4:142; Madigan and Osiek, *Ordained Women*, 173.

43. "Si cum sacrata virgine, vel cum sanctimoniali, sive cum uxore alterius; si compater cum commatre, vel frater cum sorore in Christo, secundum antiquam diffinitionem decem annis poeniteat, humana diffinitione septem. Cum devota, quae est veste mutata, si cum electa vidua vel desponsata alterius, si cum presbytera vel diacona, si cum vidua vel pagana, secundum antiquam diffinitionem decem annis poeniteat, humana diffinitione septem, Si cum vidua aequali vel publica meretrice aut ancilla alterius, secundum antiquam et humanam diffinitionem annis quinque poeniteat. Si cum laica virgine, quam nec quoniam accipit uxorem, secundum antiquam et humanam diffinitionem quatuor annis poeniteat" (included among the spurious works of Nicholas I edited by Ernest Perels in MGH, *Epistolae* 6 [Berlin: Weidmannos, 1925], 687–9). On the spurious nature of this letter and its use by later canonists, see ibid. and Jaffé, n. 2857 (2166), 1:364.

44. For the Greek and Latin text, see Josephine Mayer, *Monumenta de viduis diaconissis virginibusque tractantia*, Florilegium patristicum tam veteris quam medii aevi auctores complectens 42 (Bonn, Peter Hanstein, 1938), 11. On this text and its translation, see Macy, "Ordination," 492n44, repr. in *History of Women and Ordination*, 24; and Madigan and Osiek, *Ordained Women*, 163–64, 190. For a discussion of the meaning of *presbyterae* in the text, see Haye van der Meer, *Women Priests in the Catholic Church: A Theological-Historical Investigation*, trans. Arlene and Leonard Swidler (Philadelphia: Temple University Press, 1973), 92; Joseph Ysebaert, "The Deaconesses in the Western Church of Late Antiquity and Their Origin," in *Eulogia: Mélange oferts à Antoon A. R. Bastiaensen à l'occasion des son soixante-cinquième anniversaire*, Instrumenta patristica 24, ed. G. M. Bartelink, A. Hilhorst, and C. H. Kneepkens (Steenbruge: Abbatia S. Petri, 1991), 427; and Jean Galot, *La donna e I ministeri nella chiesa* (Assisi: Cittadella editrice, 1973), 81–83.

45. Andrieu, *Ordines Romani*, 4:142.

46. "Mulieres quae apud Graecos presyterae appellantur, apud nos autem viduae seniores, unvirae et matriculariae appellantur, in ecclesia tanquam ordinatas constitui non licebit" (c. 10 of the *Capitula synodi Laodicenae*, *Decretales Pseudo-Isidoriana*, 274). The statute, based loosely on 1 Timothy 5:2–10, is difficult to translate. "*Seniores*" can refer to elders in the technical sense of an ecclesiastical post and is the word used in the Vulgate for presbyter, e.g., Ezechiel 7:26, 2 John 1, and 1 Timothy 5:1. "*Matricularia*" is an unusual word that comes from "*matrix*" and can be used to mean "progenitress." For a detailed discussion of the interpretation of this canon, see Ida Raming, *The Exclusion of Women from the Priesthood: Divine Law or Sex Discrimination? A Historical Investigation of the Juridical and Doctrinal Foundations of the Code of Canon Law, Canon 968, 1* (Metuchen, NJ: Scarecrow Press, 1976), 21–22; and Eisen, *Women Officeholders*, 121–23. The source for the ninth-century decretals of this decree was the collection of canon law compiled by Ferrandus of Carthage c. 547, in Charles Munier, ed., *Concilia Africae A. 345-A. 525*, CCSL, 149 (Turnhout: Brepols, 1974), 305. On Ferrandus, see *ODCC* 606. For a translation of Ferrandus, see Madigan and Osiek, *Ordained Women*, 190.

47. Eisen, *Women Officeholders*, 128–29, with English translation.

48. See ibid.,129–31; and Madigan and Osiek, *Ordained Women*, 193–95, both with English translations. See also Otranto, "Priesthood, Precedent, and Prejudice: On Recovering the Women Preists of Early Christianity," trans. Mary Ann Rossi, *Journal of Feminist Studies in Religion* 7 (1991): 86–87.

49. Madigan and Osiek, *Ordained Women*, 195, with English translation.

50. Ibid., 195–96; Otranto, "Priesthood," 88–89; and idem, "Il sacerdozio della donna nell'Italiz meridionale," of his *Italia meridionale e Puglia paleochristiane: Saggi Storici*, Scavi e ricerche 5 (Bari: Edipuglia, 1991), 114–15.

51. See Eisen, *Women Officeholders*, 132–34; and Madigan and Osiek, *Ordained Women*, 197, both with English translations. See also Otranto, "Priesthood," 88.

52. See Eisen, *Women Officeholders*, 131–32; and Madigan and Osiek, *Ordained Women*, 196, both with English translations. See also Otranto, "Priesthood," 87–88.

53. "Nam si inuentus fuerit presbiter cum sua presbiteria aut diaconus cum sua diaconissa aut subdiaconus cum sua subdiaconissa, annum integrum excommunis habeatur et depositus ab omni officio clericali inter laicos se obseruare cognoscat, eo tamen permisso, ut inter lectores in psallentium choro colligatur" (DeClercq, *Concilia Galliae*, 184). This is the translation given by Madigan and Osiek in *Ordained Women*, 172. On the interpretation of this passage, see van der Meer, *Women Priests*, 94; Ysebaert, "Deaconesses," 430, 434; Roger Gryson, *The Ministry of Women in the Early Church*, trans. Jean Laporte and Mary Louise Hall (Collegeville, MN: Liturgical Press, 1976), 108; Santiago Giner Sempere, "La mujer y la potestad de orden: Incapacidad de la mujer. Arguementación histórica," *Revista española de derecho canónica* 9 (1954): 849; Martimort, *Deaconesses*, 201; and Madigan and Osiek, *Ordained Women*, 171–72.

54. "Non licet presbytero post accepta benedictione in uno lecto cum presbytera dormire nec in peccato carnali miscere, nec diacono nec subdiacono" (DeClercq, *Concilia Galliae*, 268). Madigan and Osiek, *Ordained Women*, 172–73, provide an English translation and discussion of this passage. See also van der Meer, *Women Priests*, 95; and Ysebaert, "Deaconesses," 434.

55. "Aiebat enim quod illic presbiter quidam conmissam sibi cum magno timore Domini regebat ecclesiam. Qui ex tempore ordinis accepti presbiteram suam ut sororem diligens, sed quasi hostem cauens, ad se propius accedere numquam sinebat, eamque sibimet propinquare nulla occasione permittens, ab ea sibi communione funditus familiaritatis absciderat" (Gregory the Great, *Dialogues* 4, c. 12 in *Grégoire le Grand, Dialogues*, vol. 3, ed. Adalbert de Vogüé, Sources chrétiennes 265 [Paris: Éditions du Cerf, 1980], 48).

56. "Hic ergo uenerabilis presbiter, cum longam uitae inplesset aetatem, anno quadragesimo ordinationis suae inardescente grauiter febre correptus, ad extrema deductus est. Sed cum eum presbitera sua conspiceret, solutis iam membris, quasi in mortem distensum, si quod adhuc ei uitale spiramen inesset, naribus eius adposita curauit aure dinoscere. Quod ille sentiens, cui tenuissimus inerate flatus, quantulo adnisu ualuit ut loqui potuisset, inferuescente spiritu collegit uocem atque erupit, dicens: 《Recede a me, mulier. Adhuc igniculus uiuit. Paleam tolle.》" (ibid., Grégoire le Grand, Gregory the Great, *Dialogues*, 50).

57. "Illud aetiam a quibusdam suggestum est ut, contra apostholicam discipli-nam, incogito usque in hoc tempus, in ministerium faeminae, nescio quo loco, leuiticum uideantur adsumptae; quod quidem, quia indicens est, non admittit ecclesiastica disciplina, et contra rationem facta talis ordinatio distruatur: prouiden-dum ne quis sibi hoc ultra praesumat" (Council of Nîmes, c. 2, in Munier, *Concilia Galliae*, 50).

58. See Van der Meer, *Women Priests*, 93; Ysebaert, "Deaconesses," 428–29; Gryson, *Ministry of Women*, 101; Martimort, *Deaconesses*, 193–94; Marie-Joséphe Aubert, *Des femmes diacres: Un nouveau chemin pour l'église* (Paris: Beauchesne, 1987), 134; Hünermann, *Diakonat*, 381; and Madigan and Osiek, *Ordained Women*, 184. Ysebaert, Martimort, and Madigan and Osiek read this as deaconal rather than as presbyteral.

59. "Nihilominus impatienter audivimus, tantum divinarum rerum subiisse despectum, ut feminae sacris altaribus ministrare firmentur, cunctaque non nisi virorum famulatui deputata sexum, cui non competunt, exhibere" (*Epistola* 14, in *Epistolae Romanorum pontificum genuinae et quae ad eos scriptae sunt a S. Hilaro usque ad Pelagium II*, ed. Andreas Thiel [1867; repr. New York: Georg Olms Verlag, 1974], 376–77).

60. "It is my conviction that with these expressions Gelasius intended to refer to a mandate specifically conferred by some bishops on women for the exercise of sacerdotal ministry; since bishops are referred to, Gelasius' reference can only concern the sacerdotal ordination, which allowed some women to exercise the sacrament of full priesthood" (Otranto, "Priesthood," 83). See also van der Meer, *Women Priests*, 93; Ysebaert, "Deaconesses," 431–32; Gryson, *Ministry of Women*, 105; Sempere, "La mujer," 848–49; Galot, *La donna*, 86–87; and Madigan and Osiek, *Ordained Women*, 186–88.

61. "Viri venerabilis Sperati presbyteri relatione cognouimus, quod gestantes quasdam tabulas per diuersorum ciuium capanas circumferre non desinatis, et missas ibidem adhibitis mulieribus in sacrificio diuino, quas conhospitas nominastis, facere praesumastis; sic ut erogantibus uobis eucharistias illae uobis positis calices teneant et sanguinem Christe populo administrare praesumant.... Idcirco secundum statuta partum caritati uestrae praecipimus, ut non solum huisucemodi mulierculae sacramenta divina pro inlicita administratione non polluant, sed etiam praeter matrem, auiam, sororem uel neptem intra tectum cellolae suae si quis ad cohabitandum habere voluerit, canonum sententia a sacrosanctae liminibus ecclesiae arceatur" (Letter of bishops Licinius, Melanius and Eustochius, in *Les Sources de l'Histoire du Montanisme*, ed. Pierre de Labriolle, Collectanea Friburgensia, n.s., 15 (Fribourg: Librarie de l'Université, 1913), 227–28. Translation from Madigan and Osiek, *Ordained Women*, 188. See also van der Meer, *Women Priests*, 98; Otranto, "Priesthood," 88–89; Gryson, *Ministry of Women*, 106; and Galot, *La donna*, 88–90.

62. The Latin text is given in n61 above. Translation from Madigan and Osiek, *Ordained Women*, 188.

63. "Et dum de sanctitatis vestrae sollicitudine quereremur, cur res monasterio competentes ab aliis pertulerit detinere, communis filius Epiphanius archipresbyter

vester praesens inventus respondit memoratam abbatissam usque diem obitus sui
induisse vestem monachicam noluisse, sed in vestibus quibus loci illius utuntur
presbyterae permanisse" (*Gregorius Ianuario episcopo Caralitano,* IX, 197, in *Gregorii
papae Registrum epistolorum,* ed. Paul Ewald and Ludo Moritz Hartmann, MGH,
Epistolae, 1–2, 2 vols. [Berlin: Weidmannos, 1891–99], 2:186; translation by John R. C.
Martin, *The Letters of Gregory the Great,* 3 vols., Medieval Sources in Translation 40
[Toronto: Pontifical Institute of Medieval Studies, 2004], 665–66). Martin translated
presbytera as "elderly widow."

64. "Sed res ipsius eidem loco, ex quo illic ingressa et abbatissa constituta est,
manifesto iure competere" (Ewald and Hartmann, *Gregorii papae Registrum,* 2:186).
"Rather, the property she owned clearly belonged by law to that place, from the time
she entered it and was appointed abbess" (Martin, *Letters,* 666).

65. "Nihilominus impatienter audivimus tantum sacrarum rerum subiisse
despectum, ut feminae sacris altaribus ministrare ferantur, et cuncta quae non nisi
virorum famulatui deputata sunt, sexum cui non competit exhibere" (*Epistola 7,
Zachariae Papae Ad Pipinum Majorem Domus, Itemque Ad Episcopos, Abbates, et Proceres
Francorum,* PL 89: 933C, Jaffé, 2277 [1750], "Gaudio magno," 1:266; translation in
Eisen, *Women Officeholders,* 133–34).

66. "Sexto decimo, ut unusquisque hoc provideat, ut mulieres ad altare non
accedant, nec ipsae Deo dicatae in ullo ministerio altaris intermisceantur. Quod si
pallae altaris lavandae sunt, a clericis abstrahantur et ad cancellos feminis tradantur
et ibidem repetantur; similiter a presbyteris, cum oblata ab eisdem mulieribus
offeruntur, ibidem accipiantur et ad altare deferantur" (Haito of Basle, *Capitula
ecclesiastica,* c. 16, in *Capitularia regum Frankorum,* ed. Alfred Boretius, vol. 1, MGH
[Hannover: Hahn, 1883], 364). On Haito, see the introduction to the edition by
Boretius, in ibid., 362–63. On the interpretation of this passage, see Hochstetler,
Conflict of Traditions, 99. See also van der Meer, *Women Priests,* 95.

67. For a summary of the legislation against women approaching the altar or
touching objects involved in altar service, see van de Meer, *Women Priests,* 91–96, who
argues that Haito may be the first to take so strong a stand against women ministering
at the altar.

68. "Quidam nostrorum verorum virorum relatu, quidam etiam visu didicimus
in quibusdam provintiis contra legem divinam canonicamque institutionem feminas
sanctis altaribus se ultro ingerere sacrataque vasa inpudenter contingere et indumenta
sacerdotalia praesbyteris administrare et, quod his maius, indecentius ineptiusque est,
corpus et sanguinem Domini populis porrigere et alia quaeque, quae ipso dictu turpia
sunt, exercere" (Council of Paris, 829, c. 45, in *Concilia aevi Karolini [742–842],* ed.
Albert Werminghoff, MGH, Concilia 2,1 [Hannover: Hahn, 1907], 639; translation by
van der Meer, *Women Priests,* 95). On the interpretation of this passage, see
Hochstetler, *Conflict of Traditions,* 99–100; van der Meer, *Women Priests,* 95–96;
Sempere, "La mujer," 849–50; Martimort, *Deaconesses,* 207; Aubert, *Des femmes
diacres,* 137; and Eisen, *Women Officeholders,* 134.

69. " . . . quod quorundam episcoporum incuria et negligentia provenisse nulli
dubium est. . . . ipsi adeo carnalibus desideriis et inlicitis actionibus vacabant, ut

mulieres sacratis aedibus se nullo prohibente ingererent *introferentes ea, quae non licebat*" (Werminghoff, *Concilia aevi Karolini,* 639; translation by van der Meer, *Women Priests,* 96).

70. The texts are discussed in Jean Leclercq, "Eucharistic Celebrations Without Priests in the Middle Ages," *Worship* 55 (1981): 160–65.

71. The text is a copy of a communion service for men contained in a psaltery copied at Montcassino under Abbot Odesius (1097–1105). The service from Montcassino has been edited by André Wilmart, "Prières pour la communion en deux psautiers du Mont-Cassin," *Ephemerides liturgicae* 43 (1929): 320–28.

72. The text has been edited by Jean Leclercq: "Prières médiévales pour recevoir l'eucharistie pour saluer et pour béner la croix," *Ephemerides liturgicae* 79 (1965): 327–40. See, for example, p. 331: "[E]xaudi, quaeso domine, gemitum mei famulae tuae indignae et peccatris supplicantis, et, quae de meritorum qualitate diffido, non iudicium, sed misericordiam consequi merear. Per d<ominum>."

73. Leclercq, "Eucharistic Celebrations," 165.

74. Ibid., 165.

75. Ibid., 163.

76. Cyrille Vogel and Reinhard Elze, eds., *Le Pontifical Romano-Germanique du Dixième Siécle,* Studi e testi, 226, 3 vols. (Vatican City: Biblioteca Apostolica Vaticana, 1963), 2:148–51.

77. "Surgens autem ab oratione, stat pontifex in sede sua, singilatim inponens manus capitibus eorum et benedicet eos" (ibid., 2:149).

78. "Similiter etiam feminae diaconissis et presbiterissis, quae eodem die benedicuntur" (ibid., 2:150).

79. See Andrieu, *Ordines Romani,* 4:140–42; and Martimort, *Deaconesses,* 210.

80. For text, see appendix 1. On Egbert's pontifical, see chapter 2, pp. 53–54.

81. For text, see appendix 2. On the Gregorian sacramentary, see chapter 2, pp. 54–55.

82. For text, see appendix 2. On the *Liber sacramentorum Gellonensis,* see Cyrille Vogel, *Medieval Liturgy: An Introduction to the Sources,* rev. and trans. William Storey and Neils Rasmussen (Washington, DC: Pastoral Press, 1986), 70–78.

83. For text, see appendix 2. On the *Liber sacramentorum Augustodunensis,* see Vogel, *Medieval Liturgy,* 70–78.

84. For text, see appendix 2. On the twelfth-century Roman pontifical, see Vogel, *Medieval Liturgy,* 249–51.

85. See pp. 76–77 above.

86. "Diaconissa est abbatissa, quae XX annis a Pauli jussu deminutis per manus impositionem ab episcopo ordinatur, non ante XLmum annum, ut instruat omnes christianas feminas fide et lege Dei, sicut erant in veteri lege. De qua et apostolus: Vidua eligatur non minus LX annorum. Et haec erant presbiterisse in evangelio, Anna octoagenaria; nunc vero Calcedonicus canon quadragenarium indulget" (Friedrich Maasen, "Glossen des canonischen Rechts aus dem karolingischen Zeitalter," *Sitzungsberichte kaiserliche Akademie der Wissenschaften in Wien, Philosophisch-historische*

Klasse 84 [1876]: 274). The commentary is on c. 15 of the Council of Chalcedon. On this gloss, see Martimort, *Deaconesses*, 208.

87. This would also seem to be the conclusion of Jo Ann McNamara, "Canossa and the Ungendering of the Public Man," in Berman, *Medieval Religion*, 105: "From various reforming prohibitions in the ninth century, we know that women some-times acted as acolytes (assistants to the priests in performing the Mass, usually boys) and even occasionally ventured to say Mass themselves (though without consecrating the sacrament). It seems likely, therefore, that priests' wives in smaller parishes performed similar services, encroaching on the sacred preserves of the priesthood as their secular sisters invaded the shrunken precincts of public power." Though I would argue that the Masses women said did include the consecration. This article originally appeared in *Render Unto Caesar: The Religious Sphere in World Politics,* ed. Sabrina Petra Ramet and Donald W. Treadgold (Washington, DC: American University Press, 1995), 131–50.

88. A complete discussion of the legislation referenced here is contained in Michel Dortel-Claudot, "Le prêtre et la mariage: Évolution de la législation canonique des origines au XIIe siècle," in *Mélanges offerts a Pierre Andrieu-Guitrancourt*, L'Année Canonique 17 (Paris: Faculte de Droit Canonique, 1973), 319–44. See also John Lynch, "Marriage and Celibacy of the Clergy: The Discipline of the Western Church: An Historico-Canonical Synopsis," *The Jurist* 32 (1972): 14–38, 189–212; Andrieu, *Ordines Romani*, 4:140–42; and Wemple, *Women in Frankish Society*, 131–35.

89. "...sicut enim hae quae presbyterae dicebantur, praedicandi, jubendi vel edocendi, ita sane diaconae ministrandi vel baptizandi officium sumpserant" (*Epistola ad Ambrosium, PL* 134:114C). For the entire passages summarized here, see ibid., 114A–C. On Atto, see chapter 2, n86.

90. "Possumus quoque presbyteras vel diaconas illas existimare, quae presby-teris vel diaconis ante ordinationem conjugio copulatae sunt: quas postea caste regere debent, sicut in canonibus promulgatum est" (ibid., *PL* 134: 115A). See Martimort, *Deaconesses*, 208–9. The description of deaconesses given here is similar to that given to widows by Gennadius of Marseille in a collection of ecclesial laws written in the late fifth century, see pp. 95–96 and nn101–3 below.

91. "Sunt etiam, qui eas priscis temporibus diaconas asseruere appellatas, quas nunc abbatissas nominamus, quod nobis minime congruere videtur" (ibid., *PL* 134:114C).

92. The opinions of the canonists will be discussed in chapter 4.

93. Jean Morin, *Commentarius de sacris ordinationibus secundum antiquos et recentiores latinos, graecos, syros et babylonios in tres partes distinctus* (1695; repr. Gregg Farnborough, 1969), pt. 3:144–45.

94. Martimort, *Deaconesses*, 197–206. For recent discussions of the different forms of deaconesses, see Andrieu, *Ordines Romani*, 4:139–47; Paul-Henri Lafontaine, *Les Conditions Positives de l'Accession aux Orders dans la Première Législation Ecclésiastique (300–492)* (Ottawa: Editons de l'Université d'Ottawa, 1963), 27–30; and Hochstetler, *Conflict of Traditions*, 76–82. Ysebaert, "Deaconesses," 434, suggests that

the term *diaconia* should be taken at face value as an expression of ministry: "In fact, we have to take this word as a technical term for a female minister in the church, as long as the context does not resist."

95. Following Martimort, *Deaconesses*, 201–2, the two terms will be considered to be interchangeable. See also Eisen, *Women Officeholders*, 183 and n158.

96. On Ambrosiaster, whose writings appeared c. 370–84, see *NCE* 1:346–47. The theology and influence of his commentary will be discussed in chapter 4.

97. "Sicut etiam nunc [quae sunt] in orientalibus locis diaconissae mulieres in suo sexu ministrare uidetur. In baptismo. Sive: In ministerio uerbi, quae priuatim docuisse feminas inueniumus, sicut Priscillam, cuius uir Aquila uocabatur" (Commentary on Romans 16:1 in *Pelagius's Expositions of Thirteen Epistles of St. Paul, II, Text and Apparatus Criticus*, ed. Alexander Souter, Texts and Studies 9 [Cambridge: Cambridge Univeristy Press, 1926], 121–22; English translation by Theodore de Bruyn, *Pelagius's Commentary on St Paul's Epistle to the Romans* [Oxford: Clarendon Press, 1993], 151). See also "Mulieres similiter pudicas. Similiter eas ut diaconos eligi iubet: unde intelligitur quod [h]is dicat, quas athuc hodie in oriente diaconissas appellant" (1 Timothy 3:11 in Souter, *Pelagius's Expositions*, 487).

98. See nn57–58 above.

99. "Diaconae omnimodis non ordinandae: si quae iam sunt, benedictioni quae populo impenditur capita submittant" (First Council of Orange, c. 25 in Munier, *Concilia Galliae*, 84; translation by Madigan and Osiek, *Ordained Women*, 145). On this canon, see Ysebaert, "Deaconesses," 429; Gryson, *Ministry of Women*, 102–5; Martimort, *Deaconesses*, 193–94; and Madigan and Osiek, *Ordained Women*, 145–46.

100. "In primis, quia multi, de ultimis Orientis partibus uenientis, presbyteros et diaconos se esse confingunt, . . . placuit nobis, si qui fuerint eiusmodi, si tamen communes ecclesiae causa non fuerit, ad ministerium altarii non admittantur" (Council of Nîmes, c. 1, in Munier, *Concilia Galliae*, 50).

101. "Viduitatis seruandae professionem coram episcopo in secretario habitam imposita ab episcopo ueste uiduali indicandam. Raptorem uero talium uel ipsam talis professionis desertricem merito esse damnandam" (c. 26 in Munier, *Concilia Galliae*, 85).

102. On the dating and authorship of the *Statuta*, see *NCE* 13:501. On the *Statuta* and its treatment of deaconesses, see Ysebaert, "Deaconesses," 431; Gryson, *Ministry of Women*, 104–5; Sempere, "La mujer," 848; and Madigan and Osiek, *Ordained Women*, 190–91. Gennadius used the *Apostolic Constitutions*, written in Syria c. 350–80. The *Constitutions* described the work of deaconesses in preparing women for baptism. It is possible, then, that Gennadius was not describing the practices of his own time and place. The witness of the Council of Epaon would indicate, however, that widows were active in Merovingian churches as deaconesses.

103. "Viduae uel sanctimoniales, quae ad ministerium baptizandarum mulierum eligunter, tam instructae sint ad id officium, ut possint aperto et sano sermone docere imperitas et rusticanas mulieres, tempore quo baptizandae sunt, qualiter baptizatoris ad interrogata respondeant et qualiter accepto baptismate uiuant" (c. 100 in Munier, *Concilia Galliae*, 184).

104. "Mulier, quamuis docta et sancta, uiros in conuentu docere non praesumat" (c. 37, in ibid., 172). "Mulier baptizare non praesumat" (c. 41, in ibid., 173).

105. "Veduarum consecrationem, quas diaconas uocitant, ab omni regione nostra paenitus abrogamus, sola ei paenitentiae benedictione, si converti ambiunt, inponenda" (c. 21 in DeClercq, *Concilia Galliae*, 29). On deaconesses as widows, see Ysebaert, "Deaconesses," 430; Gryson, *Ministry of Women*, 107–8; Sempere, "La mujer," 853–54; Martimort, *Deaconesses*, 196–200; Aubert, *Des femmes diacres*, 134; and Wemple, *Women in Frankish Society*, 194. On this canon, see Madigan and Osiek, *Ordained Women*, 146.

106. "Foeminae, quae benedictionem diaconatus actenus contra interdicta canonum acceperunt, si ad coniugium probantur iterum deuolutae, a communione pellantur. Quod si huiusmodi contubernium admonitae ab episcopo cognito errore dissoluerint, in communionis gratia acta penitentia reuertantur" (c. 17 in DeClercq, *Concilia Galliae*, 101).

107. "Placuit etiam, ut nulli postmodum foeminae diaconalis benedictio pro conditionis huius fragilitate credatur" (c. 18, ibid.).

108. On Remigius, see *NCE* 12:107–8.

109. "Delegoque benedictae filiae meae Helariae diaconae ancillam nomine Nocam et uitium pedaturam, que suae iungitur uineae, quam Cattusio facit, dono et partem meam de Talpusciaco transcribo pro obsequiis, que mihi indesinenter impendit" (*Testamentum*, in *Defensoris Locogiacensis monachi, Liber scintillarum*, ed. Henri Rochais, CCSL, 117 [Turnhout: Brepols, 1957], 477). The longer form of the will also includes donation to other deaconesses; "diaconae infra urbem, ... solidos II" (ibid., 478). On these references, see Martimort, *Deaconesses*, 199–200; and Aubert, *Des femmes diacres*, 134.

110. For example, the opening of the will: " ... aecclesia catholica urbis Remorum, et tu, fili fratris mei, Lupe episcope, quem precipuo semper amore dilexi, et tu, nepos meus Agricola presbyter, qui michi obsequio tuo a puericia placuisti, in omni substantia mea, que mea sorte obuenit, antequam moriar, preter id quod unicuique donauero, legauero dari ue iussero, uel unumquemque uestrum uoluero habere precipuum" (Rochais, *Liber scintillarum*, 474). Also, "Tibi autem, nepos meus Agricola presbiter, qui intra domesticos parietes meos exegisti pueritiam tuam, trado atque transcribo Merumuastem seruum et uxorem suam Meratenam et eorum filium nomine Marcouicum; eius fratrem Medouicum iubeo esse liberum" (ibid., 476).

111. For example, "Compresbiteris meis et diaconibus, qui sunt Remis, uiginti et V solidos aequaliter diuidendos in commune dimitto" (ibid., 475); and "Dono aecclesie Lugdunensi solidos X et VIII, quos presbiteri et diaconi inter se aequali diuisione distribuant" (ibid., 477).

112. See chapter 2, p. 49

113. On Radegund, see *NCE* 11:889; George, *Venantius Fortunatus, A Latin Poet*, 30–31, 161–77; and idem., *Personal and Political Poems*, 129–30. Two authors who hold that Radegund was not truly ordained are Martimort (*Deaconesses*, 199–200) and Aubert (*Des femmes diacres*, 134). For other discussions of this ordination, see Hünermann (*Diakonat*, 391) and Madigan and Osiek (*Ordained Women*, 142–43).

114. "Directa igitur a rege veniens ad beatum Medardum Novomago, supplicat instanter ut ipsam mutata vest domino consecraret. Sed memor dicentis apostoli: Si qua ligata sit coniugi, non quaerat dissolvi, differebat reginam, ne veste tegeret monacham. Adhuc beatum virum perturbabant proceres et per basilicam graviter ab altari retrahebant, ne velaret regi coniunctam, ne videretur sacerdoti, ut praesumeret principi subducere reginam non publicanam sed publicam. Quo sanctissima cognito intrans in sacrarium, monachica veste induitur, procedit ad altare, beatissimum Medardum his verbis alloquitur, dicens: Si me consecrare distuleris et plus hominem quam deum timueris, de manu tua, pastor, ovis anima requiratur. Quo ille contestationis concussus tonitruo, manu superposita consecravit diaconam" (*Vita Sanctae Radegundis*, in *Venanti Fortunati Opera pedestria*, ed. Bruno Krusch, MGH, *Auctorum antiquissimorum*, 4/2 [Berlin: Weidmannos, 1885], 41; Translation in Jo Ann McNamara and John E. Halborg, eds., *Sainted Women of the Dark Ages* [Durham, NC: Duke University Press, 1992], 75).

115. See Eisen, *Women Officeholders*, 182–83; and Madigan and Osiek, *Ordained Women*, 144, both with English translations.

116. See Eisen, *Women Officeholders*, 184–85; and Madigan and Osiek, *Ordained Women*, 144–45, both with English translations.

117. See Eisen, *Women Officeholders*, 183–84; and Madigan and Osiek, *Ordained Women*, 144, both with English translations.

118. See n53 above.

119. "Eo sub tempore directam legationem ad Pontificem prædictæ urbis sui miserunt parentes, ut ipsam mutata veste Domino consecraret. Qui eorum agnita voluntate, manu superposita consecravit diaconam" (*Vita de Sanctae Segolena*, c. 10 in *Acta sanctorum*, 24 July, 5:632). On the life of Sigolena and her hagiographer, see Isabelle Real, "Vie et Vita de Saint Ségolène, Abbesse de Troclar au VIIe siècle," *Le Moyen Âge* 101 (1995): 385–406.

120. Wemple, *Women in Frankish Society*, 142 and n81.

121. "Villa hogregia quam germana mea ermengundis, quondam dyacona, pro anime sue remedium ecclesie uirdunensi dedit, et ego ipse sub usufructuario per precatoria possedi, cum integra solidate, omnibusque ad se pertinentibus cum idem quod ibidem augmentare uel labore potuero, omnia et ex omnibus post discessum meum ad sepedicta ecclesiae uirdunensis reuertat" (*Testament des Diaconus Grimo*, 636 in *Urkundenbuch zur Geschichte der jetzt die preussischen Regierungsbezirke Coblenz und Trier bildenden mittelrheinischen Territorien*, ed. Heinrich Beyer, 3 vols. (Coblenz: In Commission bei J.Hölscher, 1860–1874), 1:7.

122. "Diaconiae St. Eustachii (al. S. Eustathii) locat in perpetuum fundum Clivus, fundum Querquetum et Placonianum ex corpore massae Calcianae partimonii Lavicani" (n. 2213, Jaffé, 1:256). "Matronae Reiigionae (al. Religione; forse religiosae) diaconissae, eiusque filii ac nepotibus locat locum, qui dicitur Iconia ex corpore patrimonii Campaniae Neopolitani" (n. 2218, Jaffé, 1:256). "Diaconiae St. Eustachii (al. S. Eustathii) locat in perpetuum fundum Cervinariola, fundum Caldariola, fundum Pomilianum..." (n. 2220, Jaffé, 1:256). In regard to Matrona, Martimort, *Deaconesses*, 202n25 quotes Andrieu, *Ordines Romani*, 4:143n3: "There is nothing to

prove that this deaconess, provided as she was with sons and nephews, was anything but the widow of a simple layman." This seems a gratuitous and inconsistent comment given that widows clearly did become deaconesses.

123. "Quam, post regimen ecclesiae suscepit, [Sergius] eam Eufimiam sponsam suam diaconissam cunsecravit [sic], et in eodem habitu permansit" (*Agnelli qui et Andreas Liber pontificalis ecclesiae Ravennatis*, ed. O. Holder-Egger, in MGH, *Scriptores rerum Langobardicarum et Italicarum saec. VI—IX*, ed. Georg Waitz [Hannover: Hahn, 1878, 377). See Martimort, *Deaconesses*, 204. On Segius and his wife, see Elliott, "Priest's Wife," 128, 131.

124. "Qui Romani, prae nimio gaudio, suum recipientes pastorem, omnes generaliter in vigilias beati Andreae apostoli, tam proceres clericorum cum omnibus clericis quamque optimates et senatus cunctaque militia, et universo populo Romano cum sanctimonilibus et diaconissis et nobilissimis matronis seu universis feminis..." *Le Liber Pontificalis*, ed. L. Duchesne (Paris: E. De Boccard, 1955), 6. On this incident, see Martimort, *Deaconesses*, 204; Aubert, *Des femmes diacres*, 136; and Wemple, *Women in Frankish Society*, 194.

125. "Considerandum vero nobis est et a populo nimis cavendum, ut nullus ex propria cognatione aut velatam, diaconam vel raptam uxorem accipiat, ne talibus rebus animam perdat et principum instititus damnatus fiat" (c. 8 in *Concilia Aevi Karolini [742–842], 1/2*, ed. Albert Wermingshoff, MGH [Hannover: Hahn, 1908], 557). On this canon, see Martimort, *Deaconesses*, 205; and Aubert, *Des femmes diacres*, 136.

126. See p. 99 above.

127. According to Umberto Nicolai, *I Vescovi di Luca* (Luca: Tipografia Bicchelli, 1966), 51, under the entry for Bishop Ottone: "Durante il suo governo, a Lucca esisteva sempre l'ufficio delle Diaconesse, cessato ormai ovunque." I want to thank Marcia Colish for this reference.

128. These authors will be discussed in chapter 4. The eleventh-century canon law collection, *Collectio canonum in Quinque libris*, included Justinian's laws regarding deaconesses, but these might be understood to apply to abbesses by this time. See l. 2, c. 198 in *de ordinatione diaconissae* as well as c. 199 and c. 200 in *Collectio canonum in V libris (libri I–III)*, ed. M. Fornasari, CCCM 6 (Turnhout: Brepols, 1970), 292–94.

129. The texts for the prayers and liturgies for the ordination of deaconesses and deacons can be found in appendix 1.

130. The liturgy takes slightly different forms in different manuscripts, as indicated in appendix 1. This discussion will follow the longer and more elaborate of the liturgies.

131. "Orariis duobus, nec episcopo quidem licet, nec prebytero uti, quanto magis diacono, qui minister eorum est. Unum igitur orarium oportet Levitam gestare in sinistro humero, propter quod orat, id est praedicat: dexteram autem partem habere liberam ut expeditus ad ministerium sacerdotale discurrat. Caveat igitur amodo Levita gemino uti orario, sed uno tantum, et puro, nec ullis coloribus, aut auro ornato" (c. 40 of the Council of Toledo, 633, in Mansi, 10:629–30). For a thorough discussion of the orarium, see Andrieu, *Ordines Romani*, 4:134–36.

132. See n86 above.

133. This is the prayer for the blessing of a widow given in two eighth-century Gallican sacramentaries. The texts were edited by Leo Mohlberg, *Missale Gallicanum Vetus (Cod. Vat. Palat. lat. 493)*, Rerum ecclesiasticarum documenta 3 (Rome: Herder, 1958), 7–8; and Leo Mohlberg, *Missale Frankorum (Cod. Vat. Reg. lat. 257)*, Rerum ecclesiasticarum documenta 2 (Rome: Herder, 1957), 17. Martimort (*Deaconesses*, 210–14) has an extensive analysis of the use of earlier rites for widows and virgins in the RGP's rite for the ordination of deaconesses.

134. Vogel, *Medieval Liturgy*, 251. The ritual continued to be copied in at least some liturgical manuscripts into the thirteenth century. For references, see Martimort, *Deaconesses*, 218.

135. Martimort, *Deaconesses*, 216.

136. For the text from Durandus, see appendix 1. On Durandus's pontifical, see Vogel, *Medieval Liturgy*, 253–55.

137. The prayers appear under the rubric, "Item oracio super ancillas dei quibus conuersis uestimenta mutantur" as "Item alia eiusdem." The texts were edited by Leo Mohlberg, *Liber Sacramentorum Romanae aeclesiae ordinis anni circuli*, Rerum ecclesiasticarum documenta 4 (Rome: Herder, 1968), 127.

138. Ysebaert, "Deaconesses," 435.

139. Ibid., 434.

140. On continent marriages in general, see Dyan Elliott, *Spiritual Marriage: Sexual Abstinence in Medieval Wedlock* (Princeton: Princeton University Press, 1993). Pages 83–93 in particular treat continent marriage among the clergy. On clerical marriage and continence, see Jo Ann McNamara, "Chaste Marriage and Clerical Celibacy," in *Sexual Practices and the Medieval Church*, ed. Vern Bullough and James Brundage (Buffalo, NY: Prometheus Books, 1982), 22–33.

141. See the reference given in n88 above. McNamara makes this point: "Since the Council of Tours had made the wives of priests virtually nuns already by forbidding them to remarry even if widowed, the only logical disposition for them was a convent" (*Sisters in Arms*, 106).

142. Jo Ann McNamara, "Chastity as a Third Gender in the History and Hagiography of Gregory of Tours," *The World of Gregory of Tours*, ed. Kathleen Mitchell and Ian Woods, Cultures, Beliefs and Traditions 8 (Leiden: Brill, 2002), 199–209.

143. McNamara, "Chaste Marriage," 24.

144. For the legislation on this *conversio*, see Dortel-Claudot, "Le prêtre," 331–32. "Some rituals of ordination even conferred a special blessing and habit upon the priest's wife" (McNamara, "Chaste Marriage," 24). "In the Gallo-Roman church a clerical wife had been required to take a vow of chastity known as a *conversio*—in essence consenting to her husband's ordination. The wife would receive a blessing and a distinct costume at the time of the ordination" (Elliott, *Spiritual Marriage*, 87). "The Gallic councils provide interesting sidelights on the status of clerical wives. Known as *episcopa, presbytera,* or *diaconissa,* they had to give their consent to their husband's ordination. At the time of ordination they too received a special blessing and wore a distinctive garb" (Lynch, "Marriage and Celibacy," 30).

145. "Si quis autem post acceptam benedictionem leviticam cum uxore sua incontinens inuenitur ab officio abiciatur" (c. 22 in Munier, *Concilia Galliae*, 84).

146. "Quosdam repperemus ardore liuidinis inflammatus abiecto militiae cingulo uomitum pristinum et inhebeta rursum coniuga repetisse adque incesti quodammodo crimine clarum decus sacerdotii uiolasse, quod nati entiam filii prodederunt" (c. 13 in DeClercq, *Concilia Galliae*, 108).

147. "Vt nullus clericorum a subdiacono et supra, qui uxores in proposito suo adcipere inhibentur, propriae, si forte iam habeat, misciatur uxori" (c. 2, DeClercq, *Concilia Galliae*, 114–15).

148. Jo Ann McNamara, "An Unresolved Syllogism: The Search for a Christian Gender System," in *Conflicted Identities and Multiple Masculinities: Men in the Medieval West*, ed. Jaqueline Murray (New York: Garland, 1999), 10. McNamara concludes, "These 'deaconesses, priestesses and bishopesses' were, as a matter of course, regulated as members of the clergy though they held no discernible office" (p. 11). I would agree, although I have argued that these ordines did have a discernible office, even if it is difficult to recover precisely what that office entailed.

149. Kim Bowes, "Personal Devotions and Private Chapels," in *Late Ancient Christianity*, ed. Virginia Burrus, *A People's History of Christianity* 2 (Minneapolis, MN: Fortress Press, 2005), 188–210. Bowes's article points out the differences and conflicts between private devotions and public liturgy, a different distinction than the one raised here. Still, her analysis is very useful as well for this argument.

150. Ibid., 206.

151. Ibid., 204.

152. Ibid., 204–5.

153. For several examples of clergy who left their possessions and positions to their children, see Anne Llewellyn Barstow, *Married Priests and the Reforming Papacy: The Eleventh-Century Debates*, Texts and Studies in Religion 12 (New York: Edwin Mellon Press, 1982), 19–45. For a discussion of married clergy as reflecting the larger pattern of society, see McNamara, "Canossa," 105–10.

154. This distinction is different than the more usual division between the secular and the clerical state that is assumed in many discussions of the eleventh-century reform movement. The distinction I am making here existed within the clerical realm itself, understanding clerical in a broader category of ministry within the church. This is not a distinction between the church and some other "secular" realm, but a dispute over the very question of how the church should be envisioned and, more importantly, governed. The distinction between the church as family and the church as monastery also played an important role in the eleventh-century reforms, and this role will be discussed further in chapter 4.

155. Married clergy and hereditary clerical posts existed in England and Normandy until at least the middle of the twelfth century. See Christopher Brooke, "Gregorian Reform in Action: Clerical Marriage in England, 1050–1200," *Cambridge Historical Journal* 12 (1956): 1–21, and idem., "Married Men Among the English Higher Clergy, 1066–1200," *Cambridge Historical Journal* 12 (1956): 187–88.

156. Hochstetler (*Conflict of Traditions*, 100–101) suggested that canonesses were the most likely women to have led the Eucharist in the Carolingian period.

157. The jurisdictional power of abbesses was also considerable. For a recent discussion of their power, see Marie Anne Mayeski, "Excluded by the Logic of Control: Women in Medieval Society and Scholastic Theology," in *Equal at the Creation: Sexism, Society, and Christian Thought*, ed. Joseph Martos and Pierre Hégy (Toronto: University of Toronto Press, 1998), 75–79.

158. See appendix 2 for the ordination rites for abbesses.

159. For a thorough analysis of confession to the abbess or her delegate within the convent, see Gisela Muschiol, *Famula Dei: Zur Liturgie in merowingischen Frauenklöstern*, Beiträge zur Geschichte des alten Mönchtums und des Benedikti-nertum 41 (Munster: Aschendorff, 1994), 222–63. For a recent discussion of the practice of penance in the early Middle Ages, see Sarah Hamilton, *The Practice of Penance: 900–1050* (Woodbridge, Suffolk: Boydell Press, 2001). Theologians into the thirteenth century continued to argue that laity, including women, had the power to hear confessions. See Paul Laurain, *De l'intervention des laiques, des diacres et des abbesses dans l'administration de la pénitence* (Paris: Lethielleux, 1897); and Georg Gromer, *Die Laienbeicht im Mittelalter: Ein Beitrag zu ihrer Geschichte*, Veröffentli-chungen aus dem Kirchenhistorischen Seminar München 7 (Munich: Lentnerschen, 1909). I want to thank Fr. Thomas O'Meara for these two references.

160. Cf. "De assidue danda confessione," and c. 7 "De non manifestandis so-rorum confessionibus," in Waldebert of Luxeuil, *Regula ad virgines*, c. 6, PL 88:1059A–1660C and "Qualiter ad confessionem omnibus diebus ueniant," in Donatus of Besançon, *Regula ad virgines*, c. 23 in Adalbert de Vogüé, "La Règle de Donat pour l'Abbesse Gauthstrude," *Benedictina* 25 (1978): 266. The *Rule* dates from the sev-enth century; see Muschiol, *Famula Dei*, 10–15.

161. Cf. cc. 18–20, in Waldebert, *Regula ad virgines*, PL 88: 1067B–1068C, and cc. 69–71, in Donatus, *Regula ad virgines*, de Vogüé, "La Regle," 304–5.

162. "Familiam quoque monasterii sive vicinos propinquos per sanctam communionem attrahebat, ut, datis confessionibus, paenitentiam pro peccatis suis agerent; ex quibus plurimis emendatis et sibi praemium adquisivit et illorum animabus lucrum fecit" (c. 6 of *Vita Bertilae Abbatissae Calensis*, in *Passiones vitaeque sanctorum aevi merovingici*, ed. B. Krusch and W. Levison, MGH, Scriptorum rerum Merovingicarum 6 [Hannover: Hahn, 1913], 106). See Muschiol, *Famula Dei*, 258. On Bertila and her *vita*, see ibid., 26. On Bertila's reputation for learning, see Stephanie Hollis, *Anglo-Saxon Women and the Church: Sharing a Common Fate* (Woodbridge, Suffolk: Boydell Press, 1992), 78, 258.

163. "Quidam uir occidit fratrem suum; et tactus penitentia, uenit ad sanctam Ytam, et egit penitudinem secundum iussionem eius" (c. 25 of *The Life of St. Ite, Virgin* in *Vitae sanctorum Hiberniae*, 2 vols., ed. Charles Plummer [Oxford: Cla-rendon Press, 1910], 2:125). The second penance occurs in c. 38, "Et postea ille egit dignam penitentiam, secundam iussionem beatissime uirginis Yte, et in vita beata obiit" (ibid., 129). See also Muschiol, *Famula Dei*, 259. On the responsibilties of the Ite, and other abbots and abbesses, to the larger community, see Bitel, *Isle of*

the Saints, 89–90. On the importance of Ite's intervetion in this case, see ibid., 170.

164. Muschiol (*Famula Dei,* 219–20) gives numerous examples of abbesses and nuns who were present on the altar.

165. Ibid., 201–6.

166. See appendix 2.

167. "Mos quippe fuerat sancte domine cotidie sacerdoti ad missam praesentare oblationem panis et vini pro salute et utilitate totius sancte ecclesie." (c. 19, in *Vita Mathildis reginae posterior,* ed. Bernard Schütte, *Die Lebenbeschreibungen der Königin Mathilde,* MGH, Scriptores rerum Germanicarum in usum scholarum 66 [Hannover: Hahn, 1994], 183. Schütte dates this work between 1107 and 1113. The story continues on to describe how Mathilda recovered the lost wine after a tame deer kept by the nuns had consumed it. An earlier version of the story is contained in the *Vita Mathildis reginae antiquior* (Schütte, *Die Lebenbeschreibungen,* 131). I want thank Jo Ann McNamara for this reference.

168. "Die Idee der kultischen Reinheit, die nach den Bußbüchern Frauen aus der Nähe des Altares verbannte, läßt sich in den Viten an keiner Stelle wiederfinden" (Muschiol, *Famula Dei,* 221).

169. "Post nocturnas et matutinas vigilias una soror de locis monasterii cum se sopori dedisset, mysticam ostendit ei Deus visionem quasi sanctae memoriae B. Aldegunda adstetisset ante altare in loco sacerdotis, et oblationes missales manibus in calicem fregisset. Et conversa ad supradictum sororem dixisset: Vade et dic sacerdoti, ut super hunc calicem missarum sollemnia canat: quia hesterna die gravis infirmitas membrorum me prohibuit communicari, hodie Domino auxiliante de corpore Christi et eius sanguine participari desidero" (c. 25 of *Vita Sanctae Aldegundis,* in *Acta sanctorum Ordinis S. Benedicti,* ed. Jean Mabillon [1688; repr. Matiscone: Fratres Protat Typographi Matisconenses, 1935], 814). On St. Aldegundis and her *vita,* see Muschiol, *Famula Dei,* 25.

170. "Mulieribus id est Christi famulabus licitum est suis ecclesiis lectiones legere et implere ministeria quae conveniunt ad confessionem sacrosancti altaris nisi ea tantummodo quae specialiter sacerdotum et diaconum sunt" (bk. 7, c. 1 of the U version, in *Die Canones Theodori Cantuariensis und ihre Überlieferungsformen,* ed. Paul Finsterwalder, Untersuchungen zu den Bußbüchern des 7, 8. und 9. Jahrhunderts, 1 [Weimer: Herman Böhlaus, 1929], 322). Finsterwalder (155–57) dates this work to 755. *Die Bussordunugen der abendländischen Kirche,* ed. F. W. H. Wasserschleben (Halle, 1851; repr. Graz: Akademische Druck-u. Verlagsanstalt, 1958), 209. See Muschiol (*Famula Dei,* 207) as well as McNamara (*Sisters in Arms,* 143), on the meaning of *confessionem* in this context.

171. These devotions are described by Janet Nelson, "Les femmes et l'évangélisation au ixe siècle," *Revue du Nord* 69 (1986): 480: "Dan sa contexte, on fait rarement mention d'un prêtre; deux ou trois moniales se tenaient à l'autel pour accueillir les pèrlerins; on versait peutêtre au pèrelin une coupe de vin du calice de l'autel, ou on lui permittait de mettre la main sur une lampe votive sur l'autel, ou on lui touchait les yeux aveugles avec le bâton de Walburgis. . . . L'alimentation rituelle

des *pauperes Christi* se faisait aussi dans l'eglise et la bénédiction des pèrelins qui repartaient comprenait quelques fois un don du pain bénit par la *materfamilias* (i.e. l'abbesse)." See also Donatus, *Regula ad virgines*, c. 56: "Cumque partes quas ipsa voluerit circumferint, protinus aut in salutatorium, aut ad portam redeant; ubi deinceps, si abbatissae visum fuerit, illa, si voluerit, praesente vel reliquis, eulogias accipiant, aut reliquum quod offere decreverint" (*PL* 87:291A).

172. See pages 89–90 above.

173. "Cumque calicem, in quo dominicum corpus et sanguis habebatur, sibi afferri iussisset, propriis manibus eum accipiendo, sancta communione participata omnibus cernentibus, animam tradidit." (c. 22 of *Vita Odiliae Abbatissae Hohenburgensis*, in Krusch and Levison, *Passiones vitaeque*, 50). On this incident, see McNamara, *Sisters in Arms*, 126–27. For similar incidents in the lives of holy women, see Anneke Mulder-Bakker, *Lives of the Anchoresses: The Rise of the Urban Recluse in Medieval Europe* (Philadelphia: University of Pennsylvania Press, 2005), 73–75.

174. The *Regula ad virgines* of Aurelian of Arles contains an addition entitled "Ordinem etiam quodmodo psallere debeatis, in hoc libello judicavimus inserendum." This section contains directions for the Divine Office that include readings from the Gospel, *PL* 68:403C–460D. On the sixth-century *Regula* of Aurelian, see Muschiol, *Famula Dei*, 10–15.

175. The details are given by Muschiol, *Famula Dei*, 343–46, 313.

176. Ibid., 94–100, discusses the importance of reading scripture for the nuns.

177. See the discussion in chapter 4 as well as Ida Raming, *The Priestly Office of Women: God's Gift to a Renewed Church*, ed. Bernard Cooke and Gary Macy, vol. 2 of *A History of Women and Ordination* (Lanham, MD: Scarecrow Press, 2004), 49–50, 54, 61, 65. According to Raming, the abbesses of the Carthusian Order sang the Epistle or Gospel at high Mass during the Middle Ages.

178. For recent studies on women preaching in the Middle Ages, see *Women Preachers and Prophets through Two Millennia of Christianity*, ed. Beverly Wayne Kienzle and Pamela J. Walker (Berkeley: University of California Press, 1998). On lay preaching in general in the Middle Ages, see Rolf Zerfaß, *Der Streit um die Laienpredigt. Eine pastoral-geschichtliche Untersuchung zum Verständnis des Predigtamtes und zu seiner Entwicklung im 12. und 13. Jahrhundert* (Frieberg: Herder, 1974). The abbesses also, of course, taught their own nuns and often ran schools for both sexes. See Muschiol, *Famula Dei*, 98–99; McNamara, *Sisters in Arms*, 135; Nelson, "Les femmes," 477–78; and Hollis, *Anglo-Saxon Women*, 78, 258.

179. "Nulla infantem de baptismo excipiat," Aurelian of Arles, *Regula ad virgines*, c. 16, *PL* 68:402A, and "Nulla cujuslibet filiam in baptismo neque divitis neque pauperis praesumat excipere" (c. 54 in Donatus of Besançon, *Regula ad virgines*, PL 87: 290C). See also McNamara, *Sisters in Arms*, 126.

180. "Auditum est, aliquas abbatis contra morem sanctae Dei ecclesiae benedictionis cum manus inpositione et signaculo sanctae crucis super capita virorum dare, necnon et velare virgines cum benedictione sacerdotali. Quod omnino vobis, sanctissimi patres, in vestris parrochiis interdicendum esse scitote" (c. 76 in Boretius, *Capitularia*, 60). See Hochstetler, *Conflict of Traditions*, 101–2. The abbesses of

Monheim blessed the pilgrims who came to the shrine of St. Walpurgis; see Nelson, "Les femmes," 480. McNamara summarizes: "Abesses, bearing the shepherd's crook, gave blessings, distributed preconsecrated wafers to their congregations and heard non-sacramental confession. Out on the missionary frontiers, they exercised many of the administrative powers of bishops" ("Unresolved Syllogism," 11).

181. See pp. 91–92 above.

182. See n90 above.

183. I have addressed some of these concerns in "Ordination" (pp. 502–7), and the complex problem of the interplay of history and theology has received a thorough and thoughtful analysis by Terrence Tilley, *History, Theology, and Faith: Dissolving the Modern Problematic* (Maryknoll, NY: Orbis Books, 2004).

184. For a recent discussion of the dangers of romanticizing the early Middle Ages as a period of equality for women, see Schulenburg, *Forgetful of Their Sex*, 403–15.

CHAPTER 4

1. Domnus papa Urbanus generalem sinodum Beneventi collegit et sententiam anathematis super Guibertum heresiarcham et omnes eius complices sinodali iudicio confirmavit." For the year 1091 of the *Chronicle* of Bernold of Constance in *Die Chroniken Bertholds von Reichenau unds Bernolds von Konstanz 1054–1000*, Ian Robinson, ed., MGH, Scriptores rerum Germanicarum, N.S 14 (Hannover: Hahnsche Buchhandlung, 2003), 484.

2. The council barely rates a mention even in the volume in which the critical edition appears. See Robert Somerville and Stephan Kuttner, eds., *Pope Urban II, The Collectio Britannica, and the Council of Melfi* (Oxford: Clarendon Press, 1996); Robert Somerville, "The Council of Clermont (1095), and Latin Christian Society," in *Papacy, Councils and Canon Law in the 11th–12th Centuries*, ed. Robert Somerville (Aldershot: Variorum, 1990), 57, 65–66 (reprint of an article by the same name in *Archivum historiae pontificiae* 12 [1974]: 55–90); and I. S. Robinson, *The Papacy 1073–1198: Continuity and Innovation* (Cambridge: Cambridge University Press, 1990), 125–26, 374.

3. "Nullus deinceps in episcopum eligatur nisi qui in sacris ordinibus religiose vivens inventus est. Sacros autem ordines dicimus diaconatus ac presbyteratus. Hos siquidem solos primitiva lege ecclesia habuit; super his solis praeceptum habemus apostoli. Subdiacones vero, quia et ipsi altaribus adminstrant, oportunitate exigente concedimus sed rarissime, si tamen spectate sine religionis et scientie, quod ipsum non sine Romani pontificis vel metropolitani licentia" (c. 1 in "The Canons of the Councils of Benevento [1091] and Troia [1093]" in Summerville and Kuttner, *Pope Urban II*, 303). The text is also given in Mansi, 20:738.

4. According to John St H. Gibaut: "This canon is noteworthy in that it understands that the orders preceding election and consecration to the episcopate are 'the diaconate and the presbyterate,'" rather than 'the diaconate or the presbyterate'" (*The "Cursus Honorum": A Study of the Origins and Evolution of Sequenial*

Ordination, Patristic Studies 3 [New York: Peter Lang, 2000], 253. "This modification is evidence of the place the presbyterate had won as an indispensable grade in the cursus toward the episcopate in the eleventh century." See also the analysis of Ludwig Ott discussed on pp. 40–41 in chapter 2.

5. "Ut nullus laicus, vel tantum subdiaconus in episcopum eligatur" (c. 3 in *The Councils of Urban II*, vol. 1, *Decreta Claromontensia*, ed. Robert Somerville [Amsterdam: Adolf Hakkert, 1972], 74–75). On the complexity of the transmission of these decrees, see Somerville, *Councils of Urban II*, 3–19. On the relationship of this decree to ordination, see Gibaut, *Cursus Honorum*, 253.

6. The debate whether the episcopacy is a separate *ordo* from the presbyterate in this and earlier periods is discussed by Roger Reynolds, "Patristic 'Presbyterianism' in the Early Medieval Theology of Sacred Orders," *Mediaeval Studies* 45 (1983): 311–42. The history of the early diffusion of this law is traced by Francis Gossman, *Pope Urban II and Canon Law*, The Catholic University of America Canon Law Series 403 (Washington, DC: The Catholic University of America Press, 1960).

7. D. 60, c. 4 in *Corpus iuris canonici*, 2 vols., ed. Emil Friedberg (Graz: Akademische Druck-und-Verlagsanstalt, 1959), 1:227. This canon is considered part of the earliest text of the *Decretum* by Anders Winroth. See his *The Making of Gratian's Decretum* (Cambridge: Cambridge University Press, 2000), 202. Winroth would date the first recension of the *Decretum* to before the 1130s (pp. 193–96).

8. "Sacri ordines tantum dicuntur sacerdotium et diaconatus, quia in illis tamen [*lire:* tantum] datur Spiritus, et ideo nulla necessitate possunt ab inferioribus tractari; sed alia possunt, ut Apostolus potest legi" (*Sententia* n. 390 in "L'École d'Anselme de Laon et de Guillaume de Champeaux," in Odo Lottin, *Psychologie et morale aux XIIe et XIIIe siècles* [Gembloux: Abbaye du Mont César, 1959], 283). According to Reynolds, the canon from Benevento also appears in the *Sentences of Magister A,* a work closely associated with the School at Laon. Reynolds, "Patristic 'Presbyterianism,'" 338n115.

9. Ivo copied the law into his *Decretum* (completed in 1094), *pars* 5, c. 72, PL 161:350D; and into his *Panormia* (compiled in 1095), bk. 3, c. 51, PL 161:1130C. On the dating of this work, see Gossman, *Pope Urban II*, 52–58; and NCE 7:680. On Ivo, see NCE 7:679–80.

10. See Marcia Colish, *Peter Lombard*, 2 vols. (Leiden: Brill, 1994), 2:616–18, especially p. 616: "The two quarters from which we first see the effort to develop a sacramental theology of holy orders, and a theology in which the way sacramental grace is seen to operate is differentiated according to the clerical rank involved, are Ivo of Chartres and the School of Laon."

11. "Sacri canones definiunt nullum in episcopum eligendum, nisi qui prius in sacris ordinibus religiose fuerit conversatus. Sacros autem ordines diaconatus et presbyteratus tantum appellandos censent; quia hos solos primitiva legitur Ecclesia habuisse, et de his solis praeceptum habemus apostoli" (bk. 2, *pars* 3, c. 13 in *De Sacramentis Christianae fidei*, PL 176:430B).

12. The passage from Romans reads: "I commend to you our sister Phoebe, a deacon of the church at Cenchreae, so that you may welcome her in the Lord as is

fitting for the saints, and help her in whatever she may require from you, for she has been a benefactor of many and of myself as well" (Rom. 16:1–2). The passage from 1 Timothy reads: "Deacons likewise must be serious, not double-tongued, not indulging in much wine, not greedy for money; they must hold fast to the mystery of the faith with a clear conscience. And let them first be tested; then, if they prove themselves blameless, let them serve as deacons. Women likewise must be serious, not slanderers, but temperate, faithful in all things. Let deacons be married only once, and let them manage their children and their households well; for those who serve well as deacons gain a good standing for themselves and great boldness in the faith that is in Christ Jesus" (1 Tim. 4:8–13). The translation of scripture used throughout is the New Revised Standard Version.

13. John Hilary Martin, "The Ordination of Women and the Theologians in the Middle Ages," *Escritos del Vedat* 36 (1986): 133–34. Martin's long article appeared in two parts, "The Ordination of Women and the Theologians in the Middle Ages," *Escritos del Vedat* 36 (1986): 115–77; and "The Ordination of Women and the Theologians in the Middle Ages (II)," *Escritos del Vedat* 36 (1988): 87–143. It has been edited and published with the Latin notes translated into English by Bernard Cooke and Gary Macy, *A History of Women and Ordination* (New York: Scarecrow Press, 2002), 1:31–160. The quote from Martin occurs in Cooke and Macy, *History*, 1:45. The passage in Ambrosiaster reads: "Sancti estote, quia et ego sanctus sum, ideoque etiam mulieres, quae inferiores videntur, sine crimine vult esse, ut munda sit ecclesia Dei. Sed Catafrygae occasionem errores captantes propter quod post diaconos mulieres adloquitur, etiam ipsas diaconissas [diaconas] debere ordinari vana presumptione defendunt, cum sciant apostolos septem diaconos elegisse. Numquid nulla mulier tunc idonea inventa est, cum inter undecim apostolos sanctas mulieres fuisse legimus?" (*Ambrosiastri qui dicitur Commentarius in Epistulas Paulinas*, ed. Henry Joseph Vogels, Corpus scriptorum ecclesiasticorum Latinorum, no. 81, pt. 1–3, 3 vols. [Vienna: Hoelder-Pichler-Tempsky, 1966–1969], 3:268).

14. "Hic inserit praeceptum de mulieribus ante et post agens de diaconibus, quod intersertum nisi ad diaconos aliquomodo pertineat, inconveniens hic ordo videtur. Ut autem quod ait de mulieribus convenienter insertum judicetur, sic exponimus: *Mulieres* quae nuptae fuerint his qui in diaconatum promoventur, *similiter* oportet esse *pudicas*, id est necesse est profiteri castitatem, sicut viros earum" (*Expositio in epistolas Pauli, Epistola I ad Timotheum*, c. 3, *PL* 153:442C). On the pseudo-Bruno gloss, see Gary Macy "Some Examples of the Influence of Exegesis on the Theology of the Eucharist in the Eleventh and Twelfth Centuries," *Recherches de Théologie Ancienne et Médiévale* 52 (1985): 64–77.

15. "Vel si placet mulieres diaconissae, scilicet moniales, similiter oportet esse pudicas, etc., sicut dicta sunt" (ibid. *PL* 153:442D). The tradition of interpreting this passage as referring to deaconesses will be discussed below.

16. "Nunc dicit quod docendi officium solis viris conveniat et quales ad illud debeant ordinari determinat" (*Biblia Latina cum Glossa Ordinaria: Facsimile Reprint of the Editio Princeps Adolph Rusch of Strassburg 1480/8*, 4 vols. [1480; repr. Turnhout: Brepols, 1992], 4:407). Mark Zier kindly checked this passage against the microfilm

of six early manuscripts from Paris, Bibliothèque nationale de France. All were probably written before 1200. All six contain the passage in question. The references are: MS lat. 310, fo. 97r; MS lat. 312, fo. 145r; MS lat. 313, fo. 143r; MS lat. 314, fo. 124r; MS lat. 654, fo. 158r; MS lat. 14785, fo. 97r.

17. "Quia non dicit mulieres debere hordinari in officiis ecclesiasticis, sed dicit mulieres ordinatorum, id est diaconorum et sacerdotum esse pudicas non dicit sobrias, etc" (Bibliothèque nationale, MS lat. 654, fo. 158r). Again, I wish to thank Mark Zier for this citation.

18. "Mulieres similiter Ambro. Cum sanctum precipit creari episcopum et diaconum plebem non disparare vult esse etiam infimo gradu mulierum ut munda sit ecclesia sed occasione horum verborum cathaphrige dicunt diaconas debere ordinari quod est contra auctoritatem" (*Biblia Latina*, 4:408, col. 2). This passage was not found in any of the early exemplars checked by Mark Zier.

19. "The known facts concerning the authorship of the *Gloss* are as follows. The central figure is Anselm of Laon. . . . Anselm was certainly responsible for the *Gloss* on St. Paul and the Psalter, probably for that on the Fourth Gospel" (Beryl Smalley, *The Study of the Bible in the Middle Ages*, 2nd ed. [Oxford: Blackwell, 1983], 60).

20. Colish, *Peter Lombard*, 2:618.

21. "Tertio queritur, an ex mulieris confessione iste sit condempnandus? In quo primum uidendum est, an mulier sacerdotem accusare ualeat? Quod sacris canonibus omnino uidetur esse prohibitum. Generaliter enim statutum est ex decretis Fabiani Papae, ut sacerdotes Domini non accusent, nec in eos testificentur, qui sui ordinis non sunt, nec esse possunt. Mulieres autem non solum ad sacerdotium, sed nec etiam ad diaconatum prouehi possunt, unde nec sacerdotes accusare, nec in eos testifi cariualent" (*Decretum*, c. 15, q. 3, *princ.*, in Friedberg, *Corpus*, 1:750). For a discussion of Gratian's position on the ordination of women, see Ida Raming, *The Priestly Office of Women: God's Gift to a Renewed Church*, ed. Bernard Cook and Gary Macy, vol. 2 of *A History of Women and Ordination* (Lanham, MD: Scarecrow Press, 2004), 5–73. Gratian's comment is included the earliest text of the *Decretum* by Winroth, *The Making of Gratian's Decretum*, 214.

22. For a recent account of Abelard's relationship to Anselm, see Michael Clanchy, *Abelard, a Medieval Life* (Oxford: Blackwell, 1997), 72–74, 80–85, 88–90.

23. Abelard's interest in the ordination of deaconesses was first noticed by F. Gillmann, "Weibliche Kleriker nach dem Urteil der Frühscholastik," *Archiv für katholisches Kirchenrecht* 93 (1913): 240–42. More recently, Alcuin Blamires (*The Case for Medieval Women in Medieval Culture* [Oxford: Clarendon Press, 1997], 200–207) has insisted on the importance of Abelard's letter detailing the history of the order of holy women: "On the contrary, it is a zealously pugnacious piece, exuding energy and a sense of discovery. In urging female 'authority' of any sort, Abelard is on unusual ground for the Middle Ages, since *auctoritas* was not in general a concept associated with women" (p. 202). See also his "*Caput a femina, membra a viris:* Gender Polemic in Abelard's Letter, 'On the Authority and Dignity of the Nun's Profession,'" in *The Tongue of the Fathers: Gender and Ideology in Twelfth-Century Latin*, ed. David Townsend and Andrew Taylor (Philadelphia: University of Pennsylvania Press, 1998),

55–79. Barbara Newman suggested that "no one went further in the ritual praise of women than Abelard" and that "his proto-feminist epistle was written to encourage the dispirited Heliose, and he goes much further than other writers were prepared to do" ("Flaws in the Golden Bowl: Gender and Spiritual Formation in the Twelfth Century," in *From Virile Woman to WomanChrist: Studies in Medieval Religion and Literature*, ed. Barbara Newman [Philadelphia: University of Pennsylvania Press], 27). For another estimation of the importance of Abelard's support of women, see Fiona Griffiths, "Brides and *Dominae:* Abelard's *Cura monialium* at the Augustinian Monastery of Marbach," *Viator* 34 (2003): 57–88; and "Men's Duty to Provide for Women's Needs: Abelard, Heloise, and their Negotiation of the *Cura monialium*," *Journal of Medieval History* 30 (2004): 1–24.

24. Since the theology contained in the other clearly genuine works of Abelard cited here is identical to that contained in Letter 7, I am assuming for the purposes of this paper that the theology contained in the letter originated with Heloise and Abelard even if they did not themselves write the letters. The letters between Heloise and Abelard have been numbered differently by different editors. In this article, the numbering found in the 1616 edition reprinted in *PL* will be used. Reference will be made to the edition by J. T. Muckle and T. P. McLaughlin, which appeared in *Mediaeval Studies* from 1953 through 1956, as well as to the edition by Eric Hicks, in his *La vie et les epistres: Pierres Abaelart et Heloys sa fame* (Paris: Champion-Slatkine, 1991).

25. The chronology of Abelard's works is difficult to ascertain. According to Buytaert, Abelard's sermons would date from 1130 to 1135; Letters 4–8, his *Commentary on Romans,* and the second redaction of the *Theologia Christiana* all date 1135–1139. See *Petri Abaelardi Opera Theologia,* ed. Eligius M. Buytaert, 3 vols., CCSM, 11–13 (Turnhout: Brepols, 1969) 1:xxii–xxv. A more recent evaluation by Constant Mews would date the *Theologia Christiana* between 1122 and 1126, the sermons between 1127 and 1132, Letters 4–8 between 1132 and 1137, and his *Commentary on Romans* between 1133 and 1137. See Constant Mews, "On Dating the Works of Peter Abelard," *Archives d'histoire doctrinale et littéraire du moyen âge* 60 (1985): 73–134.

26. "COMMENDO, scilicet precibus meis, PHOEBEN, per quam hanc epistolam Romanis de Corintho mittere creditur; diues quaedam et nobilis mulier dicitur, quae de facultatibus suis uel aliorum fidelibus illis qui erant CENCHRIS necessaria ministrabat, exemplo scilicet sanctarum feminarum quae hoc Domino seu apostolis fecisse memorantur. Haec autem negotium quoddam habebat pro quo Romam uenire necesse habebat. Pro hac igitur Romanos Apostolus adhortatur et rogat ut eam honorifice suscipiant et in suo negotio, quantum possint, adiuuent. . . . Origenes: 'Apostolica auctoritate docet etiam feminas in ministerio ecclesiae constitui. In quo officio positam Phoeben apud ecclesiam *quae est Cenchris,* magna cum laude et commendatione prosequitur, quia in necessitatibus apostolicisque laboribus adstiterit. Locus hic duo docet, et haberi feminas ministras in ecclesia et tales debere assumi in ministerium, quae adstiterint multis et per bona officia usque ad apostolicam laudem meruerint peruenire.' Hieronymus: '*In ministerio ecclesiae,* sicut et nunc in orientalibus locis diaconissae mulieres in suo sexu ministrare uidentur in baptismo siue in

ministerio uerbi, quia priuatim docuisse feminas inuenimus, sicut Priscillam cuius
uir Aquila uocabatur.' Idem, In epistola ad Timotheum: '*Adolescentiores autem uiduas
deuita* in ministerio diaconatus praeponere.' Sanctus Epiphanius *Iohanni Hierosolymitano:* 'Numquam ego ordinaui diaconissas et ad alias misi prouincias neque feci
quidquam ut ecclesiam scinderem.'—Quas itaque antiquitus diaconissas, id est
ministras, nunc abbatissas, id est matres, uocamus. Cassiodorus, super hunc
eumdem locum: 'Phoeben significat diaconissam fuisse matris ecclesiae; quod in
partibus Graecorum hodieque quasi militiae causa peragitur, quibus et baptizandi
usus in ecclesia non negatur.' Claudius quoque, in *Expositione* huius epistolae: 'Hic
locus docet etiam feminas in ministerio ecclesiae constitui, in quo officio positam
Phoeben apud ecclesiam *quae est Cenchris,* Apostolus magna cum laude et commendatione prosequitur" (Abelard, *Commentaria in epistolam,* in Buytaert, *Petri Abaelardi
Opera Theologia,* 1: 326–27).

27. "Sanctus Epiphanius *Iohanni Hierosolymitano:* 'Numquam ego ordinaui
diaconissas et ad alias misi prouincias neque feci quidquam ut ecclesiam scinderem' "
(ibid., 1:327).

28. "Et attende, quod diaconisse, etsi diaconisse dicantur, non legunt in missa
ewangelium, quod tamen in matutinis bene possunt pronuntiare, nec habent
impositionem manuum sicut diacones: habent tamen benedictionem
propriam. . . . Item post diaconissas ad diacones redit, de quibus simul agit eo, quod
sunt eiusdem officii. . . . Et ideo apostolus, quia diacones et diaconisse tam af-
fine habent officium, vicissime de illis instruit, modo post diaconissas iterum ad
diacones rediens, quod dicit oportere monogamos esse, sicut de episcopis dictum est"
(Artur Landgraf, ed., *Commentarius Cantabrigienensis in epistolas Pauli*, Publication in
Mediaeval Studies, 3 vols. [Notre Dame, IN: University of Notre Dame Press, 1937–
44], 3:575). Mews's "On Dating" argues that this work was written between 1133 and
1137.

29. "Que vita mulierum a Domino incepti, qui mulieres sanctas secum habebat
sicut postmodum apostoli, que manibus operantes sanctis viris ministrabant necessaria, in quibus quedem, que astutior erat, aliis preerat dicebatur diaconissa, id est
ministra. Sed hodie in vita monacharum, que inde inolevit, ille que presunt, vocant se
abbatissas" (Landgraf, *Commentarius Cantabrigienensis,* 1:214). "Phebe autem, de qua
loquitur apostolus in epistola ad Romanos, erat de numero harum mulierum, que, ut
sancti dicunt, Cenchris, in illo loco iuxta Corinthum, diaconissa fuit, ubi quibusdam
sacris viduis preerat, que peregrinis et illis pauperibus, qui ibi erant, ea, que poterant,
cotidie ministrabant. Et mulieres huiusmodi, que aliis in ministratione pauperum
presunt, hodie abbatisse vocantur, que convenientiori vocabulo iuxta dominicam
sententiam, que est Qui maior est vestrum, ut paulo [ante] diximus, fiat minister vester, ministre appellantur" (Landgraf, *Commentarius Cantabrigienensis,*
3:574–75).

30. "Et iste ordo mulierum diu est, quod incepit, quia et in veteri testamento et
in novo legimus fuisse diaconissas, id est mulieres, que sanctis ministrabant"
(Landgraf, ibid., 3:574).

31. "Perpendite et quanto vos honore divina gratia sublimaverit, qui vos primum suas et postmodum apostolorum habuit diaconas, cum tam illis quam istis sanctis viduis de suis facultatibus constet ministrasse. Unde et ipsas tam diaconas quam diaconissas appellare doctores sancti consuevere" (Abelard, *Sermo* 31, *PL* 178: 572A-B).

32. "Quibus pariter et feminas in hoc diaconatus ordine ab Apostolo conjunctas esse, doctores sancti multis profitentur in locis. Qui ad Romanos Epistolam scribens: *Commendo,* inquit, *vobis Phoeben sororem nostram, quae est in ministerio Ecclesiae, quae est Chencris* (Rom. 16:1). Quem quidem locum Cassiodorus in hujus Epistolae commentariis suis exponens: 'significat, inquit, diaconissam fuisse matris Ecclesiae, quod in partibus Graecorum hodie usque peragitur, quibus et baptizandi usus in Ecclesia non negatur.' Hinc et Claudius ita meminit: 'Hic locus apostolica auctoritate docet etiam feminas in ministerio Ecclesiae institui, in quo officio positam Phoeben apud Ecclesiam, quae est Chencris, Apostolus magna cum laude et commendatione prosequitur" (ibid., *PL* 178:572B-C).

33. "Hieronymus quoque illum Apostoli locum ad Timotheum scribentis exponens, dicit, 'Adolescentiores autem viduas devita in ministerio diaconatus praepoponere, nec malum pro malo detur exemplum.' Idem quoque apostolus, cum supra in eadem Epistola post episcopos etiam diaconorum vitam ordinaret, institutionem quoque diaconarum illis conjunxit" (ibid).

34. "Miror, unice meus, quod praeter consuetudinem epistolarum, immo contra ipsum ordinem naturalem rerum, in ipsa fronte salutationis epistolaris me tibi praeponere praesumpsisti, feminam videlicet viro, uxorem marito, ancillam domino, monialem monacho et sacerdoti diaconissam, abbati abbatissam" (J. T. Muckle, "The Personal Letters between Abelard and Heloise," *Mediaeval Studies* 15 [1953]: 77; and Hicks, *La vie,* 61). See also Mary Martin McLaughlin, "Peter Abelard and the Dignity of Women: Twelfth Century 'Feminism' in Theory and Practice," in *Pierre Abélard Pierre le Vénérable: Les courants philosophiques, littéraires et artistiques en occident au milieu du XIIe siècle* (Paris: Éditions du Centre National de la Recherche Scientifique, 1975), 295. On the public role such an address might have played, see Elizabeth Freeman, "The Public and Private Functions of Heloise's Letters," *Journal of Medieval History* 23 (1997): 15–28.

35. "Satis esse nostrae abritror infirmitati, si nos ipsis Ecclesiae rectoribus, et qui in sacris ordinibus constituti sunt clericis, tam continentiae quam abstenentiae virtus aequaverit, maxime quum Veritas dicit: 'Perfectus omnis erit, si sit sicut magister ejus'" (Heloise, *Epistola 6,* in Muckle, "Personal Letters," 244; and Hicks, *La vie,* 92–93). "Hinc etiam canones nostrae infirmitati consulentes decreverunt diaconissas ante quadraginta annos ordinari non debere, et hoc cum diligenti probatione, cum a viginti annis liceat diaconos promoveri" (Heloise, *Epistola 6,* in Muckle, "Personal Letters," 245; and Hicks, *La vie,* 94).

36. McLaughlin, "Peter Abelard," 287–333; and Jean Leclercq, "Ad ipsam sophiam Christum: le témoignage monastique d'Abélard," *Revue d'ascétique et de mystique* 46 (1970): 161–81. See also Clanchy, *Abelard,* 251–60.

37. "Caritate tuae, charissima soror de origine tuae professionis tam tibi quam spiritualibus filiabus tuis sciscitanti, unde scilicet monialium coeperit religio paucis, si potero, succincteque rescribam. Monachorum siquidem sive monialium ordo a Domino nostro Iesu Christio religionis suae formam plenissime sumpsit: quamvis et ante ipsius Incarnationem nonnulla huius propositi tam in viris quam in feminis praecesserit inchoatio" (Abelard, *Epistola 7* in, "The Letter of Heloise on Religious Life and Abelard's First Reply," ed. J. T. Muckle, in *Mediaeval Studies* 17 [1955]: 253; and Hicks, *La vie,* 105). A complete English translation of this letter appears in C. K. Scott Moncrieff, trans., *The Letters of Abelard and Heloise* (New York: Alfred Knopf, 1926), 131–75; and a more recent summary translation is included in Betty Radice and M. T. Clanchy, trans., *The Letters of Abelard and Heloise* (New York: Penguin, 2003), 112–29.

38. On Miriam, Anna, Deborah, Judith, and Esther, see Abelard, *Epistle 7,* in Muckle, "Letter of Heloise," 253, 261–63, 269–70; and Hicks, *La vie,* 107, 118–22, 130–31. On Elizabeth and Anna, cf. "Ac prius in Anna et Maria viduis et virginibus sanctae professionis forma est exhibita quam in Ioanne vel apostolis monasticae religionis exempla viris proposita" (*Epistle 7,* in Muckle, "Letter of Heloise," 269; and Hicks, *La vie,* 130) and "Virum Elizabeth Zachariam magnum Domini sacerdotem incredulitatis diffidentia mutum adhuc tenebat, dum in adventu et salutatione Mariae ipsa mox Elisabeth Spiritu Sancto repleta et exsultantem in utero suo parvulum sensit et, prophetiam iam de ipso completo Mariae conceptu prima proferens, plusquam propheta extitit.... Excellentius autem prophetiae donum in Elizabeth videtur completum, conceptum statim Dei Filium agnoscere, quam in Ioanne ipsum iamdudum natum ostendere. Sicut igitur Mariam Magdalenam apostolorum dicimus apostolam, sic nec istam prophetarum dicere dubitemus prophetam, sive ipsam beatam viduam Annam, de qua supra latius actum est" (*Epistle 7,* in Muckle, "The Letter of Heloise," 271; and Hicks, *La vie,* 133–34).

39. "Nec nisi feminas Domino ministrasse Scriptura commemorat Evangelica, quae proprias etiam facultates in quotidianam eius alimoniam dicarant et ei praecipue huius vitae necessaria procurabant. Ipse discipulis in mensa, ipse in ablutione pedum humillimum se ministrum exhibebat. A nullo vero discipulorum vel etiam virorum hoc eum suscepisse novimus obsequium: sed solas, ut diximus, feminas in his vel caeteris humanitatis obsequiis ministerium impendisse" (*Epistle 7,* in Muckle, "Letter of Heloise," 254; and Hicks, *La vie,* 108). "Ut hinc quoque pateat Dominum etiam in praedictione sua profiscientem ministratione mulierum corporaliter sustentari et eas ipsi pariter cum apostolis quasi inseparabiles comites adhaerere" (*Epistle 7,* in Muckle, "Letter of Heloise," 259; and Hicks, *La vie,* 116).

40. Translation is from Radice and Clanchy, *Letters,* 115. See nn8–9 above as well as "Ex quibus colligimus has sanctas mulieres quasi apostolas super apostolos esse constitutas, cum ipsae ad eos vel a Domino vel ab angelis missae suumum illud resurrectionis gaudium nuntiaverunt, quod expectabatur ab omnibus, ut per eas apostoli primum addiscerent quod toti mundo postmodum praedicarent" (*Epistle 7,* in Muckle, "Letter of Heloise," 258; and Hicks, *La vie,* 114). "Quid enim abiectius quam Maria Magdalene vel Maria Aegyptiaca secundum vitae statum pristinae? Quas vero postmodum vel honore vel merito divina amplius gratia sublimavit: illam quidem

quasi in aposotolico permanentem coenobio, ut iam supra commemoravimus..."
(*Epistle 7*, in Muckle, "Letter of Heloise," 274; and Hicks, *La vie*, 138). Abelard's high
regard for Mary Magdalene as an apostle and preacher was not unusual in the twelfth
century. For a thorough discussion of Mary Magdalene as a role model for women
preachers, see Katherine Ludwig Jansen, *The Making of the Magdalene: Preaching and
Popular Devotion in the Later Middle Ages* (Princeton: Princeton University Press,
2000), esp. 49–99.

41. "Hanc quippe Samaritanam et spiritu prophetiae repletam esse tunc constat
quo videlicet Christum et ad Iudaeos jam venisse et ad gentes venturum esse professa
est, cum dixerit: *Scio quia Messias venit qui, dicitur Christus; cum ergo venerit ille, nobis
annunitabit omnia.* Et multos ex civitate illa propter verbum mulieris ad Christum
cucurrisse et in eum credidisse, et ipsum duobus diebus apud se retinuisse qui tamen
alibi discipulis ait: *In viam gentium ne abieritis et in civitates Samaritanorum ne
intraveritis.* ... Nec tamen eos esse admissos commemorat nec illis postulantibus
tantam Christi copiam esse concessam quantam huic Samaritanae nequaquam id
petenti, a qua ejus in gentibus praedicatio coepisse videtur quam non solum conver-
terit, sed per eam, ut dictum est, multos acquisivit" (Abelard, *Epistle 7*, in Muckle,
"Letter of Heloise," 273; and Hicks, *La vie*, 136–37). See also the references to Mary
Magdalene in n40 above and to Phoebe in n42 below.

42. "Ex his profecto diaconissis Phoeben illam fuisse constat quam Apostolus
Romanis diligenter commendans et pro ea exorans, ait: *Commendo autem vobis
Phoeben sororem nostram, quae est in ministerio Ecclesiae, quae est Cenchris, ut eam
suscipiatis in Domino digne sanctis, et assistatis ei in quocunque negotio vestri indiguerit:
etenim ipsa quoque astitit multis, et mihi ipsi.* Quem quidem locum tam Cassiodorus
quam Claudius exponentes ipsam illius Ecclesiae diaconissam fuisse profitentur.
Cassiodorus: 'significat,' inquit, 'diaconissam fuisse Matris Ecclesiae, quod in partibus
Graecorum hodie usque quasi militae causa pergatur. Quibus et baptizandi usus in
Ecclesia non negatur.' Claudius: 'Hic locus' inquit, 'apostolica auctoritate docet
etiam feminas in ministerio Ecclesiae constitui. In quo officio positam Phoeben apud
Ecclesiam quae est Cenchris Apostolus magna cum laude et commendatione
prosequitur" (*Epistle 7*, in Muckle, "Letter of Heloise," 264–65; and Hicks, *La vie*,
124–25).

43. "Quales etiam ipse ad Timotheum scribens, inter ipsos colligens diaconos,
simili morum instructione vitam earum instituit. Ibi quippe ecclesiasticorum
ministeriorum ordinans gradus, cum ab episcopo ad diaconos descendisset" (*Epistle 7*,
in Muckle, "Letter of Heloise," 265; and Hicks, *La vie*, 125).

44. "Bene autem dicit hanc uirtutem non solum *apud Deum* notam, quasi
specialiter approbatam, qui ei in Euangelio centesimum assignat fructum et eam in
semetipso, de Virgine natus, tam uerbo quam exemplo praedicare uoluit, quem
uerum agnum et sine macula hi qui sine macula sunt, id est uirgines, sequi dicuntur
quocumque ierit—a quo etiam uirginitas octo Sibyllarum, beato attestante Hieronymo,
spiritum prophetiae promeruerit:—uerum et *apud homines,* cum solae uirgines Deo
consecrandae manu summi sacerdotis uelentur, et diaconissarum obtineant principatum" (bk. 2, c. 93 in *Theologia Christiana*, in Buytaert, *Opera*, 2:172–73).

45. The prayer, "Omnipotens sempiterne deus" used for the ordination of an abbot or an abbess, contains the phrases, "ut qui per manus nostre hodie impositionem abbatissa (abba) instituetur" and "multiplicato fenore eum centesimo fructu." This prayer occurs in the *Liber sacramentorum Gellonensis*, the *Liber sacramentorum Augustodunensis*, the Romano-Germanic Pontifical, and the twelfth-century Roman pontifical (see appendix 2). Abelard quoted the Gelasian pontifical, of which the *Gellonensis* and *Augustodunensis* are versions, in the *Theologia*, bk. 4, c. 122, in Buytaert, *Opera*, 326.

46. See nn29–30 and 34 above as well as "Septem vero personas ex vobis ad omnem monasterii administrationem necessarias esse credimus atque sufficere: portariam scilicet, cellariam, vestiariam, infirmariam, cantricem, sacristam, et ad extremum diaconissam, quam nunc abbatissam nominant" (T. P. McLaughlin, ed., "Abelard's Rule for Religious Women," *Mediaeval Studies* 18 [1956]: 252). Abelard continued throughout his rule to refer to the abbess as a deaconess.

47. McLaughlin, "Peter Abelard," 294. A similar estimation of the purpose of Abelard's work has been offered more recently by Blamires, "*Caput a femina, membra viris*," 57–58: "There was no foundational genealogy comparable to that which Abelard had constructed to link a highly educated nun with august female philosophical-monastic forebears. And that was why, if her husband would not respond to her emotionally, the next best thing was to challenge him (albeit strategically on behalf of 'all' the Paraclete nuns) to console her by formulating an imaginary *auctoritas* for the identity as nun into which he has rushed her at their crisis"

48. For Abelard's sources here, see Buytaert, *Opera*, 1:327.

49. "Et ideo locus hic duo pariter docet et haberi, ut diximus, feminas ministras in Ecclesia, et tales debere sumi in ministerium, quae astiterint multis, et per bona officia usque ad apostolicam laudem meruerint pervenire" (*Enarrationum in epistolas beati Pauli*, PL 111:1606A-B).

50. "*Quae est in ministerio Ecclesiae*. Sicut etiam nunc in Orientalibus locis diaconissae mulieres in suo sexu ministrare videntur in baptismo sive in ministerio verbi, quia privatim docuisse feminas invenimus, sicut Priscilla, cujus vir Aquila vocabatur: hi duo caesum Paulum virgis, vino oleoque, et aliis rebus medicati sunt. Hanc ministram esse Ecclesiae Cenchris ait: et quia multis adjutorio fuit, etiam ipsa ad adjuvandum peregrinationis causa dicitur" (*Collectanea in omnes B. Pauli epistolas, In epistolam ad Romanos*, PL 103:124A). "*Mulieres similiter pudicas*. Similiter eas ut diaconos eligi jubet. Unde intelligitur quod de his dicat, quas adhuc hodie in Oriente diaconissas appellant" (*Collectanea in omnes B. Pauli epistolas, In epistolam ad Timotheum 1*, PL 103:234B).

51. "Cenchris autem est portus Corinthi, siue ut alii dicunt, uicus iuxta Corinthum, in cuius ecclesia Phoeben significat diaconissam fuisse. Adhuc enim fertur in partibus Graecorum diaconissas mulieres ministrare, quibus nec baptizandi usus nec priuatim ministerium uerbi denegatur" (Rom. 16:1–2, in G. de Martel, ed., *Expositiones Pauli epistolarum ad Romanos, Galathas et Ephesios, ad Romanos*, CCCM 151 [Turnhout: Brepols, 1995], 153).

52. "Docet etiam feminas locus iste apostolica auctoritate in ministerio ecclesiae constitui, in quo positam Phoeben Apostolus nunc magna laude commendat, enumerans etiam gesta ejus praeclara, et dicens quia intantum omnibus astitit, et in necessitatibus praesto fuit, ut etiam mihi ipsi in necessitatibus meis apostolicis devotione mentis astiterit" (*Commentaria in epistolas divi Pauli, Expositio in epistolam ad Romanos, PL* 181:806C-D). On Herveus, see Gary Macy, *Theologies of the Eucharist in the Early Scholastic Period* (Oxford: Clarendon Press, 1984), 68 and n212.

53. "Hi ergo *adjutores ejus in Christo,* id est in Christi praedicatione, quia recte crediderant, et apostolici laboris se socios fecerant, ut et ipsi hortarentur caeteros ad fidem rectam, denique Apollo quamvis exercitatus esset in Scripturis, ab his tamen in via Domini diligentius est instructus. . . . De quibus et hoc fortasse potest intelligi, quod ex septuaginta duobus discipulis Domini fuerint, qui et apostoli jure nominantur" (*Expositio in epistolam ad Romanos, PL* 181:807B–D).

54. "*Mulieres,* id est diaconissas, *similiter* ut diacones, oportet esse *pudicas,* ut munditia castitatis in eis regnum teneat, *non detrahentes,* id est non quaerentes loquendo minuere bonam famam alicujus, sed *sobrias,* id est ab omni ebrietate immunes, et *fideles in omnibus,* dictis et factis suis, ut fidem Deo servent et hominibus" (*Expositio in epistolam ad Romanos, PL* 181:1424B-C).

55. "*Mulieres* etc. Loquendo de diacones interserit de mulieribus quas appelaverit diaconas que scilicet presbyteris ministrant sicut apostolis et ipsi domino ministrare solebant. Has ergo monet eligi similiter sicut et diacones" (London, British Library, Royal MS 2.F.i, fol. 42r1). This commentary has been identified as that of Gilbert by Friedrich Stegmüller, *Repertorium biblicum medii aevi* 2 (Madrid: Consejo Superior, 1950), 359. This exemplar, however, also contains the teaching of the Ambrosiaster gloss, identified in the margin as that of Ambrose: "Qui sanctum precipit creari episcopum atque diaconum plebem quoque vult esse non disparem iuxta illud quod dominus ait. Sancti estote quoniam ego sanctus sum (Lev. xi. 44). Ideoque et mulieres quoniam inferiores sunt vult sine crimine esse ut munda sit ecclesia. Horum verborum occasione quia scilicet ubi de diaconis agit de mulieribus loquitur, diaconas dicunt debere ordinari quod nulla auctoritas habet" (Royal MS 2.F.i, fol. 42r1). On the teaching of the Ambrosiaster, see pp. 129–30 above.

56. See chapter 2, pp. 51–52 above.

57. Ivo of Chartres, *Sermo* 2, *PL* 162:514B–516A. Hugh of St. Victor, *De sacramentis ecclesiae christianae,* 3, 6–10, *PL* 176:424A–426B. On the influence of these two texts, see Colish, *Peter Lombard,* 2:614–28.

58. C. 198–c. 216, in *Magistri Gandulphi Bononiensis Sententiarum Libri Quatuor,* ed., Ioannes de Walter (Vienna and Breslau: Aemilius Hain, 1924), 498–506.

59. *Speculum de mysteriis ecclesie,* 5, *PL* 177:350A–B. On the *Speculum,* see chapter 2, n120.

60. Bk. 4, *distinctio.* 24, c. 2–c. 9, in *Sententiae,* 2:394–400.

61. For a clear and succinct discussion of the development of canon law as well as the dating of the works of the canonists, see James Brundage, *Medieval Canon Law* (London: Longman, 1995), 44–69.

62. "Diaconissam non debere ante annos quadraginta ordinari statuimus, et hoc cum diligenti probatione. Si uero susceperit ordinationem, et quantocumque tempore obseruauerit ministerium, et postea se nuptiis tradiderit, iniuriam faciens gratiae Dei, hec anathema sit cum eo, qui in illius nuptiis conuenerit" (Friedberg, *Corpus* 1:1055; English translation in Raming, *Priestly Office*, 20). This law is included in the earliest text of the *Decretum* by Winroth, *Making of Gratian's Decretum*, 222.

63. "Si quis rapuerit, uel sollicitauerit, uel corruperit assistriam, uel diaconissam, uel monastriam, uel aliam mulierem religiosam uitam uel habitum habentem, bona ipsius, et eorum, qui huius sceleris conmunione contaminati sunt, religioso loco uendicentur, in quo talis mulier habitabat, per religiosos episcopos, et yconomos, et presides prouinciarum, et offitiales eorum: ipsi autem capitali periculo subiciantur. Mulier autem ubique inuestigetur, et cum suis rebus monasterio cautiori tradatur. Sin autem diaconissa fuerit liberos habens legitimos, pars legitima liberis eius prestetur" (*causa 27, questio* 1, c. 30 in Friedberg, *Corpus*, 1:1057). This law is included in the later texts of the *Decretum* by Winroth, *Making of Gratian's Decretum*, 222. "De persona presbiteri hoc attendendum est, si quam causam habuerit, non ab alio teneri, sed episcopus ipsius adiri debuit, sicut nouellarum constitutio manifestat, que ita loquitur de sanctissimis et Deo amabilibus, ac reuerentissimis episcopis et clericis ac monachis: 'Inp. Augustus Iustinianus Petro gloriosissimo prefecto pretorio capitulo LIII. Si quis contra aliquem clericum aut monachum, aut diaconissam, aut monastriam, aut assistriam habet aliquam actionem, doceat prius sanctissimum episcopum, cui horum unusquisque subiaceat. Ille uero causam inter eos diiudicet. Et si quidem utraque pars his, que iudicata sunt, non adquieuerit iubemus per loci iudicem executioni perfecte contradi.' Ne uero obiciatur, quia hoc de clerico loquitur, non de presbitero, sciendum est, quia superius in eadem constitutione libro L. capitulo 1. legitur appellatione clericorum etiam presbiteros et diacones contineri. Verba autem legis ista sunt: 'Presbiteros autem et diaconos, et lectores et cantores, quos omnes clericos appellamus,' et reliqua" (*causa* 11, *questio* 1, c. 38, in Friedberg, *Corpus*, 1:637). This law is included in the earliest text of the *Decretum* by Winroth, *Making of Gratian's Decretum*, 222, only up to the words "executioni perfecte contradi." The rest of the text was added later. The second text is actually a letter of Gregory the Great that quoted the Justinian law. For a discussion of these texts, see Raming, *Priestly Office*, 22; and Aimé Georges Martimort, *Les Deaconesses: Essai historique* (Rome: Edizione Liturgiche, 1982), 109–12. English translations of these laws are provided by Kevin Madigan and Carolyn Osiek, *Ordained Women in the Early Church: A Documentary History* (Baltimore: Johns Hopkins Press, 2005), 128–29.

64. The story is of a priest who separated from his *presbytera* and lived with her as a sister. For the text and a discussion of this reference, see chapter 3, p. 86 and ns55–56. Gratian commented on this text, "Presbiteram uero quam debeamus accipere, Laudicense Concilium [c. II.] ostendit, dicens." The text of the Council of Laodicea follows (Friedberg, *Corpus*, 1:122). This law is included in the earliest text of the *Decretum* by Winroth, *Making of Gratian's Decretum*, 200.

65. See chapter 3, p. 59 above. This law was included only in the later texts of the *Decretum* according to Winroth, *Making of Gratian's Decretum*, 222.

66. A thorough examination of the sources used by the *Decretum* would be necessary to determine whether Gratian or his sources deliberately excluded references to the ministry of women or whether these sources were simply not available to eleventh- and twelfth-century scholars. Such an investigation goes beyond the scope of this study but would be an important contribution to the history of women's ministries in Western Christianity.

67. "Antiquitus (*recte:* Antiquitus) diaconisssas i. e., evangeliorum lectrices in ecclesiis ordinari moris fuisse, dubium non est, quarum nulla ante quadragesimum annum ordinari debebat, nec post ordinationem matrimonium eis contrahere ullomodo licebat" (*causa* 27, *questio* 1, in *Summa Magistri Rolandi*, ed., Friedrich Thaner [1874: repr. Aalen: Scientia Verlag, 1972], 121).

68. "Antiquitus ordinabantur in ecclesiis diaconisse, i. e., evangeliorum lectrices, que quia modo non sunt in ecclesia, forsitan dicemus eas abbatissas et iste ante quadragesimum annum ordinari non debent" (text given by Gillmann, "Weibliche Kleriker," 244n3). This passage does not appear in the edition of Stephen by Friedrich von Schulte, *Summa des Stephanus Tornacensis über das Decretum Gratiani* (Giessen: Verlag von Emil Roth, 1891). Gillmann used MS. Cod. Bamburg. Patr. 118 [B. III. 21] to complete von Schulte's text. See also "Idem possit dicere de quolibet inferiori ordine. Set de hoc dicit, quia forte videtur, quoniam antiquitus fiebant diaconisse, qui ordo hodie in ecclesia non est" (text given by Gillmann, "Weibliche Kleriker," 244n5).

69. "In primitiva ecclesia permittebatur quibusdam sanctimonialibus legere evangelium, que diaconisse vocabantur, quod hodie non fit" (text given by Gillmann, "Weibliche Kleriker," 244n4).

70. "(Manus impositio) consecratoria religionis soli episcopo conpetit et est sacramentum et certis temporibus fieri debet" (text given by Gillmann, "Weibliche Kleriker," 245n2).

71. "Cum sit sacramentum, regulariter non iteratur" (text given by F. Gillmann, "Die Seibenzahl der Sacramente bei den Glossatoren des Gratianischen Decrets," *Der Katholik: Zeitschrift für katholische Wissenschaft und kirchliches Leben* 89 [1909]: 190n1). The *Summa Monacensis* described four kinds of impositions of hands in consecration and the consecration of religious parallels that of the consecration of priests and deacons. "V. videntur genere (manus impositiones), consecratoria, confirmatoria, reconciliatoria, curatoria, bendictoria. Consecratoria alia ordines, alia dignitatis, alia religionis. Consecratoria ordinis conpetit soli episcopo, quoniam manus in hac consecratoria non inponitur nisi diacono et sacerdoti, qui ab episcopo debent fieri.... Utrumque constat sacramentum et fieri debent IIII. temporibus" (ibid.).

72. Sicard described three kinds of impositions of hands under the rubric "consecratoria." "Dignitatis, ut in episcopis.... Religionis, ut in monialibus.... Ordinis, ut in sacerdotibus." Sicard added: "Et nota, quod tantum [sola] confirmatoria et consecratoria sunt proprie sacramenta ideoque nequeunt iterari" (text given by Gillmann, "Die Seibenzahl," 201n2).

73. The entire passage reads: "Quid si iudeus vel gentilis ordines et dignitatis acceperit consecrationem? R(espondent) quidam, quod esset episcopus. Econtra quod si mulier consecraretur. Item quod foris est, quomodo ordinabatur? Item nonne si

seruus daret sentenciam, retractaretur?" (text given by Raming, *Ausschluss*, 99n132).
The second edition of Ida Raming, *Der Ausschluss der Frau vom priesterlichen Amt;*
gottgewollte Tradition oder Diskriminierung? Eine rechtshistorisch-dogmatische Untersu-
chung der Grundlagen von Kanon 968 1 des Codex Iuris Canonici, contained in Raming,
Priesteramt, is an exact reproduction with the same pagination as the original.
References will be given therefore to the original edition of 1973. English translation
in Raming, *Priestly Office*, 110–111n132. Raming, *Priestly Office*, 87–88, offers further
evidence to indicate that Sicard would not accept the validity of women's orders.

74. Wolfgang Müller, *Huguccio: The Life, Works, and Thought of a Twelfth-Century*
Jurist, Modern Studies in Canon Law 3 (Washington, DC: The Catholic University of
America, 1994), 67–108, suggests a *terminus ad quem* of 1188 with some later
additions. "Alii dicunt, quod olim mulier ordinabatur usque ad diaconatum, postea
fuit prohibitum tempore Ambrosii, postea iterum ordinabantur tempore huius
concilii (the Council of Chalcedon), nunc non ordinantur" (text given in Raming,
Ausschluss, 104n157; English translation in Raming, *Priestly Office*, 112n157).

75. "Alii dicunt, quod si Monialis ordinetur, bene recipit characterem (ordinis):
quia ordinari (questio) facti est et post baptismum quilibet potest ordinari" (text given
in Raming, *Ausschluss*, 115; English translation in Raming, *Priestly Office*, 95).

76. "Satis mirandum ducimus, quomodo concilium dicaonissas post annos XL
statuat ordinanadas, cum Ambrosius dicat diaconas ordinari esse contra auctoritatem.
Ait enim, in epistol. [I] ad Timotheum super illum locum 'Mulieres similiter pudicas'
etc. 'Occasione horum verborum Catafrige dicunt diaconas debere ordinari, quod est
contra auctoritatem.' Sed aliud est eas ordinari sacramento tenus ad altaris officium,
sicut ordinantur diacones: quod quidem prohibetur: aliud ad aliquod aliud ecclesie
minsterium: quod hic permittitur. Hodie tamen huiusmodi diaconisse in ecclesia non
inveniuntur, sed fort loco earum abbatisse ordinantur" (*causa 28, questio 1, c. 23* in
Rufinus von Bologna (Magister Rufinus), Summa Decretorum, ed. Heinrich Singer
[1902; repr. Paderborn: Scientia Verlag Aalen, 1963], 437; English translation from
Raming, *Priestly Office*, 102–3nn65, 70). The anonymous commentary on the *Decretum*
known as the *Summa Parisiensis* was written c. 1160–70 and followed Rufinus in
teaching that "Mulieres. Non debet ordinari ut clerici" (*Distinctio 32, c. 19* in *The*
Summa Parisiensis on the Decretum Gratiani, ed. Terence P. McLaughlin [Toronto: The
Pontifical Institute of Mediaeval Studies, 1952], 32).

77. "Set quomodo dicit Calcedonense concilium diaconissas debere ordinari,
cum Ambrosius, qui precessit, dicat hoc esse contra autoritatem super illum locum
apostoli in prima epistola ad Timotheum" (text given in Raming, *Ausschluss*, 103n153).
"Set ordinabantur diaconisse, i.e. eligebantur et quadam sollempnitate constitue-
bantur ad aliquod officium, quod conpetit diaconis. Forte cantabant et dicebant
evangelium in matutinis et orationem et tale officium et talis prelatio dicebantur
diaconatus" (ibid., n154). "Tale officium nunc explent abbatissas in quibusdam locis
nec modo tales diaconisse apud nos inveniuntur, nisi quis dicat abbatissas esse loco
earum et de tali ordinatione loquitur concilium Calcedonense, Ambrosius loquitur
de ordinatione ad ordines" (ibid., n155). "Velo ordinationis, i.e. non ordinentur, ut sint
diaconisse. Solebant enim olim quedam monace ordinari in diaconissas, non quoad

ordinem, sed quoad ministerium, ut in matutino in lectionibus annuncient evangelium vel aliud consimile. Set modo non fit, set sine speciali institutione adhuc
quedam monace in quibusdam locis in matutino annunitiat evangelium" (ibid.,
104n156; English translation in Raming, *Priestly Office*, 112nn.153–56).

78. See n74 above.

79. "Set dico, quod mulier ordinem accipere non potest. Quid inpedit? Constitutio ecclesie et sexus, i.e. constitutio ecclesie facta propter sexum. Si ergo de facto
ordinetur femina, non accipit ordinem, unde prohibetur exercere officia ordinum"
(text given in Gillmann, "Weibliche Kleriker," 246n5; and Raming, *Ausschluss*,
105n158). Gillmann and Raming used different manuscripts of Huguccio's work.
English translation from Raming, *Priestly Office*, 112n158.

80. "Si ergo magis calet in feminam quam in virum, non recipit ordinem, si
econverso, recipere potest. Set non debet ordinari propter deformitatem et mon-
struositatem" (text given in Gillmann, "Weibliche Kleriker," 247n1; and Raming,
Ausschluss, 105n159; English translation from Raming, *Priestly Office*, 113n159).

81. "Sexus est de substantia ordinis, quia mulieres benedicuntur, non ordinantur, licet inveniatur, quod aliquando fuerunt diaconisse. Set in alio sensu dicebantur
diaconisse quam hodie diaconus. Nunquam enim habuit femina illud officium, quod
modo habet diaconus" (text given in Gillmann, "Weibliche Kleriker," 250n1; and
Raming, *Ausschluss*, 110n170; English translation from Raming, *Priestly Office*,
115n.170.

82. For a discussion of Johannes's career, see Kenneth Pennington, *Johannnis
Teutonici Apparatus glossarum in Compilationem tertiam*, Monumenta iuris canonici,
ser. A, 3 (Vatican City: Biblioteca Apostolica Vaticana, 1981), xi–xiii.

83. "Respond(eo), quod mulieris testimonium non recipiunt characterem
(ordinis) impediente sexu et constitutione Ecclesiae" (text given by Raming, *Ausschluss*, 111n177; English translation from Raming, *Priestly Office*, 116n177).

84. "Unde nec officium ordinum exercere possunt, 23. dist. c. Sacratas (c. 25):
nec ordinabatur haec: sed fundabatur super eam forte aliqua benedictio, ex qua
consequebatur aliquod officium speciale, forte legendi homilias vel Euangelium ad
Matutinas, quod non licebat alii" (text given by Raming, *Ausschluss*, 111n178; English
translation from Raming, *Priestly Office*, 116n178).

85. See n74 above.

86. "Adde: tu dic quod (mulier) ordinari non potest ut supra dictum est, et est
ratio, quia ordo est perfectorum membrorum ecclesiae, cum detur ad collationem
gratiae in altero. Mulier autem non est perfectum membrum ecclesiae sed vir" (text
given by Raming, *Ausschluss*, 117n197; English translation from Raming, *Priestly Office*,
119n197).

87. "Quam continentiam bene conservavit presbyter ille, qui presbyteram suam,
i.e. uxorem, quam in minoribus ordinibus constitutus habuit, a tempore accepti
ordinis ad se propius accedere non sinebat. Vel presbyteras intelligimus conversas
ecclesiae, quae et matricuriae appellantur, quia gerunt curas, quas matres gerere
solent; vestimenta namque abluunt, panem conficiunt et coquinatum praeparant"
(*Distinctio 32*, in *Paucapalea, Summa über das Decretum Gratiani*, ed. Johann von

Schulte [1890; repr. Aalen: Scientia Verlag, 1965], 26; English translation from Raming, *Priestly Office*, 100n40).

88. "C. 18. presbyteram, uxorem suam, quam in minoribus duxerat ordinibus, vel aliter, ut in inferiori decreto legitur. c. 19. matriculae, vel secundam aliam literam matricuriae, conversae in ecclesia religiosae feminae, quasi curam matrum de ministris ecclesiae gerentes in vestimentis lavandi, panem faciendo, coquinatum parando" (*Distinctio* 32, in Schulte, *Die Summa des Stephanus*, 50).

89. "*Presbyteram*, vel convertam quae vivit de beneficio ecclesiae, vel quae fuit uxor ejus qui est presbyter" (McLaughlin, *Summa Parisiensis*, 32; English translation in Raming, *Priestly Office*, 107n111).

90. "Potest etiam uxor sacerdotis intelligi non quam in sacerdotio accepit, set quam laicus uel in minoribus sibi ordinibus copulavit, quam contempnere, idest a cura et prouisione sua separare prohibetur" (Pars 2, c. 26, in *Summa "Elegantius in iure diuino" seu Coloniensis*, ed. Gerard Fransen and Stephan Kuttner, 3 vols., Monumenta iuris canonici, series A, 1 [New York: Fordham University Press, 1969], 1:53). On the dating of this work, see ibid., 1:xi.

91. "Dicunt tamen et aliter presbitere grandeua mulieres ad religionem conuerse, quod ex Laodicensi concilio probatur" (ibid., 1:53).

92. "Dic quod non appellatur hec presbytera, eo quod esset ordinata: nam si mulier ordinaretur, non reciperet characterem impediente sexu et constitutione ecclesie, quamvis quidam contradicunt, prout no(tatur) (C.) 27 q. 1 Diaconissam (c. 23). Sed idcirco hec appellatur, quia est ordinati socia" (text given in Raming, *Ausschluss*, 119n201; English translation from Raming, *Priestly Office*, 120n210). The contrary opinion mentioned by Guido referred back to that included in the *Glossa ordinaria* of Johannes Teutonicus (see n74 above).

93. "Nova quaedam nuper, de quibus miramur non modicum, nostris sunt auribus intimata, quod abbatissae videlicet, in Burgensi et in Palentinensi dioecesibus constitutae, moniales proprias benedicunt, ipsarum quoque confessiones in crim-inibus audiunt, et legentes evangelium praesumunt publice praedicare. Quum igitur id absonum sit pariter et absurdum, [nec a nobis aliquatenus sustinendum,] discretioni vestrae per apostolica scripta mandamus, quatenus, ne id de cetero fiat, auctoritate curetis apostolica firmiter inhibere, quia, licet beatissima virgo Maria dignior et excellentior fuerit Apostolis universis, non tamen illi, sed istis Dominus claves regni coelorum commisit" (bk. 5, t. 38, c. 10, Friedberg, *Corpus*, 2: 886–87; English translation from Raming, *Priestly Office*, 143n8).

94. "Conceditur nobis ut possimus corrigere excessus monachorum seu monialium Ordinis nostri quilibet in suo monasterio vel in filiabus suis, prout sibi competit de jure. Non licet monialibus Ordinis aliquibus personis sive religiosis sive saecularibus confiteri, nisi solummodo parti abbati vel cui ipse in hoc commiserit vices suas.... Licet nobis moniales inobedientes et rebelles ab Ordinis separare, ac privilegiis ac indulgentiis Ordini concessis omnino privare" (Distinctio 2, c. 3, par. 9, *Libellus antiquarum definitionum ordinis Cisterciensis* in *Nomasticon Cisterciense*, ed. Julien Paris and Hugo Séjalon [Solesme: Typographeo Sancti Petri, 1892], 389). On the reliability of the collections of Paris, see Marcel Pacaut, *Les Moines Blancs: Histoire*

de l'Ordre de Cîteaux (Paris: Fayard, 1993), 9. On Innocent IV's decree, see Joan Morris, *The Lady Was a Bishop: The Hidden History of Women with Clerical Ordination and the Jurisdiction of Bishops* (New York: Macmillan, 1973), 87.

95. "De monialibus tua a nobis fraternitas requisivit, per quem eis sit beneficium absolutionis impendendum, si vel in se invicem vel conversos vel conversas suas, aut clericos etiam, *in suis monasteriis servientes,* manus iniecerint temere violentas. Super hoc igitur tuae consultationi taliter respondemus, ut *auctoritate nostra* per episcopum, in cuius dioecesi *earum* monasteria fuerint, absolvantur" (Friedberg, *Corpus,* 2:903; English translation in Raming, *Priestly Office,* 146n35).

96. On this process, see *ODCH* 1396 and *NCE* 6:496–98.

97. For the dating of this work and a summary of the life of Raymond, see Xaverio Ochoa and Aliosio Diez, eds., *S. Raimundus de Pennaforte, Summa de Paenitentia,* Universa Bibliotheca Iuris, 1/B (Rome: Commentarium pro religiosis, 1976), lxiii–lxxxiii.

98. "Unde notandum quod femina non potest recipere characterem alicuius ordinis clericalis. Ambrosius super illum locum Apostoli in prima epistola at Timotheum: 'Mulieres similiter oportet esse pudicas,' ait occassione horum verborum: 'Cathafrigae dicunt diaconissam debere ordinari, quod est veritati contrarium, quia mulieres characterem non recipiunt, impediente sexu et constitutione Ecclesiae; unde nec possunt praedicare, etiam abbatissae, nec benedicere, nec excommunicare, nec absolvere, nec paenitenitas dare, nec iudicare, nec officium aliquorum ordinum exercere, quantumcumque sint doctae, sanctae vel religiosae.' ... Quidam tamen mentiuntur adhuc cum Cathaphyrgis feminam recipere characterem, etiam diaconalem et presbyteralem. Inducunt pro se: 27 q. 1 *Diaconissam* [c. 23] et *Si quis rapuerit* [c. 30], in fine. In illis expresse videtur probare de ordine diaconali. De ordine presbyeralis probant per capitulum 32 dist. *Prebyter* [c. 18]. Sed illa capitula *Diaconissam* et *Si quis* vocant diaconissam illam super quam forte fundebatur aliqua benedictio, ratione cuius consequebatur aliquod speciale officium, forte legendi homiliam in matutinis, vel aliud, quod non licebat aliis monialibus. In illo autem capitulo *Presbyter* appellatur presbytera, quia erat uxor presbyteri, vel etiam vidua, vel matricuria, id est, de rebus Ecclesiae curam habens ad instar matris familias. Et ita exponit concilium Laudicense in sequenti capitulo eiusdem distinctionis" (Titulus 23 in Ochoa and Diez, *Summa de Paenitentia,* 655–56; English translation from Raming, *Priestly Office,* 148–49n61).

99. "The church of Rome quickly eliminated from its pontificals the ritual for the blessing of deaconesses, which it was perhaps alone in using. ... The ritual was not, of course, found either in the Pontifical of Innnocent III or that of Innocent IV" (Martimort, *Deaconesses,* 218). On the pontificals of the thirteenth and fourteenth centuries, see Cyrille Vogel, *Medieval Liturgy: An Introduction to the Sources,* rev. and trans. William Storey and Neils Rasmussen (Washington, DC: Pastoral Press, 1986), 252–55.

100. According to Gillmann ("Weibliche Kleriker," 252n1), both Vincent of Beauvais (*Speculum historiale* [1254]), and John of Frieburg (*Summa confessorum* [1280/98]) copied Raymond's commentary.

101. "Mulier enim nec praedicare, nec docere potest, quia hoc officium extra-neum est a mulieribus, nec sacra vasa contingere...nec possunt velare moniales... nec absolvere eas...nec iudicare, nisi forte aliqua nobilis hoc habeat ex consue-tudine...nec arbitrium in se suscipere...nec procuratrix esse potest in iudicio...nec advocare potest in iudicio...et generaliter viri officium mulieribus est interdictum" (text given in Raming, *Ausschluss*, 140n79; English translation in Raming, *The Priestly Office*, 151n79).

102. For a summary of this teaching, see Raming, *Priestly Office*, 129–60; idem., *Ausschluss*, 134–61.

103. Jo Ann McNamara described the process by which the Gregorian reforms created "a womanless space" by looking at the role of women just before and during the early years of the reform. My own conclusions are very similar to hers. The argument is made in Jo Ann McNamara, "Canossa and the Ungendering of the Public Man," in *Medieval Religion: New Approaches*, ed. Constance Berman (New York: Routledge, 2005). See, for example, "The assumption, being henceforth fixed in the mysterious 'nature of things,' was that women could not perform sacramental functions. This assured men of a zone of 'liberty' from female interference and sexuality outside the gender system" (ibid., 110).

104. "Ideoque etiam mulieres quae in infimo gradu sunt, vult esse sine crimine ut munda sit Ecclesia. Sed Cataphrygae occasione horum verborum, quia, scilicet ubi de diaconis agit, de mulieribus loquitur, dicunt diaconas debere ordinari: quod contra auctoritatem est" (*Collectanea in epistolas Pauli, In epistolam I ad Timothaeum, PL* 192:346A).

105. "Modus talis: Primo salutat eum, deinde monet, ut pseudoapostolis resistat, postea instruit de episcopali officio docens quales debeat ordinare presbyteros et diacones, et quales debeant esse mulieres eorum; deinde quales viduas recipere debeat; postea de modo correctionis instruit eum" (ibid., *PL* 192:326D).

106. "Id est de ordinibus, nil hic dicendum eo quod decretistis disputatio de his potius quam theologis deservit" (bk. 4, c. 14, *PL* 211:1257b). See Martin, "Ordination of Women," 1:125. English translation in *A History of Women and Ordination*, vol. 1, *The Ordination of Women in a Medieval Context*, ed. Bernard Cooke and Gary Macy (New York: Scarecrow Press, 2002), 39.

107. "Si autem quaeritur quid sit quod hic vocatur ordo, sane dici potest signaculum quoddam esse, id est sacrum quiddam, quo spiritualis potestas traditur ordinatio et officium. Character igitur spiritualis, ubi fit promotio potestatis, ordo vel gradus vocatur" (bk. 4, dist. 24, c. 13 in *Senteniae* 2:405).

108. On the background of Lombard's definition, see Kenan Osborne, *Priesthood: A History of the Ordained Ministry in the Roman Catholic Church* (Mahwah, NJ: Paulist Press, 1988), 205; Colish, *Peter Lombard*, 2:614–21; and Nikolaus Häring, "Character, Signum und Signaculum: Der Weg von Petrus Damiani bis zur eigentlichen Aufnahme in der Sakramentenlehre im 12. Jahrhundert," *Scholastik* 31 (1956): 41–69, 182–212

109. "Ordo est caracter, quo spiritualis potestas et officium traditur ei qui ordinatur" (quoted in Ludwig Ott, *Das Weihesakrament*, Handbuch der

Dogmengeschichte, nos. 4, 5 (Freiburg: Herder, 1969), 48n4). On Sicard and his commentary on Gratian, see *NCE* 13:100–102.

110. Ott, *Weihesakrament*, 48–49; so reads the passage from passage from Praepositinus: "Unde dicimus, quod ordo est quoddam signaculum, quod confertur ordinatio, sine quo esse non potest." Ott does not believe Lombard intented to ascribe an indelible character to ordination. Osborne, *Priesthood*, 205, follows Ott in this interpretation.

111. "Videtur enim quod imprimatur character in consecratione episcopi, cum ibi fit chrismatis in vertice inunctio: qua ratione enim in confirmatione et baptismo, eadem ratione et in episcopi consecratione" (c. 185, *Tractatus de Sacramentis* in *Guididonis de Orchellis, Tractatus de Sacramentis ex Eius Summa de Sacramentis et Officis Ecclesiae*, ed. Damian and Odulf Van den Eynde, Franciscan Institute Publications, text series, 4 [Louvain: Nauwelaerts, 1953], 176). On Guido and his work, see ibid., v–xlvii.

112. "Consuetudine ecclesiae: quia, cum talis sacerdos ad ecclesiam rediit, non ei iterum illa potest datur—alioquin iterum ordinaretur, quod facere ecclesia non consuevit: non ergo, cum ab eccleisa recessit, illam potestatem perdidit.... Eadem ratione, si iste in heresi—quasi furtim et non militans in ecclesia—baptizando impresserit alicui signum regis nostri, scil. Christi, caracterem utique militie christiane, non est illud sacramentum repetendum, sed approbandum: si baptisma, quod recedens dedit, non esset repetendum, tunc potestatem dandi baptisma non perdidit" (*causa* 1, *questio* 1, c. 97 in Singer, *Summa*, 219. See Franz Gillmann, "Der 'sakramentale Charakter' bei den Glossatoren Rufinus, Johannes Faventinus, Sicard von Cremona, Huguccio und in der Glossa ordinaria des Dekrets," *Der Katholik: Zeitschrift für katholische Wissenschaft und kirchliches Leben* 90 (1910): 301–2.

113. "Est enim potestas aptitudinis in caractere sacramenti. Hanc vero nunquam perdimus" (quoted by Gillmann, "Der 'sakramentale Charakter' bei den Glossatoren," 303).

114. "*Quod quidam* usque *tamen quod accipit amittit.* Hic solet in questione descendere quare sacerdos catholicus in heresim lapsus sacrificandi potestatem amittit cum potestatem baptizandi sibi retineat, quod sic probatur: quia redderetur illa potestas baptizandi redeunti si eam amisisset recedens" (*causa* 1, *questio* 1, c. 97 in *Summa Simonis Bisinianensis*, ed. Peter Aimone [online edition at http: //www .unifr.ch/cdc/summa_simonis_de.php] [Fribourg, 2003], 123). Aimone dates this work between 1177 and 1179.

115. "Sic si baptisma vel ordo furtim et extra ecclesiam alicui confertur, cum redire vult, non ei auferetur illud signaculum nec repetitur, set eo approbato sociatur collegio fidelium.... Sic qui in heresi acciperet caracterem Christi scil. baptisma vel ordinem et non ab ecclesia, si postea revertitur, caracter ille non improbatur nec inmutatur, set ipso conprobato et remanente ille ceteris fidelibus iungitur, ut de cetero in ecclesia militet" (quoted by Franz Gillmann, "Der 'sakramentale Charakter' bei den Glossatoren," 304n3).

116. "Remanet ergo post mortem sacramentum baptismi. Idem dico de quolibet sacramento, in quo confertur gratia, ut de ordine, de unctione crismatis et de

omnibus, que habentur gratia anime" (quoted by Franz Gillmann, "Der 'sakramentale Charakter' bei den Glossatoren," 306n2). On Huguccio's teaching on this issue, see ibid., 303–310.

117. "Potest dici, quod quoddam signaculum, quod in ipsa unctione (extrema) confertur, sacramentum est, et tamen non oportet, quod semper maneat. Tantum enim tria sacramenta hoc habent scil. baptismus, confirmatio et ordo" (quoted by Franz Gillmann, "Der 'sakramentale Charakter' bei den Glossatoren," 311n3). On Huguccio's teaching on this issue, see ibid., 310–311.

118. The classic study of the debate over the irreversibility of orders among the eleventh-century and twelfth-century canonists is Louis Saltet, *Les Réordinations: Étude sur le Sacrement de l'Ordre* (Paris: Libraire Victor Lecoffre, 1907).

119. "Quid sit, quod vocatur ordo? Dicitur tamen, quod est quibusdam character spiritualis, id est, discretio, qua discernitur ordinatus a non ordinato. De hoc character solet queri, utrum semel susceptus aliquo modo adimatur. Hec questio decretalis est. Quidam concedunt et probabilius, quidam non" (quoted by Franz Gillmann, "Der 'sakramentale Charakter' bei Petrus Poitiers und bei Stephen Langton," *Der Katholik: Zeitschrift für katholische Wissenschaft und kirchliches Leben*, 93 [1913]: 75). See Ott, *Weihesakrament*, 72.

120. "Ordo siquidem caracter est inseparabilis, ut aiunt plerique. Sed numquid episcopus aufert ordines homicide clerico et puniendum tradit iudici seculari? Non aufert. Ergo secularis iudex potestatem habet in clericum adhuc habentem ordines suos. In quo videtur clericorum ordines derogare. Ideo dicunt alii ordinem esse separabilem et auferri" (quoted by Gillmann, "Der 'sakramentale Charaker' bei Petrus Poitiers," 75n6). See Ott, *Weihesakrament*, 72–73.

121. "Hic notandum est, quod etiam presbiter degradatus sicut excommunicatus, sicut presbiter esse non desinit, sic et quod facit factum, et quod consecrat consecratum est. Reprehendi et cogi quidem debet, ne contra Ecclesie statutum contumaciter faciat. Sed quod consecravit, non ulterius consecrandum est. Sive ergo corpus et sanguinem consecraverit, sive baptismum alicui contulerit, quod fecit, ratum erit nec iterari debebit, licet ipse consecrando et baptizando peccaverit" (*De sacramentis*, in *Maitre Simon et son group De sacramentis*, ed. Henri Weisweiler, Spicilegium Sacrum Lovaniense, Études et Documents 17 [Louvain: Spicilegium Sacrum Lovaniense, 1937], 70; see also pp. 78–81). See Ott, *Weihesakrament*, 72.

122. "Et intelligendum est quod caracter ordinis datur super caracterem baptismi. Et sicut in baptismo est caracter et ablutio exterior que significat interiorem, similiter in ordine datur caracter; et est aliquid exterius, quod est signum illius quod datur interius, sicut traditio clavium vel libri vel aliqua unctio exterior. Et sicut caracter in baptismo signum est discretionis, similiter caracter in ordine signum est excellencie" (bk. 4, *tractatus* 16, c. 1 in *Magistri Guillelmi Atlissiodorensis, Summa Aurea*, 5 vols., ed. Jean Ribaillier, Spicilegium Bonaventurianum 16–20 [Rome: Collegii S. Bonaventurae ad Claras Aquas, 1982–87], 4:368–69). On William and the *Summa Aurea*, see ibid., 5:3–24.

123. "Et licet ordo sacerdotalis dignissimus sit quantum ad dignitatem rei consecrate, tamen episcopatus dignior est quantum ad causalitatem. Episcopus enim

dat potestatem sacerdoti consecrandi corpus et sanguinem Domini" (bk. 4, *tractatus* 16, c. 2 in Ribaillier, *Summa Aurea*, 4: 372). See Ott, *Weihesakrament*, 50–51.

124. On Alexander's life and work, see *Magistri Alexandri de Hales, Glossa in Quatuor Libros Sententiarum Petri Lombardi*, 4 vols., Bibliotheca Franciscana Scholastica Medii Aevi 12–15 (Florence: Collegii S. Bonaventurae, 1951–57), 1:*7–*75.

125. "Respondemus: per hanc definitionem separatur Ordo ab aliis sacramentis. Per hoc enim quod dicitur 'signaculum,' separatur ab aliis sacramentis in quibus non imprimitur character. Per hoc autem quod dicitur 'in quo spiritualis potestas traditur,' distinguitur ab iis in quibus character tantum imprimitur: non enim in Baptismo et Confirmatione spiritualis potestas traditur super membra Ecclesiae. Per hoc autem quod dicitur 'et officium,' intelligitur quod non tantum tradatur potestas, sed executio potestatis, quantum est de virtute Ordinis, licet aliter contingat ex inidoneitate personae" (bk. 4, dist. 24 in Alexander of Hales, *Glossa*, 4: 400.

126. "Potest autem assignari altera definitio Ordinis, ex qua magis potest perpendi quis sit Ordo et quis non. Et est talis: Ordo est sacramentum spiritualis potestatis ad aliquod officium ordinatum in Ecclesia ad sacramentum communionis" (ibid., 4:401). On the importance of this definition, see Osborne, *Priesthood*, 204, whose translation is used here.

127. "Ex quod perpenditur: cum potestas Ordinis sacramentalis sit ad sacramentum communionis, et hoc pertineat ad Ordinem sacerdotalem, in eo debet stare omnis Ordo. Dignitas vero episcopalis, quae superadditur, est ratione causarum, et quia ibi suppletur potestas Domini in conferendo Ordinem sacerdotalem" (bk. 4, *distinctio* 24, in Alexander of Hales, *Glossa*, 4:401).

128. "Unde cum Beatus Thomas Cantuariensis archyepiscopus elevasset sanctum Cubertum de terra in feretrum et cum palpasset singulos eius articulos et faciem et omnia eius membra que nullam senserant putredinem eo quod vir ille virgo semper exicerat. Rex illius regni qui presens erat quisivit a beato Thoma qua presumptione ita palparet omnia membra sancti, qui respondit, 'Rex super hoc non debes mirari si manibus meis consecratis hunc tango.' Quia longe preeminentius sacramentum sicut et alii sacerdotes singulis diebus in altari tracto videlicet corpus domini sacratissimum cuius corporis ministerium commissum est tribus ordinibus ministrorum scilicet presbytero, dyacono et subdyacono sicut ostendit Clemens papa in secunda distinctio, de consecratione, capitulo 'Tribus gradibus' (c. 23)" (*Summa*, Bruges MS 247, fol. 143r1–r2). The law Robert cited is from the *Decretum*, in Friedberg, *Corpus*, 1:1321. Gratian's source here was the Pseudo-Isidorian Decretals; see Paul Hinschius, ed., *Decretales Pseudo-Isidoriana* (1863); repr. Aalen: Scientia Verlag, 1963), 47.

129. For a discussion of the adoption of this understanding of the sacrament of orders by later theologians, see Ott, *Weihesakrament*, 73–11; and Osborne, *Priesthood*, 204–18.

130. On the Fishacre's life and work, see R. James Long and Maura O'Carroll, *The Life and Works of Richard Fishacre, OP: Prolegomena to the Edition of his Commentary on the* Sentences, Bayerische Adademie der Wissenschaften, Veröffentlichungen der Kommission für die Herausgabe ungedruckter Texte aus de mittelalterlichen

Geisteswelt 21 (Munich: Verlag der Bayerische Adademie der Wissenschaften, 1999), 15–37.

131. "Hic et sequitur, quot sunt de necessitate huius sacramenti de quo sciendum, quod plura. Primum est sexus virilis, unde mulier non est susceptibilis ordinis" (quoted from Martin, "Ordination of Women," 1:144n65; English translation in Cooke and Macy, *History,* 1:144n65).

132. "Si queritur de monialibus que dicuntur diaconisse: Respondeo, non sic dicuntur quia communicent cum diacono in ordine, sed tantum in aliquo eius officii, scilicet quia licenciantur ad legendum Evangelium et dictioni aliquo" (quoted from Martin, "Ordination of Women," 1:144n65; English translation in Cooke and Macy, *History,* 1:119n65).

133. "Et nota quod femina si ordinetur, nec suscipit characterem, nec est ordinata, et de impedimento sexu et constitutionis ecclesie. Unde non potest predicare, nec possunt abbatisse benedicere, nec excommunicare, nec absolvere, nec penetentias dare, nec iudicare, nec officium aliquorum ordinum exercere" (quoted from Martin, "Ordination of Women," 1:144n65; English translation in Cooke and Macy, *History,* 1:119n65).

134. See Martin, "Ordination of Women," 1:146–47; English translation in Cooke and Macy, *History,* 1:52–54).

135. Two exhaustive studies of the theological discussions of the ordination of women from the thirteenth through the sixteenth centuries are Martin, "Ordination of Women"; Cooke and Macy, *History,* 1:56–160); and Alastair Minnis, "*De impedimento sexus:* Women's Bodies and Medieval Impediments to Female Ordination," in *Medieval Theology and the Natural Body,* ed., Peter Biller and A. J. Minnis, York Studies in Medieval Theology 1 (York Medieval Press: York, 1997), 109–39.

CHAPTER 5

1. The reception of the changes of the Gregorian reform varied from region to region. On the implementation of celibacy, see the essays in Michael Frassetto, ed., *Medieval Purity and Piety: Essays on Medieval Clerical Celibacy and Religious Reform* (New York: Garland, 1998). For a recent discussion of the implementation of the larger reform agenda, see Gerd Tellenbach, *The Church in Western Europe from the Tenth to the Early Twelfth Century* (Cambridge: Cambridge University Press, 1993).

2. "Separation from women reinforced the dislike and fear fostered by monastic polemic. We are so accustomed to thinking of the medieval clergy as violently abusive towards women that we have missed a chronological subtlety. Clerical misogyny reached a crescendo between the mid-eleventh and the mid-twelfth centuries. The struggle to separate men from women caused reformers to rave against married priests and, by implication, the whole sexual act" (Jo Ann McNamara, "The Her-renfrage: The Restructuring of the Gender System, 1050–1150," in *Medieval Masculinities: Regarding Men in the Middle Ages,* Medieval Cultures, 7, ed. Claire Lees [Minneapolis: University of Minnesota Press, 1994], 8). See also Jo Ann McNamara

"Canossa and the Ungendering of the Public Man," in *Medieval Religion: New Approaches,* ed. Constance Berman (New York: Routledge, 2005), 112–16.

3. See, for example, Elizabeth Dachowski, "*Tertius est optimus:* Marriage, Continence, and Virginity in the Politics of Late Tenth- and Early Eleventh-Century Francia," in Frassetto, *Medieval Purity,* 117–25. On Abbo of Fleury, Dachowski remarks: "Abbo was particularly concerned with differentiating the clergy from the laity, because he saw a tendency in his own day for the laity to become like clergy, in possessing church property, and the clergy to become like laity, in being married" (p. 125).

4. An interesting study of the background to the stand of the reformers is contained in Phyllis Jestice, "Why Celibacy? Odo of Cluny and the Development of a New Sexual Morality," in Frassetto, *Medieval Purity,* 81–115.

5. See Anne Llewellyn Barstow, *Married Priests and the Reforming Papacy: The Eleventh-Century Debates,* Texts and Studies in Religion, 12 (New York: Edwin Mellon Press, 1982).

6. See Christopher Brooke, "Gregorian Reform in Action: Clerical Marriage in England, 1050–1200," *Cambridge Historical Journal* 12 (1956); and idem., "Married Men Among the English Higher Clergy, 1066–1200," *Cambridge Historical Journal* 12 (1956).

7. See Kathleen Cushing, *Papacy and Law in the Gregorian Revolution: The Canonistic Word of Anselm of Lucca* (Oxford: Clarendon Press, 1998), esp. 64–102; and Klaus Schatz, "The Gregorian Reform and the Beginning of a Universal Ecclesiology," *The Jurist* 57 (1997): 123–36.

8. For details, see chapter 3, pp. 78, 80–81, 85–86, 92–93. 105–6.

9. See Barstow, *Married Priests,* 47–104 and well as James Brundage, *Law, Sex and Christian Society in Medieval Europe* (Chicago: The University of Chicago Press, 1987), 214–23.

10. "Ad haec praedecessorum nostrorum Gregorii VII, Urbani et Paschlis Romanorum pontificum vestigiis inhaerentes, praecipimus ut nullus missas eorum audiat, quos uxores vel concubinas habere cognoverit. Ut autem lex continentiae et Deo placens munditia in ecclesiasticis personis et sacris ordinibus dilatetur, statuimus quatenus episcopi presbyteri diaconi subdiaconi regulares canonici et monachi atque conversi professi, qui sanctum trangredientes propositum uxores sibi copulare praesumpserint, separentur. Huiusmodi namque copulationem quam contra ecclesiasticam regulam constat esse contractam, matrimonium non esse censemus. Qui etiam ab invicem separati, pro tantis excessibus condignam poenitentiam agant." "Id ipsum quodque de sanctimonialibus feminis si, quod absit, nubere attentaverint, observari decernimus" (cs. 7 and 8 in Norman Tanner, ed., *Decrees of the Ecumenical Councils,* 2 vols. (Washington, DC: Georgetown University Press, 1990), 1:198. The text is also given in Mansi, 21:527–28

11. Brooke, "Gregorian Reform," 20–21; and Barstow, *Married Priests,* 102–4, 133–39. For an analysis of this change from an economic and social analysis see Robert I. Moore, *The First European Revolution, c. 970–1215* (Oxford: Blackwell, 2000), 81–88.

12. Among medieval scholars, however, the term *ecclesia* (church) when it was defined as all, described the society of all the just people who had ever lived, even if they were not Christian. On this more inclusive definition of the church, see Gary Macy, "The Eleonore and Nathaniel F. Philips, Sr. Memorial Lecture, An Old Perspective—The Church in the Middle Ages," in *Religions and the American Experience,* ed. Frank T. Birtel (Hyde Prk, NY: New York City Press, 2005), 133–51.

13. "Interea et vos alloquor, o lepores clericorum, pulpamenta diaboli, projectio paradisi, virus mentium, gladius animarum, aconita bibentium, toxica convivarum, materia peccandi, occasio pereundi. Vos inquam, alloquor gynecaea hostis antiqui, upupae, ululae, noctuae, lupae, sanguisugae, Affer, affer sine cessatione dicentes. Venite itaque, audite me, scorta, prostibula, savia, volutabra porcorum pinguium; cubilia spirituum immundorum, nymphae, sirenae, lamiae, dianae, et si quid adhuc portenti, si quid prodigii reperitur, nomini vestro competere judicetur. Vos enim estis daemonum victimae ad aeternae mortis succidium destinatae. Ex vobis enim diabolus, tanquam delicatis dapibus pascitur, vestrae libidinis exuberantia saginatur" (c. 7 of *Contra Intemperantes Clericos* in *PL* 145:410A-B; English translation by Barstow, *Married Priests,* 60–61). On Peter Damian's opinion of women, see also Dyan Elliott, "The Priest's Wife: Female Erasure and the Gregorian Reform," in *Medieval Religion: New Approaches,* ed. Constance Berman (New York: Routledge, 2005), 136–45.

14. On the misgynist language of the reformers, see Barstow, *Married Priests,* 47–104; and Elliott, "Priest's Wife," 136–45.

15. "Nam solum mulier menstruale animal est, cuius contactu sanguinis fruges non germinant, acescunt musta, moriuntur herbae, amittunt arbores fructus, ferrum rubigo corrumpit, nigrescunt aera; si canes inde ederint in rabiem efferuntur" (*distinctio* 5, in *Paucapalea, Summa über das Decretum Gratiani,* ed. Johann von Schulte (1890; repr Aalen: Scientia Verlag, 1965) 11; English translation by the author).

16. "Adeo autem execrabilis et immundus est sanguis ille, sicut ait Iulius Solinus in libro de mirabilibus mundi, ut eius contactu fruges non germinent, arescant arbusta, moriantur herbe, amittant arbores fetus, nigrescant era, si canes inde ederint in rabiem efferantur" (*distinctio* 5, c. 1, in *Rufinus von Bologna (Magister Rufinus), Summa Decretorum,* ed. Heinrich Singer [1902; repr. Paderborn: Scientia Verlag Aalen, 1963], 16; English translation in Ida Raming, *The Priestly Office of Women: God's Gift to a Renewed Church,* ed. Bernard Cooke and Gary Macy, vol. 2 of *A History of Women and Ordination* [Lanham, MD: Scarecrow Press, 2004], 104n84).

17. "As parientem, ut si mulier masculum pareret, XLta diebus ab ingressu templi veluti immunda cessaret: quia puerperium in immuditia conceptum dicitur XLta diebus informe; at si feminam, spatium temporis duplicaret: sanguis enim menstruus, qui partum comitatur, usque adeo censetur immundus, ut eius tactu, sicut Solimus ait, fuges arescant et herbae moriantur. Sed quare tempus pro femina duplicatur? Solutio: quia dupla est feminei germinis maledictio; habuit enim maledictionem Adae, et insuper, 'In dolore paries,' vel quia, sicut ait peritia physicorum, feminae in conceptu manent informes duplo tempore masculorum" (text in Raming, *Der Ausschluss der Frau vom priesterlichen Amt; gottgewollte Tradition oder Diskriminierung? Eine rechtshistorisch-dogmatische Untersuchung der Grundlagen*

von Kanon 968 1 des Codex Iuris Canonici [Cologne: Böhlau, 1973], 98–99,n130; English translation in Raming, *Priestly Office*, 109n130).

18. The incident is described in Barstow, *Married Priests*, 95–96. See also Elliott, "Priest's Wife," 142–43 for a similar opinion by Peter Damian.

19. See Barstow, *Married Priests*, 142–47.

20. "Secular men living ordinary procreative lives as prescribed by their religion heard women denounced as virulent agents of moral pollution, so contagious that prudent men must flee at their approach and shun all contact with them. Many reacted by seeking escape from the terrors of conjugal life, renouncing sex and the hierarchy that sex supported" (McNamara, *"Herrenfrage,"* 6; see also McNamara, "Canossa," 112–13).

21. On the popularity of religious orders in the twelfth century, see Giles Constable, *The Reformation of the Twelfth Century* (Cambridge: Cambridge University Press, 1996), 44–87. On the spread of the friars, see C. H. Lawrence, *The Friars: The Impact of the Early Medieval Mendicant Movement* (London: Longman, 1994), 102–12. The reasons why one might enter the religious life vary greatly, but if one wished to live the fullest Christian life possible, most medievals would agree that this would entail conversion to a religious order.

22. Robert Swanson, "Angels Incarnate: Clergy and Masculinity from Gregorian Reform to Reformation," in, *Masculinity in Medieval Europe*, ed. D. M. Hadley (London: Longman, 1999), 160–77. See also Jo Ann McNamara, "An Unresolved Syllogism: The Search for a Christian Gender System," in *Conflicted Identities and Multiple Masculinities: Men in the Medieval West*, ed. Jaqueline Murray (New York: Garland, 1999), 7: "Monastic practice did, however, abandon gender or attempted to join ascetic males and females in an elite third gender that superceded the old [male] hierarchy all together."

23. "The creation of a third gender depended on the painstaking elimination of sex, and monastics expected to complete the task only when they had abandoned the earth. But, with care, women and men collaborated in the missionary age on earth. They respected one anotehr as equals in prayer. In the apostolate and its monastic virtues they achieved a circumscribed but workable syneisactism in the wilderness" (Jo Ann McNamara, *Sisters in Arms: Catholic Nuns through Two Millennia* (Cambridge, MA: Harvard University Press, 1996), 147. See also McNamara, "Herrenfrage," 12–15.

24. Prudence Allen, *The Concept of Woman*, 2 vols. (Grand Rapids, MI: W. B. Eerdmans, 1997–2002), 1:408. Stephanie Hollis, (*Anglo-Saxon Women and the Church: Sharing a Common Fate* [Woodbridge, Suffolk: Boydell Press, 1992], 78–79, 258–9 and 261–2) records the existence of a number of important schools started and staffed by Anglo-Saxon nuns.

25. Marie Anne Mayeski, "Excluded by the Logic of Control: Women in Medieval Society and Scholastic Theology," in *Equal at the Creation: Sexism, Society, and Christian Thought*, ed. Joseph Martos and Pierre Hégy, (Toronto: University of Toronto Press, l998), 71.

26. Raming, *Ausschluss*, 62–74; *Priestly Office*, 34–40. Edward Schillebeeckx also argued that the introduction of Roman law into canon law in the eleventh and twelfth

centuries made possible the new definition of ordination as a personal power bestowed on the recipient. See chapter 2, pp. 44–45.

27. On the use of Roman law in the second recension of the *Decretum*, see Anders Winroth, *The Making of Gratian's Decretum* (Cambridge: Cambridge University Press, 2000), 146–74. On the development of Roman and its use by canonists, see James Brundage, *Medieval Canon Law* (London: Longman, 1995), 44–47, 59–61.

28. Annit Arjava, *Women and Law in Late Antiquity* (Oxford: Oxford University Press, 1996).

29. "It should be noted that the more favorable situation of women in late Roman marital law was ignored by Gratian," (Raming, *Priestly Office*, 38). On power of a father in a Roman family, the *patria potestas*, see Arjava, *Women and Law*, 41–52.

30. Raming, *Priesthood*, 39.

31. See chapter 4, p. 132.

32. "Hic si quis contendat, non magis uiro, quam mulieri licitum esse, si uir alicuius eodem modo fornicetur, sciat, uirum ab Ambrosio appellatum non sexu, sed animi uirtute; mulierem quoque nominatam sentiat non sexu corporis, sed mollicie mentis" (*causa* 32, *questio* 7. c. 18, *dicta* in *Corpus iuris canonici*, 2 vols., ed. Emil Friedberg, ed., 2 vols. [Graz: Akademische Druck-und-Verlagsanstalt, 1959], 1:1145; English translation in Raming, *Priestly Office*, 61n207). Gratian quoted Ambrosiaster as Ambrose here; ibid., 26–27.

33. "Nam varium et mutabile testimonium semper femina producit" (*Extra, titulus* 40, c. 10 in Friedberg, *Corpus*, 2:914. English translation in Raming, *Priestly Office*, 147n.45). The source for this quotation is Virgil; see ibid.

34. "Sed quare sunt mulieres remotae ab officiis ciuilibus et publicis? Ratio est, quia sunt fragiles et minus discretae regulariter... Item in iudicatura specialis ratio est, quia iudex debet esse constans et non flexibilis... modo mulier est varia et fragilis... item quia non est prudens, nec erudita, sicut debet esse index per se." (text in Raming, *Ausschluss*, 151n105; English translation in Raming, *Priestly Office*, 155n105).

35. "No(ta) quod femina non est tante fidei sicut masculinus, unde potest optime adduci iste... quia in casibus in quibus femina admittitur non facit tantam fidem sicut masculus, et ideo si duo sunt viri ex una parte et duae mulieres pro contraria parte, praeferendum est testimonium virorum; nam dicitur mulier non a sexu sed a molliti[a]e mentis, ita et vir non a sexu sed a constantia et virtute animi" (text in Raming, *Ausschluss*, 160n141; English translation in Raming, *Priestly Office*, 159n141).

36. "Quid levius fumo? flamen; quid flamine? ventus, quid vento? mulier; quid muliere? nihil" (text in Raming, *Ausschluss*, 143n85; English translation in Raming, *Priestly Office*, 152n85).

37. "Moniales vero non solum per ignorantiam, sed etiam per simplicitatem, nam permissum est mulieribus ignorare iura" (text in Raming, *Ausschluss*, 149n102; English translation in Raming, *Priestly Office*, 155n102).

38. "Gratian. Hoc quamquam de sacerdotibus uideatur specialiter dictum, generaliter tamen de omnibus penitentibus oportet intelligi" (*causa* 33, *questio* 2, c. 11, *dicta*, in Friedberg, *Corpus*, 1:1155).

39. "Clericis autem conceditur, si uxores eorum peccauerint, sine mortis acerbitate habere eas in custodia, et ad ieiunia eas cogere, non tamen usque ad necem affligere." (*causa* 33, *questio* 2, c. 9, *dicta*, in Friedberg, *Corpus*, 1:1154; English translation from Raming, *Priestly Office*, 39).

40. "Judicare potest maritus uxorem, corrigendo eam . . . sed non verberando eam . . . sed temperate potest eam castigare, quia est de familia sua . . . sicut dominus seruum . . . et etiam mercenarium suam" (text in Raming, *Ausschluss*, 115n191; English translation in Raming, *Priestly Office*, 118n191).

41. "Uxores viris, et filii parentis et serui dominis subditi sunt, unde ab illis coerceri et secundum ius debent corripi, ne in causam anathematis incidant" (text in Raming, *Ausschluss*, 115n191; English translation in Raming, *Priestly Office*, 118n191). "Non tamen quod immoderate verberentur" (text in Raming, *Ausschluss*, 115n191; English translation in Raming, *Priestly Office*, 118n191).

42. "Dicitur hic quod si uxores clericorum peccauerint, eas non occidant, sed eas custodiant, ne de caetero habeant licentiam peccandi, macerando eas verberibus et fame, sed non usque ad mortem" (text in Raming, *Ausschluss*, 115n191; English translation in Raming, *Priestly Office*, 118n191).

43. "When Roman law and canon law are compared with respect to the concept of woman outside of marriage, one significant difference emerges. In Roman law, woman was mentioned only in relation to specific activities, whereas in canon law, women were classified as a group for the first time" (Allen, *Concept of Women*, 1:439).

44. Ibid., 1:328–473.

45. For an extensive analysis of medieval theologians' teaching on the ordination of women, see John Hilary Martin, "The Ordination of Women and the Theologians in the Middle Ages," *Escritos del Vedat* 36 (1986), and Alastair Minnis, "*De Impedimento sexus:* Women's Bodies and Medieval Impediments to Female Ordination," in *Medieval Theology and the Natural Body*, ed., Peter Biller and A. J. Minnis, York Studies in Medieval Theology, 1 (York Medieval Press: York, 1997).

46. The notes come from Thomas's student, Riginald of Piperno. On the notes and their reliability, see Martin, "Ordination of Women," 1:166, English translation in Cooke and Macy, *History*, 1:67. For a fuller discussion of Thomas's teaching on women, see also Mayeski, "Excluded by the Logic," 86–91; Allen, *Concept of Women*, 1:385–407, and Kari Elisabeth Børresen, "God's Image, Is Woman Excluded? Medieval Interpretation of Gen. 1, 27 and I Cor. 11, 7," in *Image of God and Gender Models in Judaeo-Christian Tradition*, ed. Kari Elisabeth Børresen (Oslo: Solum Forlag, 1991), 218–24.

47. "Circa primum tria ponit eis competere, scilicet taciturnitatem, disciplinam, et subiectionem: quae tria ex una ratione procedunt, scilicet defectu rationis in eis" (text is given in Martin, "Ordination of Women," 1:166n113; English translation in Cooke and Macy, *History*, 1:127n113).

48. "Huius autem rationem assignat, dicens, 'Non enim permittitur eis loqui,' scilicet ab Ecclesiae auctoritate; sed hoc est officium earum, ut sint subditae viris. Unde cum docere dicat praelationem, et praesidentiam, non decet eas quae subditae sunt. Ratio autem quare subditae sunt, et non praesunt, est quia deficiunt ratione,

quae est maxime necessaria praesidenti. Et ideo dicit Philosophus in *Politica* sua (bk 4, c. 11), 'quod corruptio regiminis est, quando regimen pervenit ad mulieres'" (text is given in Martin, "Ordination of Women," 1:167n115; English translation in Cooke and Macy, *History*, 1:127n115.

49. "Ad primum ergo dicendum quod per respectum ad naturam particularem, femina est aliquid deficiens et occasionatum" (*Summa theologiae, pars* 1, *questio* 92, *articulus* 1, *ad* 1,in *S. Thomae Aquinatis Summa Theologiae*, 4 vols. [Marietti: Rome, 1948], 4:451; English translation in Cooke and Macy, *History*, 1:128n119).

50. On the teaching of Aristotle, see Allen, *Concept of Women*, 1:95–21, 392–99 and 426–36.

51. "Mulier vero in respectu viri statum subiectionis habet, quod etiam naturae consonum est, quia muliebris sexus naturaliter imperfectus est, in respectu sexus virilis" (bk 4, *distinctio* 25, *articulus* 4, *questio* 1 in, *Magistri Ricardi de Mediavilla Super Quatuor Libros Sententiarum* [1591; repr. Frankfurt am Main: Minerva, 1963], 389A; English translation in Cooke and Macy, *History*, 1:134n144).

52. "Mulier vero respectu viri habet statui subiectionis. Etiam nature consonum est quia muliebris sexus naturaliter imperfectus est, cum secundum Philosophum est 'vir occasionatus,' id est imperfectus" (text in Martin, "Ordination of Women," 2:133n214; English translation in Cooke and Macy, *History*, 1:157n214).

53. "Naturaliter debilior est sexus muliebris, under communiter minus viuit: quia et minus habet caloris naturalis, ideo quanto citius finitur, tanto citius naturaliter perfici debet...Plat(o) vero dicit, quod hoc ideo est, quia citius crescit mala herba quam bona" (text in Raming, *Ausschluss*, 149n102; English translation in Raming, *Priestly Office*, 155n102).

54. "Et est ratio, quia mala herba cito crescit...alia ratio, quia naturale est, quod quanto quodcunque ens citius ad finem tendit, citius perficiatur, ut apparet in musca" (text in Raming, *Ausschluss*, 151n107; English translation in Raming, *Priestly Office*, 156n107).

55. Allen, *Concept of Women*, 1:440; Mayeski, "Excluded by Logic," 86; and McNamara, *"Herrenfrage,"* 11.

56. For a brief, but clear presentation of the problems with the introduction of Aristotle's work into theology, see *NCE* 12:759–62.

57. "Hec imago Dei est in homine, ut unus factus sit ex quo ceteri oriantur, habens inperium Dei, quasi uicarius eius, quia unius Dei habet imaginem, ideoque mulier non est facta ad Dei imaginem. Sic etenim dicit: 'Et fecit Deus hominem; ad imaginem Dei fecit illum.' Hinc etiam Apostolus: 'Vir quidem,' ait, 'non debet uelare caput, quia imago et gloria Dei est; mulier ideo uelat, quia non est gloria aut imago Dei'" (*causa* 33, *questio* 5, c. 13 in Friedberg, *Corpus*, 1:1254; English translation in Raming, *Priestly Office*, 30).

58. For a more thorough treatment of the use of the expression *imago dei* in forming a negative image of women, see Kari Elisabeth Børresen, "God's Image, Man's Image? Patristic Interpretation of Gen. 1, 27 and I Cor. 11, 7," and idem, "God's Image, Is Women Excluded?" both in Børresen, *Image of God*, 188–227.

59. "Sed quantum ad aliquid secundario imago Dei invenitur in viro, secundam quod non invenitur in muliere: nam vir est principium mulieris et finis, sicut Deus est principium et finis totius creaturae" (*Summa theologiae, pars 1, questio 93, articulus 4, ad 1*in *Summa Theologiae*, 4:456.;English translation in Cooke and Macy, *History*, 1:128n121).

60. "Vir immediatius se habet ad Deum, cum vir sit imago et gloria Dei, mulier autem viri, 1 Cor., 11: 14. Unde per viros mulieres debent in Deum reduci, non e converso" (text in Martin, "Ordination of Women," 1:175n131; English translation in Cooke and Macy, *History*, 1:130n131).

61. "Item tribus de causis dicitur vir gloria dei et non femina; primo quia potentior et gloriosior apparuit deus in creatione viri quam femine, nam precipue per homine manifestata est gloria dei cum eum fecerit per se et de limo terre contra naturam, set femina facta est de homine; secundo quia homo factus est a deo nullo mediante quod non est de femina; tertio quia deum glorificat principaliter, id est nullo medio, set femina mediante viro, quia vir ipsam feminam docet et instruit ad glorificandum deum" (text in Raming, *Ausschluss*, 108n162; English translation in Raming, *Priestly Office*, 114n162).

62. "Praeterea mulier non debet habere talem potestatem, quia non est facta ad imaginem Dei, sed vir, qui est imago et gloria Dei; et mulier debet subesse viro et quasi famula viri esse, cum vir caput sit mulieris, non e conuerso" (text in Raming, *Ausschluss*, 141n80; English translation in Raming, *Priestly Office*, 151n80).

63. "Adam per Euam deceptus est, non Eua per Adam. Quem uocauit ad culpam mulier, iustum est, ut eam in gubernationem assumat, ne iterum femina facilitate labatur" (*causa 33, questio 5, c. 18* in Friedberg, *Corpus*, 1:1255; English translation in Raming, *Priestly Office*, 66n256).

64. "Omnis natura mulierum in transgressione facta est per illam" (text in Martin, "Ordination of Women," 1:124n18; English translation in Cooke and Macy, *History*, 1:111n18).

65. "Ratio autem naturalis huic dicto consonat, quam Apostolus innuit 1. *ad Corinth*. 14 [34]. Nam natura non permittit mulierem, saltem post lapsum, tenere gradum eminentem in specie humana, siquidem est dictum sibi in poenam peccati sui Genes. 3. 'sub viri potestate eris' " (bk. 4, *distinctio 25, questio 2, Questiones in librum quartum sententiarum [Opus Oxoniensis]* in *Joannis Duns Scoti, Opera Omnia*, vol. 19 [Paris: Vivès, 1894], 140; English translation in Cooke and Macy, *History*, 1:136n152).

66. "Preterea mulier fuit causa effectiva damnationis quia fuit principium prevaricationis (*text:* privationis) et Adam per ipsam deceptus est" (text in Raming, *Ausschluss*, 117n199; English translation in Raming, *Priestly Office*, 120n199).

67. "Allicit enim blanda voc et illicit species muliebris, et tandem in rete verbi dulcis volvitur intellectus. . . . Idcirco non permittitur ei docere, quia fragilior est sexu quam vir. Et cavendum, ne sicut per serpentem seducta mortem attulit mundo, ita etiam facile ad errorem lapsa, alios ad eumdem errorem pertrahat" (text in Martin, "Ordination of Women," 2:122n196; English translation in Cooke and Macy, *History*,

1:150n196). Netter's comments are based in part on the ninth-century commentary on
1 Timothy by Haimo of Haberstadt, see PL 117:791A.

68. "Mulier semel docuit, et totum mundum subvertit." Raymond was quoting Augustine. See Raming, *Ausschluss*, 136n62. Text in ibid. English translation in
Raming, *Priestly Office*, 120n149. Raymond's teaching was copied verbatim by Vincent
of Beauvais and John of Freiburg, see F. Gillmann, "Weibliche Kleriker nach dem
Urteil der Frühscholastik," *Archiv für katholisches Kirchenreht* 93 (1913): 252n1.

69. The entire passage reads: "Mulier vero praedicandi seu docendi constantiam
non habet: quia de facili a veritate seducitur. Et ideo postquam dixit Apostolus, I Tim.
2, 'Docere mulierem non permitto' post modicum subiunxit quasi pro causa, 'Adam
non est seductus, mulier autem seducta in praevaricatione fuit.' Mulier secundo
exequendi officium doctoris non habet efficaciam, quia sexus fragilitatem patitur, qui
non sufficit in publico discurrere et laborare. Et ideo ibidem etiam cum dixisset,
'Docere mulierem non permitto': statim addidit: 'sed esse in silentio.' Mulier tertio
doctoris auctoritatem habere non potest propter sexus conditionem qui non habet
exequendi libertatem; quia sub alterius debet esse potestate, Gen. 3, 'sub potestate
viri eris et ipse dominabitur tui.' Et ideo mulieri officium docendi inhibuisset,
dicendo, 'Docere mulierem non permitto,' immediate adiunxit, 'Neque dominari in
virum' . . . Mulier quarto vivacitatem sermonis non habet in mortificandum, sed magis
provocandum peccata; et ideo super illud, 'Docere mulierem non permitto,' dicit
Glossa, 'si enim loquitur magis incitat ad luxuriam et irritatur'; et ideo dicitur
Ecclesiastici, 9, 'Colloquium illius quasi ignis exardescit'" (*articulus* 11, *questio* 2 in,
*Summae Quaestionum Ordinarium Theologi recepto praeconio Solemnis Henrici a
Gandavo*, 2 vols. [1520; repr. St. Bonaventure, NY: Franciscan Institute, 1953], 1:78a;
English translation in Cooke and Macy, *History*, 1:132n138).

70. "In ueteri lege multa permittebantur, que hodie perfectione gratiae abolita
sunt. Cum enim mulieribus permitteretur populum iudicare, hodie pro peccato, quod
mulier induxit, ab Apostolo eis indicitur uerecundari, uiro subditas esse, in signum
subiectionis uelatum caput habere" (*causa* 15, *questio* 3, *dicta*, in Friedberg, *Corpus*, 1:
750; English translation in Raming, *Priestly Office*, 25).

71. See Martin, "Ordination of Women," 1:124n18; English translation in Cooke
and Macy, *History*, 1:111n18.

72. "Et si opponas de Magdalena quae fuit Apostola, et tanquam praedicatrix
et praefecta super omnes mulieres peccatrices, respondeo quod ipsa fuit singularis
mulier, et singulariter accepta Christo, et ideo privilegium personale personam sequitur, et extinguitur cum persona" (bk. 4, *distinctio* 25, *questio* 2, *Reportatio Parisiensis*,
in, *Joannis Duns Scoti, Opera Omnia*, vol. 24 [Paris: Vivès, 1894], 370; English
translation in Cooke and Macy, *History*, 1:136n151).

73. "Tali enim gratia concessum est mulieribus publice prophetare in Veterum
Testamentum in virorum contumeliam: quia effoeminati facti erunt, sicut et foeminis
concessum est publica regimina super viros genere; et similiter in primitiva ecclesia
propter messis multitudinem et metentium paucitatem concessum est mulieribus
Marthae et Mariae publice praedicare, et iiii Philippi filiabus publice prophetare,
secundum quod habetur Act. 21" (*articulus* 11, *questio* 2 in, *Summae Quaestionum*,

1:78a. English translation in Cooke and Macy, *History*, 1:133n140). For an insightful examination of medieval discussions of the biblical precedents for women teaching, see Alastair Minnis, "*De Impedimento sexus*," 127–33.

74. See Allen, *Concept of Women*, 252: "It is interesting to note that historically, women did not participate in the development of the traditional theory of sex polarity. There were no women in the Peripatetic school, neither have any female philosophers left a record of actually arguing for Aristotle's theory, nor for any other theory that attempted to prove that women were significantly different but inferior to men."

75. Maureen Miller, "Masculinity, Reform, and Clerical Culture: Narratives of Episcopal Holiness in the Gregorian Era," *Church History* 72 (2003): 25–52.

76. On the separation of clergy and laity during this period, see Bernard Cooke, *The Distancing of God: Ambiguity of Symbol in History and Theology* (Minneapolis: Fortress, 1990), 143–84; Constable, *Reformation of the Twelfth Century*, 321–22; and Gary Macy, "The 'Invention' of Clergy and Laity in the Twelfth Century," in *A Sacramental Life: A Festschrift Honoring Bernard Cooke*, ed., Michael Horace Barnes and William P. Roberts (Milwaukee: Marquette University Press, 2003).

77. "In effect, the newly celibate clerical hierarchy reshaped the gender system to assure male dominance of every aspect of the new public sphere" (McNamara, "*Herrenfrage*," 11). "Men took this task upon themselves, alone; women were excluded from academic study of philosophy and theology, as well as from the study and practice of medicine and law. In addition, women were excluded from the hierarchical, jurisdictional, and sacramental structures of the church. Sex comlementarity, within the heart of the Catholic life of the west, as praxis and as teaching, had disappeared" (Allen, *Concept of Women*, 1: 471). "Priesthood becomes almost divine, especially through its mediation of the sacraments—particularly the eucharist—and through the notion of the priest as a Christ-substitute" (Swanson, "Angels Incarnate," 164).

78. "The Church also offered a means of expanding its womenless space by monasticizing the clergy and clericalizing the monastic movement" (McNamara, "Canossa," 110).

79. Paul-Henri Lafontaine, *L'Évêque d'Ordination des Religieux des débuts du monachisme à la mort de Louis le Pieux (840)* (Les Editions de l'Université d'Ottawa: Ottawa, 1951).

80. See, for example, Brooke, "Gregorian Reform," 19.

81. McNamara, "*Herrenfrage*," 7.

82. Allen, *Concept of Women*, 1:471.

83. Swanson, "Angels Incarnate," 164; and McNamara, "*Herrenfrage*," 22.

84. For an insightful investigation of the way in which the subordination of women in Christianity affects women in the present, see Margaret Miles, "Violence Against Women in the Historical Christian West and in North American Secular Context: The Visual and Textual Evidence," in *Shaping New Vision: Gender and Values in American Culture*, ed. Clarissa Atkinson, Constance Buchanan and Margaret Miles, Studies in Religion, 5 (Ann Arbor, MI: UMI Research Press, 1987), 13–29.

Bibliography

PRIMARY SOURCES

Abelard, *Sermo* 31, *PL* 178: 569–73.

Aimone, Peter, ed. *Summa Simonis Bisinianensis*. http://www.unifr.ch/cdc/summa_simonis_de.php Fribourg, 2003.

Alexander of Hales. *Magistri Alexandri de Hales, Glossa in Quatuor Libros Sententiarum Petri Lombardi*. 4 vols.,Bibliotheca Franciscana Scholastica Medii Aevi, 12–15. Florence: Collegii S. Bonaventurae, 1951–57.

Andrieu, Michel, ed. *Les Ordines Romani du Haut Moyen Age*. 4 vols. Spicilegium sacrum Lovaniense, Études et documents, 28. Louvain: Spicilegium sacrum Lovaniense, 1956.

———. *Le Pontifical Romain au moyen-âge, 1, Le Pontifical Romain du XIIe siècle*. Studi e testi, 86. Vatican City: Biblioteca apostolica vaticana, 1937.

Atto of Vercelli. *Epistola ad Ambrosium sacerdotem*. *PL* 134: 113–15.

Aurelian of Arles, *Regula ad virgines*. *PL* 68: 399–406.

Benedict VIII. *Epistola "Quotiens illa."* *PL* 139: 1617–23.

Benedict IX. *Epistola "Convenit apostolico."PL* 141: 1347–57.

Bernold of Constance. *Micrologus de ecclesiasticis observationibus, PL* 151: 979–95.

Beyer, Heinrich, ed. *Urkundenbuch zur Geschichte der jetzt die preussischen Regierungsbezirke Coblenz und Trier bildenden mittelrheinischen Territorien*. 3 vols. Coblenz: In Commission bei J.Hölscher, 1860–1874.

Biblia Latina cum Glossa Ordinaria: Facsimile Reprint of the Editio Princeps Adolph Rusch of Strassburg 1480/8, 4 vols. 1480; reprint, Turnhout: Brepols, 1992.

Boretius, Alfred, ed. *Capitularia regum Frankorum*. Vol. 1, MGH. Hannover: Hahn, 1883.

Bouquet, Martin and Léopold DeLisle, eds. *Recueil des Historiens des Gaul et de la France*. New ed. Paris: Victor Palm, 1869–80.

Buytaert, Eligius M., ed. *Petri Abaelardi Opera Theologia*, 3 vols., CCSM, 11–13. Turnhout: Brepols, 1969.

Calixtus II. *Epistola "Quae a praedecessoribus."* PL 163: 1283–84.

Cogitosus. *Vita Sanctae Brigidae. Acta sanctorum*, 1 Februrary, 1: 135–41.

DeClercq, Charles ed. *Concilia Galliae*. CCSL, 148A. Turnhout: Brepols, 1963.

Deshusses, Jean, ed. *Le sacramentaire Grégorien: Ses principales formes d'après les plus anciens manuscripts*. 3 vols. Spicilegium Friburgenses, 16, 24, 28. Fribourg: Éditions universitaires Fribourg, 1971–82.

Donatus of Besançon. *Regula ad virgines*, PL 87: 273–98.

Douteil, Herbert ed. *Johannis Beleth Summa de ecclesiasticis officiis*. CCCM, 41A. Turnhout: Brepols, 1976.

Duchesne, Louis, ed. *Le Liber Pontificalis*. Paris: E. De Boccard, 1955.

Dumas, Antoine, ed. *Liber sacramentorum Gellonensis*. CCSL, 159. Turnhout: Brepols, 1981.

Duns Scotus. *Joannis Duns Scoti, Opera Omnia*. 26 vols. Paris: Vivès, 1891–95.

Elze, Reinhard ed. *Die Ordines für die Weihe und Krönung des Kaisers und der Kaiserin*. MGH, Fontes juris Germanici antiqui, 9. 1960. Reprint, Hannover: Hansche Buchhandlung, 1995.

Emery, Gilles, ed. *Saint Thomas d'Aquin, Traités Les Rasions de la Foi, Les Articles de la Foi et les Sacrements de l'Église*. Paris: Cerf, 1999. English translation, *The Catechetical Instructions of St. Thomas Aquinas*: Joseph Collins. New York: Joseph Wagner, 1939.

Eustochius, Licinius, and Melanius. *Epistola*. In *Les Sources de l'Histoire du Montanisme*, ed. Pierre de Labriolle, 226–30. Collectanea Friburgensia, n.s., 15. Fribourg: Libraire de l'Université, 1913.

Ewald, Paul and Ludo Moritz Hartmann, eds. *Gregorii papae Registrum epistolorum*. MGH, *Epistolae*, 1–2. 2 vols. Berlin: Weidmannos, 1891–99. English translation: John R. C. Martin. *The Letters of Gregory the Great*. 3 vols. Medieval Sources in Translation, 40. Toronto: Pontifical Institute of Medieval Studies, 2004.

Férotin, Marius, ed. *Le Liber Ordinum en usage dans l'église Wisigothique et Mozarabe d'Espagne du cinquième au onzième siècle*. Monumenta ecclesiae liturgica, 5. Paris: Libraire de Firmin-Didot, 1904.

Finsterwalder, Paul, ed. *Die Canones Theodori Cantuariensis und ihre Überlieferungsformen*. Untersuchungen zu den Bußbüchern des 7., 8. und 9. Jahrhunderts, 1. Weimer: Herman Böhlaus, 1929.

Fornasari, Massimo, ed. *Collectio canonum in V libris (libri I–III)*. CCCM, 6. Turnhout: Brepols, 1970.

Fransen, Gerard and Stephan Kuttner. *Summa 'Elegantius in iure diuino' seu Coloniensis*. 3 vols. Monumenta iuris canonici, series A, 1. New York: Fordham University Press, 1969.

Friedberg, Emil, ed. *Corpus iuris canonici*. 2 vols. Graz: Akademische Druck-und-Verlagsanstalt, 1959.

Fry, Timothy, ed. *The Rule of St. Benedict in Latin and English with Notes*. Collegeville, MN: Liturgical Press, 1981.

Giesebrecht, Wilhelm von and Edmund von Oefele, eds. *Annales Altahenses maiores*, MGH, Scriptores rerum Germanicarum, 1. Hannover: Bibliopolii Hahniani, 1891.

Gilbert of La Porrée. *Commentaria in epistolas Pauli*. London, British Library, Royal MS 2.F.i. Folios 5–180.

Gilbert of Limerick. *De usu ecclesiae*. PL 159: 997–1004.

Gloria, Andrea. *Codex diplomatico padovanno dal secolo sesto a tuto l'undecimo*. Monumenti storici publicati dalla deputazione Veneta de storia patria, 2. Serie prima documenti, 2. Venice: A spese della Società, 1877.

Greenwell, William, ed., *The Pontifical of Egbert, Archbishop of York, A.D. 732–766*. Surtee Society, 27. London: T. & W. Boone, 1853.

Gregory I. *Epistola "Veniens quidam."* PL 77: 955–958.

Haacke, Rhaban, ed. *Ruperti Tuitiensis De divinis officiis*. CCCM, no. 7. Turnhout: Brepols, 1967.

Heiming, Odila, ed. *Liber sacramentorum Augustodunensis*. CCSL, 159. Turnhout: Brepols, 1984.

Henry of Ghent. *Summae Quaestionum Ordinarium Theologi recepto praeconio Solemnis Henrici a Gandavo*. 2 vols. 1520; reprint, St. Bonaventure, NY: Franciscan Institute, 1953.

Herveus de Bourg-Dieu. *Commentaria in epistolas divi Pauli*. PL 181: 591–1692.

Hicks, Eric, ed. *La vie et les epistres: Pierres Abaelart et Heloys sa fame*. Paris: Champion-Slatkine, 1991.

Hinschius, Paul, ed. *Decretales Pseudo-Isidoriana*. 1863. Reprint, Aalen: Scientia Verlag, 1963.

Holder-Egger, Oswald, ed. *Agnelli Liber pontificalis ecclesiae Ravennatis*. In MGH, *Scriptores rerum Langobardicarum et Italicarum saec. VI—IX*, ed. Georg Waitz, 265–391. Hannover: Hahn, 1878.

Holtmann, Robert, ed. *Die Chronik des Bischofs Thietmar von Merseburg und ihre Korveier Überarbeitung*. MGH, Scriptores rerum germanicarum, 9. Berlin: Werdmannsche Bundhandlung, 1935.

Honorius Augustodunensis. *Gemma anima*. PL 172: 541–738.

Hugh of St. Victor. *De Sacramentis Christianae fidei*. PL 176: 173–618.

Innocent III (Lothar of Segni) *De missarum mysteriis*. PL 217: 763–915.

Ivo of Chartes. *Decretum*. PL 161: 48–1022.

———. *Panormia*. PL 161: 1041–1344.

———. *Sermo 2*. PL 162: 513–19.

Janini, José, ed. *Liber ordinum episcopal [Cod. Silos, Arch. Monástico, 4]*. Studia silensia, 15. Burgos: Abadia de Silos, 1991.

John XIX. *Epistola "Quoniam semper."* PL 141: 1115–23.

————. *Epistola "Convenit apostolico."* PL 141: 1125–31 and PL 78: 1053–58.

John Moschius. *Pratum spirituale.* PL 74: 123–240.

Krusch, Bruno, ed. *Venanti Fortunati Opera pedestria.* MGH, Auctorum antiquissimorum, 4/2. Berlin: Weidmannos, 1885.

Krusch, Bruno and W. Arndt, eds. *Liber in gloria confessorum. Greogrii Turoneneis Opera.* Vol. 2, *Miracula et opera minora.* MGH, Scriptores rerum Merovingicarum. Hannover: Hahn, 1885. English translation: Raymond Van Dam. *Gregory of Tours, Glory of the Confessors,* Translated Texts for Historians, Latin series, vol. 4. Liverpool: Liverpool University Press. 1988.

Krusch, Bruno and Wilhelm Levison, eds. *Greogrii Turoneneis Libri historiarum.* MGH, Scriptores rerum Merovingicarum, 1, 2. 2nd ed. Hannover: Hahn, 1951. English translation: Lewis Thorpe. *Gregory of Tours. The History of the Franks.* New York: Penguin Books, 1974.

————. *Passiones vitaeque sanctorum aevi merovingici.* MGH, Scriptorum rerum Merovingicarum, 6. Hannover: Hahn, 1913.

Landgraf, Artur, ed. *Commentarius Cantabrigienensis in epistolas Pauli.* Publication in Mediaeval Studies. 3 vols. Notre Dame, IN: University of Notre Dame Press, 1937–44.

Leo, Friedrich, ed. *Venanti Honori Clementiani Fortunati, Opera poetica.* MGH, Auctorum Antiquissimorum, 6. Berlin: Weidmannos, 1881.

Leo I. *Epistola "Epistolas fraternitatis."* PL 54: 1197–1209.

Leo VII. *Epistola "Si instituta ecclesiastica."* PL 132: 1085–88.

Leo IX. *"Supplicantium desideriis."* PL 143: 598–604.

Lvetjohann, Christian, ed. *Sidonius domino papae Perpetuo salutem. Gai Sollii Apollinaris Sidonii Epistulae et carmina,* bk. 7, no. 9. MGH, Auctores anitquissimi, 8. Berlin: Weidmann, 1887.

Mabillon, Jean, ed. *Acta sanctorum Ordinis S. Benedicti.* 1688; reprint, Matiscone: Fratres Protat Typographi Matisconenses, 1935.

de Martel, Gérard, ed. *Expositiones Pauli epistolarum ad Romanos, Galathas et Ephesios, ad Romanos.* CCCM, 151. Turnhout: Brepols, 1995.

McLaughlin, Terence P., ed. *The Summa Parisiensis on the Decretum Gratiani.* Toronto: The Pontifical Institute of Mediaeval Studies, 1952.

————. "Abelard's Rule for Religious Women." *Mediaeval Studies* 18 (1956): 241–92.

Mittarelli, Giovanni and Anselmo Costadoni, eds. *Annales Camaldulensis ordinis Sancti Benedicti . . .* Venice: Apud Jo. Baptistam Pasquali, 1755.

Mohlberg, Leo, ed. *Missale Frankorum (Cod. Vat. Reg. lat. 257).* Rerum ecclesiasticarum documenta, 2. Rome: Herder, 1957.

————. *Missale Gallicanum Vetus (Cod. Vat. Palat. lat. 493).* Rerum ecclesiasticarum documenta, 3. Rome: Herder, 1958.

————. *Liber Sacramentorum Romanae aeclesiae ordinis anni circuli.* Rerum ecclesiasticarum documenta, 4. Rome: Herder, 1968.

Moncrieff, C. K. Scott, trans. *The Letters of Abelard and Heloise.* New York: Alfred Knopf, 1926.

Muckle, Joseph T., ed. "The Letter of Heloise on Religious Life and Abelard's First Reply," *Mediaeval Studies* 17 (1955): 240–81.

———. "The Personal Letters between Abelard and Heloise," *Mediaeval Studies* 15 (1953): 47–94.

Munier, Charles, ed. *Concilia Africae A. 345–A. 525*. CCSL, 149. Turnhout: Brepols, 1974.

———. *Concilia Galliae*. CCSL, 148. Turnhout: Brepols, 1963.

Ochoa, Xaverio and Aliosio Diez, eds. *S. Raimundus de Pennaforte, Summa de Paenitentia*. Universa Bibliotheca Iuris, 1/B. Rome: Commentarium pro religiosis, 1976.

Ò hAodha, Donncha, ed. *Bethu Brigte*. Dublin: Dublin Institute for Advanced Studies, 1978.

Paris, Julien and Hugo Séjalon, eds. *Libellus antiquarum definitionum ordinis Cisterciensis*. In *Nomasticon Cisterciense*. Solesme: Typographeo Sancti Petri, 1892.

Perels, Ernest, ed. Pseudo–Nicolas I. *Epistola*. In MGH, *Epistolae*, 6, 687–9. Berlin: Weidmannos, 1925.

Peter Damian. *Contra intemperantes clericos*. PL 145: 387–424.

Peter the Lombard. *Collectanea in epistolas Pauli*. PL 191: 1297–1696; 192: 9–520.

———. *Sententiae in IV Libris Distinctae*. 3rd. ed. 2 vols. Spicilegium Bonaventurianum, 5. Rome: Collegii St. Bonaventurae ad Claras Aquas, 1981.

Philip of Harvengt. *De institutione clericorum tractatus sex*. PL 203: 665–1206.

Plummer, Charles, ed. *Vitae sanctorum Hiberniae*. 2 vols. Oxford: Clarendon, 1910.

Pseudo-Bruno the Carthusian. *Expositio in epistolas Pauli*. PL 153: 11–568.

Rabanus Maurus. *Enarrationum in epistolas beati Pauli*. PL 111: 1273–1616.

Radice, Betty and M. T. Clanchy, trans. *The Letters of Abelard and Heloise*. New York: Penguin, 2003.

Ribaillier, Jean, ed. *Magistri Guillelmi Atlissiodorensis, Summa Aurea*. 5 vols. Spicilegium Bonaventurianum, 16–20. Rome: Collegii S. Bonaventurae ad Claras Aquas, 1982–87.

Richard the Premonstratensian. *Sermo in canone misse*. PL 177: 455–70.

Richard of Middleton. *Magistri Ricardi de Mediavilla Super Quatuor Libros Sententiarum*. 1591, reprint, Frankfurt am Main: Minerva, 1963.

Robert of Courson. *Summa*. Bruges MS 247, fols. 4v–153v.

Robert Paululus. *De officiis ecclesiasticis*. PL 177: 381–456.

Robert, Ulysse, ed. *Bullaire du Pape Calixtus II, 1119–1124: Essai de Restitution*. 2 vols. Paris: Imprimerie nationale, 1891.

Robinson, Ian, ed. *Die Chroniken Bertholds von Reichenau unds Bernolds von Konstanz 1054–1000*. MGH, Scriptores rerum Germanicarum, N.S, 14. Hannover: Hahnsche Buchhandlung, 2003.

Rochais, Henri, ed. *Defensoris Locogiacensis monachi, Liber scintillarum*. CCSL, 117. Turnhout: Brepols, 1957.

von Schulte, Johann. ed. *Paucapalea, Summa über das Decretum Gratiani*. 1890; reprint, Aalen: Scientia Verlag, 1965.

von Schulte, Stephen Friedrich, ed. *Summa des Stephanus Tornacensis über das Decretum Gratiani*. Giessen: Verlag von Emil Roth, 1891.

Schütte, Bernard, ed. *Die Lebenbeschreibungen der Königin Mathilde.* MGH, Scriptores rerum Germanicarum in usum scholarum, 66. Hannover: Hahn, 1994.

Sedulius Scotus. *Collectanea in omnes B. Pauli epistolas. PL* 103: 9–270.

Sicard of Cremona. *Mitrale. PL* 213: 14–434.

Singer, Heinrich, ed. *Rufinus von Bologna (Magister Rufinus), Summa Decretorum.* 1902. Reprint, Paderborn: Scientia Verlag Aalen, 1963.

Somerville, Robert, ed. *The Councils of Urban II.* Vol. 1, *Decreta Claromontensia.* Amsterdam: Adolf Hakkert, 1972.

Souter, Alexander, ed. *Pelagius's Expositions of Thirteen Epistles of St. Paul, II, Text and Apparatus Criticus.* Texts and Studies, 9. Cambridge: Cambridge Univeristy Press, 1926. English translation: Theodore de Bruyn. *Pelagius's Commentary on St Paul's Epistle to the Romans.* Oxford: Clarendon Press, 1993.

Speculum de mysteriis ecclesiae. PL 177: 355–80.

Tanner, Norman, ed. *Decrees of the Ecumenical Councils.* 2 vols. Washington, DC: Georgetown University Press, 1990.

Thaner, Friedrich, ed. *Summa Magistri Rolandi.* 1874: reprint, Aalen: Scientia Verlag, 1972.

Thiel, Andreas, ed. *Epistolae Romanorum pontificum genuinae et quae ad eos scriptae sunt a S. Hilaro usque ad Pelagium II.* 1867. Reprint New York: Georg Olms Verlag, 1974.

Thomas Aquinas, S. *Thomae Aquinatis Summa Theologiae.* 4 vols. Marietti: Rome, 1948.

Urban II. *Epistola "Potestatem ligandi." PL* 151: 309–11.

Van den Eynde, Damian and Odulf, eds. *Guididonis de Orchellis, Tractatus de Sacramentis ex Eius Summa de Sacramentis et Officis Ecclesiae.* Franciscan Institute Publications, text series, 4. Louvain: Nauwelaerts, 1953.

Vita de Sanctae Segolena. In *Acta sanctorum,* 24 July, 5: 630–7.

Vogel, Cyrille and Reinhard Elze, eds. *Le Pontifical Romano–Germanique du dixième siècle.* Studi e testi, 226. 3 vols. Vatican City: Biblioteca Apostolica Vaticana, 1963.

Vogels, Henry Joseph, ed. *Ambrosiastri qui dicitur Commentarius in Epistulas Paulinas.* Corpus scriptorum ecclesiasticorum Latinorum, no. 81, pt. 1–3. 3 vols. Vienna: Hoelder–Pichler–Tempsky, 1966–1969.

de Vogüé, Adalbert. *Grégoire le Grand, Dialogues,* Adalbert de Vogüé, ed. 3 vols. Sources chrétiennes, 251, 260, 265. Paris: Éditions du Cerf, 1978–80.

———. "La Règle de Donat pour l'Abbesse Gauthstrude." *Benedictina,* 25 (1978): 219–313.

Waldebert of Luxeuil. *Regula ad virgines. PL* 88: 1059–1660.

Walter, Ioannes de, ed. *Magistri Gandulphi Bononiensis Sententiarum Libri Quatuor.* Vienna and Breslau: Aemilius Hain, 1924.

Weisweiler, Henri, ed. *Maitre Simon et son group De sacramentis.* Spicilegium Sacrum Lovaniense, Études et Documents, 17. Louvain: Spicilegium Sacrum Lovaniense, 1937.

Werminghoff, Albert, ed. *Concilia aevi Karolini (742–842).* MGH, Concilia 2,1. Hannover: Hahn, 1907.

Zachary. *Epistola "Gaudio magno." PL* 89: 930–38.

SECONDARY SOURCES

Affelt, Werner and Sabine Reiter. "Die Historiae Gregors von Tours als Quelle für
Frauen im Frankenreich des sechten Jahrhunderts." In *Frauen in der Geschichte
VII: Interdisziplinäre Studien zur Geschichte der Frauen in Frühmittelalter*, eds.
Werner Affett and Annette Kuhn, 192–208. Studien Materialien, 39. Düsseldorf:
Schwann, 1986.

Allen, Prudence. The *Concept of Woman*. 2 vols. Grand Rapids, MI: W. B. Eerdmans,
1997–2002.

Ansorge, Dirk."Der Diakonat der Frau: Zum gegenwärtigen Forschungsstand." In
Liturgie und Frauenfrage, eds. Teresa Berger and Albert Gerhards, 31–65.

Arjava, Annit. *Women and Law in Late Antiquity*. Oxford: Oxford University Press,
1996.

Arnald, Francesco and Franz Blatt, eds. *Novum glossarium mediae latinitatis ab anno
DCCC usque ad annum MCC*. Copenhagen: Ejnar Munksgaard, 1900–.

Aston, Margaret. "Lollard Women Priests?" In *Lollards and Reformers: Images and
Literacy in Late Medieval Religion*, ed. Margaret Aston, 49–70. London:
Hambledon Press, 1984.

Aubert, Marie-Joséphe. *Des femmes diacres: Un nouveau chemin pour l'église*. Paris:
Beauchesne, 1987.

Audet, Jean-Paul. *Structures of Christian Priesthood: A Study of Home, Marriage, and
Celibacy in the Pastoral Service of the Church*. New York: MacMillan, 1968.

Audisio, Gabriel. *The Waldensian Dissent: Persecution and Survival, c. 1170–c.1570*.
Cambridge: Cambridge University Press, 1999.

Barnett, James and Monroe. *The Diaconate: A Full and Equal Order*. New York:
Seabury, 1981.

Barstow, Anne Llewellyn. *Married Priests and the Reforming Papacy: The Eleventh-
Century Debates*. Texts and Studies in Religion, 12. New York: Edwin Mellon
Press, 1982.

Beach, Alison. *Women as Scribes: Book Production and Monastic Reform in Twelfth-
Century Bavaria*. Cambridge: Cambridge University Press, 2004.

van Beneden, Pierre. *Aux orgines d'une terminologie sacramentelle: Ordo, ordinare,
ordinatio dans la littérature chrétienne avant 313*. Spicilegium sacrum Lovaniense,
Études et documents, 38. Louvain: Spicilegium sacrum Lovaniense, 1974.

Berger, Teresa. *Liturgie und Frauenseele: Die liturgische Bewegung aus der Sicht der
Frauenforschung*. Praktische Theologie heute, 10. Stuttgart: Kohlhammer, 1993.

Berger, Teresa and Albert Gerhards, eds. *Liturgie und Frauenfrage: Ein Beitrag zur
Frauenforschung aus liturgiewissenschaftlicher Sicht*. Pietas liturgica, 7. St. Ottilien:
Verlag Erzabtei St. Ottilien, 1990.

Berman, Constance. *The Cistercian Evolution: The Invention of a Religious Order in
Twelfth-Century Europe*. Philadelphia: University of Pennsylvania Press, 2000.

Berman, Constance, ed. *Medieval Religion: New Approaches*. New York: Routledge, 2005.

Bériou, Nicole and David d'Avray. "Henry of Provins, O.P's Comparison of the
Dominican and Franciscan Orders with the "Order" of Matrimony." In *Modern*

Questions About Medieval Sermons: Essays on Marriage, Death, History and Sanctity, eds. Nicole Bériou and David L. d'Avray, 71–75. Collano della "Società Internazionale per lo Studio del Medioevo Latino," 11. Spoleto: Centro Italiano di Studi sull'Alto Medioevo, 1994.

Biesinger, Albert. "Diakonat-Ein eigenständiges Amt in der Kirche. Historischer Rückblick und heutiges Profil." In *Diakonat-Ein eigenständiges Amt in der Kirche*, eds. Peter Hünermann, Albert Beisinger, Marianne Heimbach-Steins and Anne Jenson, 53–77.

Bitel, Lisa M. *Isle of the Saints: Monastic Settlement and Christian Community in Early Ireland*. Ithaca, NY: Cornell University Press, 1990.

———. *Women in Early Medieval Europe, 400–1100*. New York: Cambridge University Press, 2002.

Blamires, Alcuin. "*Caput a femina, membra a viris*: Gender Polemic in Abelard's Letter, 'On the Authority and Dignity of the Nun's Profession.'" In *The Tongue of the Fathers: Gender and Ideology in Twelfth-Century Latin*, David Townsend and Andrew Taylor, eds., 55–79. Philadelphia: University of Pennsylvania Press, 1998.

———. *The Case for Medieval Women in Medieval Culture*. Oxford: Clarendon, 1997.

Blumenthal, Ute-Renata. *The Investiture Controversy: Church and Monarchy from the Ninth to the Twelfth Century*. Philadelphia: University of Pennsylvania Press, 1988.

Børresen, Kari Elisabeth, ed. *Image of God and Gender Models in Judaeo-Christian Tradition*. Oslo: Solum Forlag, 1991.

Bowes, Kim. "Personal Devotions and Private Chapels." In *Late Ancient Christianity*, Virginia Burrus, ed., *A People's History of Christianity*, 2, 188–210. Minneapolis, MN: Fortress Press, 2005.

Bradshaw, Paul. *Ordination Rites of the Ancient Churches of East and West*. Pueblo Publishing Company: New York, 1990.

Brennan, Brian. "'Episcopae': Bishops' Wives Viewed in Sixth-Century Gaul." *Church History* 54 (1985): 311–23.

Brooke, Christopher. "Gregorian Reform in Action: Clerical Marriage in England, 1050–1200." *Cambridge Historical Journal*, 12 (1956): 1–21.

———. "Married Men Among the English Higher Clergy, 1066–1200." *Cambridge Historical Journal*, 12 (1956): 187–88.

Brundage, James. *Law, Sex and Christian Society in Medieval Europe*. Chicago: The University of Chicago Press, 1987.

———. *Medieval Canon Law*. London: Longman, 1995.

Cameron, Euan. *Waldenses: Rejection of Holy Church in Medieval Europe*. Oxford: Blackwell, 2000.

Canon Law Society of America. *The Canonical Implications of Ordaining Women to the Permanent Diaconate*. Washington: DC: Canon Law Society of America, 1995.

Carleton, Kenneth. "The Traditio Instrumentorum in the Reform of Ordination Rites in the Sixteenth Century." In *Continuity and Change in Christian Worship*, ed.

Robert Swanson, 172–77. Studies in Church History, 35. Woodbridge, Suffolk: Boydell Press, 1999.

Chadwick, Henry. *The Early Church*. Rev. ed. London: Penguin Books, 1993.

Chenu, Marie-Dominique. "Un cas de platonisme grammatical au XIIe siècle." *Revue des sciences philosophiques et théologiques* 51 (1957): 666–68.

Cholij, Roman. *Clerical Celibacy in East and West*. Leominster, Herefordshire: Fowler Wright Books, 1989.

Clanchy, Michael. *Abelard, A Medieval Life*. Oxford: Blackwell, 1997.

Colish, Marcia. *Peter Lombard*, 2 vols. Leiden: Brill, 1994.

Congar, Yves. "My Path–Findings in the Theology of Laity and Ministries." *The Jurist* 32 (1972): 169–88.

———. "Note sur une valeur des termes "ordinare, ordinatio"." *Revue des sciences religieuses* 58 (1984): 7–14.

Connell, Charles W. "In a Different Voice: Heloise and the Self–Image of Women of the 12th Century." In *The Worlds of Medieval Women: Creativity, Influence, Imagination*, eds. Constance Berman, Charles Connell and Judith Rice Rothschild, 24–40. Morgantown: West Virginia University Press, 1985.

Constable, Giles. "The Ceremonies and Symbolism of Entering Religious Life and Taking the Monastic Habit, from the Fourth to the Twelfth Century." *In Segni e Riti nella Chiesa altomedievale occidentale*, 2: 771–834. Settimane di Studio del Centro italiano di Studi sull'Alto Medioevo, 33. 2 vols. Spoleto: Presso La Sede del Centro, 1987.

———. "The Orders of Society in the Eleventh and Twelfth Centuries." In *Medieval Religion: New Approaches*, ed. Constance Berman, 68–94. New York: Routledge, 2005.

———. *The Reformation of the Twelfth Century*. Cambridge: Cambridge University Press, 1996.

Cooke, Bernard. *The Distancing of God: Ambiguity of Symbol in History and Theology*. Minneapolis: Fortress, 1990.

Corsi, Dinora, ed. *Donne cristiane e sacerdozio: Dalle origini all'età contemporanea*. Rome: Viella, 2004.

Cushing, Kathleen. *Papacy and Law in the Gregorian Revolution: The Canonistic Word of Anselm of Lucca*. Oxford: Clarendon Press, 1998.

Dachowski, Elizabeth. "*Tertius est optimus*: Marriage, Continence, and Virginity in the Politics of Late Tenth- and Early Eleventh-Century Francia." In *Medieval Purity*, ed. Michael Frassetto, 117–25.

Daniélou, Jean. *The Ministry of Women in the Early Church*, 2nd ed. Leighton Buzzard, Bedfordshire: Faith Press, 1974.

Davies, J. G. "Deacons, Deaconesses and the Minor Orders in the Patristic Period." *Journal of Ecclesiastical History*, 14 (1963): 1–15.

Delehaye, Hippolyte. *A Travers Trois Siècles: L'oeuvre des Bollandists, 1615–1915*. Brussels: Bureaux de la Société des Bollandistes, 1920.

Delhaye, Phillippe. "Retrospective et prospective des ministeres feminins dans l'eglise," *Revue théologique de Louvain*, 3 (1972): 55–75

Dortel-Claudot, Michel. "Le prêtre et la marriage: Évolution de la legislation canonique des origins au XIIe siècle." In *Mélanges offerts a Pierre Andrieu–Guitrancourt*, 319–44. L'Année Canonique, 17. Paris: Faculte de Droit Canonique, 1973.

DuCange, Charles, ed. *Glossarium mediae et infimae latinitatis.* 1883–87. Reprint. Graz: Akademische Druck-U. Verlagsanstalt, 1954.

Eisen, Ute. *Amsträgerinnen in frühen Christentum. Epigraphische und literarische Studien.* Göttingen: Vandenhoeck & Ruprecht, 1996. English translation: *Women Officeholders in Early Christianity: Epigraphical and Literary Studies.* Collegeville, MN: Liturgical Press, 2000.

Elliott, Dyan. "The Priest's Wife: Female Erasure and the Gregorian Reform." In *Medieval Religion*, ed. Constance Berman, 123–55.

———. *Spiritual Marriage: Sexual Abstinence in Medieval Wedlock.* Princeton: Princeton University Press, 1993.

Elms. Susanna, "Vergini, Vedove, Diaconesse-Alcuni osservazioni sullo sviluppo dei cosiddetti 'ordini femminili' nel quarto secolo in oriente," *Codex Aquilarensis: Cuadernos de Investigación del Monasterio de Santa Maria la Real*, 5 (1991): 77–90.

Espín, Orlando O. "Toward the Construction of an Intercultural Theology of Tradition," *Journal of Hispanic/Latino Theology*, 9 (2002): 22–59.

Études sur le sacrement de l'ordre. Lex orandi, 22. Paris: Éditions du Cerf, 1957. English translation *The Sacrament of Holy Orders: Some Papers and Discussions concerning Holy Orders at a Session of the Centre de Pastorale Liturgique, 1955.* London: Aquin Press, 1962.

Faivre, Alexander. *Naissance d'une Hiérarchie: Les Premières Étapes du Cursus Clérical.* Théologie Historique, 40. Paris: Éditions Beauchesne, 1977.

Ferguson, Everett et al., eds. *Studies in Early Christianity: A Collection of Scholarly Essays.* New York: Garland Publishing, 1993.

Fiorenza, Elisabeth Schüssler. *In Memory of Her: A Feminist Theological Reconstruction of Christian Origins.* New York: Crossroad, 1983.

FitzGerald, Kyriaki Karidoyanes. *Women Deacons in the Orthodox Church: Called to Holiness and Ministry.* Rev. ed. Brookline, MA: Holy Cross Orthodox Press, 1999.

———. "The Nature and Characteristics of the Order of the Deaconess." In *Women and the Priesthood*, ed. Thomas Hopko, 93–137.

Fransen, Gerard. "The Tradition in Medieval Canon Law." In *Sacrament of Holy Orders*, 202–18.

Frassetto, Michael, ed. *Medieval Purity and Piety: Essays on Medieval Clerical Celibacy and Religious Reform.* New York: Garland, 1998.

Freeman, Elizabeth. "The Public and Private Functions of Heloise's Letters." *Journal of Medieval History* 23 (1997): 15–28.

Fuchs. Vinzenz. *Der Ordinationstitel von seiner Entstehung bis auf Innozenz III.* Amsterdam: P. Shippers, 1963.

Fuhrmann, Horst. *Einfluß und Verbreitung der pseudoisidorischen Fälschungen.* 2 vols. Schriften der Monumenta Germaniae historica, 24. Stuttgart: Hiersemann, 1972.

Galot, Jean. *La donna e i ministeri nella chiesa.* Assisi: Cittadella editrice, 1973.

George, Judith. *Venantius Fortunatus, A Latin Poet in Merovingian Gaul.* Oxford: Clarendon Press, 1992.

———. *Venantius Fortunatus, Personal and Political Poems.* Liverpool: Liverpool University Press, 1995.

Gräf, Hermann J. "Ad monacham faciendum: Die Mönchsprofess nach einem Fest-Sakramentar von Venedig aus dem II. Jh." *Ephemerides liturgicae,* 88 (1974): 353–69.

Gossman, Francis. *Pope Urban II and Canon Law.* The Catholic University of America Canon Law Series, 403. Washington, DC: The Catholic University of America Press, 1960.

Gibaut, John St. H. *The "Cursus Honorum": A Study of the Origins and Evolution of Sequential Ordination.* Patristics Studies, 3. NewYork: Peter Lang, 2000.

Gillmann, Franz. "Der 'sakramentale Charakter' bei den Glossatoren Rufinus, Johannes Faventinus, Sicard von Cremona, Huguccio und in der Glossa ordinaria des Dekrets." *Der Katholik: Zeitschrift für katholische Wissenschaft und kirchliches Leben,* 90 (1910): 300–13.

———. "Der 'sakramentale Charakter' bei Petrus Poitiers und bei Stephen Langton." *Der Katholik: Zeitschrift für katholische Wissenschaft und kirchliches Leben,* 93 (1913): 74–76.

———. "Die Seibenzahl der Sacramente bei den Glossatoren des Gratianischen Decrets." *Der Katholik: Zeitschrift für katholische Wissenschaft und kirchliches Leben* 89 (1909): 182–215.

———. "Weibliche Kleriker nach dem Urteil der Frühscholastik." *Archiv für katholisches Kirchenrecht,* 93 (1913): 239–53.

———. *Zur Lehre der Scholastik vom Spender der Firmung und des Weihesakraments.* Ferdinand Schöningh, 1920.

Griffiths, Fiona. "Brides and *Dominae*: Abelard's *Cura monialium* at the Augustinian Monastery of Marbach." *Viator* 34 (2003): 57–88.

———. "Men's Duty to Provide for Women's Needs: Abelard, Heloise, and their Negotiation of the *Cura monialium.*" *Journal of Medieval History,* 30 (2004): 1–24.

Gromer, Georg. *Die Laienbeicht im Mittelalter: Ein Beitrag zu ihrer Geschichte.* Veröffentlichungen aus dem Kirchenhistorischen Seminar München, 7. Munich: Lentnerschen, 1909.

Gryson, Roger. *Le ministère des femmes dans l'Église ancienne.* Recherches et synthèses, section d'histoire, 4. Éditions J. Duculot: Gembloux, 1972. English translation: *The Ministry of Women in the Early Church.* Collegeville, MN: Liturgical Press, 1976.

Gvosdev, Matushka Ellen. *The Female Diaconate: An Historical Perspective.* Minneapolis, MN: Light and Life, 1991.

Gy, Pierre-Marie. "Les anciennes priéres d'ordination," *La Maison-Dieu* 138 (1979): 93–122. English translation: "Ancient Ordination Prayers," *Studia liturgica* 13 (1979): 70–93.

———. "Notes on the Early Terminology of Christian Priesthood," *Sacrament of Holy Orders,* 98–126.

Häring, Nikolaus. "Character, Signum und Signaculum: Der Weg von Petrus Damiani bis zur eigentlichen Aufnahme in der Sakramentenlehre im 12. Jahrhundert." *Scholastik*, 31 (1956): 41–69, 182–212.

Hamilton, Sarah. *The Practice of Penance: 900–1050.* Woodbridge, Suffolk: Boydell Press, 2001.

Hauke, Manfred. *Der Empfänger de Weihesakraments: Quellen zur Lehre und Praxis der Kirche, nur Männern des Weihesakrament zu spenden.* Würzgrug: Echter, 1999.

———. *Die Problematik um das Frauenpriestertum vor dem Hintergrund der Schöpfungs- und Erlösungsordnung.* Paderborn: Bonifatius-Drukerei, 1986. English translation *Women in the Priesthood? A Systematic Analysis in the Light of the Order of Creation and Redemption.* San Francisco: St. Ignatius Press, 1988.

Hochstetler, Donald. *A Conflict of Traditions: Women in Religion in the Early Middle Ages: 500–840.* Lanham, M.D.: University Press of America, 1992.

Hollis, Stephanie. *Anglo-Saxon Women and the Church: Sharing a Common Fate.* Woodbridge, Suffolk: Boydell Press, 1992.

Hopko, Thomas, ed. *Women and the Priesthood.* Rev. ed. Crestwood, NY: St. Vladimir's Seminary Press, 1999.

Hünermann, Peter. "Conclusions Regarding the Female Diaconate," *Theological Studies* 36 (1975): 325–33.

———. "Theologische Argument für Diakonatsweihe von Frauen." In *Diakonat-Ein eigenständiges Amt in der Kirche,* eds. Peter Hünermann, Albert Biesinger, Marianne Heimbach-Steins and Anne Jenson, 98–128.

Hünermann, Peter, Albert Biesinger, Marianne Heimbach-Steins and Anne Jenson, eds., *Diakonat: Ein Amt für Frauen in der Kirche-Ein frauengerechtes Amt?* Ostfildern: Schwabenverlag, 1997.

Jansen, Katherine Ludwig. *The Making of the Magdalen: Preaching and Popular Devotion in the Later Middle Ages.* Princeton: Princeton University Press, 2000.

Jestice, Phyllis. "Why Celibacy? Odo of Cluny and the Development of a New Sexual Morality." In *Medieval Purity*, ed. Michael Frassetto, 81–115.

Jorissen, Hans. "Theologische Bedenken gegen die Diakonatsweihe von Frauen." In *Diakonat-Ein eigenständiges Amt in der Kirche,* eds. Peter Hünermann, Albert Biesinger, Marianne Heimbach-Steins and Anne Jenson, 86–97.

Juncker, Joseph. "Die Summa des Simon von Bisignano und seine Glossen." *Zeitschrift der Savigny-Stiftung für Rechtsgeschichte. Kanonistische Abteilung,* 15 (1926): 326–500.

Jungmann, Joseph. *The Mass of the Roman Rite: Its Origin and Development (Missa Sollemnia).* 2 vols. New York: Benziger Brothers, 1955.

Kalsbach, Adolf. *Die altkirchliche Einrichtung der Diakonissen bis zum ihrem Erlöschen.* Frieburg im Breisgau: Herder, 1926.

Kantorowicz, Ernst. *The King's Two Bodies: A Study in Medieval Political Theology.* Princton, NJ: Princeton University Press, 1997.

Karras, Valerie. "Female Deacons in the Byzantine Church," *Church History* 73 (2004): 272–316.

————. "The Liturgical Functions of Consecrated Women in the Byzantine Church," *Theological Studies* 66 (2005): 96–116.

Kienzle, Beverly Wayne and Pamela J. Walker, eds. *Women Preachers and Prophets through Two Millennia of Christianity*. Berkeley: University of California Press, 1998.

Kraemer, Ross Shepard and Mary Rose D'Angelo, eds. *Essays in Women and Christian Origins*. New York: Oxford University Press, 1999.

Laeuchli, Samuel. *Power and Sexuality: The Emergence of Canon Law at the Council of Elvira*. Philadelphia: Temple University Press, 1972.

Lafontaine, Paul-Henri. *Les Conditions Positives de l'Accession aux Orders dans la Première Legislation Ecclésiastique (300–492)*. Ottawa: Editons de l'Université d'Ottawa, 1963.

————. *L'Évêque d'Ordination des Religieux des débuts du monachisme à la mort de Louis le Pieux (840)*. Les Editions de l'Université d'Ottawa: Ottawa, 1951.

Laurain, Paul. *De l'intervention des laiques, des diacres et des abbesses dans l'administration de la pénitence*. Paris: Lethielleux, 1897.

Lawrence, Clifford H. *The Friars: The Impact of the Early Medieval Mendicant Movement*. London: Longman, 1994.

Leclercq, Jean. "Ad ipsam sophiam Christum: le témoignage monastique d'Abélard." *Revue d'ascétique et de mystique* 46 (1970): 161–81.

————. "Eucharistic Celebrations Without Priests in the Middle Ages." *Worship* 55 (1981): 160–65.

————. "Prières médiévales pour recevoir l'eucharistie pour saluer et pour béner la croix." *Ephemerides liturgicae* 79 (1965): 327–40.

Lécuyer, Joseph. *Le Sacrement de l'Ordination: Recherche Historique et Théologique*. Théologie Historique, 65. Paris: Éditions Beauchesne, 1983.

Legrand, Hervé. "Traditio perpetuo servata? La non-ordination des femmes: Tradition ou simple fait historique?" In *Rituels: Mélanges offerts à Pierre-Marie Gy, O.P.*, eds. Paul De Clerk and Éric Palazzo, 393–416. Paris: Cerf, 1990.

Long, R. James and Maura O'Carroll. *The Life and Works of Richard Fishacre, OP: Prolegomena to the Edition of his Commentary on the Sentences*. Bayerische Adademie der Wissenschaften, Veröffentlichen der Kommission für die Herausgabe ungedruckter Texte aus de mittelalterlichen Geisteswelt, 21. Munich: Verlag der Bayerische Adademie der Wissenschaften, 1999.

Lottin, Odo. *Psychologie et morale aux XIIe et XIIIe siècles*. Gembloux: Abbaye du Mont César, 1959.

Lynch, John. "Marriage and Celibacy of the Clergy: The Discipline of the Western Church: An Historico-Canonical Synopsis." *The Jurist* 32 (1972): 14–38, 189–212

Maasen, Friedrich. "Glossen des canonischen Rechts aus dem karolingischen Zeitalter." *Sitzungsberichte kaiserliche Akademie der Wissenschaften in Wien, Philosophisch–historische Klasse* 84 (1876): 235–98.

Macy, Gary. "Demythologizing 'the Church' in the Middle Ages," *Journal of Hispanic/ Latino Theology* 3 (1995): 23–41.

———. "The Eleonore and Nathaniel F. Philips, Sr. Memorial Lecture, An Old Perspective—The Church in the Middle Ages." In *Religions and the American Experience*, ed. Frank T. Birtel, 133–51. Hyde Park, NY: New York City Press, 2005.

———. "The Future of the Past: What Can the History Say about Symbol and Ritual." In *Practicing Catholic: Ritual, Body, and Contestation*, ed. Bruce Morrill, S.J., Susan Rodgers, and Joanna E. Ziegler, 29–37. New York: Palgrave-Macmillan Press, 2006.

———. "Heloise, Abelard and the Ordination of Abbesses," *Journal of Ecclesiastical History* 57 (2006): 16–32.

———. "The Iberian Heritage of U.S. Latino/a Theology." In eds. Orlando O. Espín and Gary Macy, *Futuring Our Past: Explorations in the Theology of Tradition*, 43–83. Maryknoll, NY: Orbis, 2006.

———. "The 'Invention' of Clergy and Laity in the Twelfth Century." In *A Sacramental Life: A Festschrift Honoring Bernard Cooke*, eds. Michael Horace Barnes and William P. Roberts, 117–35. Milwaukee: Marquette University Press, 2003.

———. "The Ordination of Women in the Early Middle Ages." *Theological Studies* 61 (2000): 502–7. Reprinted in *A History of Women and Ordination: Volume 1: The Ordination of Women in a Medieval Context*, eds. Bernard Cooke and Gary Macy, (New York: Scarecrow Press, 2002), 1–30.

———. "Some Examples of the Influence of Exegesis on the Theology of the Eucharist in the Eleventh and Twelfth Centuries." *Recherches de Théologie Ancienne et Médiévale*, 52 (1985): 64–77.

———. *Theologies of the Eucharist in the Early Scholastic Period*. Oxford: Clarendon Press, 1984.

———. *Treasures from the Storehouse: Essays on the Medieval Eucharist*. Collegeville, MN: Liturgical Press of America, 1999.

———. "Was there a 'the Church' in the Middle Ages?" In *Unity and Diversity in the Church*, ed. Robert Swanson, 107–116. Studies in Church History, 52. Blackwell: Oxford, 1996.

Madigan, Kevin and Carolyn Osiek. *Ordained Women in the Early Church: A Documentary History*. Baltimore: Johns Hopkins Press, 2005.

Makowski, Elizabeth. *"A Pernicious Sort of Woman" Quasi-Religious Women and Canon Law in the Later Middle Ages*. Studies in Medieval and Early Modern Canon Law, 6. Washington, DC: Catholic University of America Press, 2005.

Martimort, Aimé Georges. "A propos des ministères féminins dans l'Eglise." *Bulletin de littérature ecclésiastique* 74 (1973): 103–8.

———. *Les Diaconesses: Essai historique*. Rome: Edizione Liturgiche, 1982. English translation: *Deaconesses: An Historical Study*. San Francisco: Ignatius Press, 1986.

Martin, John Hilary. "The Ordination Of Women And The Theologians In The Middle Ages," *Escritos del Vedat*, 36 (1986): 115–77 and "The Ordination Of Women And The Theologians In The Middle Ages (II)," *Escritos del Vedat*, 36 (1988): 87–143. English Translation: Bernard Cooke and Gary Macy, *A History Of Women And Ordination*, vol. 1. New York: Scarecrow Press, 2002. Pp. 31–160.

Mayer, Josephine. *Monumenta de viduis diaconissis virginibusque tractantia.* Florilegium patristicum tam veteris quam medii aevi auctores complectens, 42. Bonn: Peter Hanstein, 1938.

Mayeski, Marie Anne. "Excluded by the Logic of Control: Women in Medieval Society and Scholastic Theology." In *Equal at the Creation: Sexism, Society, and Christian Thought,* eds. Joseph Martos and Pierre Hégy, 70–95. Toronto: University of Toronto Press, 1998.

———. *Women at the Table: Three Women Theologians.* Collegeville, MN: Liturgical Press, 2005.

McLaughlin, Mary Martin. "Peter Abelard and the Dignity of Women: Twelfth Century 'Feminism' in Theory and Practice." In *Pierre Abélard Pierre le Vénérable: Les courants philosophiques, littéraires et artistiques en occident au milieu du XIIe siècle,* 287–333. Paris: Éditions du Centre National de la Recherche Scientifique, 1975

McNamara, Jo Ann and John E. Halborg, eds. *Sainted Women of the Dark Ages.* Durham, NC: Duke University Press, 1992.

McNamara, Jo Ann. "An Unresolved Syllogism: The Search for a Christian Gender System." In *Conflicted Identities and Multiple Masculinities: Men in the Medieval West,* ed. Jaqueline Murray, 1–24. New York: Garland, 1999.

———. "Canossa and the Ungendering of the Public Man." In *Medieval Religion,* ed. Constance Berman, 102–22. This article originally appeared in *Render Unto Caesar: The Religious Sphere in World Politics,* eds. Sabrina Petra Ramet and Donald W. Treadgold, 131–50. Washington, DC: American University Press, 1995.

———. "Chaste Marriage and Clerical Celibacy." In *Sexual Practices and the Medieval Church,* eds. Vern Bullough and James Brundage, 22–33. Buffalo, NY: Prometheus Books, 1982.

———. "Chastity as a Third Gender in the History and Hagiography of Gregory of Tours." In *The World of Gregory of Tours,* eds. Kathleen Mitchell and Ian Woods, 199–209. Cultures, Beliefs and Traditions, 8. Leiden: Brill, 2002.

———. "The *Herrenfrage*: The Restructuring of the Gender System, 1050–1150." In *Medieval Masculinities: Regarding Men in the Middle Ages,* ed. Clare Lees, 3–29. Medieval Cultures, 7. Minneapolis: University of Minnesota Press, 1994.

———. *Sisters in Arms: Catholic Nuns through Two Millennia.* Cambridge, MA: Harvard University Press, 1996.

Meer, Haye van der. *Priestertum der Frau? Eine theologiegeschichtliche Untersuchung,* Quaestiones disputatae, 42. Freiburg: Herder, 1969. English translation: *Women Priests in the Catholic Church: A Theological–Historical Investigation.* Philadelphia: Temple University Press, 1973.

Melton, J. Gordon and Gary L. Ward, eds. *The Churches Speak on Women's Ordination: Official Statements from Religious Bodies and Ecumenical Organizations.* Detroit: Gale Research, Inc., 1991.

Metz, René. "Benedictio sive consecratio virginum." *Ephemerides liturgicae* 80 (1966): 265–93.

Mews, Constant. "On dating the works of Peter Abelard." *Archives d'histoire doctrinale et littéraire du moyen âge,* 60 (1985): 73–134.

Miles, Margaret. "Violence Against Women in the Historical Christian West and in North American Secular Context: The Visual and Textual Evidence." In *Shaping New Vision: Gender and Values in American Culture*, eds. Clarissa Atkinson, Constance Buchanan and Margaret Miles, 13–29. Studies in Religion, 5. Ann Arbor, MI: UMI Research Press, 1987.

Miller, Maureen. "Masculinity, Reform, and Clerical Culture: Narratives of Episcopal Holiness in the Gregorian Era." *Church History*, 72 (2003), 25–52.

Minnis, Alastair. "*De impedimento sexus*: Women's Bodies and Medieval Impediments to Female Ordination." In *Medieval Theology and the Natural Body*, eds. Peter Biller and A. J. Minnis, 109–39. York Studies in Medieval Theology, 1. York Medieval Press: York, 1997.

Moore, Robert I. *The First European Revolution, c. 970–1215*. Oxford: Blackwell, 2000.

Morgan, John and Teri Wall, eds. *The Ordination of Women: A Comprehensive Bibliography (196)–1976)*. Wichita, KS: Institute of Ministry and the Elderly, 1977.

Morin, Jean. *Commentarius de sacris ecclesiae ordinationibus secundum antiquos et recentiores latinos, graecos, syros et babylonios in tres partes distinctus*. 1695; reprt. Farnborough: Gregg, 1969.

Morris, Joan. *The Lady Was a Bishop: The Hidden History of Women with Clerical Ordination and the Jurisdiction of Bishops*. New York: Macmillan, 1973.

Mortari, Luciana. *Consacrazione Episcopale e Collegialità: La Testimonianza della Chiesa Antica*. Testi e Ricerche di Scienze Religiose, 4. Florence: Vallecchi Editore, 1969.

Müller, Gerhard. *Der Empfänger de Weihesakraments: Quellen zur Lehre und Praxis der Kirche, nur Männern des Weihesakrament zu spenden* (Würzgrug: Echter, 1999).

———. *Priestertum und Diakonat: Der Empfänger des Weihesakramentes in schöpfungstheologischer und christologischer Perspektive*. Freiburg: Johannes Verlag, 2000. English translation: *Priesthood and Diaconate: The Recipient of the Sacrament of Holy Orders from the Perspective of Creation Theology and Christology*. San Franciso: St. Ignatius Press, 2002.

Müller, Wolfgang. *Huguccio: The Life, Works, and Thought of a Twelfth-Century Jurist*. Modern Studies in Canon Law, 3. Washington, DC: The Catholic University of America, 1994.

Mulder-Bakker, Anneke. *Lives of the Anchoresses: The Rise of the Urban Recluse in Medieval Europe*. Philadelphia: University of Pennsylvania Press, 2005.

Murray, Jacqueline, ed. *Conflicted Identities and Multiple Masculinites: Men in the Medieval West*. New York: Garland, 1999.

———. "Masculinizing Religious Life: Sexual Prowess, the Battle for Chastity and Monastic Identity." In *Holiness and Masculinity in the Middle Ages*, eds. P. H. Cullum and Katherine J. Lewis, 24–42. Cardiff: University of Wales Press, 2004.

Muschiol, Gisela. *Famula Dei: Zur Liturgie in merowingischen Frauenklöstern*. Beiträge zur Geschichte des alten Mönchtums und des Benediktinertum, 41. Munster: Aschendorff, 1994.

Nelson, Janet. "Les femmes et l'évangélisation au ixe siècle." *Revue du Nord* 69 (1986): 471–85.

Newman, Barbara. "Flaws in the Golden Bowl: Gender and Spiritual Formation in the Twelfth Century." In *From Virile Woman to WomanChrist: Studies in Medieval Religion and Literature*, Barbara Newman, ed., 19–45. Philadelphia: University of Pennsylvania Press.

Nicolai, Umberto. *I Vescovi di Luca*. Luca: Tipografia Bicchelli, 1966.

Osborne, Kenan. *Priesthood: A History of the Ordained Ministry in the Roman Catholic Church*. Mahwah, NJ: Paulist Press, 1988.

Otranto, Georgio. "Il sacerdozio della donna nell'Italia meridionale." *Italia meridionale e Puglia paleochristiane: Saggi storici*. Scavi e ricerche, 5. Bari: Edipuglia, 1991, 94–121.

———. "Note sul sacerdozio femminile nell'antichità in margine a una testimonianza di Gelasio I." *Vetera Christianorum* 19 (1982): 341–60. English translation in Mary Ann Rossi, "Priesthood, Precedent, and Prejudice: On Recovering the Women Priests of Early Christianity." *Journal of Feminist Studies in Religion* 7 (1991): 73–93.

Ott, Ludwig. *Das Weihesakrament*. Handbuch der Dogmengeschichte, no. 4, 5. Freiburg: Herder, 1969.

Pacaut, Marcel. *Les Moines Blancs: Histoire de l'Ordre de Cîteaux*. Paris: Fayard, 1993.

Pennington, Kenneth. *Johannnis Teutonici Apparatus glossarum in Compilationem tertiam*. Monumenta iuris canonici, ser. A, 3. Vatican City: Biblioteca Apostolica Vaticana, 1981.

Pien, Jean. *Tractatus Prœliminaris De Ecclesiœ Diaconissis*. In *Acta Sanctorum*, eds. J. Bollandus et al., September, 1, i–xxviii. Antwerp: Bernard Albert Vander Plassch, 1746.

Ratigan, Virginia Kaib and Arlene Anderson Swidler, eds. *A New Phoebe: Perspectives on Roman Catholic Women and the Permanent Diaconate*. Sheed and Ward: Kansas City, MO, 1990.

Raming, Ida. *Der Ausschluss der Frau vom priesterlichen Amt; gottgewollte Tradition oder Diskriminierung? Eine rechtshistorisch-dogmatische Untersuchung der Grundlagen von Kanon 968 1 des Codex Iuris Canonici*. Cologne: Böhlau, 1973. English translation: *The Exclusion of Women from the Priesthood: Divine Law or Sex Discrimination?: A Historical Investigation of the Juridical and Doctrinal Foundations of the Code of Canon Law, Canon 968, 1*. Metuchen, NJ: Scarecrow Press, 1976.

———. *Priesteramt der Frau: Geschenk Gottes für eine erneuerte Kirche: Erweiterte Neuauflage von 'Der Ausschluss der Frau vom priesterlichen Amt' (1973) mit ausführlicher Bibliographie (1974–2001)*. Münster: LIT, 2002. English translation: Bernard Cooke and Gary Macy, eds., *A History of Women and Ordination*, vol. 2, Ida Raming, The *Priestly Office of Women: God's Gift to a Renewed Church*. New York: Scarecrow Press, 2004.

Reynolds, Roger. "'At Sixes and Sevens'—and Eights and Nines: The Sacred Mathematics of Sacred Orders in the Early Middle Ages." *Speculum* 54 (1979): 669–84.

———. *The Ordinals of Christ From Their Origins to the Twelfth Century*. Beiträge zur Geschichte und Quellenkunde des Mittelalters, 7. Berlin: Walter de Gruyter, 1978.

————. "Patristic 'Presbyterianism' in the Early Medieval Theology of Sacred Orders." *Mediaeval Studies*, 45 (1983): 311–42.

Robinson, Ian S. *The Papacy 1073–1198: Continuity and Innovation*. Cambridge: Cambridge University Press, 1990.

Pankowski, Arcadius. *De Diaconisses: Commentatio archaelogica*. Ratisbon: George Joseph Manz, 1866.

Real, Isabelle. "Vie et Vita de Saint Ségolène, Abbesse de Troclar au VIIe siècle." *Le Moyen Âge*, 101 (1995): 385–406.

Reininger, Dorothea. *Diakonat der Frau in der Einen Kirche: Diskussionen, Entscheidungen und pastoral-praktische Erfahrungen in der christlichen Ökumene und ihr Beitrag zur römisch–katholischen Diskussion*. Ostfildern: Schwabenverlag, 1999.

Saltet, Louis. *Les Réordinations: Étude sur le Sacrement de l'Ordre*. Paris: Libraire Victor Lecoffre, 1907.

Schäfer, K. H. "Kanonissen und Diakonissen." *Römische Quartalschrift für christliche Altertunskunde und Kirchengeschichte*, 24 (1910): 49–90.

Schatz, Klaus. "The Gregorian Reform and the Beginning of a Universal Ecclesiology." *The Jurist*, 57 (1997), 123–36.

Schillebeeckx, Edward. *Kerkelijk ambt: Voorgangers in de gemeente van Jezus Christus*. Blemendaal: H. Nelissen, 1980. English edition: *Ministry: Leadership in the Community of Jesus Christ*. New York: Crossroads, 1981.

Schulenburg, Jane. *Forgetful of Their Sex: Female Sanctity and Society, ca 500–1100*. Chicago: University of Chicago Press, 1998.

Sempere, Santiago Giner. "La mujer y la potestad de orden: Incapacidad de la mujer. Argumentación histórica." *Revista española de derecho canónica* 9 (1954): 841–69.

Smalley, Beryl. *The Study of the Bible in the Middle Ages*. 2nd ed. Oxford: Blackwell, 1983.

Somerset, Fiona. "Eciam Mulier Women in Lollardy and the Problem of Sources." In *Voices in Dialogue: Reading Women in the Middle Ages*, eds. Linda Olson and Kathryn Kerby–Fulton, 245–60. Notre Dame, Ind.: University of Notre Dame Press, 2005.

Somerville, Robert and Stephan Kuttner, eds. *Pope Urban II, The Collectio Britannica, and the Council of Melfi*. Oxford: Clarendon Press, 1996.

Somerville, Robert. "The Council of Clermont (1095), and Latin Christian Society." In *Papacy, Councils and Canon Law in the 11th–12th Centuries*, ed. Robert Somerville, 55–90. Aldershot: Variorum, 1990. Reprint of an article by the same name in *Archivum historiae pontificiae*, 12 (1974): 55–90.

————. "Ordinatio abbatis in the Rule of St. Benedict." *Revue benedictine*, 77 (1967): 246–63.

Stegmüller, Friedrich. *Repertorium biblicum medii aevi*. 5 vols. Madrid: Consejo Superior, 1950.

Stengel, Edmund. "Die Grabschrift der ersten Abtissin von Quedlinbug." *Deutches Archiv für Geschichte des Mittelalters* 3 (1939): 36–70.

Swanson, Robert. "Angels Incarnate: Clergy and Masculinity from Gregorian Reform to Reformation." In *Masculinity in Medieval Europe*, ed. D. M. Hadley, 160–77. London: Longman, 1999.

Tellenbach, Gerd. *The Church in Western Europe from the Tenth to the Early Twelfth Century*. Cambridge: Cambridge University Press, 1993.

Thiermeyer, Abraham-Andreas. "Der Diakonat der Frau." *Theologische Quartalschrift*, 173 (1993): 226–36.

Thurston, Bonnie Bowman. *The Widows: A Women's Ministry in the Early Church*. Minneapolis: Fortress Press, 1989.

Tilley, Terrence. *History, Theology, and Faith: Dissolving the Modern Problematic*. Maryknoll, NY: Orbis Books, 2004.

———. *Inventing Catholic Tradition*. Maryknoll, NY: Orbis Books, 2000.

Torjesen, Karen Jo. *When Women Were Priests*. San Francisco: HarperSanFrancisco, 1993.

Vogel, Cyrille. *Medieval Liturgy: An Introduction to the Sources*. Rev. ed. Washington, DC: Pastoral Press, 1986.

Wahl, Joseph A. *The Exclusion of Women from Holy Orders, Abstract of a Dissertation*. The Catholic University of America Studies in Sacred Theology, second series, 110. Washington, DC: The Catholic University of America Press, 1959.

Weidemann, Margarete. *Geschichte des Bistums Le Mans von der Spätantike bis zur Karolingerzeit*. 4 vols. Römisch-Germanische Zentralmuseum, Forschungsinstitut für vor-und frühgeschichte, Monographien, vol. 56. Mainz: Verlag des Römisch–Germanische Zentralmuseum, 2002.

Wemple, Suzanne Fonay. "Women from the Fifth Century to the Tenth Century." In *A History of Women in the West*, vol. 2, *Silences of the Middle Ages*, ed. Christine Klapisch-Zuber, 181–213. Cambridge, MA: Harvard University Press, 1992.

———. *Women in Frankish Society: Marriage and the Cloister, 500 to 900*. Philadelphia: University of Pennsylvania Press, 1981.

White, Susan. *A History of Women in Christian Worship*. Cleveland: The Pilgrim Press, 2003.

Wijngaards, John. *No Women in Holy Orders? The Women Deacons of the Early Church*. Norwich: Canterbury Press, 2002.

———. *The Ordination of Women in the Catholic Church: Unmasking a Cuckoo's Egg Tradition*. New York: Continuum, 2001.

Wilmart, André. "Prières pour la communion en deux psautiers du Mont-Cassin." *Ephemerides liturgicae*, 43 (1929): 320–28.

Winroth, Anders. *The Making of Gratian's Decretum*. Cambridge: Cambridge University Press, 2000.

Witherington, Ben. *Women in the Earliest Churches*, Society for New Testament Studies, Monograph Series, 59. Cambridge: Cambridge University Press, 1988.

Ysebaert, Joseph. "The Deaconesses in the Western Church of Late Antiquity and Their Origin." In *Eulogia: Mélange offerts à Antoon A. R. Bastiaensen à l'occasion des son soixante-cinquième anniversaire*, eds. G. M. Bartelink, A. Hilhorst and C. H.

Kneepkens, 423–36. Instrumenta patristica, 24. Steenbruge: Abbatia S. Petri, 1991.

Zagano, Phyllis. *Holy Saturday: An Argument for the Restoration of the Female Diaconate in the Catholic Church*. New York: Crossroad Publishing, 2000.

Zerfaß, Rolf. *Der Streit zum die Laienpredigt. Eine pastoral-geschichtliche Untersuchung zum Verständnis des Predigtamtes und zuer sienen Entwicklung im 12. und 13. Jahrhundert*. Frieberg: Herder, 1974.

Index

abbess, 35, 53, 61–62, 66, 70, 74, 76,
    79, 80–88, 91, 93- 95, 97, 98,
    109, 113, 172, 189, 191, 195,
    206, 207, 210, 213, 214, 215
  ordination of, 14, 20, 27, 30, 33,
    34, 35, 36, 37, 38, 39, 40, 41, 49,
    64, 66, 81–82, 98–99, 101,
    102, 126, 130–131, 140, 143–155,
    173, 175, 176, 177, 181, 189, 190,
    210, 214, 215
  powers of, 14, 51, 58, 76–77,
    82–85, 102–104, 109, 125, 181,
    185, 198, 199, 200, 201, 216,
    217, 222
abbot, 41, 82, 103, 113, 125–126, 180,
    181, 198–199, 207, 216
  ordination of, 27, 30, 33, 36, 37,
    38, 39, 40, 41, 64, 80, 81–82,
    86, 140, 141–146, 148–149,
    152–155, 171, 173, 175, 176,
    177, 210
Abelard, 42–43, 93–96, 100, 104,
    109, 110, 124, 178, 181, 204–10
acolyte, order of, 28, 33, 34, 37,
    38, 39, 40, 96, 176, 191
Adam, 114, 122–23, 229–230

Aegidius de Bellamera, 118, 120
Agde, Council of, 55, 74
Aimone, Peter, 219
Aldegundis, 83–84, 199
Alexander II, 25, 168
Alexander of Alexandria, 45
Alexander of Hales, 28, 29,
    107–08, 169, 221
Allen, Prudence, ix, 116, 119–20,
    125, 126, 225, 227, 228
Ambrose of Milan, 91, 94, 98, 99,
    103, 122, 211, 226
Ambrosiaster, 67, 91–92, 98, 192,
    203, 211, 226
Andrieu, 59, 140, 142, 152, 166, 177,
    186, 190, 194–95
Anna, deaconess, 69
Anna, prophetess, 64–65, 71, 95,
    135, 141, 190, 208
Anselm of Canterbury, 173
Anselm of Lucca, 180–81, 223
Ansorge, Dirk, 16, 163
Apostolic Constitutions, 12–13,
    161, 192
Aristotle, 116, 117, 119–21, 126,
    228, 231

Arjava, Annit, 117, 226
Atto of Vercelli, 36, 65–66, 85, 174, 191
Aubert, Marie-Joséphe, 15–16, 18, 162,
    176, 188, 189, 193, 195
Audisio, Gabriel, 180
Aurelian of Arles, 200
Ausonia, deaconess, 69
Auxerre, Council of, 60, 75
Avitus, 56

Baldovin, John, 3
Balsamon, Theodore, 8, 159
baptism, 66, 67, 74, 77, 78, 106, 107,
    161, 192, 200, 205, 210, 214, 219,
    220, 221
Barstow, Anne, ix, 197, 223, 224, 225
Bassett, William, ix
Beleth, John 43, 44, 47, 179
van Beneden, Pierre, 29, 163, 170
Benedict IX, 35, 173
Benedict VIII, 35, 173
Benevento, Council of, 28, 63, 89–91,
    92, 96, 99, 100, 201, 202
Berger, Teresa, ix, 16, 159, 160, 163
Berman, Constance, 32–33, 171, 181, 191,
    218, 223, 224
Bernard of Botone, 105, 107, 118
Bernard of Chartres, 43, 44, 47
Bernold of Constance, 44, 89, 179, 201
Bertila, 83, 198
Biesinger, Albert, 16, 164, 185
bishop, order of, viii, 7, 8, 14, 17, 18, 19,
    20, 23, 25, 26, 27, 31, 33, 34, 35–36,
    38, 39, 41, 44, 48, 53–58, 59, 60, 61,
    62, 63, 64, 65, 67, 68, 69, 70, 71,
    72, 73, 74, 75, 76, 77, 78, 79, 80, 81,
    82, 83, 86, 87, 88, 89, 90, 91, 94,
    95, 98, 103, 106, 107, 112, 113, 131,
    163, 164, 168, 173, 182, 183, 185, 184,
    185, 188, 201
Bitel, Lisa, 180, 185, 198–99
Blamires, Alcuin, 204, 210
Børresen, Kari Elisabeth, 227, 228
Bowes, Kim, 77–78, 197

Brennan, Brian, 55, 57, 182, 183, 184
Brianson, Gui, 120
Brigid of Ireland, 54, 58, 64, 87, 104,
    182, 184–85
Brooke, Christopher, 197, 223
Brundage, James, 172, 196, 211, 223, 226
Bruno the Carthusian, 91–92, 105, 203
Buytaert, Eligius, 178, 205, 206,
    209, 210
Byzantine Church, 13, 17–18, 20, 21,
    157, 165

Calixtus II, 36, 173
Cameron, Euan, 178
canoness, 35, 49, 81, 198
Canons of Theodore, 84, 199
Carleton, Kenneth, 167–68
Carthusian Order, 14, 200
Cassiodorus, 94, 95, 96, 206, 207, 209
Celestine III, 25
celibacy, viii, 57, 59, 87, 112–15, 116–17,
    125, 126, 191, 196, 198, 222, 223
Chadwick, Henry, 34, 172
character, of a sacrament, 29, 31, 98, 101,
    102, 103, 104, 105, 106–08, 109,
    110, 170, 214, 215, 216, 217, 218, 219,
    220, 221, 222
Charlemagne, 30, 85
chastity, viii, 39, 60, 71, 196
Chenu, Marie-Dominique, 43, 163, 178
Cistercian Order, 32–33, 103, 115, 171
Clanchy, Michael, ix, 204, 207, 208
Clark, Anne, ix
Claudius of Turin, 94, 95, 96, 206,
    207, 209
Clermont-Ferrand, Council of, 89
Clothar, 68
Cogitosus, 184–85
Colish, Marcia, ix, 92, 195, 202, 204,
    211, 218
Collins, Mary, 3
communion service, 3, 4, 8, 23, 28, 51,
    63, 68, 70, 72, 76, 83, 84, 85, 86,
    108, 190, 198, 200, 221

confession, 41, 42, 51, 82, 83, 86, 102, 103, 110, 125, 198, 199, 201, 216
Congar, Yves, ix, 15, 16, 18, 29, 30–31, 33, 38, 41, 170, 171
Constable, Giles, ix, 32, 33, 171, 225, 231
continence, viii, 54, 56, 57, 59, 73, 74, 75, 79, 86, 87, 112, 113, 115, 116, 183, 196, 223
Cooke, Bernard, 157, 159, 166, 177, 181, 200, 203, 218, 222, 224, 227, 228, 229, 230, 231
Courson, Robert, 108
Cronopius, Bishop of Périgueux, 57
cross, as cause of consecration, 45–46
cursus honorum, 25–26, 168
Cushing, Kathleen, 180–181, 223
Cuthbert, 108

Dachowski, Elizabeth, 223
Damian, Peter. 31, 113, 168, 218, 224, 225
Daniélou, Jean, 10, 160
deacon, viii, 8, 17, 18, 19, 21, 24, 25, 26, 28, 33, 35, 42, 60, 80, 84, 91, 95, 96, 100, 108, 110, 164, 165, 202, 203, 204, 206, 207, 210, 211, 212, 213, 214, 215, 217, 218, 222, 223
  ordination of, 7, 9, 10, 12, 13, 14, 16, 20, 37, 39, 70, 71, 72, 73, 81, 86, 88, 90, 107, 133–34, 135, 137–41
deaconess, 66–70, 8, 9, 14, 19–20, 40, 49, 50, 53, 58, 59, 60, 65, 74, 78, 79, 80, 81, 82, 85–86, 91, 92, 93–94, 95, 96, 97, 98, 101, 102, 110, 113, 115, 185, 187, 191, 192, 193, 194, 195, 203, 205, 206, 207, 209, 210, 211, 212
  ordination of, 7, 8, 9, 10, 11–13, 14, 15, 16–18, 20–21, 28, 35, 36, 37–38, 39, 40, 41, 63–64, 70–73, 74–75, 98–99, 99–101, 102, 103–104, 105, 109, 114, 126, 130–31, 133–42, 157, 158, 162, 163, 164–65, 173, 175, 176, 177, 195, 196, 204, 214, 215, 217, 218, 222
  powers of, 19, 62–63, 66, 67, 71, 73, 74–77, 87, 88, 181, 197, 213

Deborah, 123–24, 208
DeClercq, Charles, 182, 187, 193, 197
Decretum, 52, 90, 92, 97, 98, 99, 101, 104, 105, 106, 112, 114, 117, 119, 121, 122, 202, 204, 212, 213, 214, 215, 221, 224, 226
Donatus of Besançon, 198, 200
doorkeeper, 26, 28, 37, 38, 39, 40
Dortel-Claudot, Michel, 191, 196
Duns Scotus, 123, 124, 229, 230
Durandus, William, 30, 72–73, 104, 196

Eastern Church, 6, 11, 12, 13, 15, 16, 17–18, 67, 93, 94
Egbert, Bishop of York, 37–38, 64, 70–71, 133–34, 175, 190
Eisen, Ute, ix, 18, 53, 54, 157, 165, 181, 182, 186, 187, 189, 192, 194
Elizabeth, 95, 208
Elliott, Dyan, 181, 195, 196, 224, 225
Emengaud, deaconess, 69
emperor, ordination of, 33, 34, 113, 125, 172
empress, ordination of, 33, 34, 125
Epaon, Council of, 67, 192
Ephifania, deaconess, 59
Ephiphanius, 158, 159
episcopa, 14, 49, 53–54, 58, 59, 65, 66, 74, 75, 76, 79, 80, 86, 88, 113, 182, 196
Espín, Orlando, 167, 181
Eucharist, 5, 15, 21, 28, 31, 32, 41–47, 50, 60, 61, 63, 76, 107–08, 126, 160, 162, 165, 169, 170, 178, 188, 190, 198, 231
Eufrasia of Vienne, 56, 183
Eugenius IV, 24
Eumerius, Bishop of Nantes, 57
Euphemia, deaconess, 69
Eustochius, Bishop, 61, 188
Eve, 122
exorcist, 26, 28, 33, 34, 37, 38, 39, 40, 96, 176, 177
Expositiones Pauli epistolarum, 96, 210

Ferrandus of Carthage, 186
Fishacre, Richard, 109, 221
FitzGerald, Kyriaki Karidoyanes, 17,
    164–65
Flavia, presbytera, 60
Fransen, Gerard, 27, 169, 216
Freeman, Elizabeth 207
Fuchs, Vinzenz, 27, 29, 31, 169
Fuhrmann, Horst, 185

Galot, Jean, 13, 16, 161, 186, 188
Gandulf of Bologna, 96
Gelasius I, 14, 61, 188
Gelasius II, 25
Gennadius of Marseilles, 67, 191, 192
George, Judith, 183, 184, 193
Gibaut, John St. H., 25–26, 168, 201, 202
Gilbert, Bishop of Limerick, 36, 173
Gilbert of La Porrée, 96, 211
Gillmann, Franz, ix, 204, 213, 215, 217,
    219, 220, 230
Glossa ordinaria on the Decretales, 105,
    107, 118, 122
Glossa ordinaria on the Decretum, 101,
    107, 109, 116
Glossa ordinaria on scripture, 92, 93, 94,
    98, 105–06, 112, 203–04, 230
Gospel, reading by women, 62, 70, 74,
    77, 85, 99, 100, 101, 102, 103, 110,
    200, 213, 214–15, 216, 222
Gossman, Francis, 202
Gratian of Bologna, 52, 90, 92–93, 97,
    99, 100, 101, 105, 110, 112, 117,
    118–19, 123–24, 202, 204, 212,
    221, 226
Gregorian Reform, 79, 111, 112–115, 126,
    180–81, 197, 218, 222, 223
Gregorian Sacramentary, 38, 64, 71, 73,
    163, 175, 190
Gregory I (the Great), 38, 235, 44, 45, 60,
    76, 97, 102, 178–79, 187, 189, 212
Gregory II, 59, 61–62, 69, 185
Gregory VII, 25, 31, 39, 89, 112
Gregory IX, 103, 105

Gregory of Tours, 55, 56–57, 61, 74, 87,
    183, 184, 196
Gryson, Roger, 11–13, 15, 16, 158, 161, 187,
    188, 192, 193
Guido de Baysio, 101, 102, 123, 216
Guido of Orchelles, 106, 219, 238
Gy, Pierre-Marie, ix, 27, 29–30, 38,
    169, 170

Haito, Bishop of Basle, 62, 189
Heimbach-Steins, Marianne, 16,
    164, 240
Helaria, deaconess, 68, 69, 193
Heloise, 93, 94, 95, 96, 109, 110, 116,
    181, 205, 207
Henry of Ghent, 123, 124, 230
Herveus de Bourg-Dieu, 96, 211
Hildeburga of Le Mans, 54
Hinschius, Paul, 185, 221
Hochstetler, Donald, 181, 189, 191,
    198, 200
Hollis, Stephanie, 198, 200, 225
Honorius Augustodunensis, 44,
    179, 235
Hostiensis, 118, 120
Hugh of St. Cher, 123, 124
Hugh of St. Victor, 27, 90, 96, 165,
    168, 211
Huguccio, 98, 99, 100, 101, 106, 107,
    122, 214, 215, 219, 220
Humbert of Silva Candida, 31
Hünermann, Peter, ix, xiii, 16–17, 18–19,
    26, 164, 166, 167, 185, 188, 193

Innocent, 235
Innocent II, 25
Innocent III, 25, 34, 43, 46, 47, 102, 103,
    125, 178, 216, 217
Innocent IV, 103, 217
Innocent V, 122, 229
Isidore of Seville, 39, 118
Ite, 83, 198–199
Ivo, Bishop of Chartres, 90, 96, 168,
    202, 211

Jansen, Katherine, 209
Januarius, bishop of Caligliari, 61
Jenson, Anne, 16, 164, 185
Jerome, 93, 94
Jestice, Phyllis, 223
Johannis Teutonicus, 98, 100–01, 109,
    119, 216
John, bishop of Syracuse, 44
John XIX, 35, 173
John of Crema, 114
John of Frieburg, 217, 230
Jorissen, Hans, 16–17, 26, 19, 164
Jungmann, Joseph, 179
Junia, 96

Kale, *presbytera*, 60
Kalsbach, Adolf, 9, 158, 159
Kantorowicz, Ernst, 172
Karras, Valerie, 17, 165
kings, ordination of, 27, 30, 33, 34, 113,
    125, 172
Kirkely, Evelyn, 3

Laeuchli, Samuel, 183
Lafontaine, Paul-Henri, 191, 231
Langton, Stephen, 107
Laodicea, Council of, 59, 66, 97,
    102, 212
Laon, School of, 90, 92, 93, 202, 204
Lateran, Fourth Council of, 31, 46, 47,
    98, 101, 112, 170
Lateran, Second Council of, 112
Lateran, Third Council of, 31, 112, 170
Lawrence, C. H., 225
Leclercq, Jean, 63, 94, 190, 207
lector, 26, 28, 33, 34, 37, 38, 39, 40, 176,
    177, 212
Leo I (the Great), 34, 55, 183
Leo III, 69
Leo VII, 59, 70, 185
Leo IX, 35, 74, 173
Leontius, Bishop of Bordeaux, 56, 184
Leta, *presbytera*, 60
Liber pontificalis, 25, 55, 195

Liber sacramentorum Augustodunensis, 64,
    81, 145, 189, 210, 235
Liber sacramentorum Gellonensis, 64, 81,
    144, 190, 210
Logan, Donald, ix
Long, R. James, 221
Lord's Prayer, as consecration, 44–45,
    178–79
Luscombe, David, ix
Lynch, John, 191, 196

Macy, Gary, 20, 157, 159, 166, 177, 178,
    179, 180, 181, 186, 200, 203, 204,
    211, 218, 222, 224, 227, 228, 229,
    230, 231
Madigan, Kevin, 53, 59, 167, 181, 185,
    186, 187, 188, 192, 193, 194, 212
Mariam, 81, 145, 146, 147, 149, 151,
    155, 208
Martia, *presbytera*, 60, 65, 77
Martimort, Aime Georges, 11, 12, 13, 14,
    15, 16, 66, 72, 158–59, 161, 162, 173,
    176, 185, 187, 188, 189, 190, 191,
    192, 193, 194, 195, 196, 212, 217
Martin, John Hilary, ix, 91, 203, 207,
    218, 222, 227, 228, 229, 230
Mary, Mother of Jesus, 72, 102–03,
    208, 216
Mary Magdalene, 95, 124, 208, 209, 230
Master Simon, 107, 220
Matilda, 83, 199
Mayer, Josephine, 9, 159, 186
Mayeski, Marie Anne, ix, 116–17, 180,
    198, 225, 227, 228
McLaughlin, Mary Martin, 94, 95–96,
    207, 210
McNamara, Jo Ann, ix, 75, 76, 115, 116,
    125, 126, 130, 174, 180, 181, 185, 191,
    194, 196, 197, 199, 200, 201, 218,
    222–23, 225, 228, 231
Médard, bishop of Noyen, 68–69
Meer, Haye van der, 11, 12, 13, 160, 186,
    187, 188, 189, 190
Mel, 54, 182

Metz, René, 28, 169
Mews, Constant, ix, 205, 206
Miles, Margaret, 231
Miller, Maureen, ix, 125, 231
Minnis, Alastair, ix, 222, 227, 231
miter, of an abbess, 81, 82, 86–87
Monheim, 84, 200–01
Moore, Robert, 180, 223
Morin, Jean, 7–8, 9, 10, 12, 23, 24, 35,
    66, 158, 159, 167, 168, 191
Morris, Joan, ix, 13–14, 162, 185, 217
Moschius, John, 43
Mozarabic rite, 36–37, 38, 81, 82,
    143–44, 175
Müller, Gerhard, 19, 26, 166
Müller, Wolfgang, 214
Muckle, Joseph T., 205, 207, 208, 209
Mulder-Bakker, Anneke, 200
Muschiol, Gisela, 83, 198, 199, 200

Namatius, Bishop of Clermont-Ferrand,
    55, 56
Nelson, Janet, 199–200, 201
Netter, Thomas, 123, 229–30
Newman, Barbara, 205
Nîmes, Council of, 61, 67, 188, 192
Nicolai, Umberto, 195
Nicolas de Tudeschis, 118

O'Carroll, Maura, 221
Ochoa, Xaverio, 217
Odilia, 84, 173
Ò hAodha, Donncha, 182
Orange, Council of, 67, 74, 75, 192
orarium, 71, 72, 73, 74, 134, 135, 142, 195
Ordines Romani, 26, 186, 190, 191, 194,
    195, 233
Origen, 93, 95, 96, 205
Orso, Bishop of Olivolo, 34, 68, 172
Orthodox Church, 10, 15, 17–18, 19,
    164, 165
Osborne, Kenan, 168, 169, 218, 219, 221
Osiek, Carolyn, 53, 59, 167, 181, 185, 186,
    187, 188, 192, 193, 194, 212

Otranto, Giorgio, ix, 14, 15, 61, 162,
    187, 188
Ott, Ludwig, ix, 28, 167, 168, 169, 172,
    202, 218, 219, 220, 221
Otto II, 30
Otto III, 30

Pacaut, Marcel, 216–17
Pankowski, Arcadius, 9, 159
Paris, Council of, 62, 70, 189
Paschal I, 53
Paucapalea, 101, 114, 215, 224
Paul VI, 26
Paululus, Robert, 44, 179
Pelagius, 67, 192
Pennington, Kenneth, 215
Peter the Lombard, 28, 29, 45, 52, 96,
    105, 106–07, 109, 112, 165, 168,
    169, 202, 218, 219
Peter of Poitiers, 106, 107, 220
Philip of Harvengt, 36, 64, 96, 174
Phoebe, 91, 93, 95, 96, 202, 205, 206,
    207, 209, 210, 211
Pien, Jean, 8, 9, 14, 158
Pius XII, 24
Placidina, 56, 184
porter, 33, 34
Praepositinus, 106, 219
presbytera, 14, 15, 40, 49, 53, 58–66, 70,
    74, 75, 76, 77, 79, 80, 85, 86, 88,
    97, 99, 101, 102, 104, 105, 110, 113,
    114, 115, 165, 185, 186, 187, 189, 191,
    196, 212, 215, 216, 217
priest, order of, viii, 8, 10, 11, 12, 13, 14,
    15, 16, 17, 19, 20, 21, 24, 25, 26, 27,
    28, 30, 31, 32, 33, 34, 35, 36, 37, 38,
    39, 40, 41–47, 49, 48, 50, 51, 53,
    55, 58, 59, 60, 61, 62, 63, 64, 65, 66,
    67, 68, 69, 71, 72, 73, 74, 75, 76,
    77, 78, 79, 80, 83, 84, 86, 88, 89,
    90, 91, 92, 93, 95, 97, 99, 101,
    102, 103, 104, 105, 106, 107, 108,
    109, 110, 112, 113, 114–15, 117, 118,
    124, 125, 126, 131, 132, 160, 161,

164–65, 166, 167, 168, 172, 173, 174, 175, 177, 178, 183, 185, 187, 188, 189, 191, 192, 196, 197, 201, 202, 211, 212, 213, 217, 218, 221, 222, 223, 231
Prisca, 96
Priscus, 56, 184
psalmist, 39, 40
Pseudo-Isidorian Decretales, 59, 70, 185, 186, 221

queens, ordination of, 20, 33, 34, 113, 125

Rabanus Maurus, 96
Radegund, 68, 69, 73, 163, 193
Rainold, Archbishop of Rheims, 33
Raming, Ida, ix, 11, 12, 20, 117, 159, 160, 161, 186, 200, 204, 212, 214, 215, 216, 217, 218, 224, 225, 226, 227, 228, 229, 230
Raymond of Peñafort, 103, 104, 105, 123, 217, 230
Real, Isabelle, 194
Reininger, Dorothea, 18–19, 160, 161, 165
Remigius, Bishop of Reims, 68, 78, 171, 193
Reynolds, Roger, 168, 202
Ribaillier, Jean, 220, 221
Richard of Middleton, 120, 228
Richard the Premonstratensian, 45, 180
Richild, 34, 172
Robert of Flamesbury, 101
Robinson, Ian, 201
Roman law, 30, 31, 32, 117–19, 121, 124, 126, 225, 226, 227
Roman pontificals, 26, 28, 30, 40–41, 64, 72–73, 104, 140–42, 152–55, 177, 190, 210, 217
Romana of Olivolo, 34, 68, 172
Romano-Germanic Pontifical, 33, 38–40, 63, 71, 72, 75, 81, 82, 134–40, 146–52, 176–77, 190, 196, 210

Rome, Council of, 69, 185
Romuldus, Bishop of Constance, 25
Rufinus, 98–99, 100, 106, 114, 214, 219, 224
Rule of Benedict, 33
Rupert of Deutz, 44, 179

Saltet, Louis, 220
sanctimonialia, 93, 180
Schatz, Klaus, 223
Schillebeeckx, Edward, 31–32, 42, 170, 225
Schütte, Bernard, 199
Schulenburg, Jane, 180, 201
Sedulius Scotus, 96, 210
Segenfrid, Bishop of LeMans, 54
Sempere, Santiago, 9–10, 159, 173, 187, 188, 189, 192, 193
Sergius, Archbishop of Ravenna, 69, 195
Sicard of Cremona, 44, 98, 106, 114, 179, 213, 214, 219
Sidonius Apollinaris, Bishop of Clermont, 56, 78, 183
Sigolena, deaconess, 69, 85, 194
Simon of Bisignano, 106, 219
Siricius, 53
Smalley, Beryl, 204
Somerville, Robert, 171, 201, 202
Speculum de mysteriis ecclesiae, 43, 45, 96, 178, 211
Stegmüller, Friedrich, 211
Stengel, Edmund, 185
stole, 7, 8, 23, 71, 72, 73, 135, 137, 139, 140, 141, 158
subdeacon, 8, 12, 19, 24, 26, 33, 34, 35, 37, 40, 41, 42, 60, 65, 68, 69, 74, 89, 108, 112, 113, 168, 173, 175, 176, 177, 182, 187, 197, 201, 202, 223
Summa Coloniensis, 101–02, 216, 234
Summa Monacensis, 97–98, 104, 213
Summa Parisiensis, 101–02, 214, 21

Susanna, 56–57, 184
Swanson, Robert, ix, 115, 125, 168, 181, 225, 231

Tellenbach, Gerd, 222
Theodora, *episcopa*, 53, 58, 69, 181
Thierry of Chartres, 43, 44, 47
Thietmar, Bishop of Merseburg, 36, 174
Thomas Aquinas, 24, 120–21, 167, 234, 238
Thomas of Canterbury, 108
Thurston, Bonnie, 157
Tilley, Terrence, 157, 167, 201
Toledo, Council of, 71, 74, 195
Torjesen, Karen Jo, 157
Tours, Councils of, 54, 55, 60, 69, 75, 182, 187, 196

Urban II, 28, 33, 89, 171, 201, 202
Urbicus, Bishop of Clermont, 56, 74, 184

veil, 72, 105, 124
Venantius Fortunatus, 56, 57, 68, 78, 183, 184, 193
Via, Jane, ix
virgin, order of, 9, 28, 35, 36, 37, 38, 39, 40, 41, 49, 59, 64, 71, 72, 73, 74, 76, 95, 147, 148, 159, 169, 174,

175, 176, 177, 180, 186, 196, 198, 200, 208
Vogel, Cyrille, 72, 134, 146, 171, 175, 176, 177, 190, 196, 217

Waldebert of Luxeuil, 198
Waldensians, 43, 45, 46, 47, 180
Wemple, Suzanne, ix, 57, 180, 181, 184, 191, 193, 194, 195
widow, order of, 9, 11, 18, 35, 38, 39, 40, 41, 49, 59, 64, 66, 67–68, 71, 73, 74, 75, 76, 94, 104, 157, 161, 174, 175, 176, 177, 182, 186, 189, 190, 191, 192, 193, 196, 207, 217, 218
Wijngaards, John, 20–21, 167
William of Auxerre, 107, 220, 221
Winigris, 34
Winroth, Anders, 202, 204, 212, 226
Witherington, Ben, 157

Ysebaert, Joseph, 16, 73, 163, 186, 187, 188, 191, 192, 193, 196

Zachary, 59, 62, 70, 185, 189
Zagano, Phyllis, 19–20, 166
Zerfaß, Rolf, 200
Zier, Mark, ix, 203, 204